College Writing

College Writing

Keeping It Real

Lee Brewer Jones

Alyse W. Jones

Georgia Perimeter College

Longman

New York   San Francisco   Boston
London   Toronto   Sydney   Tokyo   Singapore   Madrid
Mexico City   Munich   Paris   Cape Town   Hong Kong   Montreal

Editor-in-Chief: Joseph Opiela
Senior Acquisitions Editor: Steven Rigolosi
Marketing Manager: Melanie Goulet
Supplements Editor: Donna Campion
Production Manager: Joseph Vella
Project Coordination, Text Design, and Electronic Page Makeup: Shepherd, Inc.
Cover Design Manager: John Callahan
Cover Designer/Cover Illustration: Neil Flewellyn
Photo Research: Photosearch, Inc.
Manufacturing Buyer: Al Dorsey
Printer and Binder: R.R. Donnelley & Sons, Inc.
Cover Printer: Phoenix Color Corp.

For permission to use copyrighted material, grateful acknowledgement is made to the copyright holders on pp. 371–372, which are hereby made part of this copyright page.

Library of Congress Cataloging-in-Publication Data

Jones, Lee Brewer.
　　College writing : keeping it real / Lee Brewer Jones ; Alyse W. Jones.
　　　　p.　cm.
　　Includes index.
　　ISBN 0-321-06741-X
　　　1. English language—Rhetoric. 2. English language—Grammar. 3. Report writing. I.
Jones, Alyse W. II. Title.

PE1408 .J833 2000
808′.042—dc21   00-059807

Please visit our website at http://www.ablongman.com

ISBN 0-321-06741-X

1 2 3 4 5 6 7 8 9 10—DOC—03 02 01 00

To Eli and Esther, our finest collaborations yet

Brief Contents

Detailed Contents

Supplemental Readings 307

Additional Writing Assignments 345

A ny faculty member who joins an exhaustive search for a composition textbook (whether for Freshman Comp or Developmental English) probably owns, at the end of the process, an extensive collection of books. Some are plain awful, others serviceable, and a few quite good. Chances are that such a professor has found parts of one textbook most attractive and parts of another most useful. He or she may have thought, "If I ever write a textbook, I will do things differently. I'll have a more unified approach, better readings, units of grammar that students can understand more clearly."

This line of thinking, developed over a decade each of teaching by the authors, has resulted in *College Writing: Keeping It Real.* Although we have read and liked many items and strategies in other texts, we still wanted to say it all a little differently, organize it more toward the theme of "keeping it real," and produce a book that reaches students more fully. In *College Writing: Keeping It Real,* we present sound rhetorical principles in an understandable, unified format. At the same time, we have developed new approaches and innovative assignments geared toward the "real-life" writing situations students encounter in both the academy and the outside world. Our ultimate goal is to make composition classes relevant while keeping our students involved and energized to succeed.

Organization

We have carefully planned the structure of *College Writing: Keeping It Real,* beginning with a narrative assignment. In doing so we grant narrative the important place that it deserves, especially but not exclusively for students moving from predominantly oral cultures into the written culture of the academy. Three detailed chapters discussing the writing process follow. Subsequent chapters present and culminate in several different types of writing assignments, giving teachers and students a wide variety of choices. *College Writing: Keeping It Real* then concludes with appendices of additional readings and alternate writing assignments. This book comprises the following chapters:

Features

We have incorporated many special features to help students become more proficient and confident writers in the classroom and beyond. Thus, *College Writing: Keeping It Real* does the following:

- organizes around a coherent approach, James Kinneavy's **communication triangle,** which focuses on the interplay among the writer "I," the reader "you," and the subject "it." The communication triangle requires writers to consider which of the pronouns is/are their primary concern(s).

- includes assignments that have students understand not only the **how** of the essay but also the **why.**

- acknowledges a variety of learning styles and consistently offers multiple exercises that appeal to those varied styles.

- offers **writing process strategies** as potentially helpful activities rather than individual absolutes without which no good writing may occur.

- includes numerous **solo and collaborative activities.**

- helps students organize their thoughts with **charts, diagrams, and worksheets.**

- celebrates **diversity** in student writings as well as in student and professional readings.

- uses both the processes of writing and of reading to **promote critical thinking.**
- teaches grammar and usage in an approachable way that reflects students' concerns for **ethos** rather than exclusively error avoidance.
- **integrates grammar and usage instruction into chapters** and yet keeps these units sufficiently discrete that they may be taught individually.
- includes **computer tips** and recommendations for using **electronic media,** including the Internet.
- encourages students—as they read, write, and think—to **keep it real,** not only in the vernacular sense of avoiding pretense and unnecessary artifice, but also in the pedagogical sense of thinking always of the communication triangle and the ways a writing situation reflects the varying emphases of the triangle.

The Teaching and Learning Package

Available with *College Writing: Keeping It Real* is an extensive **Instructor's Manual.** The instructor's manual contains much practical, helpful material. In it we provide a general introduction to using the textbook, specific tips for teaching each chapter, sample syllabi, and answers to the questions and activities (ISBN 0-321-06743-6).

Also Available:

The Writer's ToolKit Plus. This CD-ROM offers a wealth of tutorial, exercise, and reference material for writers. It is compatible with either a PC or Macintosh platform and is flexible enough to be used either occasionally for practice or regularly in class lab sessions. For information on how to bundle this CD-ROM FREE with your text, please contact your Longman sales representative.

Electronic Test Bank for Writing. Available in December 2000, this electronic test bank features more than 5,000 questions in all areas of writing, from grammar to paragraphing, through essay writing, research, and documentation. With this easy-to-use CD-ROM, instructors simply choose questions from the electronic test bank, then print out the completed test for distribution (ISBN 0-321-08117-X).

The Longman Developmental English Package

In addition to the Instructor's Manual described above, a website is available to support *College Writing: Keeping It Real.* For additional quizzes and Internet links, visit us at **http://www.awl.com/jones.**

A series of other innovative supplements is available for both instructors and students. All of these supplements are available either free or at greatly reduced prices.

For Additional Reading and Reference

The Dictionary Deal. Two dictionaries can be shrinkwrapped with this text at a nominal fee. *The New American Webster Handy College Dictionary* is a paperback reference text with more than 100,000 entries. *Merriam Webster's Collegiate Dictionary,* tenth edition, is a hardback reference with a citation file of more than 14.5 million examples of English words drawn from actual use. To shrinkwrap a dictionary with this text, please contact your Longman sales consultant.

Penguin Quality Paperback Titles. A series of Penguin paperbacks is available at a significant discount when shrinkwrapped with any Longman Basic Skills title. Some titles available are John Steinbeck's *The Pearl,* Julia Alvarez's *How the Garcia Girls Lost Their Accents,* Mark Twain's *Huckleberry Finn, Narrative of the Life of Frederick Douglass,* Harriet Beecher Stowe's *Uncle Tom's Cabin,* Dr. Martin Luther King, Jr.'s *Why We Can't Wait,* and plays by Shakespeare, Miller, and Albee. For a complete list of titles or more information, please contact your Longman sales consultant.

The Pocket Reader, First Edition. This inexpensive volume contains eighty brief readings (1–3 pages each) on a variety of themes: writers on writing, nature, women and men, customs and habits, politics, rights and obligations, and coming of age. Also included is an alternate rhetorical table of contents (ISBN 0-321-07668-0).

100 Things to Write About. This 100-page book contains 100 individual assignments for writing on a variety of topics and in a wide range of formats, from expressive to analytical. Ask your Longman sales representative for a sample copy (ISBN 0-673-98239-4).

Newsweek Alliance. Instructors may choose to shrinkwrap a 12-week subscription to *Newsweek* with any Longman text. The price of the subscription is 57 ¢ per issue (a total of $6.84 for the subscription). Available with the subscription is a free "Interactive Guide to *Newsweek*"—a workbook for students who are using the text. In addition, Newsweek provides a wide variety of instructor supplements free to teachers, including maps, Skills Builders, and weekly quizzes. For more information on the Newsweek alliance, please contact your Longman sales consultant.

Electronic and Online Offerings

The Longman English Pages Web Site. Both students and instructors can visit our free content-rich Web site for additional reading selections and writing exercises. From the Longman English pages, visitors can conduct a simulated Web search, learn how to write a resume and cover letter, or try their hand at poetry writing. Stop by and visit us at **http://www.awl.com/ englishpages.**

The Longman Electronic Newsletter. Twice a month during the spring and fall, instructors who have subscribed receive a free copy of the Longman Developmental English Newsletter in their e-mailbox. Written by experienced classroom instructors, the newsletter offers teaching tips, classroom activities, book reviews, and more. To subscribe, visit the Longman Basic Skills Web site at **http://www.awl.com/basicskills,** or send an e-mail to **Basic Skills@awl.com.**

Daedalus Online. Longman Publishers and The Daedalus Group are proud to offer the next generation of the award-winning Daedalus Integrated Writing Environment. Daedalus Online is an Internet-based collaborative writing environment for students. The program offers prewriting strategies and prompts, computer-mediated conferencing, peer collaboration and review, comprehensive writing support, and secure, 24-hour availability.

For educators, Daedalus Online offers a comprehensive suite of online course management tools for managing an online class, dynamically linking assignments, and facilitating a heuristic approach to writing instruction. For more information, visit **http://www.awl.com/daedalus,** or contact your Longman sales representative.

***Teaching Online: Internet Research, Conversation, and Composition,* Third Edition.** Ideal for instructors who have never surfed the Net, this easy-to-follow guide offers basic definitions, numerous examples, and step-by-step information about finding and using Internet sources. Free to adopters (ISBN 0-321-07760-1).

***Researching Online,* Fourth Edition.** A perfect companion for a new age, this indispensable new supplement helps students navigate the Internet. Adapted from *Teaching Online,* the instructor's Internet guide, *Researching Online* speaks directly to students, giving them detailed, step-by-step instructions for performing electronic searches. Available free when shrinkwrapped with *College Writing: Keeping It Real.* For more information, contact your Longman sales consultant (0-321-08408-X).

For Instructors

Competency Profile Test Bank, Second Edition. This series of 60 objective tests covers ten general areas of English competency, including fragments; comma splices and run-ons; pronouns; commas; and capitalization. Each test is available in remedial, standard, and advanced versions. Available as reproducible sheets or in computerized versions. Free to instructors (Paper version: ISBN 0-321-02224-6; Computerized IBM: ISBN 0-321-02633-0; Computerized Mac: ISBN 0-321-02632-2).

Diagnostic and Editing Tests, Third Edition. This collection of diagnostic tests helps instructors assess students' competence in Standard Written English for purpose of placement or to gauge progress. Available as reproducible sheets or in computerized versions, and free to instructors (Paper: ISBN 0-321-08382-2; Computerized IBM Version: 0-321-08782-8; Computerized MAC Version: 0-321-08784-4).

ESL Worksheets, Third Edition. These reproducible worksheets provide ESL students with extra practice in areas they find the most troublesome. A diagnostic test and post-test are provided, along with answer keys and suggested topics for writing. Free to adopters (ISBN 0-321-07765-2).

80 Practices. A collection of reproducible, ten-item exercises that provide additional practices for specific grammatical usage problems, such as comma splices, capitalization, and pronouns. Includes an answer key, and free to adopters (ISBN 0-673-53422-7).

CLAST Test Package, Fourth Edition. These two 40-item objective tests evaluate students' readiness for the CLAST exams. Strategies for teaching CLAST preparedness are included. Free with any Longman English title (Reproducible sheets: ISBN 0-321-01950-4; Computerized IBM version: ISBN 0-321-01982-2; Computerized Mac version: ISBN 0-321-01983-0).

TASP Test Package, Third Edition. These 12 practice pre-tests and post-tests assess the same reading and writing skills covered in the TASP examination. Free with any Longman English title (Reproducible sheets: ISBN 0-321-01959-8; Computerized IBM version: ISBN 0-321-01985-7; Computerized Mac version: 0-321-01984-9).

Teaching Writing to the Non-Native Speaker. This booklet examines the issues that arise when non-native speakers enter the developmental classroom. Free to instructors, it includes profiles of international and permanent ESL students, factors influencing second-language acquisition, and tips on managing a multicultural classroom (ISBN 0-673-97452-9).

For Students

Learning Together: An Introduction to Collaborative Theory. This brief guide to the fundamentals of collaborative learning teaches students how to work effectively in groups, how to revise with peer response, and how to co-author a paper or report. Shrinkwrapped free with this text (ISBN 0-673-46848-8).

A Guide for Peer Response, **Second Edition.** This guide offers students forms for peer critiques, including general guidelines and specific forms for different stages in the writing process. Also appropriate for freshman-level course. Free to adopters (ISBN 0-321-01948-2).

Thinking Through the Test, **by D.J. Henry.** This special workbook, prepared specially for students in Florida, offers ample skill and practice exercises to help student prep for the Florida State Exit Exam. To shrinkwrap this workbook free with your textbook, please contact your Longman sales representative. Also available: Two laminated grids (one for reading, one for writing) that can serve as handy references for students preparing for the Florida State Exit Exam.

Acknowledgments

Many people have helped us immeasurably in writing this book. First, we want to thank our local Longman representative, John Cross, who encouraged us to take this project from the idea stage to a formal proposal. Steven Rigolosi, our acquisitions editor, provided positive feedback and friendly encouragement from start to finish as well. Liza Rudneva, Melanie Goulet, and especially Jennifer Krasula helped keep ideas germinating, and Jennifer excerpted some of the better ones in the Longman e-newsletter.

We would also like to thank the following reviewers from across the country for their invaluable feedback as we wrote and revised the manuscript: Kathy Albertson, Georgia Southern University; Bob Baron, Mesa Community College; Judith Boschult, Phoenix College; Kathy Britton, Florence-Darlington Technical College; Duncan Carter, Portland State University; Judith Gallagher, Tarrant County College; Geert Hendriks, Butte College; Laura Knight, Mercer County College; Mary Ann Lee, Longview Community College; Mary Ann Leiby, El Camino College; Clyde Moneyhun, Youngstown State University; David Rollison, College of Marin; Victoria Sarkisian, Marist College; Nancy Schneider, University of Maine at Augusta; Holly Young, Arkansas State University–Beebe.

Closer to home, we want to thank Georgia Perimeter College professor Margo Eden-Camann for allowing us to use a version of her chart outline in the book. In addition, GPC colleague Jack Riggs kindly authorized our publication of his short story, which our students (and we hope you, too) love. Claudia Shorr of the Gwinnett System Center Library assisted with the research for the Persuasive Job Application Letter and helped refine the concept at a conference presentation. Moreover, we express our sincere gratitude to every former student who signed a permission slip and allowed us to include what we hope you will agree are some excellent examples of student achievement in composition. Without their demonstrated learning, neither this book nor our confidence to write it could ever have been possible.

Finally, we want to thank our parents, the late E.B. and Nelle Jones, and Sandy and Barbara Warren, for teaching us to love reading, writing, and learning.

Lee Brewer Jones
Alyse W. Jones
Lawrenceville, Georgia

Memories: Narrating a Real Experience

True or False: If you write an essay that is free of grammatical errors and that shows good organization, you will have written a good essay. The answer is *maybe*. Avoiding problems with grammar and having a clear organizational pattern certainly help any essay, and this textbook will offer many exercises to help you with grammar, punctuation, usage, organization, and development. However, to write an essay that has a real chance to succeed, an essay where you **keep it real,** you also need to pay attention to purpose as well as to grammar and organization.

Think about some of the purposes behind the essays you have written or expect to write. Of course, receiving a good grade tops the list. Different assignments will also make assumptions about purpose that you will heed as you produce your best product. For example, suppose an assignment asks you to teach a 16-year-old how to do his own laundry. The essay you would write in response would have the obvious purpose of providing information about sorting, detergents, water levels, and fabric softeners. In other words, it would **inform** the reader about these matters. It would also have the less obvious purpose of **persuading** the teenager that he actually could do the job and that you had the information to help him do it. This hypothetical how-to essay is a real assignment that you will encounter in Chapter 7.

On the other hand, what would you do if an assignment asked you to tell about a past experience that really happened to you? What purposes would drive this essay? First of all, you would want to tell the story accurately, so you would search your memory thoroughly. In addition, you would probably want to find a point to the story because, as we show in this chapter, people like a story to have a moral or a lesson to remember. Last, but certainly not least, you would want to **express** your own feelings and thoughts as the experience occurred and as you reflect upon it. After all, it is your story, and you have every right to show how you feel about

1

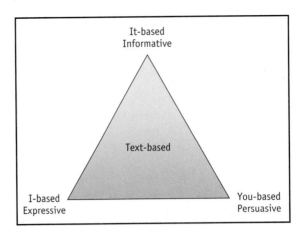

Figure 1.1 The Communication Triangle

the various moments and events in it. And you will do so—beginning, in fact, in just a few minutes.

The idea that writing may **express, inform, persuade,** or perform some combination of the three makes up James Kinneavy's theory of the communication triangle. Figure 1.1 illustrates what we mean.

With the triangle before you, notice that at one angle, we have written the word *I*, at the second *it*, and at the third *you*. Each of these pronouns expresses one of the **purposes** of writing. When you focus on any one of the angles, you begin to see that some of your writing is I-based, or expressive; other writings are it-based, or referential; still other writings are you-based, or persuasive. You may even choose to focus upon the entire plane of the triangle and imagine a fourth type of writing, text-based, or literary. You will encounter each of these types of writing in this book.

Keep in mind, however, that just as the three angles that make up the communication triangle share lines, so also will many of your essays involve more than one purpose; the second purpose is often less obvious or emphasized less as you write. The how-to example illustrates an essay with twin purposes, one more apparently important and the other less so. In moving around the angles of the communication triangle, you will frequently reach back to the previous angle or ahead to the next one as your essay leads you to do. Blending purposes poses no hindrance to your writing well; indeed, your awareness of moving from purpose to purpose will help you write clearly and exactly. Best of all, by staying focused on purpose(s) from beginning to end, you will have a much better chance of keeping it real.

So do you begin every essay by thinking carefully about your purpose and whether you primarily want to express, inform, or persuade? In time, you may very well do so. For now, however, we will begin with the assumption that the absolute best way to improve your writing skills is to write. Your very first activity, then, will be to perform a writing, or rather a prewriting, activity.

Focused Freewriting #1

At the top of a blank page of paper write the following heading: "I'll never forget the time when. . ." Now time yourself five minutes, and begin writing whatever pops into your head. Write continuously, fill each line entirely before moving to the next, and do not hold your pen too tightly. Let the ideas flow from your brain, down your arm, and directly to the page. Do not be concerned with grammatical correctness, with spelling, with neatness, or even whether what you are writing "makes sense." Simply get ideas to the page as quickly as possible and do not stop writing.

Look over your page. Did you tell about an event? Did you perhaps write about more than one event? Probably you have the beginning of a story.

Story form is one way we humans make sense of our world. It is one way we create order. You intuitively understand what story means. Probably you have enjoyed certain stories during life, beginning in childhood. Children love stories. Often they ask to hear a favorite one over and over. Perhaps is a well-known fable such as "The Three Bears" or a personal story like "The story of when I was born."

Readers or listeners have certain expectations when they approach a story. Think about the four-year-old who says, "Tell me a story." What are some characteristics of story? Consider the fable of "The Three Bears." The story begins with "Once upon a time, there were three bears." "Once upon a time" signals the beginning of the story. Fables characteristically end with "They all live happily ever after," which signals the conclusion of the story. Another signal of the conclusion might be "The moral of the story is. . . ." What comes between the beginning and the ending is the "meat" or the "middle" or the "body" of the story. Thus, we see that all complete stories have beginnings, middles, and endings. In a story essay or *narrative essay,* these parts are called the introduction, the body, and the conclusion.

One of the ways good writers write well is by second-guessing their readers. In other words, to be a better writer, you should think like a reader. Think about a story you liked. In fact, it could even be one you heard. Now on a sheet of paper jot down what you liked about this story. In other words, what made this particular story memorable? Was it the language? Was it a suspenseful plot? Was it the descriptions of characters or places?

In this first assignment, you will have the chance to tell a real-life story to real readers, your classmates and instructor.

The Assignment: Telling about a Real Experience

Primary Purpose: Expressive

Audience: Your classmates and instructor

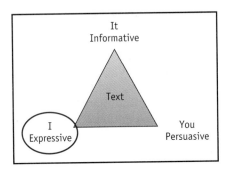

Step 1: Gathering Ideas

Choosing Your Story/Developing Details

The first step in any writing project is deciding what to say. Which story will you tell? It may be you have so many ideas, it will be hard to stick to just one. Or it may be that your mind is a blank and you can think of nothing that is worth writing or hearing about. In either case, do not despair. Several techniques are available to aid in this beginning stage of writing. In fact, you have already practiced one such technique, focused freewriting, at the beginning of this chapter.

Freewriting

Freewriting is designed to help us come up with something to say. True freewriting begins with a blank page with no given topic. We simply start writing with the first thought that pops into our heads and continue until time is up or until we fill a predetermined number of pages. Focused freewriting differs only in that we start with a topic in mind. Now try your hand at some more focused freewriting. By the way, if you find yourself not writing at any point and seemingly unable to do so, write your name or "I am stuck" over and over until you continue onto a new thought, but do not stop writing!

Focused Freewriting #2

Choose two of the following three topics and freewrite for five minutes (or until you fill two pages). Remember that the only rule is that you write nonstop until the task is complete. Hold your pen loosely to avoid hand cramping.

1. Frightening times in my life

2. Embarrassing times in my life

3. Proud moments in my life

━━━━━━━━

You have now completed three focused freewritings. Perhaps you already have an idea or ideas for your story. Maybe you even have some of the details of the event floating through your mind. But perhaps not. Do not fear. You are still getting warmed up! Try your hand at another popular prewriting technique called clustering. The finished product of clustering is called a cluster diagram.

Clustering

Like freewriting, the main reason we use clustering is to come up with ideas. In addition, clustering helps us begin to sort out ideas floating around in our minds. Clustering is unlike plain freewriting, but just like focused freewriting in that we start with some focus (or topic) in mind. Take a look at the sample cluster diagram in Figure 1.2 with the focus "My Most Memorable Moments."

Notice that a cluster diagram starts in the middle of the page and works out toward the edges. Think of the diagram as having levels. At the center is our focus. Next we branch out with the first level. Clustering is similar to a free association mind game. Remember the familiar scene of the psychiatrist asking his or her patient to play a word association game? You may have seen such a scenario in films or old television programs. The doctor says, "When I say black, what word comes to mind?" The patient may respond with "white" or perhaps "dark" or "night." When we cluster, we play a similar game. We ask ourselves this question: When I think of memorable moments in my life, what pops into my mind? Now we simply start filling in with these ideas. Again, as with freewriting, we don't really want to consider whether or not these ideas are right or interesting or valid. And we certainly are not yet interested in whether or not we spell correctly. We just write them in as quickly as possible. Thus, at this first level the writer came up with "getting married," "birth of my son," "my grandmother's death," "birth of my daughter," "winning first place," and "my father's death."

When we move out to the next level in our cluster diagram, we create a new focus. We now ignore the original focus of "memorable moments" and move on the one of our new focuses such as "getting married." Then, with "getting married" as her new focus, our writer came up with three ideas: "getting engaged," "preparing for the wedding," and "the ceremony." At the next level, with "preparing for the wedding" as a focus, she branched out with "ordering cake," "catering," "bartending," and "music." Notice how we work from a relatively broad (general) focus, moving outward to more and more narrow (specific) details.

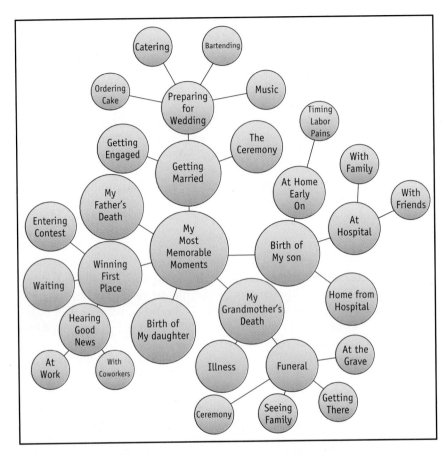

Figure 1.2 Cluster Diagram with Focus on "My Most Memorable Moments"

With clustering, generally no one tells us when we are finished with each level or when we have finished the diagram. We finish when we feel we have exhausted our well of ideas. Now try clustering on your own.

Clustering Activity

Choose two of the following three topics, and complete two cluster diagrams.

1. My happiest moments

2. My disappointments or failures

3. Times I have learned lessons

One way to think about writing is by seeing it as a series of decisions we must make. Now it is time to make a decision. Look back over all your freewritings and cluster diagrams. Consider the stories you might relate in your narrative essay. Then choose two so that you have a Plan A and a Plan B. Now fill in the following blanks.

My Plan A: The event that happened to me that I would like to relate to

my classmates and instructor: _____

My Plan B: A second event that I will tell about if for some reason

Plan A does not work out: _____

Telling Your Story Out Loud

Now since stories really should be heard, this next prewriting activity may help you think through your essay before you write it. Use your Plan A story.

Collaborative Activity

Find a partner. Consider where your story begins. Where should it end? Tell your partner your story from beginning to end. Listen carefully to your partner's story. After hearing the story, ask your partner any questions you may have.

Using Your Five Senses—Sensory Details

Group Activity

Think of at least two historical events that you can remember, such as the O.J. Simpson verdict or the school shootings in Littleton, Colorado. Discuss the events with some classmates who also remember them. What makes the events memorable to so many people? What images do you see and hear when you close your eyes and think of the events? Are those images the same for your classmates? As a group make a list of the images to share with the rest of your class.

Five Senses Activity

Now consider your own story, the one you related to a classmate. Close your eyes and see yourself back at the beginning of the event. Now in your "mind's eye," see yourself reliving the whole event from beginning to end. Focus your attention only on what you can see around you. What do you see? You may want to speak your response to this question into a tape recorder. Play back the tape, and write down a list of what you saw. Include as many visual details on the list as you can. Then close your eyes once again, and see yourself at the beginning of your story. Relive the story, but this time focus on what you hear. Tape yourself telling what you heard as you lived through your story. Then play back the tape and write down your list. Repeat this activity focusing on what you could feel. Then do it a final time, focusing this last time on the senses of smell and taste.

———

You now have four lists of sensory details. You should try to include many of these details when you write your story. Why? It is extremely important to put yourself in your reader's position, to think like a reader. You've probably noticed that some writing is easy to "get into" and some is very difficult to relate to. One of the ways to make your writing easy to "get into" is by including lots of details that let us see, hear, feel, smell, or taste what is happening. Our senses allow us to make sense of the world. Everything a baby learns must come through one or more of his or her senses.

Consider the situation of Helen Keller, a woman who became a scholar, an author, and a famous advocate for the disabled. You may be familiar with her story. Helen was born with all five of her senses functioning, but an illness in her infancy left her blind and deaf. Unable to reach their daughter by showing or speaking to her, Helen's parents were unable to teach her about the world, and she grew uncontrolled and wild. Annie Sullivan, her teacher, was finally able to reach her through her sense of touch, by finger spelling into her hand. Until this revelation, Helen was shut out from her world. Likewise, too few sensory details and we may be shut out from a story. Instead of shutting out your readers, draw them in.

Exercise: Reading and Listing

Read the following essay, "Mrs. Bertha Flowers," by Maya Angelou. When you have completed the essay, review it, and list at least five details that appeal to your sense of sight, five to your sense of hearing, five to your sense of touch, and five to your senses of smell and/or taste. Hint: you may want to pay special attention to Paragraphs 2, 14, and 45.

Mrs. Bertha Flowers

by Maya Angelou

1   For nearly a year, I sopped around the house, the Store, the school and the church, like an old biscuit, dirty and inedible. Then I met, or rather got to know, the lady who threw me my first life line.

2   Mrs. Bertha Flowers was the aristocrat of Black Stamps. She had the grace of control to appear warm in the coldest weather, and on the Arkansas summer days it seemed she had a private breeze which swirled around, cooling her. She was thin without the taut look of wiry people, and her printed voile dresses and flowered hats were as right for her as denim overalls for a farmer. She was our side's answer to the richest white woman in town.

3   Her skin was a rich black that would have peeled like a plum if snagged, but then no one would have thought of getting close enough to Mrs. Flowers to ruffle her dress, let along snag her skin. She didn't encourage familiarity. She wore gloves too.

4   I don't think I ever saw Mrs. Flowers laugh, but she smiled often. A slow widening of her thin black lips to show even, small white teeth, then the slow effortless closing. When she chose to smile on me, I always wanted to thank her. The action was so graceful and inclusively benign.

5   She was one of the few gentlewomen I have ever known, and has remained throughout my life the measure of what a human being can be.

6   Momma had a strange relationship with her. Most often when she passed on the road in front of the Store, she spoke to Momma in that soft yet carrying voice, "Good day, Mrs. Henderson." Momma responded with "How you, Sister Flowers?"

7   Mrs. Flowers didn't belong to our church, nor was she Momma's familiar. Why on earth did she insist on calling her Sister Flowers? Shame made me want to hide my face. Mrs. Flowers deserved better than to be called Sister. Then, Momma left out the verb. Why not ask, "How *are* you, *Mrs.* Flowers?" With the unbalanced passion of the young, I hated her for showing her ignorance to Mrs. Flowers. It didn't occur to me for many years that they were as alike as sisters, separated only by formal education.

8   Although I was upset, neither of the women was in the least shaken by what I thought an unceremonious greeting. Mrs. Flowers would continue her easy gait up the hill to her little bungalow, and Momma kept on shelling peas or doing whatever had brought her to the front porch.

9   Occasionally, though, Mrs. Flowers would drift off the road and down to the Store and Momma would say to me, "Sister, you go on and play." As I left I would hear the beginning of an intimate conversation. Momma persistently using the wrong verb, or none at all.

10   "Brother and Sister Wilcox is sho'ly the meanest—" "Is," Momma? "Is"? Oh, please, not "is," Momma, for two or more. But they talked, and from the side of the building where I waited for the ground to open up and swallow me, I heard the soft-voiced Mrs. Flowers and the textured voice of my grandmother merging and melting. They were interrupted from time to time by giggles that must have come from Mrs. Flowers (Momma never giggled in her life). Then she was gone.

11   She appealed to me because she was like people I had never met personally. Like women in English novels who walked the moors (whatever they were) with their loyal dogs racing at a respectful distance. Like the women who sat in front of roaring fireplaces, drinking tea incessantly from silver trays full of scones and crumpets. Women who walked over the "heath" and read morocco-bound books and had two last names divided by a hyphen. It would be safe to say that she made me proud to be Negro, just by being herself.

12   She acted just as refined as whitefolks in the movies and books and she was more beautiful, for none of them could have come near that warm color without looking gray by comparison.

13   It was fortunate that I never saw her in the company of powhitefolks. For since they tend to think of their whiteness as an evenizer, I'm certain that I would have had to hear her spoken to commonly as Bertha, and my image of her would have been shattered like the unmendable Humpty-Dumpty.

14   One summer afternoon, sweet-milk fresh in my memory, she stopped at the Store to buy provisions. Another Negro woman of her health and age would have been expected to carry the paper sacks home in one hand, but Momma said, "Sister Flowers, I'll send Bailey up to your house with these things."

15   She smiled that slow dragging smile, "Thank you, Mrs. Henderson. I'd prefer Marguerite, though." My name was beautiful when she said it. "I've been meaning to talk to her, anyway." They gave each other age-group looks.

16   Momma said, "Well, that's all right then. Sister, go and change your dress. You going to Sister Flowers's."

17   The chifforobe was a maze. What on earth did one put on to go to Mrs. Flowers' house? I knew I shouldn't put on a Sunday dress. It might be sacrilegious. Certainly not a house dress, since I was already wearing a fresh one. I chose a school dress, naturally. It was formal without suggesting that going to Mrs. Flowers' house was equivalent to attending church.

18   I trusted myself back into the Store.

19   "Now, don't you look nice." I had chosen the right thing, for once.

20   "Mrs. Henderson, you make most of the children's clothes, don't you?"

21   "Yes, ma'am. Sure do. Store-bought clothes ain't hardly worth the thread it take to stitch them."

22   "I'll say you do a lovely job, though, so neat. That dress looks professional."

23   Momma was enjoying the seldom-received compliments. Since everyone we knew (except Mrs. Flowers, of course) could sew competently, praise was rarely handed out for the commonly practiced craft.

24   "I try, with the help of the Lord, Sister Flowers, to finish the inside just like I does the outside. Come here, Sister."

25   I had buttoned up the collar and tied the belt, apronlike, in back. Momma told me to turn around. With one hand she pulled the strings and the belt fell free at both sides of my waist. Then her large hands were at my neck, opening the button loops. I was terrified. What was happening?

26   "Take it off, Sister." She had her hands on the hem of the dress.

27   "I don't need to see the inside, Mrs. Henderson, I can tell . . ." But the dress was over my head and my arms were stuck in the sleeves. Momma said, "That'll do. See here, Sister Flowers, I French-seams around the armholes." Through the cloth film, I saw the shadow approach. "That makes it last longer. Children these days would bust out of sheet-metal clothes. They so rough."

28   "That is a very good job, Mrs. Henderson. You should be proud. You can put your dress back on, Marguerite."

29   "No ma'am. Pride is a sin. And 'cording to the Good Book, it goeth before a fall."

30   "That's right. So the Bible says. It's a good thing to keep in mind."

31   I wouldn't look at either of them. Momma hadn't thought that taking off my dress in front of Mrs. Flowers would kill me stone dead. If I had refused, she would have thought I was trying to be "womanish" and might have remembered St. Louis. Mrs. Flowers had known that I would be embarrassed and that was even worse. I picked up the groceries and went out to wait in the hot sunshine. It would be fitting if I got a sunstroke and died before they came outside. Just dropped dead on the slanting porch.

32   There was a little path beside the rocky road, and Mrs. Flowers walked in front swinging her arms and picking her way over the stones.
      She said, without turning her head, to me, "I hear you're doing very good school work, Marguerite, but that it's all written. The teachers report that they have trouble getting you to talk in class." We passed the triangular farm on our left and the path widened to allow us to walk together. I hung back in the separate unasked and unanswerable questions.

33   "Come and walk along with me, Marguerite." I couldn't have refused even if I wanted to. She pronounced my name so nicely. Or more correctly, she spoke each word with such clarity that I was certain a foreigner who didn't understand English could have understood her.

34   "Now no one is going to make you talk—possibly no one can. But bear in mind, language is man's way of communicating with his fellow man and it is language alone which separates him from the lower animals." That was a totally new idea to me, and I would need time to think about it.

35   "Your grandmother says you read a lot. Every chance you get. That's good, but not good enough. Words mean more than what is set down on paper. It takes the human voice to infuse them with the shades of deeper meaning."

36   I memorized the part about the human voice infusing words. It seemed so valid and poetic.

37   She said she was going to give me some books and that I not only must read them, I must read them aloud. She suggested that I try to make a sentence sound in as many different ways as possible.

38   "I'll accept no excuse if you return a book to me that has been badly handled." My imagination boggled at the punishment I would deserve if in fact I did abuse a book of Mrs. Flowers'. Death would be too kind and brief.

39   The odors in the house surprised me. Somehow I had never connected Mrs. Flowers with food or eating or any other common experience of common people. There must have been an outhouse, too, but my mind never recorded it.

40   The sweet scent of vanilla had met us as she opened the door.

41   "I made tea cookies this morning. You see, I had planned to invite you for cookies and lemonade so we could have this little chat. The lemonade is in the icebox."

42   It followed that Mrs. Flowers would have ice on an ordinary day, when most families in our town bought ice late on Saturdays only a few times during the summer to be used in the wooden ice-cream freezers.

43   She took the bags from me and disappeared through the kitchen door. I looked around the room that I had never in my wildest fantasies imagined I would see. Browned photographs leered or threatened from the walls and the white, freshly done curtains pushed against themselves and against the wind. I wanted to gobble up the room entire and take it to Bailey, who would help me analyze and enjoy it.

44   "Have a seat, Marguerite. Over there by the table." She carried a platter covered with a tea towel. Although she warned that she hadn't tried her hand at baking sweets for some time, I was certain that like everything else about her the cookies would be perfect.

45   They were flat round wafers, slightly browned on the edges and butter-yellow in the center. With the cold lemonade they were sufficient for childhood's lifelong diet. Remembering my manners, I took nice little lady-like bites off the edges. She said she had made them expressly for me and that she had a few in the kitchen that I could take home to my brother. So I jammed one whole cake in my mouth and the rough crumbs scratched the insides of my jaws, and if I hadn't had to swallow, it would have been a dream come true.

46   As I ate she began the first of what we later called "my lessons in living." She said that I must always be intolerant of ignorance but understanding of illiteracy. That some people, unable to go to school, were more educated and even more intelligent than college professors. She encouraged me to listen carefully to what country people called mother wit. That in those homely sayings was couched the collective wisdom of generations.

47   When I finished the cookies she brushed off the table and brought a thick, small book from the bookcase. I had read *A Tale of Two Cities* and found it up to my standards as a romantic novel. She opened the first page and I heard poetry for the first time in my life.

48   "It was the best of times and the worst of times . . ." Her voice slid in and curved down through and over the words. She was nearly singing. I wanted to look at the pages. Were they the same that I had read? Or were there notes, music, lined on the pages, as in a hymn book? Her sounds began cascading gently. I knew from listening to a thousand preachers that she was nearing the end of her reading, and I hadn't really heard, heard to understand, a single word.

49   "How do you like that?"

50   It occurred to me that she expected a response. The sweet vanilla flavor was still on my tongue and her reading was a wonder in my ears. I had to speak.

51   I said, "Yes, ma'am." It was the least I could do, but it was the most also.

52   "There's one more thing. Take this book of poems and memorize one for me. Next time you pay me a visit, I want you to recite."

53   I have tried often to search behind the sophistication of years for the enchantment I so easily found in those gifts. The essence escapes but its aura remains. To be allowed, no, invited, into the private lives of strangers, and to share their joys and fears, was a chance to exchange the Southern bitter wormwood for a cup of mead with Beowulf or a hot cup of tea and milk with Oliver Twist. When I said aloud, "It is a far, far better thing that I do, than I have ever done . . ." tears of love filled my eyes at my selflessness.

54   On that first day, I ran down the hill and into the road (few cars ever came along it) and had the good sense to stop running before I reached the Store.

55   I was liked, and what a difference it made. I was respected not as Mrs. Henderson's grandchild or Bailey's sister but for just being Marguerite Johnson.

56   Childhood's logic never asks to be proved (all conclusions are absolute). I didn't question why Mrs. Flowers had singled me out for attention, nor did it occur to me that Momma might have asked her to give me a little talking to. All I cared about was that she had made tea cookies for *me* and read to *me* from her favorite book. It was enough to prove that she liked me.

Collaborative Activity

In groups of three to five, discuss your details with your classmates. Revise your list so that it contains the absolute strongest details, for each sense, that you can find. Also, briefly discuss the following questions.

1. Why does Angelou include so many sensory details in her story? What effect(s) do the details have upon the reader?

2. At which points in the essay does Angelou most clearly **express** herself, the way that she personally feels about what she is seeing, hearing, touching, smelling, and tasting?

3. How do you interpret what happens at the very end of the essay? Why are the words "she liked me" so powerful? What do these words suggest will be the long-term effect that Mrs. Flowers will have upon Maya. Does the conclusion suggest that Angelou writes not only to express but also to inform and perhaps even to persuade?

Using Dialogue

We have discussed how effective sensory details can be in a story. Let's now focus on aural or hearing details. One relatively easy way to let us hear what is happening in your story is to include dialogue. In other words, at important moments let us hear what people in your story are saying.

Dialogue Activity

Think of three to five characters in your story. Pretend you are each. Write down, word for word, at least three comments you can "hear" each saying. Also write, word for word, a dialogue at least five sentences long between two characters.

Don't worry if you can't remember exactly what someone actually said. But do try to be completely honest to the voice of the speaker. In other words, have the characters speak just the way they would speak in real life.

Step 2: Organizing Ideas

Now that you have collected ideas and gathered information, it is time to move on to organizing your information. You actually began this step when you decided when your story begins and where it ends. Now consider your story for a moment. Not everything that happened while your story took place is equally important. Say, for example, your story starts when you woke up one morning and ends when you went to bed that night. Many small events make up your larger story. Perhaps you brushed your teeth, flossed, and showered before eating breakfast. Those events may or may not be significant occurrences in your story, but probably they are not.

Focusing Your Story

You'll want to be sure to emphasize those details that are most important. In doing so you will bring focus to your narrative. To help you understand focus it may help to think about the last movie you saw. Moviemaking is storytelling. How does the filmmaker tell the audience something important is happening? Sometimes music or lighting cues viewers. Another big hint is when the camera zooms in for a close-up, thereby letting viewers know they are witnessing a key scene.

Activity: Drawing Key Scenes

No matter how sloppily, draw pictures to show three to five key moments in your story. Show your drawings to a classmate, and ask him or her to give you a "word picture" to match what he or she sees. Write down some of the key words you hear and use them in your narrative. You can always repeat the activity and create your own word pictures when no partner is available.

Now that you have determined your key scenes, how will you emphasize them? Easy. Focus on these key moments by supplying more specific details about these moments. Unimportant moments should be mentioned in brief, without going into much detail, or left out altogether.

Making Connections Through Time—Chronological Order and Time Transitions

We have already noted that your story is made up of a series of events, some key moments, some less significant, some relatively insignificant. You must choose which to include, which to emphasize, and which to omit. What we have not discussed is moving from one event to the next. Every time your story moves from one event to the next, you will leave a gap. Some gaps, or points in the story when you skip over or summarize several insignificant events, will be huge like canyons while others will be more like cracks. You can build bridges over these gaps by including transitions in your essay. Your readers will need time transitions to get them from idea to idea, from event to event as they read your narrative. You should tell your story in chronological order, the order in which it occurred. You should also be sure to include transitions that make connections across gaps in time.

The simplest time transitions are *first, last,* and *finally.* But simplest is not always best. What are some other ways to signal movement in your narrative? Consider words and phrases like *before, after, meanwhile, later, at the same time, eventually, soon, next,* and *then.*

Developing a Thesis Statement

Before you begin writing, it is a good idea to be able to say why you are telling your classmates this particular story. Fill in the blanks in the following sentence.

_____, *overall, was a* _____ *experience.*

You have just written a working thesis statement for your narrative essay. A thesis statement is a sentence that tells readers the main idea of your essay. It is a promise to your readers that everything that follows will relate to it and support it. "Working" means that you may choose to revise this thesis statement later. Having your working thesis statement should also help you to make final decisions about which details you might leave out of your essay.

We usually find the thesis statement near the end of the introduction. The second most common placement is in the conclusion. If an essay's thesis (main idea) is never directly stated, it is called an implied thesis.

Step 3: Writing

By now you have come up with many ideas, and you have decided which ideas to include in your story. In addition, you have thought about ordering your ideas and connecting them logically. You are ready to write your essay. Here is an example of what one particular student produced in response to this same assignment.

My First 2-Wheel Bicycle

By Shaun Crouse

1   Most people seem to remember their childhood better than any other time in their life. This is so true for me. I can recall my childhood off the top of my head, especially that special moment when I received my first bike, a two-wheel bicycle to be exact. This was indeed a triumphant moment in which I went from childhood to manhood. This point in which I got my bike was also special for the simple reason that the assembling of the bike brought my father and me close. I will never forget the time that I received my first two-wheel bicycle. To this day I can still feel the handlebars in my hands and the bicycle seat between my little legs. This moment in my life happened during the spring time like this.

2   I knew every kid on my street. We all hung with each other, threw parties together, and spent the night at each other's house. This was even true about sharing bikes. Every child of proper age had a bike, a tricycle or a two-wheeler. We each had our own forms of traveling. Yet, as the ages of the children grew, so did their advance-

ments from tricycle to two-wheeler with training-wheels to the full life-size two-wheeler bicycle. I was one of few young children who did not have a two-wheeler bicycle, at least not yet. At that time I was not alone having the tricycle as my get around, and I loved my tricycle.

3   Soon Mike, my best friend, and I were the only two kids left without a two-wheeler bicycle. All that changed when Mike came over to my house with "the gang" on his new bike, a cheap one, but a new two-wheel bicycle to ride up to the convenience store. I was flabbergasted, a little depressed and lonely, but I went with them. I rode on my tricycle while the rest of them rode on their bicycles. That night my mother and I carried on the conversation of me having a bicycle like the others. Of course my father was involved, and the question of allowing me to be considered an adult-child with responsibilities arose.

4   For about two hours I had the first lecture in my life. Soon my mother said, "How about this sweetie. You practice riding a two-wheeler, and get good at it, and well, I'll talk to your father into allowing you to get a bike." I reminded her, "A Huffy bike." She smiled.

5   For two weeks, I practiced and practiced on my neighbor's bike. Of course I fell and fell. Nevertheless, I got better and better. It really seemed hard for any of the neighbors to miss me riding, falling, and riding some more. During the two weeks of hard military, two-wheel bicycle training, Mike approached me about what I thought of the bell on his bicycle. "Neat," I exclaimed. Then he looked at my tricycle in the garage and smirked. "Don't worry," I said. "I'll have one soon." That exact night my mother brought me in from riding my bicycle to eat dinner. "Honey, I have some good news." "What?" I said with applesauce down my chin. "I talked to your father and told him of the progress you've made in the last two weeks. When he gets home, we'll go get that new Huffy bike." "Really mom, really!!" I could barely control myself. Finally, I will be a man, a man with a bike.

6   Maybe I got a little too worked up, but we did it. We started the journey to K-Mart. As we were walking towards the bike department, my mother would grin and wink at me. My father, on the other hand, just stared at the prices of certain items and shook his head. "There they are guys." I ran toward the bikes as if they may disappear or something. I giggled and laughed as my parents, hand-in-hand, slowly walked towards all the excitement. My mother and I looked around while my father compared prices. As the anxiety grew inside of me, I could feel the moment of when I would get my bike approaching. Right at that moment, I saw the coolest, fastest, two-wheel bicycle ever made, the Huffy Power Bike 2000. "Padding included," my dad stated while I was drooling on the box. "Can I have it dad, please?" "Ummm" was the only word that exited his mouth. After heavy debate and configuration, an agreement was settled. I got the bike. "Thanks mom," I said. Because I knew she really helped me out in getting the bike.

7   My smile didn't move from my face all the way home. As soon as we got home, my dad and I put the power machine together, padding and stickers too. I could tell there was something missing when the two hour long project was completed, but I couldn't figure it out. "Oh honey, don't forget these," my mother yelled from the kitchen. "Accessories," my dad said, "just what this bike needs," streamers, and a police horn and a bell. After the following hour passed of converting a normal bike to a deluxe-loaded screaming machine, the time came for a test-run. "Can I take the bike . . . ," was as far as I got until my dad said that I had to go to bed and I could ride it the next morning, Saturday.

8   The next morning, I woke up early to ride my bicycle. I told my mother what I was about to do. She moaned, still half asleep. I rolled out the Huffy, and slightly looked down at my lonely tricycle, and continued on. "Wow Shaun, you got a bike," all the kids said. They couldn't take their eyes off of my bike. It was a special and beautiful moment for me. After the show was over, the gang and I rode off towards wherever the bikes lead us to. The wind felt so good at a faster speed, and the height was tremendously breathtaking. All the neighbors watched as I showed off the Huffy. My parents proudly watched me outside, yet I believe my father was looking for problems with the bike. I rode and rode, never getting off. I was happy that I finally made it to the big leagues.

9   That afternoon we had a neighborhood barbeque. You sure can smell a lot more at a faster speed and at a greater height. My dream had come true. That night after I parked my bike into the garage, I looked at my tricycle, lonely and dirty, and asked my dad, "What is going to happen to my tricycle?" "We'll probably give it to another young child." I felt bad but also glad that perhaps another kid would go through the same experiences that I did. At night in bed I dreamed of my new bike and all the journeys that would follow.

Notice that Shaun, the student author, chose to tell about a memorable event in his life, getting his first two-wheel bicycle. Can you see that his essay, as do all essays, has an introduction, a middle (or body), and a conclusion? In this case, the first paragraph is an introduction, the last paragraph is a conclusion, and all the paragraphs in between make up the body of the essay.

Activity

With a partner, answer the following questions regarding Shaun's essay.

1. What do we learn from the first paragraph of the essay? In particular, what do we learn about Shaun's purpose for the essay?

2. What do we learn from the second paragraph? Might we consider it introductory as well?

3. Can you find a thesis statement, or a statement of the main idea? Copy it down.

4. What happens in the conclusion of the essay?

5. What are the key scenes in Shaun's narrative? How do these key scenes help him "keep it real"?

6. Write down two examples of places where dialogue lets us "hear" the story.

7. Write down two examples of good visual details.

8. Write down two examples of good "feeling" details.

9. Write down three or more examples of time transitions.

Now write your story. After you finish, repeat the activity above with your partner, but answer the questions about your own narratives. Consider any changes or additions you could make to improve your essay.

Activity

Read your story out loud to yourself, but instead of saying "I," plug in the name of someone you don't like very much. How would you respond if the story told about this person? Pull the name of someone you don't know from the telephone book, and plug in that person's name. How does your perspective change now? Do you need to revise any details or observations to keep the points clear? Do you want to change some of your points?

Activity

Ask yourself how another person in your story felt about the experience. What would he or she have considered the moral of the story? Will incorporating his or her viewpoint change or improve your story?

Grammar and Usage: Recognizing and Using "True Blue Verbs" for Strong Sensory Details

Consider the following sentences from Shaun Crouse's essay:

My mother and I **looked** around while my father **compared** prices.
I **rolled** out the Huffy, slightly **looked** down at my lonely tricycle, and **continued** on.

Also note the following from Maya Angelou's essay:

> *I **had buttoned** up the collar and **tied** the belt, apronlike, in back. Momma **told** me to turn around. With one hand she **pulled** the strings and the belt **fell** free at both sides of my waist. Then her large hands **were** at my neck, opening the button loops. I **was** terrified. What **was happening?***

Each of the sentences cited contains very strong details that a reader may easily imagine. What makes the details strong? Look carefully at the high-lighted words. What do these words have in common?

After evaluating the words emphasized, you may notice that all of them, except *were* and *was,* show an action occurring. That is, some-one *looked* in one sentence while someone *pulled* in another. These words, again except for *were* and *was,* are all **action verbs.** The words *were* and *was* are also verbs. Perhaps you remember them from high school as **linking verbs.** All of the highlighted words, then, are verbs, and since they actually function within their clauses as verbs with sub-jects, we will call them **true blue verbs.** If you make a point of using several true blue verbs, especially those that show actions, in each paragraph, you will almost inevitably find yourself writing strong sen-sory details.

Unfortunately, not all verbs function as true blue verbs. Sometimes a verb functions, instead, as a **verbal** and can trick you into making a sen-tence error if you fail to distinguish between it and a true blue verb. Look at the three examples below.

> **Walking** home after school yesterday afternoon.
>
> **Encouraged** by the grades on the first three essays.
>
> With the ability **to score** at will against the weak defense.

Each highlighted word or phrase is a verb form but is a verbal rather than a true blue verb because it has no subject and fails to function as a verb within a clause. You will probably also note that neither of the examples is a sentence. You would be wise to infer from the examples that *every sentence must have at least one true blue verb.* Finally, you may note three rules about true blue verbs and verbals from the examples above:

1. A verb that ends in *-ing* is a verbal. It can become a true blue verb only if it has a linking verb helper, such as *am, is, are, was, were, have been, has been, had been,* or *will have been* in front of it.

2. A verb that has the word *to* directly in front of it is always a verbal.

3. A verb that ends in *-ed* is a true blue verb only if it is preceded by a noun that can function as its subject.

vt missing p. 22

Now let's follow the directions for the exercise below and apply what we have just discussed. Use extreme caution around words ending in *-ing* or *-ed* or words with *to* in front of them. Also, remember that sometimes a true blue verb includes a main verb and a helper, as "I *had buttoned* up the collar" from Angelou illustrates.

Exercise 1

To determine whether a sentence is a complete sentence, you must first be able to find the true blue verbs. Circle all of the true blue verbs in the following constructions. Please note that some constructions will have one true blue verb, some more than one, and some none at all.

1. One of my favorite movies is *Raiders of the Lost Ark.*

2. Harrison Ford wonderfully portrays Indiana Jones

3. By the end, Indiana has encountered many obstacles.

4. He uses his brains rather than his brawn to outwit them.

5. Indiana Jones always fights the Nazis, who are trying to recover many valuable artifacts, such as the Ark of the Covenant.

6. You never know where Indiana will appear next.

7. In another movie, he searches for the Holy Grail.

8. Running and having enemies shoot at him never seem to tire Indiana out.

9. As long as he has his rope and a pistol.

10. River Phoenix, as young Indiana, encounters snakes and explains Indiana's lifelong fear of the slithery creatures.

11. Yesterday, I saw a penny on the sidewalk, and I stopped to pick it up.

12. The old saying claims that picking up a penny brings a person good luck.

13. Learning this lesson from my grandparents during my childhood in the 1960s.

14. When I see a penny, I quickly check to see whether it is showing "heads" or "tails."

15. Of course, if you don't pick up the penny, your good luck goes!

16. The next time I see a penny, I'll grab it as always, if it is on "heads."

17. After all, possibly gaining good luck never hurt anybody.

18. But pennies will only buy so much nowadays; we need to talk about five dollar bills!

19. "To be or not to be: that is the question."—Shakespeare

20. " 'Twas brillig, and the slithy toves did gyre and gimble in the wabe."—Lewis Carroll (Charles Lutwidge Dodgson)

Exercise 2: Collaborative Activity

Apply what you have learned about true blue verbs to your own essay. With a partner, read over your entire essay, and find as many true blue verbs as you can. Remember that action verbs convey sensory details more clearly than linking verbs. Revise as many linking verbs into action verbs as you can, and see how much more lively your writing becomes!

Writing Process

Getting Started: Gathering Ideas and Organizing

What Is the Writing Process?

Picture this scene. You are sitting in a college math class surrounded by classmates as your professor finishes an explanation of ways to solve quadratic equations. While you copy the final problem into your notebook and begin thinking about lunch, the professor says, "Wait just a moment. I've finished grading your exams, and I'll return them to you now." Immediately you perk up and listen.

Your hands begin to sweat while you wait to hear your name. As your professor shifts back and forth handing out papers, you think about the fact that math has always been a difficult subject for you. You try to remember all the types of problems that were on this test. Then you think about a math test you failed in high school, and you remind yourself that this exam will count 25 percent of your grade for this course. Then, as you lean over and reach out for the exam paper, already you can see a grade circled near the top of the test. You take your exam, look closely at it, and breathe a small sigh of relief. Your score is 85!

To experience this type of success on a major exam usually requires a good deal of effort, and part of that effort is planning to meet the goal of passing the exam (or passing with a B, or an A). With such effort, you will experience the satisfaction of earning a high grade frequently during your college career. But keep in mind that you rarely, if ever, just happen to make an 85 (or a 45, for that matter) on an exam. You must take certain steps to meet the goal of succeeding on the exam. In other words, people follow a process of some sort to achieve a goal or final product. The product in this example is a test score of 85.

So what might be involved in scoring well on a major math exam? Put another way, the question looks like this:

Product: A good score on the math exam

Process: Steps to achieve this product or goal?

Some items might not be obvious at first. For one, you should be sure to go to each class meeting. You should be on time and stay the whole period so that you won't miss any information that might prove to be important later on. You should ask questions when they arise and approach the teacher if you have additional questions or need clarification after class. You should do all the homework assigned each night so that you don't fall behind. You could go to a math lab if one is available to check your work with a tutor or to get extra help if you don't understand a lesson completely.

Then, of course, you should begin studying for the test several days before it is scheduled. Review all the problems that have been worked in class. You might also work extra problems of the same type just to be sure you can handle anything that appears on the exam.

Process for Succeeding on a Math Exam

1. Go to each class.
2. Be on time.
3. Stay for the entire class.
4. Ask questions as a way to stay involved during class.
5. See the teacher to ask for clarification on difficult topics.
6. Do all homework completely and on time.
7. Go to the Math Lab or tutor for help.
8. Begin study for the exam several days in advance.
9. Review all the material the exam will cover.
10. Work extra problems of the sort you expect on the exam.

Now consider another example. I love fresh, juicy, homegrown tomatoes, and I want to enjoy these delicacies all summer long. Therefore, my product or goal is several healthy tomato plants, bowed over with the weight of bright, red tomatoes. Unfortunately, such plants don't just appear in my back yard at the end of July.

If I want a successful garden, then I must begin a process in April or May. I'll have to prepare the soil by tilling it, and by adding plant food, fertilizer, and any other necessary nutrients. Then I have to acquire gardening tools and be sure my garden hoses and nozzles are in working order. In addition, I have to decide whether to grow my plants from seed or from seedling plants. I need to decide on the species, and I need to decide where to purchase them. I have to sow, plant, and water the seedlings. I must weed and nurture the plants. I will need to examine them closely for signs of disease or insect infestations. Later, I will stake the plants so that they won't touch the ground and rot. Finally, I may enjoy those ripe, juicy tomatoes many weeks after I begin the process.

If a friend comes to visit and I serve him slices of my tomatoes, he only sees and enjoys the final product. Similarly, when we attend a play, we see and enjoy the show. We don't see the months of preparation and rehearsal that preceded the production. When we buy a new sofa, we don't see the production line, the excess pieces of lumber, or the extra pieces of cloth and loose threads cut away from the upholstery. In addition, we don't see the initial test production pieces that failed while the machines were being set to specific standards.

So it is with writing. We often think of writing as just that, the final product, the article we read in the magazine or newspaper, the book as it appears on the library's shelf, or the essay we hand in to our English teacher for a grade. In other words, we tend to focus on the product, or where we want to end up, rather than the process, or how we may get there. Understand, then, that writing is both a product (the essay, the short story, or novel in its final form) and a process.

Activity: Writing Process

Think about a time when you wrote an important paper for a class or for work. Then list the steps you took to complete this writing task from beginning to end. Try to be as specific as you can.

Individual writing processes certainly may vary, and various models of the writing process may include different numbers of steps. Yet nearly all models include at least four stages. Keeping that in mind, we now present the following four-step model of the writing process.

The Writing Process

Step 1: Gathering Ideas
Step 2: Organizing
Step 3: Writing
Step 4: Revising

Our model of the writing process is *linear* in that it shows separate, distinct stages and implies that after completing the first step, the writer moves to the second, followed by the third, and finally the fourth step to finish. But in reality, writing is not a perfectly straightforward process. It is a *circular* process. Writing is a complex task that usually includes several stops and starts. Sometimes we need to take a step back. For example, while organizing ideas, we may discover that we don't have enough to say; therefore, we need to gather more information. Other times we may begin revising early on in the process, as in the case of the writer who rewrites her introduction before moving on to write the body of her essay. The steps may also seem to blend together so that it is not clear when you are completing one step and moving to the next.

Getting Ready to Write: The First Two Steps (Prewriting)

The word *prewriting,* which literally means *before writing,* refers to everything you do before you actually write a first draft. The remainder of this chapter concerns itself with this first half of the writing process: **gathering ideas** and **organizing ideas.**

Step 1: Gathering Ideas

Almost everyone has experienced the horrible feeling of sitting at a blank page (or blank computer screen) and having no ideas or "nothing to say." This feeling, often called writer's block, may be caused by several reasons, including having too broad a topic, trying to say something entirely original, trying to sound like someone other than yourself, or being overly concerned about grammar, punctuation, and word choice too early in the writing process. Happily, several techniques have helped and continue to help writers get started writing. Before you start practicing some of these techniques, realize that some of them will work better for you than others. Your preferences may relate to your topic or writing assignment, to the writing situation (you may have three weeks to finish the essay, or three hours), or to your individual learning style (whether or not, for example, you learn best by reading words or by looking at charts).

Keep in mind, also, that sometimes when you don't know what to say, the best option may be to jump in and just start writing. Peter Elbow's book *Writing With Power* describes several writing processes, including the following "open-ended writing process" that may lead you to produce a rough draft when "you sense you have something to write but you don't quite know what." As you read the essay, pay particular attention to Elbow's extensive use of nonstop freewriting. Then answer the questions that follow the selection.

The Open-Ended Writing Process

by Peter Elbow

1   The open-ended writing process is at the opposite extreme from the direct writing process. It is a way to bring to birth an unknown,

unthought-of piece of writing—a piece of writing that is not yet in you. It is a technique for thinking, seeing, and feeling new things. This process invites maximum chaos and disorientation. You have to be willing to nurse something through many stages over a long period of time and to put up with not knowing where you are going. Thus it is a process that can change you, not just your words.

2   As the most creative and unmethodical writing process, I associate it with poems or stories or novels. But it will also lead you to essays. It has led me to parts of this and my previous book about writing.

3   Ideally you should not choose in advance what you are going to end up with. Perhaps you start out thinking and hoping for a poem, but you may well end up with a story in prose, a letter to someone, an essay that works out one of your perplexities. The open-ended writing process goes on and on till the potential piece of writing is fully cooked and grown. Sometimes this happens quickly, sometimes you nurse it through decades (though I will suggest some ways to hasten the process a bit).

4   I think of the open-ended writing process as a voyage in two stages: a sea voyage and a coming to new land. For the sea voyage you are trying to lose sight of land—the place you began. Getting lost is the best source of new material. In coming to new land you develop a new conception of what you are writing about—a new idea or vision—and then you gradually reshape your material to fit this new vision. The sea voyage is a process of divergence, branching, proliferation, and confusion; the coming to land is a process of convergence, pruning, centralizing, and clarifying.

5   To begin the sea voyage, do a nonstop freewriting that starts from wherever you happen to be. Most often you just start with a thought or a feeling or a memory that seems for some reason important to you. But perhaps you have something in mind for a possible piece of writing: perhaps you have some ideas for an essay; or certain images stick in mind as belonging in a poem; or certain characters or events are getting ready to make a story. You can also start by describing what you wish you could end up with. Realize of course that you probably won't. Just start writing.

6   The open-ended writing process is ideal for the situation where you sense you have something to write but you don't quite know what. Just start writing about anything at all. If you have special trouble with that first moment of writing—that confrontation with a blank page—ask yourself what you *don't* want to write about and start writing about it before you have a chance to resist. First thoughts. They are very likely to lead you to what you are needing to write.

7   Keep writing for at least ten or twenty or thirty minutes, depending on how much material and energy you come up with. You have to write long enough to get tired and get past what's on the top of your mind. But not so long that you start pausing in the midst of your writing.

8   Then stop, sit back, be quiet, and bring all that writing to a point. That is, by reading back or just thinking back over it, find the center or focus or point of those words and write it down in a sentence. This may mean different things: you can find the main idea that is there; or the new idea that is trying to be there; or the imaginative focus or center of gravity—an image or object or feeling; or perhaps some brand new thing occurs to you now as very important—it may even seem unrelated to what you wrote, but it comes to you now as a result of having done that burst of writing. Try to stand out of the way and let the center of focus itself decide to come forward. In any event, don't worry about it. Choose or invent something for your focus and then go on. The only requirement is that it be a single thing. Skip a few lines and write it down. Underline it or put a box around it so you can easily find it later. (Some people find it helpful to let themselves write down two or three focusing sentences.)

9   If this center of gravity is a feeling or an image, perhaps a mere phrase will do: "a feeling that something good will happen" or "mervyn the stuffed monkey slumped under the dining room table." But a complete sentence or assertion is better, especially if the focus is an idea or thought or insight. Try, that is, to get more than "economics" or "economic dimension"—since those words just vaguely point in a general direction—and try for something like "there must be an economic reason for these events."

10   You have now gone through a cycle that consists of nonstop writing and then sitting back to probe for the center. You have used two kinds of consciousness: immersion, where you have your head down and are scurrying along a trail of words in the underbrush; and perspective, where you stand back and look down on things from a height and get a sense of shape and outline.

11   Now repeat this cycle. Use the focus you just wrote down as the springboard for a new piece of nonstop writing. There are various ways in which you can let it bounce you into new writing. Perhaps you just take it and write more about it. Or perhaps that doesn't seem right because what you already wrote has finished an idea and the focusing sentence has put the lid on it. If you write more about it, you would just be repeating yourself. In this case, start now with what comes next: the next step, the following thing, the reply, the answering salvo. Perhaps "what comes next" is what follows logically. Perhaps the next thing is what comes next in your mind even though it involves a jump in logic. Perhaps the next thing is a questioning or denial of what you have already written: arguments against it, writing in an opposite mood, or writing in a different mode (from prose to poetry). Stand out of the way and see what happens.

12   Whatever kind of jump it is, jump into a second burst of nonstop writing of however long you can keep it up. Long enough to get tired and lose track of where you started; not so long that you keep pausing

and lose momentum. And then, again, stop and come out from the underbrush of your immersion in words, attain some calm and perspective, and find the summing up or focus or center of gravity for this second piece of writing.

13   The sea voyage consists of repeating this cycle over and over again. Keep up one session of writing long enough to get loosened up and tired—long enough in fact to make a bit of a voyage and probably to pass beyond what happened to be in mind and in mood. But usually a piece of open-ended writing takes several or even many long sittings. One of the major ingredients in the open-ended process is time and the attendant changes of mood and outlook.

14   As you change modes from writing to focusing and back to writing and back to focusing, practice letting the process itself decide what happens next—decide, for example, whether your focusing sentence springboards you into a new treatment of the same material, into a response to that material or into some other new topic or mode that "wants" to come next. If it sounds a bit mystical to say "Let it decide," I don't mean to rule out hard conscious thinking. "Letting it decide" will often mean realizing you should be rigorously logical at this point in the writing cycle. As you practice the open-ended writing process, you will get better at feeling what kind of step needs to be taken at any given point. The main thing is not to worry about doing it right. Just do it a lot.

15   As you engage in this sea voyage, invite yourself to lose sight of what you had in mind at the beginning, invite digressions, new ideas, seeds falling from unexpected sources, changes of mind. You are trying to nurse your thoughts, perceptions and feelings through a process of continual transformation—cooking and growing.

16   The sea voyage is most obviously finished when you sight new land—when you get a trustworthy vision of your final piece of writing. You see that it's an argument and where it is going; or you see it is a poem and feel the general shape of it.

17   To come to land you need to get this vision clearer and more complete. Perhaps your first glimpse showed you what is central: now you need to write out that central event or idea more fully. If what is emerging is primarily conceptual, such as an essay, you may well need to make an outline. You won't be able to see your structure clearly until you go through all you have written to find the points that feel important, write each one into a complete sentence, and then put these sentences into the most logical or easily understood order. Even for a long story or poem, you may need some kind of schematic representation of the whole so you can see it all in one glance.

18   But perhaps it is too early for any outline or overview. Perhaps you cannot really get this final vision clear and right except by plunging into a new draft in your present frame of mind—starting the first scene of the story or novel, the first line of the poem, the introductory

thought for your essay—and just plowing along. Perhaps *doing it* is more helpful at this point than any method of planning or outlining.

19   What if you keep writing and writing and you sense that the sea voyage is really done, but you lack any glimpse of land. You feel you have gotten down everything you can get down, you are beginning to repeat yourself, there is no more divergence. You've succeeded in getting productively lost, but now this unknown territory starts to get depressingly familiar.

20   You can try to hasten the convergent process of coming to land. Go back over all the centers or focuses you have written down in the course of the sea voyage. Ponder them for a while. Then engage in some nonstop writing on the basis of them. Start writing "I don't yet know what all this writing is really about, but here's what the important elements seem to be: . . ." Of course you can't put them in the right or logical order—that's just what you don't know. You are trying to bring them together into the same burst of energy and attention. You might write something like this:

There's writing that sounds like the writer talking, there's writing that somehow just resonates in some mysterious way, there's radio announcer speech with great energy and liveliness but sounding completely fake, there's _____, and there's _____. How can I make sense of it all.

You are trying to get the important elements to bounce against each other in a tight place.

21   Keep this burst of writing—this attempt to figure out what your writing is about—as long as you can. Perhaps a center will emerge. If not, go on to the step of standing back and looking for a center. If that isn't the final center, then go on to another wave of writing. Keep this up for a while. Keep up, that is, the same process you used for the sea voyage, but instead of using it for divergence and getting lost, use it for convergence and getting found. If this doesn't work, you may simply have to stop and rest. Give your writing more time in a drawer unlooked at. Anything that takes this long simply to emerge is probably important. Some complicated and important reordering of things is trying to take place inside you. . . .

22   There is some danger that I have made the open-ended writing process sound too complicated. I could describe it more simply as follows: just start writing, keep writing, don't stop writing except for eating, sleeping, and living, and keep the process going till you have figured out what you are writing, and when you have done that, keep writing still until you get it right. This is the heart of the process and if it is what you do and it works, terrific. But I am trying to emphasize two additional elements that may well be part of your process without your paying much attention to them: first let yourself start without knowing where you are going and even get more lost as you proceed; and second, alternate between nonstop writing and pausing to focus what you've written. As long as your nonstop writing is going well there

is no need, of course, to stop and focus. But if you are writing and writing without getting anywhere, it will help to move deliberately back and forth between immersion and perspective. Doing so will help each wave of writing carry you farther and make each pause not just a rest but an occasion for progress. . . .

23   After you have your vision of your final piece and after you have worked out that vision in a new draft—perhaps starting with an outline—you need of course to revise and polish your way to your final draft. Sometimes the open-ended writing process yields a draft that needs little revising, sometimes lots.

Questions

1. Explain how the open-ended writing process "invites maximum chaos and disorientation."

2. What does Elbow mean when he says writing this way is like going on a sea voyage? Why must you lose sight of land for this process to be effective?

3. What is the focus or "center of gravity" of a freewriting? List four possibilities.

Freewriting

Elbow's open-ended process involves extensive use of a particular strategy for gathering ideas or coming up with something to say. This technique is called *freewriting*. Let's review our definition of freewriting. Freewriting certainly is not the same as essay writing, and there are really only two rules: (1) Write continuously for the full length of time preselected, such as ten minutes, and (2) **do not stop.** If you make a mistake, wait until you finish the time before going back to correct it. Other than these two rules, allow yourself the freedom to write without restriction. Simply spill the thoughts from your brain straight onto the page. Don't worry if your hand can't keep up with your brain. Don't worry if your thoughts lead you off your original track. Remember, according to Elbow, it may even be necessary for you to lose track of where you originally began. If you want to go back to a topic, you may do so at any time. And if you find that you have nothing to say, just write "I have nothing to say" or "I'm stuck." Something else to write eventually will come to you!

Two variations on freewriting are *focused freewriting* and *looping*. With focused freewriting, instead of just beginning with the first thought that pops into your mind, you begin by writing about a particular topic. Elbow's open-ended writing process describes looping. Looping means completing a freewriting, finding the "center of gravity" or focus, and then writing a focused freewriting with this focus as the starting point. You might, then, choose a new focus and loop again. Theoretically this process may continue as many times as you find it useful in helping you gather ideas and hone in on what you really want to say.

Activity

Freewrite for ten minutes. Read over your writing, and circle a center of gravity. Then write that focus at the top of a new page, and complete a ten-minute focused freewriting. Choose a center of gravity, and repeat the process once more.

Collaborative Activity

In a small group, take turns reading a freewriting or a freewriting and loop aloud. As you listen to each of your partners, write down at least three ideas or phrases that stick in your mind. Also, list at least three questions that occur to you as you listen.

After everyone reads, consider these questions as a group:

1. What made ideas or phrases memorable?

2. What would you hope to learn from follow-up questions?

Brainstorming a List

Another helpful way to get started is to make a list of everything that comes to mind on a particular topic. If you have little or no idea of what to write about, you might even want to list possible ideas for topics. Your goal is similar to your goal when freewriting, to write down everything that pops into your brain as quickly as you think of it. At this point, do not even allow yourself to think about whether what you list is right or wrong, a good idea or a bad idea, spelled correctly or incorrectly.

Right now, none of that matters. You will want to let your creative mind be free and make as big a list as you can.

Activity

Choose one of the following topics, and brainstorm a list of ideas.

A. Planning vacations (for example, looking at brochures, getting maps, seeing an agent)

B. Children's games (for example, outdoor games, board games, rainy day games)

C. My favorite high school teacher

D. Transportation problems

E. Striving to be successful

Discussing/Dialoguing

This technique might actually be the most common although we might not often consider talking to other people about their thoughts as a prewriting technique. The fact is, though, that we do get many ideas by talking with friends, neighbors, colleagues, and others. Most of these conversations are informal. In other words, we don't necessarily set out to gather ideas or information for a piece of writing. We just find ideas in everyday conversation just as we may suddenly have a wonderful idea for an essay while driving to work or while cooking dinner. On the other hand, we may purposefully seek out discussion on a specific topic because we know we want to or need to write about it soon.

Collaborative Activity

With a partner, choose one of the following topics, and discuss it for about ten minutes. Jot down your ideas. Finally, be ready to share your discussion with the rest of your class.

A. The 1950s

B. Technology in the workplace

C. Healthy living

Clustering

Now let's review the technique called *clustering*. It is another tool at your disposal when you are gathering ideas for a piece of writing. As with other prewriting strategies for coming up with ideas, when you produce a cluster diagram, you will want to free your mind to explore many options. Try not to stop and think too much; just make as many associations as you can.

Clustering Type 1. Write your topic in the center of a page. Circle it. Then think of what comes to mind when you think of that topic. Draw spokes out from the topic to your ideas, and circle them. Now choose one of your ideas, and make it your next focus. What comes to mind? Branch off this new focus with all your associations or ideas. Now you can go back and choose a different focus. Repeat the process, working outward to develop the diagram. Your ideas should become more and more detailed and specific as you work outward. The following activity presents a partially completed cluster diagram (Figure 2.1).

Activity

Complete the following cluster diagram.

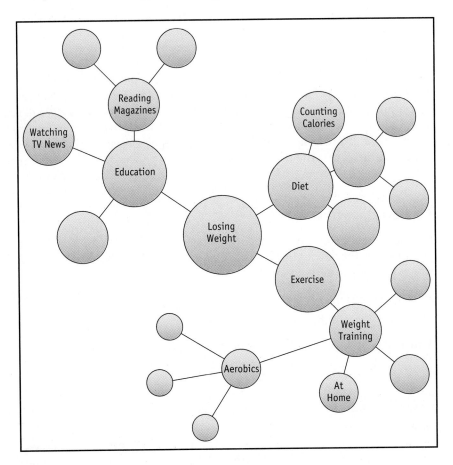

Figure 2.1 Example of a Cluster Diagram

Clustering Type 2. This variation on the traditional cluster diagram may be particularly helpful when you are under time pressure and need to be able to collect your thoughts as quickly as possible. You may also find it works well for certain topics. For whatever reason, feel free to experiment with this type of clustering at any time. To produce this type of cluster dia-

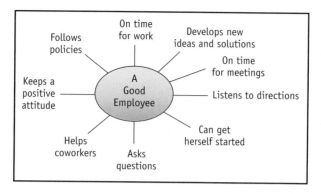

Figure 2.2 Example of a Cluster Diagram

gram start with your topic, again, circled at the center of a clean page. Then make as many associations (i.e., come up with as many ideas as you can) that relate to your topic. Radiate them out like many spokes on a wheel. See the example in Figure 2.2.

Now look over all your ideas and see which ones go best with each other. Try to come up with two to four groups. Choose a geometric shape to represent each group. For example, draw rectangles around one set, triangles around another, and diamonds around a third. If you don't have enough ideas, brainstorm more, or if you like, you may elect to change your original topic. See the completed example in Figure 2.3.

Keeping a Journal

A journal is not necessarily the same as a diary. Writers may write down their ideas, their beliefs, their thoughts, and/or their feelings in journals. There are set rules for journal writing. Many writers find it extraordinarily helpful to keep a journal, a place to jot down ideas. Your instructor may require you to keep a journal as part of your course. He or she may allow you to write about almost anything, or the assignments may be quite specific. For example, you may be asked to respond to certain assigned readings or to class assignments. Or your journal may become a place for you and your instructor to write to each other.

Even if you are not required to keep one, consider setting aside a notebook or folder in which to jot down your thoughts and ideas. Write down as many ideas as you can as they come to you. Look over your journal entries on occasion. When you can't think of what to say, delve into your journal. Think of your journal musings as seeds waiting to germinate. Today's fleeting thought just may grow to become next month's (or next year's!) excellent essay topic.

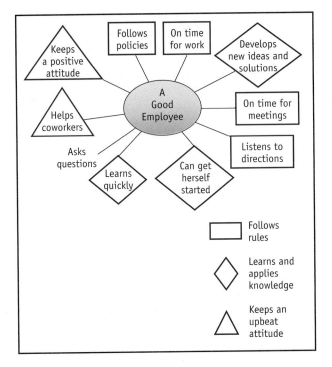

Figure 2.3 Completed Example of a Cluster Diagram

Step 2: Organizing Ideas

After you have gathered your information, you are ready to move on in the writing process to organizing that information. No matter which techniques you used to collect information (and using a variety of different techniques usually yields the best results), you should strive to have more information than you could possibly use in your essay. Thus, as you look to organize your ideas, you will have two goals. First, you will need to decide what information to keep and what to discard. And second, you will need to decide in what order to put the information that you decide to include in your rough draft.

Categorizing

Organizing your essay may seem a daunting task at first glance, or it may seem quite obvious. For example, you may have produced several freewritings that are completely disorganized but contain several good, but buried, kernels of ideas that you want to use in your essay. Furthermore, the lists you have brainstormed may contain some terrific ideas, and many not-so-terrific. Now is the time to cross those not-so-terrific ideas off the list. If you simply start writing now, beginning with the first idea left on the list and ending your final sentence with the last idea on the list, you will probably have one completely confusing essay that won't make much sense to anyone, possibly including yourself! You will need to create categories for the items on your list. Consider the following example. *Stop*

Brainstorming

Reasons many Americans are overweight

TV	Fad diets
Laziness	Long work day
Desk jobs	Depressed so they eat
Fast food	Large portions of food
High-fat diets	No time to exercise
Lack of exercise	Drink huge sodas
Eat to relieve stress	Eat when bored
Eat for comfort	Tired
Prepackaged foods	

Category I: Eating for the wrong reasons	Category II: Poor diet	Category III: Inactive lifestyle
Eat to relieve stress	Fast food	TV
Eat for comfort	High-fat diets	Desk jobs
Depressed so they eat	Prepackaged foods	Long work day
Eat when bored	Large portions	No time to exercise
	Huge sodas	Laziness
		Tired

The following activity gives you some practice in categorizing.

Collaborative Activity

Look back over the list you made in response to the brainstorming activity and at a partner's list. Then together, organize each list (first one and then the other) by developing two to four categories and placing items under the categories where they fit. You may elect to leave some items out. You may also brainstorm more items to fit under categories if you like.

A well-developed cluster diagram may have already led you to see your best method of organizing a particular essay. Clustering, in fact, has an advantage over some other prewriting techniques in that it is also an organizational tool. Look back at the cluster in Figure 2.1 for a moment. Each large "branch" might represent one body paragraph of an essay. Or, if the topic had been quite broad to begin with, we might select just one branch as the topic of an entire essay. In the cluster diagram in Figure 2.2 the ideas are organized by grouping them together. That organizational process was the first step in establishing categories. Then, we went to the next step and made category headings for each of the groups. Now we should decide which idea should go first in the essay. We might, for example, decide to discuss learning and applying knowledge in the first body paragraph (the first paragraph following the introductory paragraph), then the importance of following company rules in the second body paragraph, and last, the importance of keeping an upbeat attitude in a third body paragraph.

Ordering

When it comes to deciding how to put major ideas of your essay in order, you have a few options. The option you choose may very well be dictated by the sort of essay you are writing. In the example about the good employee, we decide to save the point about a good employee's attitude for last because we think that having an upbeat attitude is the most important characteristic of a good employee. Putting key ideas in order from least important to most important is called **climactic order.** Using climactic order should serve you well in writing many essays. Ordering ideas in this manner may keep readers more interested all the way through the essay. Furthermore, since readers usually remember best the last item they read (and readers tend to be a forgetful group), you can be more certain that your readers will remember the most important point than if you had said it earlier in the essay.

If you are telling a story, you will probably use **chronological order,** which means putting items in the order in which they actually happened. You could, for example, tell about your recent cruise vacation beginning when you left your home and ending as you return to your front door. If you are relating what a place looks like, you would use **spatial order,** which might mean describing, for example, the inside of an old barn starting at the left side and moving to the right. Or you might start up at the roof, then move to the loft, and continue down to the dirt floor of the barn. You might describe the appearance of your friend's seven-year-old son by starting with his baseball cap and ending with his untied shoelaces. All these examples rely on using spatial order to organize your material. When we talk about order, we refer not only to how to order the main ideas in an essay, but also the order of ideas within a single section of an essay or individual paragraph.

Activity

1. Using climactic order, write a paragraph explaining why you like or dislike babysitting children.

2. Using spatial order, write a paragraph describing one of your friends or neighbors.

3. Using narrative order, write a paragraph describing your trip to school today.

―――――――

Outlining

When you began this discussion of organization, you may have immediately thought of outlining. The word "outline" may seem like an old friend to you, or it may send a shiver down your spine. If the latter is true, you may be happy to know that contrary to popular belief, there are other ways to outline besides the traditional Roman numerals and letters. In fact, you may have already discerned that a cluster diagram may also be thought of as a sort of outline. In any case, outlining can be an extremely useful tool in helping you gather your thoughts and organize your ideas prior to writing a rough draft.

Some writers develop a detailed outline fairly early in their writing process. Others begin working from a scratch outline, write for a while, find some direction in what they want to say, write a more detailed outline, and then proceed with a rough draft. Remember to be flexible. It is not necessarily a good thing to be married to your outline. You may find that sticking to your outline while writing an essay is the best way to proceed. However, the next time you write, you may find that you need to change your outline to match your growing and changing essay as you write a rough draft. In other words, in this case you would need to consider your outline a rough blueprint that you may amend as the need arises.

Scratch Outlines. A scratch outline is the most basic type of outline. It gives only the roughest idea of your plan for an essay. Here is a scratch outline for our sample essay explaining some of the reasons why so many Americans become overweight.

    I. Introduction
   II. Eating for the wrong reasons
 III. Poor diets
 IV. Inactive lifestyles
   V. Conclusion

Notice that we decided to keep our ideas in this order because we believe eating for the wrong reason is the least important and inactive lifestyle is the most important reason Americans tend to weigh too much.

Topic Outlines. Topic outlines are more formal than scratch outlines and require you to have thought through your essay a bit more. In this type of outline, you express your ideas in a balanced or parallel manner and show how ideas relate to each other within the essay by using indentation, Roman numerals and numbers, and uppercase and lowercase letters. Remember that as you plan your paper, you do not need to use all the ideas that you have gathered; furthermore, you may combine ideas at this point, and you may even think of some new ones. Remain open to new thoughts as you plan your paper. Topic outlines usually begin with a complete sentence summing up the main idea of the paper. A topic outline of our sample paper might look like this:

Main Idea: Many Americans become overweight because they eat for the wrong reasons, have poor diets, and live relatively inactive lifestyles.

   I. Eat for the wrong reasons
      A. To relieve stress
          1. Stress from work
             a. from dealing with customers/clients
             b. from dealing with the boss
          2. Stress from home
             a. housekeeping duties
             b. arguments with family members
      B. To relieve depression
          1. Clinical depression
             a. millions take antidepressants
             b. many "binge eat"
          2. The blues depression
             a. when having a bad day
             b. when facing a "life situation"
      C. To relieve boredom
          1. when living alone
          2. when family/roommate is out-of-town
  II. Have poor diets
      A. Too much fast food
          1. high in calories
          2. high in fat
      B. Too much prepackaged food
          1. heat-and-eat convenience
          2. pay a price in calories and fat
      C. Too many huge portions
          1. all-you-can-eat bars
             a. at steakhouses
             b. at pizza places
          2. larger size for little cost at fast-food restaurants
          3. 40-ounce sodas at quick-marts
 III. Live Inactive Lifestyles
      A. Long hours at desk jobs
          1. sitting all day
          2. fatigue
             a. too tired to cook
             b. too tired to exercise

  B. Too much TV
    1. watching TV instead of being outside
      a. could be walking
      b. could be going to a gym
      c. could be gardening
    2. conducive to snacking
      a. potato chips
      b. nuts
      c. buttery popcorn

Chart Outlines. Chart outlines, developed by Professor Margo Eden-Camann, are another way to help you organize your ideas. In a chart outline, you show relationships among your ideas by placing them near each other in some sort of spatial arrangement. The chart in Figure 2.4, in which you write your topic at the base, shows the ideas growing upward and outward.

The chart outline is arranged in levels. The first level always represents the major divisions in an essay. In this case, since our essay will be relatively short, each item on this level may represent one developed body paragraph. The second level from base shows the items we plan to discuss in each major section of our essay. If we wanted, we could continue upward to a fourth level, which would include even more specific details. If you appreciate maps, charts, and diagrams, you may find chart outlines a helpful technique to add to your writer's bag of tricks.

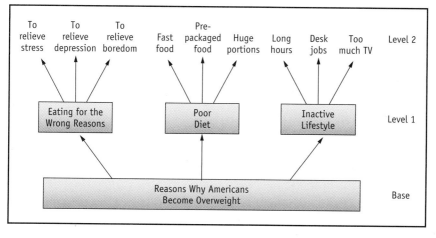

Figure 2.4 Chart Outline

Activity

Create a scratch outline, a chart outline, and a topic outline for an essay explaining your reasons for selecting the college you currently attend.

Grammar and Usage: Clause Identification

Examine each of the following groups of words, and tell what you find:

1. Typing on computers is much faster than typing on manual typewriters.
2. Because computers allow you to correct mistakes without erasing.
3. Certainly something to remember in purchasing a machine.

Undoubtedly, you have noted that the three groups of words are related, with each adding information to the group that came before. Now look at the groups grammatically, and see if anything stands out. The first group of words makes sense all by itself and has a good true blue verb, *is,* a linking verb. We would call this group of words a sentence. If we deleted the first group of words, the second could not stand alone because it begins with the word *because,* even though it does have a good true blue verb, *allow,* an action verb. The third set of words is even more problematic than the first two. It certainly does not stand alone, and although at first glance *remember* and *purchasing* have true blue verb potential, further examination reveals that the word *to* transforms "remember" into an infinitive, or verbal, and the *-ing* on "purchasing" calls for a helping verb, which is nowhere to be found. Therefore, group three contains no true blue verb at all.

Group #1 is an example of a clause that is also a complete sentence. Group #2 is an example of a clause that is not a complete sentence but would be if not begun with the word *because.* Group #3 is an example of a group of words that is neither a complete sentence nor a clause because it has no true blue verb. From these three examples, we should be able to deduce a good working definition of a clause, and here it is:

A clause is any group of words that contains at least one true blue verb. The clause includes the true blue verb(s), subject(s), anything that comes after the verb(s) and answers the question "What?", and/or anything that describes any of the above parts of the clause.

Thankfully, this definition is much simpler than it may at first appear. Let's use it to examine each of the three examples above. *Stop*

1. *Typing on computers is much faster than typing on manual typewriters.* We have already identified a true blue verb, *is,* in this group, so we know for certain that we have a clause. A true blue verb must have a subject, and in this case *typing* fills the bill. Don't be deceived by *on computers,* which is a prepositional phrase describing the subject and is therefore also part of the clause. The part of the group after the verb, *much faster than typing on manual typewriters,* answers the question "What?" about the words *typing is* or describes one of the other words after the verb. For example, *much* describes *faster* and *manual* describes *typewriters.* In the case of this example, then, we will say that the entire group of words constitutes one clause.

2. *Because computers allow you to correct mistakes without erasing.* We can subject this group of words to the same analysis as Group #1. We begin with the true blue verb, *allow,* and move on to its subject, *computers.* The word *you* tells what computers allow, and *to correct mistakes without erasing* tells what computers allow you. Finally, *because* introduces the clause and describes the true blue verb. Once again, the entire group of words is one clause. Note, however, that a clause is not necessarily a sentence, and the reason this clause is not a sentence is the word *because.*

3. *Certainly something to remember in purchasing a machine.* We begin our analysis of this group of words by looking for the true blue verb, and we remember that there is none. What about the subject or the word(s) following the true blue verb(s) and answering the question "What?"? Any time spent looking for such items is time wasted. Since this group of words has no true blue verb, it is not a clause—stop, period, end of discussion. This group, like the second group, is a sentence fragment, but for a different reason, as we will see later.

Exercise 1

Underline each clause in the following constructions. Remember that sometimes you will find one clause, sometimes more than one, and sometimes none at all.

1. Many Americans proudly remember our 1980 Olympic Ice Hockey team.

2. In the semifinals, Americans defeated a more experienced Russian team.

3. Then they defeated the Finnish team, and they won the gold medal.

4. After the last game ended, announcer Al Michaels said, "Do you believe in miracles?"

5. Most people will never forget watching those upset wins.

6. Did Shakespeare or someone else call parting sweet sorrow?

7. I used to wonder what he meant by that expression.

8. After all, something sweet should not bring sorrow, and something sorrowful should not seem sweet.

9. Suffering the experience of someone leaving you alone.

10. That hardly sounds like a good time to me.

11. When I make friends, I do not like to lose them at all.

12. Some students play sports; hence, we call them student athletes.

13. If a student athlete strives diligently in both endeavors, then he or she exemplifies the Latin expression "mens sana in corpore sano."

14. Which means a healthy mind in a healthy body.

15. Unfortunately, some schools abuse the idea of student athletes; thus, the schools and individuals all suffer.

16. Racing down the highway the other morning, a student accidentally saw two pink arms waving up and down.

17. The arms belonged to a lost child, but the student soon managed to find the child's family.

18. When they saw their child again, the parents were overjoyed.

19. "I caught this morning morning's minion, kingdom of daylight's dauphin, dapple-dawn-drawn Falcon, in his riding. . . ."—Gerard Manley Hopkins

20. "He learned the arts of riding, fencing, gunnery/And how to scale a fortress—or a nunnery."—George Gordon (Lord Byron)

Exercise 2

Choose five sentences from a recent piece of your own writing, and underline each of the clauses.

C h a p t e r

Writing Process

Writing a Draft

Often in life getting started is the hardest part of doing something. After a long, hard day at the office, you may not be thrilled at the thought of sweating at the gym. But once you arrive and get started, the rest of your exercise routine may just fall into place. Ask any English teacher with four stacks of papers to grade how hard it is to get started. Students do not own the market when it comes to procrastination. Yet once begun, almost any task becomes less daunting. Remember that by the time you produce a rough draft, you should be well into the process of writing your essay. You will have already asked yourself "What will I say?" and "How should I say it?"

Thesis Statements

Prior to writing a draft, it is usually a good idea to write a **thesis statement** for a paper. *Thesis* means main idea, and a thesis statement tells the main point of the entire essay, usually in a one-sentence statement. A thesis statement cannot be phrased as a question. It should not be too broad, and it should not be a simple statement of fact. If the thesis statement is too broad, you will have great difficulty writing the body of your essay. Likewise, you will have great difficulty finding enough to say about an undisputed fact. Thus, the following three would not make good thesis statements for 500-word essays:

A question: Should children play with guns?

Too broad: The United States needs to clarify its foreign policy.

A fact: Plants help us breathe by using carbon dioxide and giving off oxygen.

We produced a statement of main idea or thesis statement in the previous chapter at the top of our topic outline for an essay explaining why Americans tend to be overweight. The thesis statement for that essay is:

Many Americans become overweight because they eat for the wrong reasons, have poor diets, and live relatively inactive lifestyles.

All thesis statements contain at least two elements: the **topic** and a limiting of the topic, frequently called the **controlling idea.** The topic of our essay is Americans. But what about Americans? Will the essay discuss the history of people coming to America? Will the essay discuss American political views? Will it argue for a way Americans can coexist peacefully? There are an infinite number of possible essays we could write with the topic Americans. The controlling idea tells us which of these papers about Americans we are about to read. Our controlling idea is that they become overweight. Any thesis statement that consists of just the topic and a controlling idea is called a **general thesis statement.** An example of a general thesis statement is the following:

Contrary to popular opinion, skunks really do make excellent house pets.

Following the introductory phrase *contrary to popular opinion,* we discern the topic, *skunks,* and the controlling idea, *really do make good house pets.* Our example about Americans and weight, however, happens to be an **enumerated thesis statement** because it also presents a plan for the development of the essay. It lists the main points that we plan to make in the body of our essay; thus, the plan is *because they eat for the wrong reasons, have poor diets, and live relatively inactive lifestyles.* These are the three points we will make and develop in the body paragraphs. If your thesis statement is enumerated, it is important to make the parts of the plan as balanced or parallel as you can so the thesis statement reads smoothly and is pleasing to the ear.

Activity

In the following thesis statements, circle the topic and underline the controlling idea. If it also has a plan for the essay's development, draw a rectangle around it. Finally, determine if the thesis statement is a general thesis statement or an enumerated thesis statement, and write G or E the space provided.

1. __G__ (High school students) should be allowed to leave the school grounds for lunch.

2. __E__ (Student athletes) learn valuable employment skills because they must learn to manage their time carefully and to be team players.

3. __E__ (You,) too, can learn to bathe a dog in three simple steps.

4. ___G___ Randy Smith is the best friend anyone could have.

5. ___E___ You should consider a variety of possible sources including books, newspaper and magazine articles, and World Wide Web pages.

6. ___E___ A successful vacation requires careful planning.

7. ___G___ Reading books to children encourages them to use their imaginations.

8. ___E___ Walking 45 minutes every day will help you decrease stress, think more clearly, and become more fit.

Activity

Devise both general and enumerated thesis statements for each of the following papers.

1. A 500-word essay about the harmful effects of sun exposure

2. A 500-word essay describing the characteristics of a perfect mate

3. A 500-word essay explaining why some people choose to smoke cigarettes

The most common placement for the thesis statement is in the introduction of your essay, usually near the end of the introduction. The second most common place to find a thesis statement is at the end of the essay. Very occasionally, you will read something that never states the main idea directly, yet you can figure it out from reading the piece of writing. Then we say the essay has an **implied thesis.**

Possible Strategies for Developing Essays

An essay must make its point or develop in a logical manner if it is to make sense and make some contribution to readers' perceptions or understanding. Writers have several strategies at hand to help explain themselves and make their point clearly. The following **patterns of development** have been central to the teaching of writing for many years. Each is effective for informing and also has uses for expressing and persuading. Rather than thinking of them as patterns that someone one day sat down and made up, think of them as representing patterns in the way our brains make sense of the world around us. For example, if you witness an old lady in the grocery store picking up a grapefruit, squeezing it, picking up another in the other hand and squeezing it, realize that she is at that moment making use of the pattern called **comparison/contrast.**

When you have something to say or write, use the pattern (or a combination of these patterns) that is best suited for that particular piece of writing. Ask yourself, "What is my main purpose in writing this essay?" and choose the pattern that best suits that purpose and the point you want to make. Keep in mind that although you will have a main pattern of development, you may also employ supplemental patterns as your essay develops. For example, while writing an essay in which your primary purpose is to explain reasons for teen violence (cause/effect), you might compare teens today with teens in the '70s (comparison/contrast). We have listed several patterns of development, and an example of an essay using each pattern, in the following table.

Patterns of Development

Pattern	Purpose	Example
Narration	Tells about an event	First child's birth
Description	Explains the appearance of a person, place, or thing	Person young people should admire
Exemplification	Provides examples	Most people are selfish
Process	Tells how to do something	How to pull an "all-nighter"
Classification	Breaks the topic down into categories	Types of movies kids enjoy
Comparison/contrast	Shows similarities or differences	Contrast two theories about love
Cause/effect	Explains why something happened or analyzes its effects	The causes and prevention of tooth decay
Definition	Explains what a word or concept means	What is the gender bias?

Transitions

As you write your essay and progress from one idea to the next, think frequently of the reader who will be trying to follow your thoughts. Although we writers may know exactly what we mean to say, our readers can easily become lost as we move from point to point. To help our readers follow, we must provide **transitions.** The prefix *trans* has to do with getting from one place to another. We see it in many words including *translate* (to move from one language to another), *transport* (to move from one place to another), and *transmit* (to send a signal from one point to another).

Think of a transition as a bridge to help readers cross over the gaps created in your writing as you move from one point to another, from idea to idea. Without these bridges, you will leave many such gaps in your writing. For instance, when you finish your introduction and move to the body of your essay, you will leave a gap. Each time you finish making one main point and move on the next, there will be a gap. Then, when you move from the body to begin to conclude your essay, you will create another gap. In addition, you will want to provide additional transitions within paragraphs so that they will be cohesive as well. *Cohesion* basically means that the thoughts stick together. Another way to think of transitions is that they are the glue that holds ideas together. Some gaps will be larger than other gaps. Moving from one major point to another or skipping several days when telling a story may create a gap like a canyon. Moving from one example to the next within the same paragraph leaves a smaller gap that might be more like crossing over a creek bed. In general the larger gaps may require the larger bridges or transitions. In some cases, an entire paragraph may function as a transition.

There are two ways to make bridges or transitions for your readers. The first is to repeat key words. The second is to use a transitional word or expression.

Repeating Key Words

When moving from one paragraph to another, you can use the technique of repeating a key word or words to build a bridge effectively. For instance, if the final sentence of a paragraph is *For safety's sake, nearly every child should learn to swim by age five,* then the first sentence of the next paragraph might be *Although learning to swim is extremely important, many children will first master learning to ride a bicycle.* Notice how we repeat key words *learn, swim,* and *learning* to build a bridge to the next body paragraph. You can use this technique make your ideas "stick together" within a single paragraph as well. Consider the following example.

> *One of my earliest* memories *involves a trip to a* beach *when I was three or four, at the most. I think the* beach *is at the shore of a lake, not the sea. In this* memory, *my parents and my brother, then an infant in my mother's arms, are with me. My mother walks toward me from the edge of the water as my wriggling brother turns his head to the side. My father stands beside a green lounge chair underneath which rests a transistor radio. This is where the* memory *ends. Early* memories *are often like a snapshot photo; we* remember *only a moment, which seems frozen in our minds forever.*

Do you see how the repetition of certain key words keeps the paragraph flowing smoothly?

Activity

Write a paragraph about a hobby you enjoy. Use the repetition of key words to make your paragraph's ideas "stick together."

Collaborative Activity

Swap paragraphs from the previous activity with a partner. See if you can pick out the key words from your partner's paragraph.

———

Transitional Words and Phrases

In addition to repeating key words, you can make transitions by using certain words and phrases that signal a certain kind of gap is coming in your writing. For example, the gap might be in time, or it might be a gap created when moving from one idea to the next, or it could be the gap created when finishing the last point and moving toward a conclusion. These signal words and phrases function very well as bridges and will help your readers immensely in getting from point to point in your writing. First, you will need to decide what type of gap you have. Are you moving on to an additional idea? Are you about to make a contrasting point? Is it a concluding point? Then choose a transition from that category. The following chart presents many of the most common transitional words and phrases.

Transitional Words and Phrases

To signal movement in time: first, second, third, later, earlier, before, after, during, meanwhile, then

To signal movement in space: above, below, beside, near, to the right, to the left, behind, in front of

To signal an additional idea is coming: furthermore, in addition, also, next, moreover, first, second, third, then

To signal a contrasting idea is coming: but, although, however, in contrast, yet

To signal a similar idea is coming: likewise, similarly

To signal an example is coming: for example, for instance, such as

To signal a conclusion is coming: to conclude, to sum up, in summation, in closing, finally, therefore, thus

Activity

In the following paragraph, fill in the blanks with appropriate transitional words or phrases. Feel free to add commas if necessary.

Returning to school after years in the workforce can be a daunting experience. _Similarly_ *a returning student may fear being perceived as odd*

or different if he or she is much older than the rest of the class.
Furthermore *a returning student often has many responsibilities to jug-*
gle. First *, he or she often must balance family, work, and school*
demands. Also *if the student is a single parent, the family*
demands are often more extreme. But *with support from family*
members or special programs at school, these students will find their
transition back to school easier to negotiate. Finally *anyone who*
really wants to go back to school should at least give it a try.

Body Paragraphs

Topic Sentences

Unless they themselves are serving as a transition, most body paragraphs are made up of a **topic sentence** and **support.** In general, the
topic sentence is a statement that tells the main point of that particular
paragraph. Think of the topic sentence as functioning somewhat like an
umbrella. It must be broad enough to cover all the details or points you
mention in that paragraph. If your topic sentence doesn't match the
details, you will need to change the details to fit under the topic sentence, or you may amend the topic sentence to include more information. When everything you mention in your paragraph fits with the topic
sentence, your paragraph will have unity. In other words, everything will
be relevant.

Usually you will find topic sentences at the beginning of body paragraphs. The second most common placement is at the end of the paragraph. Occasionally you may come across a body paragraph that never
states its topic directly, but you understand the main point anyway because
the details are so good. Furthermore, you will not find a topic sentence in
a paragraph that is functioning solely as a transition between main ideas
in a paper (transitional paragraphs generally are not necessary in essays
under about 1,000 words).

The topic sentences are written in bold print in the following examples. The second you will recognize from earlier in this chapter.

Example 1
I left my last job for two main reasons. *First of all, the hours were*
wrong for me. The manager kept scheduling me for the night shift even
though I have a six-year-old child to see off to school at 9 A.M. I was
exhausted all the time. Then, when I finally started to adjust to the

schedule, I would find myself on the day shift. Furthermore, I earned only eight dollars an hour. I found it hard to pay the rent, buy us clothes, and keep food on the table. Never mind any extras like an occasional movie or miniature golf for my daughter. Luckily, after a few months, I found my current job with steady daytime hours and somewhat better pay.

Example 2
One of my earliest memories involves a trip to a beach when I was three or four, at the most. I think the beach is at the shore of a lake, not the sea. In this memory, my parents and my brother, then an infant in my mother's arms, are with me. My mother walks toward me from the edge of the water as my wriggling brother turns his head to the side. My father stands beside a green lounge chair underneath which rests a transistor radio. This is where the memory ends. **Early memories are often like a snapshot photo; we remember only a moment, which seems frozen in our minds forever.**

Support

The support in your body paragraphs may include specific details, facts, and/or examples. Supporting details are frequently the reason why it is easier to "get into" one piece of writing while another seems uninteresting and unapproachable.

First of all, some details are better than others, and some of the best details to use are **showing details.** Showing details are generally preferable to details that do not show. Writing that the classroom has four white walls is not a showing detail about the classroom. Nearly every room does, and what conclusion can readers draw? Showing details are those details that allow readers to draw some conclusion or make an inference. Drawing conclusions and making inferences mean almost the same thing. Here are examples of showing details and possible inferences a reader might be led to make.

Showing Detail: The professor's desk is covered with papers, books, pencils, and several unwashed coffee cups.

Inferences: The professor is sloppy.
              The professor has been too busy to clean up his office.

Showing Detail: Bobby flew into the room, stomped to his desk, threw down his books, and dropped into his seat.

Inferences: Bobby is angry.
              Bobby is frustrated.

Showing Detail: Teachers of the twenty-first century, who make every-day use of many types of computer systems and software, frequently teach simultaneously in several cities on closed circuit television or even over the Internet.

Inference: Teachers must keep abreast of new technology.

Showing details help us "get into" the paper. Readers prefer the details rather than being told the inference. If a writing teacher has ever said, "Show me; don't tell me," he or she meant for you to supply the details, and let the reader draw the inference. Instead of saying Bobby is angry, let your reader see him stomping and storming and throwing down his books. Allowing readers to make their own inferences gives them a way to become more involved in what you are saying. To sum up, you will want to avoid details that show little, that do not allow any inferences, and you will want to avoid making the inferences for your reader. Strive to support your point with showing details that allow readers to make inferences.

Activity

For each of the following statements, list six to eight showing details that support the sentence. After you complete your lists, put a star next to those details that are the "most showing."

A. My neighbor's dog is vicious.

B. My five-year-old cousin is a brat.

C. The Johnsons' yard is gorgeous.

Collaborative Activity 1

Fill in the blank in the following sentence:

My bedroom is a _____ room.

Then list five showing details that support the statement.
Finally, take turns reading *only the list* of showing details to your classmates as they try to infer what is in the blank.

Collaborative Activity 2

With three or so classmates, choose one of the following, and write a narrative paragraph set in that location. Choose one person to write, and skip *three* lines between every written line. Then swap papers with another group. As a group, add showing details to the paragraph you receive. Be creative with these paragraphs. Next, swap papers a second time so you have yet another paragraph, and again add showing details. Then choose someone to read, and take turns reading the final paragraphs out loud. How much did your paragraph change? Were some changes for the better? Were there any additions that detract from the paragraph?

Locations:

1. In the middle school cafeteria

2. At the bus stop

3. At a baseball game

4. An afternoon at the beach

5. In an amusement park

If you look back over the showing details in this section, you will see that many of the best showing details are also **sensory details,** which means they let readers see, hear, touch, smell, or taste. Whenever you can evoke one of the reader's five senses, you will help draw him or her into your writing.

Introductions

In a relatively short essay of 400 to 600 words, a paragraph is generally a suitable length for the introduction. In a lengthy piece of ten, fifteen, twenty, or more pages, however, the introduction will probably need to be longer. Introductory paragraphs are a special type of paragraph that do not function in the same way as body paragraphs.

Collaborative Activity

With a partner, brainstorm a list of the characteristics of a good introduction.

Although you may have come up with more characteristics, the role of the introductory paragraph is generally in three parts: (1) to get the reader's attention, (2) to supply background information, and (3) in most cases, to state the thesis of the essay.

Observed on posters at college campuses in recent years:

SEX!
Now that we've gotten your attention, ...

In all cases, a sales pitch follows for a business, organization, club, etc. Why does the poster begin with the provocative word SEX? The next words answer the question: SEX is an attention grabber. Such grabbers are also called *hooks* because you want to hook your reader right from the start, then continue to reel him or her in as the essay progresses. Good writers think about getting and keeping their readers' attention. Of course, they can't simply begin every essay with SEX!

Other ways to grab the readers' attention are the following:

1. Ask a question.

2. Start with a direct quotation.

3. Begin with a shocking, odd, unusual, or particularly interesting fact.

Do the best you can to get your readers' attention right from the start. After all, if you don't, chances are they will stop reading immediately. But if you hook your readers, they will read on, and you will need a way to move smoothly toward the body of your essay.

There are several different ways to shape introductions. Some of the most common are called the inverted funnel introduction, the funnel introduction, the contrast introduction and the anecdotal introduction.

Inverted Funnel Introduction

The inverted funnel introduction is rarely your best option, but if you are strapped for time (such as when taking an exam), it may be your fastest route to a complete rough draft. This introduction is called an inverted funnel because it begins with a specific thesis statement and broadens as it continues; thus, it creates the shape of a funnel resting on its base, narrow at the top and broad at the bottom. Its shape is a triangle with a base at the bottom and point at the top. The inverted funnel introduction begins with a general thesis statement that is then broken down into its parts or plan for development. The thesis statement is written in bold in the following example.

> **Successful family vacations require careful thought and planning.** *The smartest travelers will first decide what type of vacation they would like and whether or not the activities will be age-appropriate for the children. They will then research by talking to friends, by going to the library, or by looking on the Internet. Finally, they will gather maps and any other material that will help their trip go smoothly.*

Funnel Introduction

The funnel introduction is so called because it is broad at the top and narrows down toward the end, becomes more and more specific, and concludes with the thesis statement (either general or enumerated). It is roughly the shape, then, of a funnel resting on its tip or a triangle with a point at the bottom and base at the top. The funnel is usually a better choice than the inverted funnel as it is more liable to pique your reader's interest. Try to use an attention-grabber at the beginning.

> *Have you ever returned home with your family badly needing a vacation from your vacation? Many of us have. Often the vacation's failure to relax us results from too many unexpected mishaps due to insufficient preparation. Spending hours driving around in search of a room, taking clothing for the wrong season, and not knowing the local food specialties often deprive vacationers of a good time.* **Successful family vacations require careful thought and planning.**

Contrast Introduction

A contrast introduction begins and changes direction partway through. This change of direction takes your reader in an unexpected turn that may pique his or her interest. The change of direction hinges on a contrast transition such as *but, yet,* or *however.*

> *After waiting and saving all year, the family is ready to partake in one of the greatest American traditions—the family vacation. As they head out, everyone looks forward to a week to remember. However, these memories they could do without. After three days of rain, getting lost, and bored, screaming children, the family heads home early.* **Successful family vacations require careful thought and planning.**

Anecdotal Introduction

An anecdote is a short story. Anecdotal introductions, then, very briefly tell a story. Another name for this type of introduction is a narrative opening. Beginning with an anecdote is usually a good attention-grabber.

> *Jo and her husband had failed twice before, once with a ski trip and once at the beach. This time they had vowed to make their family vacation a success. Jo began thinking about the Disney World vacation months in advance. She talked to several families whom she saw regularly at her neighborhood swimming pool about their recent trips to the amusement park. Next, she located several guidebooks, including two that catered specifically to budget-conscious families. Then she asked her husband, Sam, to use his Internet-access at work to find out what he could about places to stay nearby. This time Jo was certain the whole family would be happy.* **Successful family vacations require careful thought and planning.**

Activity

Choose one of the following topics, and narrow it to a thesis statement. Then write an inverted funnel introduction, funnel introduction, a contrast introduction, and finally, an anecdotal introduction for the topic you choose.

1. Characteristics of a good neighbor

2. Ways to land a good job

3. Keeping a relationship together

Conclusions

Many writers find that sometimes their conclusions just seem to fall into place while other times they are quite difficult to write. Concluding paragraphs, like introductory paragraphs, have a very special function.

Collaborative Activity

With a partner, list the characteristics of a good conclusion.

In general, a conclusion has two key functions: (1) sum up and tie together any loose threads in the essay, and (2) leave the readers something to think about. A ho-hum conclusion accomplishes only the first function. This conclusion gets the job done, but only minimally, and tends to be a bit boring, especially in shorter essays. A stronger conclusion goes farther to leave readers something to think about after they finish the essay. One way to accomplish this is to save a point that you might make in a body paragraph and present it in the conclusion.

You may, in planning your essay or in writing it, decide that a particular detail would serve you well in the conclusion. If you do this, you will need to be sure that the point is not so big that it seems you are bringing up a whole new side issue in the conclusion. Doing so would only serve to confuse readers. A second way to leave readers with something to think about is to look toward the future. This method is almost always effective.

A Conclusion That Summarizes

To sum up, the happiest travelers will take the time to plan family vacations with care. They will consider the best type of vacation for their family, and they will do their research. Furthermore, they will consider fully and gather everything they will need to make the week go as smoothly as possible. Only then will they be reasonably assured of a successful trip.

A Conclusion That Summarizes and Does More

To sum up, the happiest travelers will take the time to plan family vacations with care. They will choose the best type of vacation for their family, do their research, and gather together everything they will need to have a good trip. Once they experience a successful family vacation, they will face the next one with much more confidence and very little trepidation. In fact, they may even be ready to tackle a two-week vacation the next year!

 Computer Tip *Computers have changed the way most writers write. In some ways, using a computer will make the process of writing simpler for you. Revising, for example, becomes an easier and much neater process. Using a computer will probably speed up your writing and revising and save you time in the long run. However, writing on a computer can become a frustrating experience if you are not "computer smart." Here are some potential pitfalls that you must be aware of:*

1. *Always save your essay in at least two different places. For example, save to a diskette, and then save again on a back-up diskette! If you are working on your own computer, save it again to the hard drive just to be extra safe.*

2. *Do not leave your diskettes in direct sunlight or anywhere it gets very hot (such as in your car) for any length of time.*

3. *Save your work frequently (every ten or fifteen minutes). If you are working on a computer that is set to back up automatically, that's fine. But don't assume that you are unless you know for a fact. The safest course is assume you aren't, and get in the habit of saving every ten minutes or so. If you lose power (someone kicks your cord, or electrical outage occurs), you will lose everything that you haven't saved.*

4. *Make sure that the computer is finished working and that the light beside the disk drive goes off before you remove the diskette.*

5. *Do not rely too much on spell-checkers and grammar-checkers.*

6. *If you know you will have to have a printout right away, make sure the printer is working and has paper before you begin.*

In addition, remember that when writing on a computer, you will need to double-space essays most of the time. Furthermore, you don't need to press Enter at the end of lines; the program automatically formats paragraphs for you. Do press Enter at the ends of paragraphs, and remember to press Tab to indent each paragraph.

Keeping Your Audience in Mind

Earlier in this chapter we discussed the significance of keeping your purpose in mind when you choose a pattern for developing your essay. In fact, much of this book focuses on the importance of understanding your purpose when writing. Just as important, however, is knowing your audience. When writing, always use a "you attitude." That is, as you write, try to put yourself in your readers' place and think like your readers will think. Likewise, when you read (and you will read a great deal during your college career), think about the way the piece was written. As you continue to write (and read), you will find that thinking like your readers will begin to be second nature, and your writing will improve because of it.

The following essay, by popular novelist Amy Tan, brings up several issues involving varieties of spoken English, prejudice against immigrants, the American system of education, and the relationship between Tan and her mother. Yet she sums up all by making a statement about her need of having a specific audience in mind when writing.

Mother Tongue

by Amy Tan

1   I am not a scholar of English or literature. I cannot give you much more than personal opinions on the English language and its variations in this country or others.

2   I am a writer. And by that definition, I am someone who has always loved language. I am fascinated by language in daily life. I spend a great deal of my time thinking about the power of language—the way it can evoke an emotion, a visual image, a complex idea, or a simple truth. Language is the tool of my trade. And I use them all—all the Englishes I grew up with.

3   Recently, I was made keenly aware of the different Englishes I do use. I was giving a talk to a large group of people, the same talk I had already given to half a dozen other groups. The nature of the talk was about my writing, my life, and my book, *The Joy Luck Club*. The talk was going along well enough, until I remembered one major difference that made the whole talk sound wrong. My mother was in the room. And it was perhaps the first time she had heard me give a lengthy speech, using the kind of English I have never used with her. I was saying things like, "The intersection of memory upon imagination" and "There is an aspect of my fiction that relates to thus-and-thus"—a speech filled with carefully wrought grammatical phrases, burdened, it suddenly seemed to me, with nominalized forms, past perfect tenses, conditional phrases, all the forms of standard English that I had learned in school and through books, the forms of English I did not use at home with my mother.

4   Just last week, I was walking down the street with my mother, and I again found myself conscious of the English I was using, the English I do use with her. We were talking about the price of new and used furniture and I heard myself saying this: "Not waste money that way." My husband was with us as well, and he didn't notice any switch in my English. And then I realized why. It's because over the twenty years we've been together I've often used that same kind of English with him, and sometimes he even uses it with me. It has become our language of intimacy, a different sort of English that relates to family talk, the language I grew up with.

5   So you'll have some idea of what this family talk I heard sounds like, I'll quote what my mother said during a recent conversation which I videotaped and then transcribed. During this conversation, my mother was talking about a political gangster in Shanghai who had the same last name as her family's, Du, and how the gangster in his early years wanted to be adopted by her family, which was rich by comparison. Later, the gangster became more powerful, far richer than my mother's family, and one day showed up at my mother's wedding to pay his respects. Here's what she said in part:

6   "Du Yusong having business like fruit stand. Like off the street kind. He is Du like Du Zong—but not Tsung-ming Island people. The local people and putong, the river east side, he belong to that side local people. That man want to ask Du Zong father take him in like become own family. Du Zong father wasn't look down on him, but didn't take seriously, until that man big like become a mafia. Now important person, very hard to inviting him. Chinese way, came only to show respect, don't stay for dinner. Respect for making big celebration, he shows up. Mean gives lots of respect. Chinese custom. Chinese social life that way. If too important won't have to stay too long. He come to my wedding. I didn't see, I heard it. I gone to boy's side, they have YMCA dinner, Chinese age I was nineteen."

7   You should know that my mother's expressive command of English belies how much she actually understands. She reads the *Forbes* report, listens to *Wall Street Week,* converses daily with her stockbroker, reads all of Shirley MacLaine's books with ease—all kinds of things I can't begin to understand. Yet some of my friends tell me they understand 50 percent of what my mother says. Some say they understand 80 to 90 percent. Some say they understand none of it, as if she were speaking pure Chinese. But to me, my mother's English is perfectly clear, perfectly natural. It's my mother tongue. Her language, as I hear it, is vivid, direct, full of observation and imagery. That was the language that helped shape the way I saw things, expressed things, made sense of the world.

8   Lately, I've been giving more thought to the kind of English my mother speaks. Like others, I have described it to people as "broken" or "fractured" English. But I wince when I say that. It has always both-

ered me that I can think of no way to describe it other than "broken," as if it were damaged and needed to be fixed, as if it lacked a certain wholeness and soundness. I've heard other terms used, "limited English," for example. But they seem just as bad, as if everything is limited, including people's perceptions of the limited English speaker.

9   I know this for a fact, because when I was growing up, my mother's "limited" English limited *my* perception of her. I was ashamed of her English. I believed that her English reflected the quality of what she had to say. That is, because she expressed them imperfectly her thoughts were imperfect. And I had plenty of empirical evidence to support me: the fact that people in department stores, at banks, and at restaurants did not take her seriously, did not give her good service, pretended not to understand her, or even acted as if they did not hear her.

10   My mother has long realized the limitations of her English as well. When I was fifteen, she used to have me call people on the phone to pretend I was she. In this guise, I was forced to ask for information or even to complain and yell at people who had been rude to her. One time it was a call to her stockbroker in New York. She had cashed out her small portfolio and it just so happened we were going to go to New York the next week, our very first trip outside California. I had to get on the phone and say in an adolescent voice that was not very convincing, "This is Mrs. Tan."

11   And my mother was standing in the back whispering loudly, "Why he don't send me check, already two weeks late. So mad he lie to me, losing my money."

12   And then I said in perfect English. "Yes, I'm getting rather concerned. You had agreed to send the check two weeks ago, but it hasn't arrived."

13   Then she began to talk more loudly. "What he want, I come to New York tell him front of his boss, you cheating me?" And I was trying to calm her down, make her be quiet, while telling the stockbroker, "I can't tolerate any more excuses. If I don't receive the check immediately, I am going to have to speak to your manager when I'm in New York next week." And sure enough, the following week there we were in front of this astonished stockbroker, and I was sitting there red-faced and quiet, and my mother, the real Mrs. Tan, was shouting at his boss in her impeccable broken English.

14   We used a similar routine just five days ago for a situation that was far less humorous. My mother had gone to the hospital for an appointment to find out about a benign brain tumor a CAT scan had revealed a month ago. She said she had spoken very good English, her best English, no mistakes. Still, she said, the hospital did not apologize when they said they had lost the CAT scan and she had come for nothing. She said they did not seem to have any sympathy when she told them she was anxious to know the exact diagnosis, since her husband and son had both died of brain tumors. She said they would not give

her any more information until the next time and she would have to make another appointment for that. So she said she would not leave until the doctor called her daughter. She wouldn't budge. And when the doctor finally called her daughter, me, who spoke in perfect English—lo and behold—we had assurances the CAT scan would be found, promises that a conference call on Monday would be held, and apologies for any suffering my mother had gone through for a most regrettable mistake.

15   I think my mother's English almost had an effect on limiting my possibilities in life as well. Sociologists and linguists probably will tell you that a person's developing language skills are more influenced by peers. But I do think that the language spoken in the family, especially in immigrant families which are more insular, plays a large role in shaping the language of the child. And I believe that it affected my results on achievement tests, IQ tests, and the SAT. While my English skills were never judged as poor, compared to math, English could not be considered my strong suit. In grade school I did moderately well, getting perhaps B's, sometimes B-pluses, in English and scoring perhaps in the sixtieth or seventieth percentile on achievement tests. But those scores were not good enough to override the opinion that my true abilities lay in math and science, because in those areas I achieved A's and scored in the ninetieth percentile or higher.

16   This was understandable. Math is precise: there is only one correct answer. Whereas, for me at least, the answers on English tests were always a judgment call, a matter of opinion and personal experience. Those tests were constructed around items like fill-in-the-blank sentence completion, such as, "Even though Tom was _____, Mary thought he was _____." And the correct answer always seemed to be the most bland combinations of thoughts, for example, "Even though Tom was shy, Mary thought he was charming," with the grammatical structure "even though" limiting the correct answer to some sort of semantic opposites, so you wouldn't get answers like, "Even though Tom was foolish, Mary thought he was ridiculous." Well, according to my mother, there were very few limitations as to what Tom could have been and what Mary might have thought of him. So I never did well on tests like that.

17   The same was true with word analogies, pairs of words in which you were supposed to find some sort of logical sentence relationship—for example, "*Sunset* is to *nightfall* as _____ is to _____." And here you would be presented with a list of four possible pairs, one of which showed the same kind of relationship: *red* is to *stoplight, bus* is to *arrival, chills* is to *fever, yawn* is to *boring*. Well, I could never think that way. I knew what the tests were asking, but I could not block out of my mind the images already created by the first pair, "*sunset* is to *nightfall*"—and I would see a burst of colors against a darkening sky, the moon rising, the lowering of a curtain of starts. And all the other pairs of words—red, bus, stoplight, boring—just threw up a mass of

confusing images, making it impossible for me to sort out something as logical as saying: "A sunset precedes nightfall" is the same as "a chill precedes a fever." The only way I would have gotten that answer right would have been to imagine an associative situation, for example, my being disobedient and staying out past sunset, catching a chill at night, which turns into feverish pneumonia as punishment, which indeed did happen to me.

18   I have been thinking about all this lately, about my mother's English, about achievement tests. Because lately I've been asked, as a writer, why there are not more Asian Americans represented in American literature. Why are there few Asian Americans enrolled in creative writing programs? Why do so many Chinese students go into engineering? Well, these are broad sociological questions I can't begin to answer. But I have noticed in surveys—in fact, just last week—that Asian students, as a whole, always do significantly better on math achievement tests than in English. And this makes me think that there are other Asian-American students whose English spoken in the home might also be described as "broken" or "limited." And perhaps they also have teachers who are steering them away from writing and into math and science, which is what happened to me.

19   Fortunately, I happen to be rebellious in nature and enjoy the challenge of disproving assumptions made about me. I became an English major my first year in college, after being enrolled as pre-med. I started writing nonfiction as a freelancer the week after I was told by my former boss that writing was my worst skill and I should hone my talents toward account management.

20   But it wasn't until 1985 that I finally began to write fiction. And at first I wrote using what I thought to be wittily crafted sentences, sentences that would finally prove I had mastery over the English language. Here's an example from the first draft of a story that later made its way into *The Joy Luck Club,* but without this line: "That was my mental quandary in its nascent state." A terrible line, which I can barely pronounce.

21   Fortunately, for reasons I won't get into today, I later decided I should envision a reader for the stories I would write. And the reader I decided upon was my mother, because these were stories about mothers. So with this reader in mind—and in fact she did read my early drafts—I began to write stories using all the Englishes I grew up with: the English I spoke to my mother, which for lack of a better term might be described as "simple"; the English she used with me, which for lack of a better term might be described as "broken"; my translation of her Chinese, which could certainly be described as "watered down"; and what I imagined to be her translation of her Chinese if she could speak in perfect English, her internal language, and for that I sought to preserve the essence, but neither an English nor a Chinese structure. I wanted to capture what language ability tests can never reveal: her

intent, her passion, her imagery, the rhythms of her speech and the nature of her thoughts.

22   Apart from what any critic had to say about my writing, I knew I had succeeded where it counted when my mother finished reading my book and gave me her verdict: "So easy to read."

Questions

1. Explain how the title of this essay "Mother Tongue" constitutes a play on words.
2. How many types of English does Tan mention by the end of her essay? What are they?
3. How did Tan realize that "That was my mental quandary in its nascent state" is a terrible sentence? Do you agree that it is awful? Why or why not?
4. Why did Tan consider her writing successful when her mother pronounced it "so easy to read"? Do you agree that a piece of writing is successful when it is easy to read? What does this have to do with knowing your audience?

Grammar and Usage: Review of True Blue Verbs and Clauses

Analyze the three following constructions from Amy Tan's "Mother Tongue."

1. Lately, I've been giving more thought to the kind of English my mother speaks.
2. Because lately I've been asked, as a writer, why there are not more Asian Americans represented in American literature.
3. "Du Yuson having business like fruit stand."

Although the instructions state that you are to "analyze" these constructions, what exactly are you to do? Do you read them aloud and try to make sense or nonsense of them? Do you count the words and expect some formula to tell you what they contain? Do you simply stare at the page until some supernatural inspiration tells you what you have before you?

Of course, you do none of these. But if you have not yet much experience in analyzing groups of words, getting started can be daunting. It needn't be. In any situation where you must analyze or diagram or otherwise dissect a sentence or construction, your first step, always, is to *find the true blue verb(s)*.

Now, which of the constructions have true blue verbs? What about the first one? *Giving* has true blue verb potential, but it ends in *-ing*. Therefore, it must have a helper. Does it? Yes, *I've* is a contraction for *I* *have,* and *have been* is an acceptable helper for *giving.* And what about *speaks?* Is it also a true blue verb and, more importantly, if it is, is its subject separate from the *I* of the first one? Again, *speaks* is an acceptable true blue verb, and it has a separate subject, *mother.* Thus, if we remind ourselves that a clause is any group of words that contains at least one true blue verb, we will realize that construction #1 contains not one, but two clauses. We may also instinctively sense that this group of words is a sentence.

What about the second group of words? As with the first, we begin by searching for a true blue verb. We should be able to locate two, *have been asked* (with *have* again pulled out of *I've*) and *are.* These two true blue verbs take separate subjects, *I* and *Asian Americans,* and so we have two clauses. Yet if we read this construction aloud, something may sound not quite right about it, and we may realize that, despite the two clauses and despite Amy Tan's considerable skill as a writer, this construction is not a sentence. Yet if we drop the word *because* from the very beginning, we will have a sentence. Tan has used this non-sentence deliberately, as you will see if you examine it in the context of her text, because she wants to form a concrete link to the previous sentence.

Finally, the third group of words is an example of the English that Amy Tan says her mother speaks. In analyzing this group of words, we must remember the first rule of grammar analysis: find the verb. Since this group of words has no true blue verb (*Having* lacks a helper), it is neither a clause nor a sentence, and we need say no more about it.

So far we have determined that construction #1 has two clauses and is a sentence, while construction #2 has two clauses and is not a sentence, and construction #3 is just a group of words. Now we must ask ourselves how to divide the clauses. When does the first clause in #1 or #2 end and the second begin? This question takes us to the second part of the definition of a clause: the clause includes the true blue verb(s), subject(s), and anything that comes after the verb(s) and answers the question "What?" and/or describes any of the above parts of the clause.

In the first construction, we have already identified the true blue verb *have been giving* and the subject *I* in the first part. *Lately* tells when the speaker has been giving, *thought* tells what the speaker has been giving, and *to the kind of English* describes or tells what the thought has been about. Afterwards, *speaks* is the true blue verb of its clause with the subject *mother,* which is described by *my.* Thus, we would say that every word from *lately* to *English* is part of the first clause while *my mother speaks* is the second clause.

Moving on to the second construction, we find the true blue verb *have been asked* and subject *I* followed by *as a writer,* which describes *I* and is preceded by *because,* which modifies the *have been asked.* Later, the true blue verb *are* takes *Asian Americans* as its subject. *Represented in American literature* comes after the verb and tells what Asian Americans are (actually, are not, as the sentence says) while *why* describes the verb and *there* is a filler word that helps unify the clause. Thus, in this sentence, we would say that the first clause extends from *because* to *writer,* and the second begins with *why* and ends with *literature.*

What can we say about the third group of words? The temptation may arise to begin analyzing, but don't forget that there is no verb. Consequently, there is neither a beginning nor an ending of a clause in the third construction.

Exercise 1

Using the definition of clause and the previous examples, circle each true blue verb and draw a box around its subject in these constructions. Then write the first and last words of every clause. Some constructions will have one clause, some more than one, and some none.

1. The author Toni Morrison is a major literary figure today.

2. One of her most famous novels, *Song of Solomon,* tells the story of a youth's strange growth to manhood.

3. Macon ("Milkman") Dead, III, comes to learn about his family and its history.

4. Morrison has also achieved fame because she wrote the novel *Beloved.*

5. Although *Beloved* is often difficult to understand, in 1998 it was made into a major motion picture starring Danny Glover and Oprah Winfrey.

6. Unfortunately, *Beloved* did not fare as well at the box office as its stars and author had hoped it would do.

7. Because some people had trouble with the idea of the main character driving off all her living loved ones while she tried to comfort her dead daughter Beloved.

8. Morrison won a Pulitzer Prize after she wrote *Song of Solomon.*

9. Then, in 1993, becoming the first African American woman ever to win the Nobel Prize for literature.

10. Now most critics speak favorably of Morrison's depictions of African American lives and struggles, two subjects frequently discussed today.

11. Some people prefer attempting success to not trying at all.

12. Most of us have more respect for one who makes the effort than for one who refuses even to try.

13. Doing your best, no failure at all. *Phrase*

The - come 14. The man in the boat, over by the shores of Lake Superior, enduring the drought and enjoying the gentle rains to come. *Phrase*

He - left 15. He left.

Since - month 16. Since he had not had a meal in a restaurant for several months, he *He - while* decided to head ashore and to become a "land-lubber" for a while.

Soon - return 17. Soon he will return, for he will grow tired of the hustle and bustle of *For - city* automobiles in the city.

He - boat 18. He truly enjoys sleeping on the deck of his boat, with just a layer of *The - sleep* stars overhead and the sounds of animals singing him to sleep.

Shall - day 19. "Shall I compare thee to a summer's day?"—Shakespeare

A - minds 20. "A foolish consistency is the hobgoblin of little minds."—Ralph Waldo Emerson

Note: You should have noticed by now that every structure that is not a clause is not a sentence, but not every structure that is a clause is a sentence. Why are some clauses sentences while others are not? When you can determine the difference between a group of mere words and a clause, and a clause that is a sentence versus one that is not, you will be able to eliminate **sentence fragments** from your writing.

Exercise 2

Choose five sentences from a piece of your own writing. Copy them in your notebook. Then circle each true blue verb, and draw a box around its subject. How many clauses do you find in each of your sentences?

Writing Process

Making It Better: Revising Your Essay

Why Revise? What Is Revising Anyway?

Do you remember when you first learned to ice skate, roller skate, snow ski, or water ski? Can you remember learning how to ride a bicycle? Your first attempts may not have been particularly successful. In the early stages of learning any of these activities, you probably spent as much time on the ground as you did upright. Learning may have taken some time. You may have grown tired and frustrated; you may have been sore from the bumps and bruises. At times, you probably wanted to give up, but you kept getting back up. Then with practice, you probably achieved at least some success, and with much more practice, you may even have achieved excellence.

You may be familiar with the old saying that "practice makes perfect." Although we will probably never attain perfection, in the long run practicing usually leads to improvement. Therefore, we learn to ride a bike by riding. We learn to play a musical instrument by practicing it. We become more accurate basketball players by shooting lots of hoops, and we become more able and proficient with a new computer program the more we use it. Likewise, we writers learn to write better by writing. And we can often improve what we have written by revising it.

Revision Is Both Linear and Circular

Revision is the last stage of the writing process.

Four-Stage Writing Process
1. Gathering ideas
2. Organizing ideas
3. Writing
4. Revising

After writing, it is almost always a good idea to focus your energy on revising your draft. This often means using your time wisely so that you have time for this important step. You should always consider a first draft to be a rough draft. Your second and maybe your third or fourth drafts may end up being rough drafts as well. The writing process does not have to end until either you are finished and satisfied with what you have written or your instructor or employer says your time is up.

Yet revising is like all the other steps in the writing process in that it is circular, which means that revising is really not restricted to a distinct step. Remember our model of the writing process is linear and does not show steps backward, but we may very well be jumping back and forth among steps. For example, you may decide to revise a body paragraph before going on to write the next one. Thus, we may be writing and revising simultaneously. Still, it is good when finished with a draft to look over the entire piece with an eye toward revision.

Revising Means "Seeing Again"

Revising frequently means different things to different people. For example, to one person, revising may mean correcting errors someone has marked. To another it may mean correcting all grammatical and punctuation mistakes in a piece of writing. To another it may mean rewriting the whole paper. Such vastly different ideas about revising can lead to miscommunication between students and instructors and employers and supervisors.

First, let's look at the word *revising*. It is made up of three parts, the prefix *re,* the root word *vis,* and the suffix *ing.* "Vising," of course, has to do with seeing. We see the prefix *re* in many words including revitalize, reactivate, redo, and rethink. It means to do over, or to do again. If we put the parts together, then, we find that revising literally means "seeing again." And although we associate revising with writing, it actually does have much to do with seeing.

When we revise, we must see again, and we must try to see our writing as clearly as possible. The less clearly we see, the less effectively we can revise, and the more clearly we see, the more effectively we can revise. Say, for example, that you have a term paper due in the morning. You stay up late and finish writing it. Then at midnight, you again read over it. After the third or fourth reading, you realize that your eyes are floating over the page. You are not seeing the writing at all! Nearly all of us have had the experience of not being able to see our own writing anymore. When this happens, revising simply cannot happen.

Thus, the goal is to achieve the opposite, to see your writing as clearly as possible. Writers need to see their writing with fresh eyes. One thing to keep in mind is that you will want to put as much distance between yourself and your writing as you can. In general, writers are too close to their work to see it clearly. They wrote it, they created it, and it is very familiar to them. In a sense, critiquing one's own writing is like a parent critiquing the behavior of his or her own child. Writers may lack the perspective to make clear judgments.

Activity: Seeing with Fresh Eyes

List as many ways as you can think of to make your own writing seem more distant to you. One idea, for example, might be to take a break from your writing and come back to revise it later.

Collaborative Activity: Comparing with Classmates

Compare your list of ways to see your own writing more clearly with two classmates. Go back to the previous exercise and add their ideas to your own.

Were you and your classmates able to think of several ways to distance yourself from your own writing? Almost anything that makes your essay appear odd, unusual, or different should help you see it more clearly. You may have mentioned reading the essay aloud to yourself, having someone read it back to you, or reading it into a tape recorder and playing it back. Have you ever noticed how weird your own voice sounds on tape? This "weirdness" can be quite helpful. You might have mentioned peer editing, which means sharing your essay with someone who really does have fresh eyes for your writing.

You might also have considered working backward through your essay, either sentence by sentence, or paragraph by paragraph. When writers read over their writing, their mind often sees what it wants to see instead of what is actually on the page. This is the reason why it is so hard to find typos while reading straight through, even if you reread many times. Yet if you look at individual words, typos are much easier to find. So you might look at the last word of your essay, then the second to last, third to last, and so on. You may try the same method to check for sentence fragments or fused sentences, or sentences that are just not smoothly phrased. Start with the last sentence in your conclusion. Then look at only the second to last sentence, and so on. Use this backward method one last time to check individual paragraphs for completeness and unity. The first step is to read only the concluding paragraph, and make revisions if you like. Next read the final body paragraph. Continue working backward through your essay until you conclude with the first paragraph. When you take words, sentences, and paragraphs out of context, you will see them more clearly and you should be able to do a better job revising them.

How Is an Essay Like a House? Structure and Polish Revision

Writing an essay is something like building a house. By comparing the building of essays and the building and selling of houses, we can better understand revising and all it entails. First of all, an outline for an essay is similar to the blueprint drawings for a house. Both represent the plans for building. Next, there are similarities in the way houses and essays are actually put together. They both have structure and polish.

Let's talk about houses first. Think about a time when you saw a house or building under construction. Fairly early on in the process, a construction crew framed the house. At that point you could already see the **structure** of that house. You could tell roughly how big the house would be, whether or not it had two stories, the slant of the roof, and whether or not it had any gables. You could also tell if it had no garage, a one-car garage, or a two- or three-car garage.

As the construction progressed, the later stages did not result in structural changes at all. These later stages involved more the **polish** of the house. Examples of polish items would be vinyl or wood siding, brick, exterior and interior paint, wallpaper, carpeting, molding, and light fixtures.

Structure and polish are important in both houses and essays. A solid, good-looking house must have solid structure and attractive polish. Neither one will do the job alone. In fact perfect polish may actually hide structural flaws. Newspapers and television news shows tell the sad stories of people who purchase beautiful "dream homes" for hundred of thousands of dollars, only to discover a year or so later that the builder has taken shortcuts. The builder may have used inferior, cheaper building materials, or not hammered in enough nails, or used thinner wood beams than were necessary. These homeowners find themselves the unhappy owners of homes with seeping water or with cracks in floors or walls, for example. Solid structure in a house is so important that if buyers do not know enough about construction, they may decide to hire a building inspector to do this important job for them. Home inspection, in fact, is big business nowadays. Polish can hide structural flaws, but if buyers know where and how to examine the structure, they can find the problems. When you make a huge investment like buying a home, you will want to be sure it is structurally sound.

Yet polish is also a consideration. For example, who would want to move into a new home that looks sloppy, dirty, or just plain ugly? Who wants to spend $100,000 on an unattractive property? The homes that sell quickly are homes that have nice paint jobs inside and out, that appear tidy, that have new carpet, ceramic tile, or linoleum. Realtors say that homes that smell nice sell faster. In fact, real estate agents recommend that sellers bake if they know their house will be shown to prospective buyers.

Now let's consider essays. What is the structure of an essay? An essay with a solid structure has several characteristics. First, it has a clear thesis, or main idea. It is focused. The points it makes are clearly stated, and they are supported well with many facts, details, and examples. Each paragraph is a unified unit without irrelevant or detracting details. In addition, the essay moves smoothly from one idea to the next. Essays with these qualities have good structure. When your essay has a solid structure, it will be easily understood and well supported. On the other hand, if your essay has faulty structure, no amount of polish can fix the problem.

What is the polish of an essay? Polish concerns are different from structural concerns. Good polish makes your essay presentable; it makes it "look good." It also helps your credibility as a writer. Polish issues include following grammar and usage rules, using punctuation correctly, and spelling correctly.

Again, both structure and polish are important concerns when writing. We should make one more point here. A polish problem, such as a misspelled word or missing comma, is generally a "quick-fix" problem, whereas modifying structure tends to be more involved—and in the case of the house, more costly. You might be willing to buy a house for a good price even if it has bad polish because you know you can fairly easily and cheaply paint, wallpaper, and replace worn carpets. On the other hand, very poor polish—that is, many grammatical and punctuation errors—can become a structural problem, just as a house that is not maintained with fresh coats of paint and new roof shingles may end up falling in after many years. In other words, with both houses and essays if you totally ignore polish, structure will eventually be affected.

Now let's talk about revision, again in terms of houses and essays. You can structurally alter a house, but it involves some measure of rebuilding. An example of a structural change is an addition on a home. Structural changes in your essay will involve some rewriting. You can also alter the polish. An example of this would be a fresh coat of paint. Fixing polish in your essay may not involve a lot of rewriting.

By now, you probably realize that revision means more than just correcting punctuation and spelling mistakes. When revising your writing, you need to consider both the structure and the polish, and since revising means *seeing again,* revising your writing involves your seeing the structure and the polish of your essay as clearly as possible.

Therefore, there are two ways of revising: **structural revision** and **polish revision.**

Activity: Revising

Think about a time that you had the opportunity to revise your own writing. What exactly did you do to improve your essay? Did you correct spelling errors? Did you add any new information? What else might you have done? Being as specific as you can, explain in a paragraph or in a list exactly what changes you made when you had an opportunity to revise.

Collaborative Activity: Revising

Compare your paragraph or list of specific revision practices with those of two or three other classmates in a small group. Add their ideas about revision to yours.

Collaborative Activity: Revising for Structure vs. Revising for Polish

Now look over all the ideas about revision, and place each item on the following chart.

Revising

Structural	Polish
Add supporting details	Fix spelling mistakes

Structural Revision

Let's now look at the changes a student, Quisha Bennett, made as she revised an essay telling about a memorable event in her life—her high school graduation. Quisha wrote three drafts of her paper. Read her first draft now.

Graduation Day (First Draft)

By Quisha Bennett

The day of graduation was so hectic. I had so much to do in order to prepare for my senior beach trip leaving the next day, family, and the graduation ceremony itself. When my family from out of town had arrived that morning, I was so happy. They had traveled all the way from Georgia to attend my special ceremony. I tried to spend as much time as I could with my family and thank them for coming. I knew that in the next few hours I would be getting to attend the all-night graduation party or leaving town.

I started feeling overwhelmed with fear and happiness. I had finally achieved my first and most important step in adulthood and education. It was also an achievement of not dropping out or getting pregnant, like so many girls at my high school did.

It was finally time for the ceremony, the real thing. I was very nervous because I would be the first group of people to walk out into that huge cheering crowd. As I was walking, I saw all of my family and friends yelling and taking pictures. In the crowd I saw my boyfriend. He waved, blew me a kiss, and whispered "I Love You." I took my diploma and shook hands with my principal. I had did it without a sweat.

This experience was the best of my life and the most important. Although it took 12 years to reach that point, I wouldn't change it for the world. I would just encourage more high school students to accomplish that goal.

As you read Quisha's first revised draft of "Graduation Day" you will probably notice some changes. As you read the next version, consider the following questions:

- Do you think the revisions are helpful?
- Do they make you more interested or less interested in what she is saying?

When you finish reading, answer the questions that follow the essay.

Graduation Day (Second Draft)

By Quisha Bennett

The day of graduation, June 20, 1998, was so hectic. I had so much to accomplish on that day with no time pending. I needed to pack for my senior beach trip that was leaving the next day, clean up my house for family arriving, and the graduation ceremony. When my family from out of town arrived that morning, I was so happy. They had traveled all the way from Georgia to Virginia to attend my special ceremony. I tried to spend as much time with them as I could, and thank them for coming. I knew that in the few hours after graduation I would be attending the all-night graduation party or leaving town.

The time was 2:00 p.m. and the ceremony was ready to begin. Our entire senior class was outside waiting for the music to start so that we could begin our march. As I was standing there looking at all the people, I started to feel overwhelmed with fear and happiness. I had finally achieved my most important step in adulthood and education, which was fearful. It was also an achievement to not drop out or get pregnant, like so many girls at my high school did.

It was finally time for the ceremony and the music had begun. I was very nervous. My group was the first to walk out into that huge cheering crowd. As I was walking, I saw all of my family and friends yelling and taking pictures. In the crowd I saw my boyfriend. He waved, blew me a kiss, and whispered "I love you." I took my diploma and shook hands with my principal. I had done it without a sweat.

This experience was the best of my life and the most important. Although it took 12 years to reach that point, I would not change it for the world. I would just encourage more high school students to accomplish that goal.

Questions

1. What additions did the author make to the introduction? Which do you think are the most important and why?
2. What changes did she make in the first body paragraph? Do you think they improve the essay? Why or why not?
3. The author made very few revisions in the second body paragraph, which has some specific details that let us see what was happening at the graduation. List at least two of these vivid details.

Quisha continued working on her essay and produced the following final draft. As you read this next version, you should notice much more structural revision. Once again, respond to the questions following the essay.

Graduation Day (Third Draft)

By Quisha Bennett

The day of graduation, June 20, 1998, was so hectic. I had so much to accomplish on that day with no time pending. I needed to pack for my senior beach trip that was leaving the next day, to clean up my house for family arriving, and to prepare for the graduation ceremony. I had planned for our senior beach trip, so I was in charge of everything. I needed to make sure that ten people could fit into two cars, that everyone was packed and that their deposit money for the beach apartment was correct. With my mom yelling in the background, "Quisha, you need to help clean up before everyone arrives," cleaning was definitely another priority.

When my family from out of town arrived that morning, I was so happy. They had traveled all the way from Georgia to Virginia to attend my special ceremony. I tried to spend as much time with them as I could and thank them for coming. I knew that in the few hours after graduation I would be attending the all-night graduation party or leaving town.

That morning and half of the afternoon, my senior class was practicing for hours for the ceremony. I seemed like forever and a day before we got it right. We then had to move outside to where the graduation was going to take place. We were instructed how to walk, where to sit, and how to approach the stage. After practice was over, I went home and started getting ready.

The time was 2:00 p.m. and the ceremony was ready to begin. Our entire senior class was outside waiting for the music to start so that we could begin our march. As I was standing there looking at the people, I started to feel overwhelmed with fear and happiness. I had finally achieved my most important step in adulthood and education, which was scary. It was also an achievement to not drop out or get pregnant, like so many girls at my high school did.

It was finally time for the ceremony and the music had begun. I was very nervous. My group was the first to walk out into that huge cheering crowd. As I was walking, I saw all of my family and friends yelling and taking pictures. In the crowd I saw my boyfriend. He waved, blew me a kiss, and whispered "I love you." I took my diploma and shook hands with my principal. I had done it without a sweat. After the graduation, my mom threw a party to celebrate at my house. All of my friends and family were there. We had food, cake, music, and gifts.

The next day I had to say good-bye to my family with hugs, kisses, and thank you. I was very tired from the all night graduation party. It was time for us to pack up the cars and head out of town, now adults.

This experience was the best of my life and the most important. Although it took 12 years to reach that point, I would not change it for the world. I would just encourage more high school students to accomplish that goal.

Questions

1. How does this draft better show that the author was very busy as she prepared for her graduation from high school?

2. Explain how the author has further developed her ideas about the visiting family.

3. The author added two paragraphs to her essay. What are they about? Do they add to your reading of this essay in any way?

4. Make one suggestion for improving the structure of this essay.

Computer Tip

Using a computer to write your essays has considerable advantages over the old paper and pen method when it comes to structural revision. Simply put, it makes the job of revising easier. With a few points and clicks of the mouse, you can move or remove even large chunks of your writing. If you change your mind, another click or two puts everything back where it was. When you decide to make an addition, you simply insert writing wherever you like. No more scratching outs, copying over, or cutting and pasting pages. You always work on a perfectly "clean" copy.

Polish Revision: Correctness and Precision

As we noted earlier, good polish makes an essay more readable, presentable, and credible. In fact, if an essay has grammatical mistakes and misspelled words, no matter how important or structurally sound its argument, its writers will probably not be taken seriously. For this reason, no one who wants to get the job sends out a resume or cover letter with these kinds of mistakes.

The fact is our intelligence is often judged on the basis of how we use language. A case in point is the famous African-American abolitionist leader Frederick Douglass. In the 1840s, when Douglass gave his antislavery speeches, many Americans doubted that a black man, born a slave, could actually have the intelligence to write the speeches he was delivering. It was in the face of such criticism that Douglass wrote *Narrative of the Life of Frederick Douglass.* In his case, correctness was an absolute necessity, for in proving that he could write "correct English," he also proved his intelligence to many doubters.

Another polish issue we haven't yet mentioned is word choice. Think carefully about each word you have used. Using precise words is essential. Consider this quotation by Mark Twain, author of *Tom Sawyer* and *Huckleberry Finn:*

> *The difference between the almost-right word & the right word is really a large matter—it's the difference between the lightning bug and the lightning.*

In addition, if you can write the same thing in thirty words or in fifteen, you should write it in fifteen. Get rid of unnecessary words in favor of simplicity. Don't ever add words just to make your essay longer or attempt to sound "more important" by using more or bigger words. Even the federal government is trying to improve in this regard.

Consider the following news article published in *The Atlanta Constitution* on June 2, 1998. After you read the article, answer the questions that follow.

In Plain English: Feds Must Prune Prose

By Marcy Gordon, Associated Press

1   **Washington**—Taking aim at government gobbledybook, Vice President Al Gore announced a directive Monday requiring bereaucrats to use plain English.

2   Starting Oct. 1 in official Washington, these are in: common, everyday words; pronouns such as "you"; the active, not passive voice; and short sentences. Clutter and unnecessary technical terms are out.

3   The change, ordered by President Clinton, applies to all new federal documents, other than regulations, that explain how to get a benefit or service or how to comply with an agency requirement.

4   By New Year's Day, federal regulations will fall under the plain English knife.

5   The change is designed to help ordinary citizens and small businesses.

6   "By using plain language, we send a clear message about what the government is doing, what it requires and what services it offers," Clinton wrote in announcing the initiative. "Plain language saves the government and the private sector time, effort and money."

7   And Gore, who has led the administration's campaign to reinvent government, told a group of small business owners from around the country: "Short is better than long. Active is better than passive. Clarity helps advance understanding."

8   Government rules that took 72 words to explain will be chopped to around six, Gore said. Unfamiliar phrases will be simplified: for example, "means of egress" becomes "exit routes."

9   He said a number of agencies, notably the Small Business Administration and the Veterans Benefit Administration, already have made great progress rewriting their rules into plain English.

10   The assault on jargon and convoluted language started at the Securities and Exchange Commission, which began developing a plain English rule several years ago with the mutual fund industry.

11   The SEC adopted a rule in January requiring that key sections of mutual fund prospectuses and similar financial documents be written simply and clearly.

12   The push to improve investors' understanding will cost U.S. companies an estimated $56 million.

13   "I applaud the administration for directing federal employees to write in plain language," SEC Chairman Arthur Levitt Jr. said. "I'm sure the American public will be grateful when they read clear, well-written government documents."

14   Marc Beauchamp, spokesman for the North American Securities Administrators Association, said, "Clearly you have to strike a balance between full disclosure and the classic comic book version. But it's harder to commit fraud in plain English."

Questions

1. According to the article, how will citizens and businesses benefit from the government's use of plain English?
2. List four or five specific examples of changes the government writers will have to make to comply with the new rules.
3. What is meant by the phrase "government gobbledygook"?
4. What is meant by the phrase "plain English knife"?
5. Is it better to say the same thing in thirty words or in ten words?

 Computer Tip

If you are using a computer to write your essay, you may have a spell-checker and/or grammar-checker available to you as you work on polish revision. Many students come to rely on these tools, but they are not nearly always reliable. Do not make the common mistake of overrelying on a spell-checker or grammar-checker! Spell checkers do not read. They merely check to see that each word is in a dictionary. Therefore, they cannot differentiate between words like there and their or to, too, and two. And grammar checkers are notorious for giving bad advice. The fact is, you must understand a good deal about grammar to tell the bad advice from the good.

More on Peer Editing—Revising Together

Earlier in this chapter, we talked about the benefits of seeing our writing with fresh eyes as we revise. We mentioned letting someone else look over your rough drafts and give you feedback. Sometimes you will have the opportunity to do just this in class. This type of activity is usually called *peer editing.*

For many years, most college professors would have thought you were cheating if you and your classmates went over each other's essays. Today, except in a testing situation where collaboration is expressly forbidden, peer editing gives you a great opportunity to improve your essays and strengthen your writing.

As we mentioned earlier, getting responses from others can be invaluable as you revise, partly because it is so hard to see your own writing clearly. Second, learning to be a careful reader and editor of another's writing is a necessary skill for success in college and in the workforce. Use the following Editing Sheet as you complete the Peer Editing Activity that follows.

Editing Sheet

Author's Name: _____

Editor's Name: _____

1. What is the main idea or thesis of the essay? Copy it here.
2. List two to four key points that support the main idea of the essay.
    1)
    2)
    3)
    4)
3. What is the best part of the essay and why?
4. Every essay can be improved. What is the weakest part and why?
5. Do you see any mistakes in grammar, punctuation, or spelling?
6. Do you see any places where the author used the wrong word or where he or she might use a better word?

Collaborative Activity: Peer Editing

For this activity, you may use any essay you have already written. In groups of three, take turns reading your essay out loud to the group. Then swap papers around so that you do not have your own. Next, fill out an editing sheet about your classmate's essay. When everyone finishes, swap papers again and fill out a second sheet. Give your written comments to the person who wrote the essay. Collect the comments you receive from classmates so that you may consider them as you revise your essay.

Grammar and Usage: Types of Clauses and Clause Combiners

What are the differences between the following clauses?

1. Jessica is an extremely capable and reliable friend.
2. Because Jessica is an extremely capable and reliable friend.

A close review of these two clauses immediately reveals the obvious difference that the second begins with *because* while the first does not. How important is that difference? As we continue, we realize that the first clause is a sentence; however, the second is not. Why is this so? Since we have already determined that the only difference between the two clauses is the word *because,* we may conclude that the second clause is not a sentence "because." In other words, the word *because* keeps the second clause from being a sentence. The same would be true if the clause also began with a variety of words, which are listed later in this section.

Other than omitting *because,* is it possible to turn the second clause into a sentence? It certainly is. We simply need to change the period to a comma and proceed with another clause that does not begin with a word like *because.* In other words, we will have a perfectly acceptable sentence if we write, "Because Jessica is an extremely capable and reliable friend, I feel free to ask her advice on any subject."

This recognition allows us to draw a distinction: a clause that begins with a word like *because* is a fragment (in other words, not a sentence) while a clause that does not begin with a word like *because* is a sentence. What, you may ask, about a clause with no true blue verb? Remember: no true blue verb means NO CLAUSE and therefore no sentence. So we may safely say that any group of words containing no true blue verb is a fragment and any clause that begins with a word like *because* is a fragment. Only a clause that does not begin with a word like *because* may be a sentence. But note that this rule does not mean that we cannot begin a sentence with *because:* as the sentence "Because Jessica is an extremely capable and reliable friend, I feel free to ask her advice on any subject" shows, a sentence may begin with a word like *because* if it contains a second clause (*I feel free to ask her advice on any subject*) that does not.

What are some other words like *because?* Here is a short list that you may find helpful:

after	although	as	before	how
if	since	though	unless	until
when(ever)	where(ever)	whether	while	

These words are known as **subordinating conjunctions.** As the term *subordinating* implies, they make a clause a "sub" sentence, or not a real sentence. In this book, you will also see these words called **yellow lights.** We have selected this term because we believe it is easier to remember than *subordinating conjunctions* and also because it indicates what you should do as you use these words: proceed with caution. Remember that a clause that begins with a yellow light and stands alone is a fragment, but a sentence that has two clauses, with only one of them beginning with a subordinating conjunction is perfectly acceptable.

There is also a short list of relative pronouns that may be used as yellow lights. They include:

that	what	which
whose	whom(ever)	who(ever)

The relative pronouns are like subordinating conjunctions in that they prevent a clause from being a sentence. They differ in that a subordinating conjunction at the beginning of a sentence calls for a comma in the middle: When I arrived home from school, I went to bed. A relative pronoun, on the other hand, does not: Whoever wins the game will satisfy me. Both subordinating conjunctions and relative pronouns, however, are yellow lights as this book defines them.

Thus far in this unit, we have defined the difference between **dependent clauses** (a.k.a fragments) and **independent clauses** (a.k.a sentences). The difference is as simple as one word, the yellow light that occurs at or near the very beginning of a dependent clause. Now that you can define and understand yellow lights, you have also discovered the first of three very good ways to combine sentences.

Consider the following:

Delores ate a taco with spoiled meat.
Delores had to go to the doctor.

In an essay, we would consider these sentences short and choppy and would look for ways to combine them. A yellow light used in either of two places will do just fine. For example, we could write "Because Delores ate a taco with spoiled meat, she had to go to the doctor." On the other hand, we could reverse the order of the clauses and say, "Delores had to go to the doctor because she ate a taco with spoiled meat."

Either of the revised sentences makes a vast improvement on the two choppy sentences we originally had. Notice, however, that we punctuate the sentences differently. If the yellow light is a subordinating conjunction that comes at the *beginning* of the sentence, a comma at the end of the first clause is necessary. If, on the other hand, the yellow light is a subordinating conjunction that comes in the *middle* of the sentence, a comma is *not* necessary. Finally, if we use a relative pronoun as a yellow light, it will not require a comma at all unless the relative pronoun is *which,* which (as you can see) comes in the middle of a sentence and usually requires a comma.

Are yellow lights the only way to combine sentences? No, they are only one of several good ways. One combiner that you have doubtless used many times is the **coordinating conjunction,** or FANBOYS word. **FANBOYS** is an acronym that represents

For
And
Nor
But
Or

Yet

So

You may use a FANBOYS word to combine any two independent clauses. For example, let us return to Delores and her stomach problems:

Delores ate a taco with spoiled meat.
Delores had to go to the doctor.

Again, these sentences are short and choppy as written. But if we use the FANBOYS word *so,* we can make a tremendous improvement. Now the sentence reads "Delores ate a taco with spoiled meat, so she had to go to the doctor." As you can see, a FANBOYS word combines clauses nicely. The only problem, in fact, with this combiner is that you may tend to overuse it. Hence, it is important to make yourself familiar also with yellow lights and with a third type of combiner we are about to discuss.

Undoubtedly you have seen writers, including the writers of this text, use words like *however, therefore, consequently,* and the like. In everyday speech, most of us do not use these words anywhere near as frequently as we use simpler words like the FANBOYS. Take a minute, though, and ask yourself who *does* use these words in ordinary discourse. Politicians? Yes, to a degree. Clergy? Again, somewhat. But more than anyone else, we believe, lawyers use these words as part of the way they do business. Thus, while the formal terms for such words are **conjunctive adverbs** and **transitional expressions,** we will simply call them **lawyer words.** This term should help you remember a good number of them. Here is a more extensive list:

after all	also	as a result	besides
consequently	finally	for example	furthermore
hence	however	in addition	indeed
in other words	instead	likewise	moreover
nevertheless	next	nonetheless	on the other hand
still	then	therefore	thus

This list does not include every word that can possibly be used as a lawyer word, but it does include enough to get you through virtually any writing situation you may encounter in college or elsewhere (unless you *do* become a lawyer).

How do lawyer words work as combiners? To see, we will take a final look at Delores. You may recall that

Delores ate a taco with spoiled meat.
Delores had to go to the doctor.

In using a lawyer word to combine these two clauses, we have many options. Here are several:

> Delores ate a taco with spoiled meat; therefore, she had to go to the doctor.
>
> Delores ate a taco with spoiled meat; thus, she had to go to the doctor.
>
> Delores ate a taco with spoiled meat; she had, therefore, to go to the doctor.
>
> Delores ate a taco with spoiled meat; she had to go to the doctor, therefore.

As you can see, lawyer words are slightly more complicated than the other combiners because they require a semicolon *and* a comma whenever they combine sentences. They can also be more fun than the other combiners because, as the examples have shown, they can move around in the second clause. The semicolon always goes at the end of the first clause, but you have the option of putting the lawyer word there or moving it deeper into the second clause so that it functions not only as a lawyer word but also as an **interrupter** (and thus requires the extra comma). Look at the previous examples for clarification on this point.

By now you should have begun to realize that although *because, so,* and *therefore* are grammatically different and require different punctuation (possibly even no punctuation) when they combine clauses, they are also quite similar. All three of these words are appropriate for combining the two sentences about Delores, and they all have essentially the same meaning.

The fact that combiners, when punctuated appropriately, may often be used interchangeably, is very good news for writers. It means that we have options for writing and that we may use a good deal of sentence variety. Here is another example of three different combiners used to express the same point.

I love my dog Brutus.
Brutus is ugly.

We may use a yellow light: I love my dog Brutus *although* he is ugly.

We may opt for a FANBOYS word: I love my dog Brutus, *but* he is ugly.

Or we may select a lawyer word: I love my dog Brutus; *however,* he is ugly.

As you can see, three different types of combiners may link these two choppy sentences correctly so long as we remember the rules that govern punctuating the three types. **A special note on yellow lights, FANBOYS, and lawyer words:** A word like *since, and,* or *in addition* is not necessarily a yellow light, FANBOYS word, or lawyer word every time it is used. In fact, these words apply *only* when the word is specifically used to combine two or more clauses. *Since* may simply be a preposition: "I haven't seen you since last Thursday." Likewise, *and* may simply combine two items: "Skiing and snow boarding are two thrilling activities." Finally, *in addition* may be nothing more than an interrupter. "Alejandro has tremendous talents with the saxophone. He is, in addition, a good soccer player." Keep this note in mind as you approach the following exercise.

Exercise 1

Directions: Circle the yellow lights, FANBOYS words and lawyer words in the following constructions. Do not, however, circle a word that does not function to combine clauses.

1. When Radesh announced his resignation, he surprised us all.

2. He had worked for the company four years and three months.

3. He did good work; however, he did not find opportunities for advancement at his position.

4. Now I expect him to find a new job and enjoy it more because he has so much training and experience.

5. Since he had run out of promotion opportunities here, he made a wise decision, in my opinion.

6. He is bright and capable; therefore, he will rise quickly in his new position, no matter who else works there.

7. If this pollen doesn't go away, I will die!

8. Two of my best friends, Jane and Maria, had to go to the hospital last night with allergies.

9. The doctor said that she may have to put them on long-term medicine if they don't get better soon.

10. They seemed concerned; nevertheless, they are improving rapidly.

11. Maybe they will be able to come home and convalesce there.

12. After finishing the test, the careful student went back over all of the difficult questions.

13. After she examined all of them, she corrected a few mistakes and thereby improved her grade ten points.

14. When Sigmund Freud, who invented psychoanalysis, was a little boy, his father said that he would never amount to anything.

15. Many years later, while writing of *The Interpretation of Dreams,* Freud remembered that moment.

16. Perhaps it helped to influence his theory about how the first few years form a person's character for life.

17. After many people grow up, they have very strong memories about events from their very early years.

18. Some people have very good memories, and some very bad.

19. "Though this be madness, yet there is method in 't."—Shakespeare

20. "I wak'd, she fled, and day brought back my night."—Milton

Exercise 2

Choose two or three paragraphs from one of your own essays, and circle the yellow lights, FANBOYS words, and lawyer words. Again, do not circle words that do not combine clauses. Do you tend to use any one type of combiner more frequently than the others? If so, be sure to practice using the other combiners in your next writing endeavor.

Summarizing a Real Essay or Article

Have you ever taken a history test that covered several chapters in a textbook? Or has a friend ever handed you an article from the newspaper or a journal and asked, "What do you think of this?"

Chances are that both of these situations are at least partly familiar to you. In any event, success at taking the history test or responding to your friend's question requires you to develop certain **critical reading** skills: namely that you learn how to recognize **main ideas, supporting details,** and **conclusions.** You also need a certain ability to "read between the lines" or do what teachers call drawing **inferences.** Finally, you must master the **vocabulary** essential for understanding the text before you.

Because books, essays, and articles will be thrust in front of you throughout your college career and possibly in your real-world career as well, it will prove helpful to learn certain writing strategies that grow out of critical reading. In particular, the ability to write summaries will help you earn a grade, reply to a memorandum, or maybe even earn a promotion. This chapter offers two different yet very useful strategies for writing summaries: **GRASP,** developed by University of Georgia reading education professor David Hayes, and **SQ3R.**

Summaries and the Communication Triangle

Where do you think summaries belong on the communication triangle? Do you write summaries primarily to express yourself? To persuade a reader? To convey information? If you guessed the third of those alternatives, you have accurately surmised the purpose of summaries. A summary is all about "it," with "it" being the subject matter covered in the text you are reading and summarizing. You generally will not need to inject your personal opinion into a summary, nor will you need to try to convince a reader of your accuracy. A good summary takes a longer document and pulls out the most important information so that a reader may have access to that information without having to read (or reread) the entire document.

The Assignment: Writing a Summary

Aim or Purpose: Informative

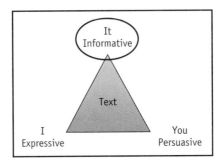

Audience for Summaries

Very often you are your own audience for the summaries you write. Occasionally, however, you will also write for other individuals who are unwilling or unable to read the actual source. A good example of a summary written for an audience is the familiar yellow and black paperback volume that students have clung to and professors have lamented for more than forty years: Cliff Notes. If you produce a summary of a work for someone else, you are in a sense writing a Cliff Notes version of the work for that person. And your work is not necessarily helping the other person "cheat": for example, you may be offering a summary of a report to a colleague or superior at work, which your coworker will then use in determining whether to read the original source. This type of summary may also call for your opinion or evaluation, but understand that the opinion part is separate from the summary itself. A summary merely restates briefly what another author or authors have already said.

A Word about Summaries and Plagiarism

Plagiarism, in brief, means that you use someone else's words and/or ideas without making it clear you are doing so. If you are writing a summary for yourself only, you need not concern yourself with plagiarism. Likewise, if a coworker asks you to summarize a particular source, plagiarism is no worry. If, however, you are writing a summary of a source that you later may use in producing an essay, you need to remember to keep an accurate and full record of the source, including its author, title, and page number(s). The primary example of this sort of writing is the research essay, or term paper. In such a paper, you need to give credit to any author(s) whose ideas you use in producing your own essay. Furthermore, in looking over your summary, if you see that you have retained any of the original wording (one or two very common words may be acceptable) from your source, you must be sure to put those words that you haven't changed in quotation marks. Otherwise, you run the risk of committing plagiarism.

Strategy One for Writing Summaries: GRASP

The following selection is from a history textbook. We will use it to demonstrate the **Guided Reading and Summary Procedure** (GRASP). Read the selection straight through from beginning to end. Do not pause to reread unless a passage is totally incomprehensible to you. When you have completed reading it, list in your notebook every detail that you can remember from the passage. Do not worry about whether the detail seems important or unimportant; if you can remember it, list it. But first, proceed directly into the selection from the textbook.

The Treatment of German, Italian, and Japanese Americans

By John Garraty

1   World War II affected the American people far more drastically than World War I had, but it produced much less intolerance and fewer examples of the repression of individual freedom of opinion. People seemed able to distinguish between Italian fascism and Italian Americans, and between the government of Nazi Germany and Americans of German descent in a way that had escaped their parents. The fact that few Italian Americans admired Mussolini and that nearly all German Americans were anti-Nazi helps explain this. So does the fact that both groups were prepared to use their considerable political power to protect themselves against abuse.

2   But the underlying public attitude was more important. Americans went to war in 1941 without illusions and without enthusiasm, determined to win but expecting only to preserve what they had. They therefore found it easier to tolerate dissent and to concentrate on the real foreign enemy without venting their feelings on domestic scapegoats.

3   The one flagrant example of intolerance was the relocation of the West Coast Japanese in internment camps in Wyoming, Arizona, and other interior states. About 110,000 Americans of Japanese ancestry, the majority of them native-born citizens, were rounded up and sent off against their will. Not one was accused of sabotage or being an enemy agent.

4   The Japanese Americans were properly indignant but also baffled, in some cases hurt more than angry. "We didn't feel Japanese. We felt American," one woman, the mother of three small children, recalled many years later. A fisherman remembered that besides his nets and all his other equipment, he had to leave behind a "brand-new 1941 Plymouth." "We hadn't done anything wrong. We obeyed the laws," he told

an interviewer. "I lost everything." Then he added, almost plaintively, "But I don't blame anyone. It was a war."

5   The government's excuse was fear that some of the Japanese *might* be disloyal. Nevertheless, racial prejudice (the "yellow peril") and frustration at not being able to strike a quick blow at Japan in retaliation had much to do with the callous decision to force people into camps. The Supreme Court upheld the relocation order in *Korematsu* v. *United States* (1944), but in *Ex Parte Endo* it forbade the internment of loyal Japanese American citizens. Unfortunately the latter decision was not handed down until December 1944.

Now, without referring back to the passage, list everything that you remember from it on a page in your notebook. Do not try to prioritize the items on your list, and don't worry about grammar or complete sentences. Just list. You may want to list more than one item per line.

Now that you have listed everything you can remember from "The Treatment of German, Italian, and Japanese Americans," review your list, but still don't look back to the passage. If you see obvious errors in your list, correct them. Also, if new items occur to you, list them. You want your list to be as thorough as it can be, based upon your first reading of the selection.

What sorts of details do you find yourself remembering? Did the image of the fisherman being forced to leave behind his new automobile make an impression upon you? Do you remember his statement "But I don't blame anyone. It was a war"? Do the facts that most German Americans were squarely against the Nazis and that most Italian Americans disapproved of Mussolini stick in your head? Of the details listed above, do all seem equally important? For now, that does not matter. Your only concern so far is accuracy.

The next step is to look back over the text to verify your list. Skim the passage as needed, but do not take the time necessary to reread every word. Your sole purpose this time is to make sure that your list is both accurate and complete. When you finish, make any needed corrections, additions, or subtractions to your list. Copy your revised list, minus strikethroughs, onto another page.

By now, you should have begun to develop a sense of which details are more important in the passage and which are less so. You have probably come to realize that not every fact is as important as every other fact. Review your list, and highlight or draw stars next to the information that you consider the most crucial to the passage.

You are now almost ready to begin writing your summary. To begin, locate the main idea or **thesis** of the passage. It may not be stated word for word; if not, state it as clearly as possible in your own words. Write down your interpretation of the main idea.

Return now to the highlighted items on your list. These will be the key supporting details for the summary. Put them into some sort of order that makes sense to you. As you make these decisions, you may simply want to write a number beside each important detail.

The last step before you begin writing is to evaluate the end of the passage and see if you think it points toward a conclusion or allows you to draw any inferences. In your own words, restate this conclusion or inference in your notebook.

At this point, you may be pleasantly surprised to discover that in prewriting your GRASP summary, you have essentially written the summary! In no more than one paragraph, summarize "The Treatment of German, Italian, and Japanese Americans." Begin with your statement of the main idea, follow with the key supporting details you have found, and end with the conclusion to the essay or any inferences that it inspires. Write your summary in your notebook now.

We can hardly overemphasize the fact that there are many "right" ways to summarize this textbook selection. As a point of reference, you may want to consider this version:

> *Although there was not much organized mistreatment of German Americans and Italian Americans during World War II, there was prejudice toward and systematic abuse of Japanese Americans. The United States government forced many honorable American citizens of Japanese heritage into camps in the Western United States. Not only were they forced to live in these camps for most of the duration of the war, but they also lost their possessions. For example, one fisherman said that he had to leave behind his new automobile along with all his fishing equipment. For their part, the Japanese Americans, many of whom were born in the United States and considered themselves more American than Japanese, tended to be confused and hurt by their mistreatment. Unfortunately, the Supreme Court condoned the imprisonment of these "loyal Japanese American citizens" until near the end of 1944.*

Your summary may look very much like the one above, or it may look completely different. In all likelihood, you will have included much of the same information and a very similar main idea and conclusion. The finished product will give you an opportunity to refresh yourself on the textbook selection in only a few seconds, where you needed several minutes to read and understand the passage the first time.

Strategy Two for Writing Summaries: SQ3R

While GRASP offers an excellent method for writing summaries, particularly of short works, not all works or all writers are best suited for using GRASP. An alternate method is **Survey Question Read Recite Recall** (SQ3R).

Unlike GRASP, SQ3R is nonlinear, meaning that you do not begin by simply reading the source from start to finish. Instead, SQ3R begins with two steps, surveying the text and asking questions about it, before you formally begin the reading stage.

You will soon use SQ3R to produce a summary of an article from a popular magazine. To begin, ask yourself what you will do when you **survey** the article. What do fairly lengthy magazine articles usually look like? Do they run from start to finish with no breaks? Or do they include pictures, sidebars, and subheadings to help the reader comprehend the article more easily? Of course, photographs and subheadings are popular features of magazine articles. Taking a close look at them can help you understand the organization and the important topics in an article. As you examine these items, try to make predictions about what the article will say. Putting this step to work for you, whether in a long article or several chapters of a book, can give you the mindset to learn quickly and efficiently.

After you have surveyed the article, ask yourself some **questions** about it. Every journalism major learns that a newspaper reader picks up an article expecting to find, right away, the answer to several key questions known as the **reporter's questions:**

Who?

What?

When?

Where?

Why?

How?

Apply these questions to a text you are about to read, and see if they also help focus you as you begin to read. In addition, develop a few questions of your own. What are some fair questions to ask about any text, be it an article, a book, or a few chapters? List five good questions.

With your questions in hand (including the reporter's questions) and your instructions on how to survey in your mind, examine the following article, "Save Now, Live Later." Remember that you are not actually reading the article at this time. Instead, you are examining it and asking yourself about it in such a way as to make the actual reading easier and more productive when you do it. Allow yourself several minutes to look over the article fully.

Save Now, Live Later

By Steven D. Kaye, Anne Kates Smith, Pamela Sherrid and Jonathan Sapers, with Bureau Reports

Do you really need that big-screen TV or new suit? Today's workers who want a secure retirement have to start saying 'No'

1   Let's go back in time, to David and Jeanne Wetherby's house in Portsmouth, Va., circa 1970. With five kids, the four-bedroom home can get

a bit crowded, but the four girls don't mind sharing rooms. David, a 43-year-old engineer with General Electric, earns about $35,000. Jeanne, also 43, plans meals a month ahead and buys food in bulk. The girl's home-sewn clothing is passed down, and down again. Dad's Fiat gets him to work—usually—and Mom has her Ford wagon, bought used. Cars for the teenagers? Hardly. Every month, as they have since they got married in 1951, David and Jeanne put 6 percent of his pay into a savings plan at work.

2 Baby boomers and generation X-ers, take note: Living like the Wetherbys did 25 years ago may be your only hope of a secure future. In today's era of $25,000 minivans, $1,000 big-screen TVs, $95 sneakers and $4-per-pound prewashed lettuce, the virtue of thrift seems almost quaint. In 1994, Americans on average saved an abysmal, decades-low 3.8 percent of their income after taxes. The amount ticked up—barely—to 4.5 percent in 1995. Credit card debt rose by a fourth last year, the biggest jump in a decade.

3 David and Jeanne Wetherby, meanwhile, spend 10 months of the year on their boat in the Caribbean. At 69, they have a house in New Hampshire, a condo in Florida, $500,000 in investments and the Felicidad, the 40-foot ketch that David helped build.

4 As the modest and unassuming couple readily acknowledge, much of their security comes from a triple dose of economic good fortune: soaring real-estates values, a generous pension and Social Security. The five-bedroom house in Lee. N. H., built in 1979 for $90,000, is now worth about a quarter million dollars. David's company-provided pension will pay at least $2,700 monthly, for life, and Social Security adds $1,300—enough to live on and then some. But many of today's workers face a triple whammy instead. Guaranteed pensions are being replaced with "defined contribution" plans, such as 401(k)'s, that employees must largely fund themselves. With Social Security's trust fund projected to go bust by 2030, the system is almost guaranteed *not* to fulfill its promises to many of today's under-50 workers. And with real-estate prices rising slowly, if at all, homeowners certainly can't count on a windfall.

5 To provide just a modest $35,000 of annual retirement income from age 65 to age 90, in 1996 dollars, today's 40-year-old will need $1.7 million—that's no typo—by age 65. Today's 25-year-old will need $3 million. Even with $50,000 already saved, the 40-year-old would have to start putting away an additional $12,000 yearly. Merrill Lynch's just released "Baby Boom Retirement Index," a kind of yearly ding on the head for boomers, shows that most would need to triple their saving rate to retire at 65 without a severe decline in living standards. Financial journalist Phillip Longman, in his recent book *The Return of Thrift,* calls the behavior of most of today's consumers "slow-motion bankruptcy." Thrift will return forcibly, Longman says, when today's workers try to retire and find that if they do, they'll lose their grip on the middle class.

6   With the price of fabric these days, it's cheaper to buy clothes at a discount store than to make them. And who has time? Times *have* changed, but even in the '90s some young people have chosen an aggressively thrifty life. *U.S. News* searched out five "Wetherbys," folks who have decided to downscale their lives now in order to upscale their futures.

THEIR MONEY IS TIME

7   In July of 1992, Chicagoans Mike and Linda Lenich owed $51,000 on their house, car and credit cards and were spending $200 more than they took in. Today, the Leniches are debt free, and their savings of $100,000 adds about $600 a month to their income. Mike, 41, earns $68,900 as a Commonwealth Edison manager; Linda, 39, a quilt maker, brings in about $3,100. He is planning his retirement in the next couple of years.

8   The Leniches credit their transformation from freewheeling suburbanites to supersavers (they stash away 35 to 40 percent of their earnings) to the New Road Map Foundation, a nonprofit group in Seattle that promotes, among other things, financial independence. The group's philosophy is crystallized in the bestselling *Your Money or Your Life* by Joe Dominguez and Vicki Robin (Penguin, $11.95). The first step is to track spending, which the Leniches did in notebooks they carried everywhere. Real progress came when they began defining every purchase in terms of hours worked. "We decided we had enough *stuff*," says Mike. "Our money is buying our time back."

9   Out went the health club memberships, Mike's book-a-week habit—even Cheerios. In their place: walks with Linda, trips to the library and oatmeal bought in bulk at a warehouse club, for a savings of $1,670 a year. Mike, who used to get itchy for a new car at 80,000 miles, is still driving his 1986 Dodge Daytona, with 175,000 miles. And the couple have decided to stay in their $90,000, three-bedroom rancher—despite Mike's 94-mile round-trip commute—rather than pay more for closer-in housing. Linda even makes her own giftwrap out of inside-out potato chip bags. But they've also been to Europe three times in three years. "We're not living the life of the Unabomber," says Linda.

10   But the Leniche's premium on security may be a drag on their investments. Mike figures they can live on $1,500 to $2,000 a month after he retires, and the focus now is on generating enough income to cover that. All but about $4,000 in stock (Com-Ed and Butler International) is tucked away in cash, Treasury bonds with yields ranging from 6.25 to 7.63 percent and the guaranteed investment contract option in Mike's 401(k) yielding 6.8 percent. "They're not going to keep up with taxes and inflation," says Gig Harbor, Wash., financial planner Terri Jiganti Stewart. But with retirement approaching, says Mike, "we'll need the money to live."

FREELANCING'S PERILS

11   When Bruce Jones, 41, and Louise Miller, 32, married in 1988, they planned to use the cash they'd received to buy a bed. Instead, they

bought the tools and materials with which they made the bed, the dresser and the night table.

12   That impulse explains the Norwood, Mass., couple's $266,000 nest egg. On Jones's income as a self-employed graphic designer—he typically earns $55,000 to $60,000 while Miller is a full-time mom—the couple sock away $15,000 to $20,000 a year, on average. Jones's mantra—don't live to your paycheck—has guided him his whole adult life. Out of college in 1978, he lived on $50 of his $100-a-week paycheck; the rest, he banked.

13   These days, the couple's strategems are a bit more sophisticated. Take the "big check, little check" system. Normally, Jones banks 41 percent of the gross profit from each check his business collects—the amount needed for taxes, Social Security and major expenses. Saving all of these payments until they're due produces $5,000 to $6,000 in interest income yearly. The remaining 59 percent goes to business expenses and Jones's income. But when an extra-large check arrives, the couple put the whole thing to work immediately and cover expenses with subsequent smaller checks. In the years that Jones's income beats the average, they invest the extra—sometimes as much as $30,000.

14   Rather than trade up when they bought their home in 1993, the couple paid less than the selling price on their old house. Jones reasoned that the $700-a-month mortgage on the $139,000 home would be affordable even if his business went bust and he had to get a job for $35,000 a year. The couple do admit to the occasional splurge: trips to the local do-it-yourself store and, for Miller, a can of General Foods International Coffee a week.

15   The largest chunk of the couple's portfolio is in stocks (Bradlee's, Chubb, Hewlett-Packard) and Fidelity stock funds: Equity-Income II, Growth & Income, Blue Chip Growth, Contrafund, Low-Priced Stock and Select funds in telecommunications, health care, regional banks, home finance and defense and aerospace. Last year's highly satisfying showing: Their funds' returns ranged from 25 to 53 percent.

REFORMED SUPERSHOPPER

16   The epiphany that saved John Hutchinson's financial life came in 1988 in a shopping mall near his home in Oakland, Calif. Two years before, on his 18th birthday, he had taken control of a $50,000 inheritance from his parents—and become a spending machine.

17   Within eight weeks, he had bought $7,000 worth of clothes, electronics and Christmas gifts. Within 18 months, he had burned up $20,000—on more clothes, jewelry, dinners out. In a rare act of frugality, he bought a used Volvo for $7,400. But by his 20th birthday, Hutchinson, who was earning $4.50 an hour at a hot-tub salon, had run through $30,000 and built up $8,000 in credit card debt.

18   The stupidity of it hit him that day in the mall. "I was walking along, holding shopping bags full of stuff I didn't need, and I suddenly realized, 'I need to *stop*.' "

19   John decided then and there to build upon what was left of his parents' legacy, not waste it. He locked up his last $20,000 in a five-year certificate of deposit, then took a second job, shipping computers, to pay down debt. For the first time, he picked up *Fortune*, *Forbes* and *Money*.

20   Flash forward to the John Hutchinson of today, a tall 28-year-old with a ready smile and decidedly more discipline. Standing in his bedroom, in the family house he and his two sisters inherited, he tugs at his blue T-shirt. "Three dollars and 99 cents," he reveals. "Why should I spend more?" In fact, this John Hutchinson hardly spends at all. His small wooden desk has seen better days; an old RCA TV sits on an equally used dresser. He quit his gym, saving $20 a month. The Volvo—now 17 years old—has a broken odometer, but John guesses 185,000 miles. His share of the mortgage: $350 a month.

21   And, boy, has he socked money away. After the CD matured three years ago, he took $5,000 to buy a laptop computer (he had become a part-time business student at San Jose State) and an engagement ring for his girlfriend, Norma. (The wedding is this month.) That left $20,000, which he deployed into four mutual funds, Gabelli Growth, Janus, a Benham bond fund and Vanguard Star, a balanced fund. Since then—taking three classes and working nights at a supermarket—he has put $50 from every weekly paycheck into Safeway stock and $75 into a savings account, a total of $6,500 per year. After taxes, that leaves about $265 per week to take home.

22   Hutchinson's portfolio today is worth $40,000. About half is in cash, a down payment on a house. There's $2,000 in Safeway stock and $6,500 in an IRA account, with $4,500 of that in the stock of casino operator Circus Circus and $2,000 in Treasury notes. ("There are three things human need to survive," Hutchinson says. "Food, a place to live and entertainment.") An additional $6,000 is in the Gabelli Growth Fund; he has $3,500 in a 401(k).

23   John expects to graduate next Christmas, and he has been eyeing a small, neighborhood food store near his house that's for sale. He's been stocking shelves for someone else; why not do it for himself? He'd need to keep saving like mad, of course, but that shouldn't be a problem. "Norma," John says, "is more of a scrooge than I am."

MASTERS OF MODERATION

24   Chris and Jennie Zhen have an income that could support a lavish yuppie lifestyle. She earns $50,000 a year as a computer programmer for Donaldson, Lufkin & Jenrette, and he expects to generate $100,000 this year as a computer consultant. But the Zhens have lived in a cramped, one-bedroom apartment in Brooklyn since they got married in 1987. "This is good enough," they said—even after son Kevin arrived in 1993. No matter that Chris's home office occupies a huge chunk of

the living room and that Kevin's toys take up much of the rest. Or that the Zhens haven't seen a movie since 1993's *Cliffhanger*. By routinely saving as much as 50 percent of their earnings, Chris, 36, and Jennie, 30, have amassed more than $300,000.

25   Like other supersavers, the Zhens have an aversion to debt. They bought their apartment for $78,000 with $30,000 down: it was paid off in eight years. There are few dinners out, no fancy electronics and Jennie buys clothes for the family at end-of-season sales. With Jennie's mother taking care of Kevin, child-care costs are only $100 a week.

26   Now, with the birth of a baby girl and Kevin facing pre-school, the Zhens are headed for the suburbs. Their destination: a $360,000 house in Holmdel, one of New Jersey's top school districts. While five bed-rooms and a 1-acre yard may seem palatial the Zhens, who plan to put 50 percent down, could afford more. In fact, they chose the cheapest house in the 10-year-old subdivision. Furniture? In the future. The first priority is to put an extra $10,000 toward the mortgage every year, in order to pay it off in 10 years.

27   Is a house the place for so much capital? "Normally, the answer would be 'No,' " says New York financial planner Connie Chen—and Chris's aunt. Real estate is hardly a sure thing; the Zhens' apartment lost a quarter of its value in New York's melt-down. Plus, they'll raid their investments, evenly split between cash, municipal bonds and individual stocks, including highflying Intel.

28   But the Zhens will hardly be "house poor." They've got $100,000 in retirement accounts, $40,000 they can tap in Chris's company and a year's worth of house payments in reserves. Anyway, managing money well is also about sleeping at night, Chen notes. The Zhens are quite well rested, thank you.

A NEW BEGINNING

29   Five years ago, optician Donald Gaudiomonte was earning $75,000 and living with his wife and kids in a five-bedroom home in New Milford, N.J. Then, as his clients joined health care plans that refused to pay an independent optician, Donald's income fell by half. Two years ago, the family's $168,000 house was threatened with foreclosure.

30   A friend stepped in with the needed cash, but Donald, 46, and his wife, Janet, 41, knew that big changes had to come. Their business struggles had led the couple to seek comfort in their Christian faith—and spirituality brought a belief in the virtue of a simpler life. Seven months ago, they moved to a three-bedroom apartment, drastically cut-ting their housing costs. Now, instead of clothes from Saks Fifth Avenue and a new car every three years, the couple's priority is saving for April, 10, and Peter, 8, and for retirement, says Donald—an audiophile who used to "easily spend $800" for a turntable needle.

31   Their savings goal: $300 to $400 a month. Their income has started to inch back up, now that Donald has found a niche in "vision ergonomics," consulting to computer users at companies such as Lucent Technologies and AT&T. With what Janet brings in waitressing at a local bar on weekends, they hope to make $38,000 this year. But most of their savings will come from slashing monthly housing costs from $1,500 to $650. Accounting for the lost mortgage deduction, they come out more than $3,000 ahead annually. House prices in their area are rising so slowly that the Gaudiomontes figure there are better places to invest. Sean Bookstaver, the financial planner at American Express Financial Advisor that the Gaudiomontes went to for guidance two weeks ago, recommends they automatically have a sum moved monthly from their checking account into one or two growth-stock funds. They'll start with some of the $25,000 proceeds from their house.

32   Janet has developed her own ways to keep cash from flying; to cap impulse buying at the grocery store, each child gets $5 to buy snacks. The teenage years may bring demands for fancy sneakers and video games, but for now, says Janet, "we don't think the children feel deprived. They see us happily doing with less." For their sake, it would be lucky if the lesson lasts.

At this point, what do you believe you can say about "Save Now, Live Later?" You should feel fairly confident in stating that the topic of the article is retirement savings. The article will provide a variety of tips to help investors take the steps needed now for them to enjoy profitable retirements later. Examples illustrate individuals, couples, and families at various stages of life who have used or are using successful retirement investment strategies. Moreover, the subheadings indicate that the article will discuss both positive strategies and potential pitfalls to consider in investing. You also can predict that although the article comes from a popular magazine (*U.S. News and World Report*), it will employ the vocabulary of finance. Therefore, you may want to have a dictionary handy—just in case. Now, with your mind prepared and your interest level hopefully raised fairly high (Who doesn't want to have a secure retirement?), you should be ready to read "Save Now, Live Later" successfully.

Read the article. As you do, feel free to take notes on your own paper or in the margins of your text. What matters more than anything else now is that you understand the article and that the lessons illustrated by examples become clear to you. When you have finished reading the article, reread any parts that were unclear or particularly interesting to you. The more time you spend with the article, the more familiar and friendly it should become.

The step that follows reading, **reciting,** is very important in successful comprehension and summary writing. First of all, let's be clear about what reciting is not: it is not simply reading the article's words aloud to yourself and expecting something magical to occur as a result. Reciting, instead, is a very active step in your reading and writing process. Reciting means that you find key notions or examples in the article and put them into your own words. This way, you help yourself to gain knowledge, and by activating your sense of hearing as well as your sense of sight, you make the material more likely to stick in your memory. While simply reading aloud is generally a waste of time (unless that is your preferred reading style upon first encountering the source), reciting is time very well invested (to use the language of "Save Now, Live Later").

As you recite, try to identify the main idea, key supporting details, and conclusion or suggested inferences of "Save Now, Live Later." Jot down these items on a sheet of paper.

As you wrote down this information, you moved from the recite stage of SQ3R into the actual summarizing stage, **review.** Take your time to go back over the article, your notes, and your replies to the questions. Review this information for accuracy and completeness. When you believe you have reached as full an understanding of "Save Now, Live Later" as you are likely to reach, produce a summary on your own paper. As with your summary of "The Treatment of German, Italian, and Japanese Americans," it is wise to try to limit yourself to one paragraph, with the main idea, key supporting details, and conclusion or inferences listed in that order. If, however, you find that your material is too long to fit into a single paragraph, you may consider a mini-essay. Fully explain the article's main idea in the first paragraph. Then, use one or more paragraphs to flesh out supporting details. Finally, in a short finishing paragraph, describe the conclusion to the article or the inferences that it inspires you to reach.

Try to the greatest extent possible to keep your summary brief. Remember that the purpose of a summary is to give a much shorter version of the actual text. Still, do not fail to produce a complete account of the important information simply for the sake of being brief.

Collaborative Activity: Exchange of Summaries

Working with two or three classmates, review the summaries that each of you has written in response to "Save Now, Live Later." Look for details or topics common to each summary and also for details or topics unique to each. What are some characteristics of the summaries that have most effectively translated the article into one paragraph or a mini-essay? What are some flaws to avoid next time? Discuss the various strengths and weaknesses of the summaries, and be prepared to defend your own view of what works best and what doesn't work as well.

A Second View of Familiar Material

To give yourself additional practice writing summaries using both the techniques you have learned in this chapter, produce a second summary of "The Treatment of German, Italian, and Japanese Americans" and "Save Now, Live Later." For variety, however, use SQ3R in writing your summary of "The Treatment of German, Italian, and Japanese Americans" and GRASP in writing your summary of "Save Now, Live Later." As you use a different technique on each essay, do different items stand out? Or do you find that your summaries are very similar? If so, is that similarity a result primarily of familiarity?

Assignment: Write a Summary Using GRASP or SQ3R

The following opinion piece, "What's Wrong with Black English?" was written by Rachel Jones when she was a college student. Using your choice or your instructor's choice of GRASP or SQ3R, summarize "What's Wrong with Black English?" in one well-written paragraph.

What's Wrong with Black English?

by Rachel L. Jones

1   William Labov, a noted linguist, once said about the use of black English, "It is the goal of most black Americans to acquire full control of the standard language without giving up their own culture." He also suggested that there are certain advantages to having two ways to express one's feelings. I wonder if the good doctor might also consider the goals of those black Americans who have full control of standard English but who are every now and then troubled by that colorful, grammar-to-the-winds patois that is black English. Case in point—me.

2   I'm a 21-year-old black born to a family that would probably be considered lower-middle class—which in my mind is a polite way of describing a condition only slightly better than poverty. Let's just say we rarely if ever did the winter-vacation thing in the Caribbean. I've often had to defend my humble beginnings to a most unlikely group of people for an even less likely reason. Because of the way I talk, some of my black peers look at me sideways and ask, "Why do you talk like you're white?"

3   The first time it happened to me I was nine years old. Cornered in the school bathroom by the class bully and her sidekick, I was offered the opportunity to swallow a few of my teeth unless I satisfactorily explained why I always got good grades, why I talked "proper" or "white." I had no ready answer for her, save the fact that my mother had from the time I was old enough to talk stressed the importance of

reading and learning, or that L. Frank Baum and Ray Bradbury were my closest companions. I read all my older brothers' and sisters' literature textbooks more faithfully than they did, and even lightweights like the Bobbsey Twins and Trixie Belden were allowed into my bookish inner circle. I don't remember exactly what I told those girls, but I somehow talked my way out of a beating.

"WHITE PIPES"

4   I was reminded once again of my "white pipes" problem while apartment hunting in Evanston, Ill., last winter. I doggedly made out lists of available places and called all around. I would immediately be invited over—and immediately turned down. The thinly concealed looks of shock when the front door opened clued me in, along with the flustered instances of "just getting off the phone with the girl who was ahead of you and she wants the rooms." When I finally found a place to live, my roommate stirred up old memories when she remarked a few months later, "You know, I was surprised when I first saw you. You sounded white over the phone." Tell me another one, sister.

5   I should've asked her a question I've wanted an answer to for years: how does one "talk white"? The silly side of me pictures a rabid white foam spewing forth when I speak. I don't use Valley Girl jargon, so that's not what's meant in my case. Actually, I've pretty much deduced what people mean when they say that to me, and the implications are really frightening.

6   It means that I'm articulate and well-versed. It means that I can talk as freely about John Steinbeck as I can about Rick James. It means that "ain't" and "he be" are not staples of my vocabulary and are only used around family and friends. (It is almost Jekyll and Hyde-ish the way I can slip out of academic abstractions into a long, lean, double-negative-filled dialogue, but I've come to terms with that aspect of my personality.) As a child, I found it hard to believe that's what people meant by "talking proper,"; that would've meant that good grades and standard English were equated with white skin, and that went against everything I'd ever been taught. Running into the same type of mentality as an adult has confirmed the depressing reality that for many blacks, standard English is not only unfamiliar, it is socially unacceptable.

7   James Baldwin once defended black English by saying it had added "vitality to the language," and even went so far as to label it a language in its own right, saying, "Language [i.e., black English] is a political instrument" and a "vivid and crucial key to identify." But did Malcolm X urge blacks to take power in this country "any way y'all can"? Did Martin Luther King Jr. say to blacks, "I has been to the mountaintop, and I done seed the Promised Land"? Toni Morrison, Alice Walker and James Baldwin did not achieve their eloquence, grace and stature by using only black English in their writing. Andrew Young, Tom Bradley and Barbara Jordan did not acquire political power by saying, "Y'all

crazy if you ain't gon vote for me." They all have full command of standard English, and I don't think that knowledge takes away from their blackness or commitment to black people.

SOULFUL

8   I know from experience that it's important for black people, stripped of culture and heritage, to have something they can point to and say, "This is ours, *we* can comprehend it, *we* alone can speak it with a soulful flourish." I'd be lying if I said that the rhythms of my people caught up in "some serious rap" don't sound natural and right to me sometimes. But how heart-warming is it for those same brothers when they hit the pavement searching for employment? Studies have proven that the use of ethnic dialects decreases power in the marketplace. "I be" is acceptable on the corner, but not with the boss.

9   Am I letting capitalistic, European-oriented thinking fog the issue? Am I selling out blacks to an ideal of assimilating, being as much like white as possible? I have not formed a personal political ideology, but I do know this: it hurts me to hear black children use black English, knowing that they will be at yet another disadvantage in an educational system already full of stumbling blocks. It hurts me to sit in lecture halls and hear fellow black students complain that the professor "be tripping dem out using big words dey can't understand." And what hurts most is to be stripped of my own blackness simply because I know my way around the English language.

10   I would have to disagree with Labov in one respect. My goal is not so much to acquire full control of both standard and black English, but to one day see more black people less dependent on a dialect that excludes them from full participation in the world we live in. I don't think I talk white, I think I talk right.

Now that you have completed your summary of Jones, revise it both for structure and for polish. Structurally, make certain that you have followed a useful summary format. In most cases, this means beginning with Jones' main idea, followed by her main points, and ending with her conclusion or the inferences she causes the reader to draw. Make certain that no unnecessary material is included in the summary. Remember that the purpose of your summary, whether your audience is yourself or another potential reader, is to give a brief but thorough account of what Jones says. Whether or not you agree with Jones is not an appropriate element for this summary.

In revising for polish, review carefully for verbs, sentences, spelling, and other grammatical concerns. Read your summary aloud to ensure that it sounds good and flows smoothly from the tongue. This chapter's grammar and usage unit on combining independent clauses using conjunctive adverbs and transitional expressions may help you as you revise for polish. Remember that all the work you put into writing an effective summary shows through most clearly when you express the ideas clearly and accurately.

―――

Grammar and Usage: Subject-Verb Agreement

Subjects are either singular or plural, and so are verbs. When we say that subjects must agree with their verbs, what we mean is that a singular subject (only one of something) must have a singular verb. Likewise, a plural subject (two or more) must have a plural verb. You can not pair a singular subject with a plural verb or a plural subject with a singular verb. Thus, the following sentences are correct.

> This year, **they hope** to earn $38,000.
>
> His small wooden **desk has seen** better days; an old RCA **TV sits** on an equally used dresser.

Here are some special issues to keep in mind regarding subject-verb agreement.

The *s* Rule. When you are writing in the present tense (happening now) and the subject is *he, she, it,* or a word that could be replaced with *he, she, it,* or *they,* the following rule generally holds true: **If the subject ends with an "s," then the verb will not. If the subject does not end with an "s," then the verb will.**

> **John expects** to graduate next Christmas, and **he has** been eyeing a small, neighborhood food store near his house that's for sale.
>
> A **helicopter circles** overhead.   Four **helicopters** circle overhead.
> The **cart crashes** to the floor.   **Carts crash** to the floor.

This rule does not apply to compound subjects or the subject "they."

> **Jeremy races** home after work.   **Jeremy and his wife race** home after work.
>
> Each day **she works** diligently.   Each day **they work** diligently.

Notice that in all the examples above, the singular verb ends in *s,* and the plural verb does not end in *s.* This is exactly backwards from the way nouns work. In general, nouns become plural when we add *s* and singular when we delete the *s.*

Hard-to-find Subjects. Sometimes the subject is separated from its verb by a modifier (describing word), a phrase or a clause and, therefore, may be somewhat difficult to locate. If you make a mistake in locating the subject and choose a word that is not the subject of that verb, you may make a mistake in subject-verb agreement. Remember to locate the verb(s) first. Then to find the subject of a verb, ask yourself the question, "Who or what did the action?" You may have to look back behind a phrase or clause to find the answer.

> The **bear** from these woods **is** huge and frightening. (Who or what is huge and frightening? The answer is the *bear.*)
>
> The **boys,** who currently live on the island of Guam, **are visiting** Josephine. (Who are visiting Josephine? The answer is the *boys.*)
>
> House **prices** in their area **are rising** so slowly that the Gaudiomontes figure there are better places to invest. (Who or what are rising? The answer is *prices.*)

There Is/There Are. When a sentence or clause starts with the word *there,* it is *never* the subject. In this case, you must look beyond the verb to locate the real subject of *is, are, was,* or *were.* Look again at the third example from above, the sentence that ends with "there are better places to invest." The subject of *are* is not *there,* but *places.*

> House prices in their area are rising so slowly that the Gaudiomontes figure there **are** better **places** to invest.

Here are few more examples:

> He also suggested that there **are** certain **advantages** to having two ways to express one's feelings.
>
> There **were** three pregnant **elephants** at the city zoo.
>
> There **was** a pregnant **elephant** at the city zoo.

Compound Subjects. Most compound subjects (connected with "and") are considered plural and must have plural verbs.

> **David and Jeanne Wetherby,** meanwhile, **spend** 10 months of the year on their boat in the Caribbean.
>
> **Running and jumping are** two favorite activities of young children.

An exception occurs when the two items are thought of generally as one.

> **Ham and eggs is** just about my favorite breakfast.

Either/Or. Two singular subjects joined by either/or require a singular verb.

> Either Sue or Joan **works** as a housekeeper in this motel.

If one subject is singular and the other plural, the verb agrees with the nearest subject.

Either he or the girls **want** to eat fast food.

Neither the swimmers nor the runner **likes** this facility.

Some Words Are Always Singular. Certain pronouns are always singular and, therefore, always require singular verbs when we use them as subjects. They include *everyone, each, every, everybody, anybody, anyone, either, and one.*

Each of us **has come** to visit.

Only **one needs** to do this job.

Some Words Can Be Singular or Plural. Some (although not many) words can be singular or plural. Certain pronouns are singular or plural depending on whether or not the items involved are countable. They are plural if the items involved can be counted; they are singular if the items involved cannot be counted. These words are the following: *some, all, any, none, half,* and *most.*

Some coins **are falling** from the girl's change purse.

Some money **is missing** from the piggy bank.

None of the men **are working.**

None of the air **is** fit to breathe.

In a few cases, whether or not a word is singular or plural is merely a matter of personal preference; however, you must be consistent within a particular essay. Some examples of these words are *team, family,* and *couple.*

*And the **couple have decided** to stay in their $90,000, three-bedroom rancher—despite Mike's 94-mile round-trip commute—rather than pay more for closer-in housing.*

(In this case, *has decided* would be fine if you were consistent throughout the paper.)

Tricky and/or Irregular Verbs. Certain verbs may pose particular problems for you, and if this is the case, it is best just to memorize the singular and plural forms of those verbs for which you confuse the singular and plural forms. Here are some that tend to cause the most problems.

Singular	Plural
The boy **has**	The boys **have**
The boy **does**	The boys **do**
The boy **is**	The boys **are**
The boy **was**	The boys **were**

Exercise 1

Directions: Each of the following groups of sentences contains at least one error in subject-verb agreement. Combine each group into one complete sentence without any errors in subject-verb agreement.

1. I loves cats.
   I loves dogs.
   I hate snakes.

2. The radio is loud.
   The radio have lots of power.
   The radio play a crescendo.

3. Terry found a job.
   Terry works at a golf course.
   Terry like golf.

4. Going to school is hard.
   Going to school costs a lot of money.
   Going to school take a lot of time.

5. Sally loves to eat popcorn.
   Sally's parents loves to eat popcorn.
   Sally hates to eat caramel popcorn.

6. She run three miles twice a week.
   She is a very fast runner.
   She stay in shape.

7. Mom and I looks at cars frequently.
   We want to buy a Honda.
   We do not know how much we can afford.

8. The ribs are burning.
   The grill is too hot.
   Someone need to close the lid on the grill.

9. There is food and drinks for all.
   Everyone deserves to eat.
   Everyone worked hard.

10. There was a spaceship and aliens in the movie.
    That movie had many special effects.
    The special effects was gory.
    The special effects was scary.

Exercise 2

Write a paragraph about an action film you have seen. Circle each verb. Then draw a line through each verb's subject or subjects. Does each verb agree with its subject? Why or why not?

Chapter

"Allow Me to Introduce": Profiling a Real Person

What Is Personality?

Fill in the following blanks with words that describe people you know:

1. I have a friend who is a _____ person.
2. My neighbor is a _____ person.
3. My English instructor is a _____ person.
4. I have a relative who is a _____ person.
5. I am a _____ person.

The adjectives that you chose for the blanks help to describe several individuals' personalities. Perhaps you may have heard that someone has a "great personality," or "a great deal of personality," "little personality," or "the personality of a stump." What do such comments mean? What is personality? First of all, everyone has personality. It has something to do with the way we come across to others. It also has something to do with the individual traits and characteristics that distinguish each of us from the other. Our individual personalities embody our beliefs, our emotional states, and our behaviors or actions. Our personalities may change over time. We may also choose to develop certain aspects of our personalities.

As you work through this chapter, you will think and write about personality a great deal. When you conclude, you will have produced a personality profile. We have discussed the word *personality*. Now consider the word *profile*. A side view of something is called a profile; an outline of something is also sometimes called a profile. These definitions imply that a profile may not be the complete picture. A written profile usually means a listing of someone's most significant accomplishments. A personality profile essay discusses some of the significant features of one's personality. In other words, it answers the question, "What kind of person is he or she?" It probably will not represent a complete and total picture of an individual because people are extremely complex. Yet a personality profile should give readers some keen insights into the person who is the subject.

You may have seen personality profiles in magazines, in your local newspaper, in your college newspaper, or on television. Journalists frequently profile television and movie stars, athletes, business tycoons, and other celebrities. Yet they also may profile everyday individuals whom they deem noteworthy for any of several reasons, including their contributions to their communities or their willingness to take on challenging tasks.

The topic of your personality profile will be one of your classmates. Likewise, you will be the topic of a classmate's essay. By the time you finish, the members of your class will know a great deal more about each other. Your purpose in this assignment is primarily to inform. Your audience will be your classmates and instructor.

The Assignment: Profiling a Real Person

Aim or Purpose: Informative

Audience: Your Classmates and Instructor

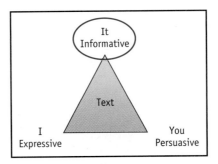

Step 1: Gathering Ideas

Developing a Generic List of Questions

First, we need to gather as much information as we can about our topic, which in this case is a person. One way to do this might be to observe the individual as much as possible in as many different situations as possible and to take notes about what he or she says and does. Obviously, this tactic would be very time consuming and logistically difficult. Yet even if we were able to do this, we would still need to talk to this person to find out what he or she thinks. So what is our best option? To gather information for our personality profile, we will borrow a helpful tool from journalists—the interview.

A successful interview requires at least two items. The first item is preparation; the second is flexibility. You can prepare for interviewing a classmate by thinking in advance of some good questions to ask. In developing questions for the interview, avoid questions that lead to "yes" or "no" answers. *Don't ask,* "Do you like music?" *Do ask,* "What is some of your favorite music, and why?" In addition, think of good interview questions as dividing into two basic types: short answer and open-ended. Ask short answer questions to obtain some general background information about the person. Examples of a couple of short answer questions would be "Where were you born?" and "What is your major?" Open-ended questions require more thought and cannot be answered in a word or two. "What is some of your favorite music, and why?" is open-ended. Other examples might be "If you could suddenly change one thing about yourself, what would it be and why?" or "What do you see yourself doing five years from now, and why?" Open-ended questions are very important because they will require your subject to express his or her thoughts, opinions, and beliefs. In other words, they will hopefully elicit glimpses into personality.

Activity 1: Generating a List of Interview Questions

Alone or with a partner, create a list of twenty interview questions. Be sure to remember to leave space for your interviewee's responses. Make sure that at least ten of your questions are open-ended. The rest may be short answer questions. Remember to avoid all questions that may be answered with a simple "yes" or "no."

Activity 2: Sharing Questions in Small Groups

Now compare your list of questions with others in a small group of three or four. Share your questions with your partners in the group, and feel free to "borrow" from each other. Add any good interview questions you hear to the list of questions you have already prepared. You can never be too prepared before an interview!

Identifying a Subject and Interviewing

You have now almost prepared to tackle your interview. Your instructor may assign you to pairs for interviewing or you may have the option of choosing your own interview subject. In either case, once you know the subject of your personality profile, you are ready to begin the interview process.

Earlier we noted that a successful interview requires two items. The first was preparation, and you are now well prepared. Now the second item—flexibility—comes into play. Consider all your prepared questions as only a starting point. Be ready to think of other questions on the spot, and don't feel that you have failed if you don't ask all your prepared questions. Be aware of which questions prompt the most response. Then try to keep your subject talking about these issues. In other words, be ready to ask follow-up questions to delve deeper. You may think of these follow-up questions at that moment. For example, if during the course of the interview, your subject tells you that she holds a black belt in karate and has competed in local and state competitions, you would definitely want to know more about this seemingly significant part of her life.

As you interview, you will need to take a good deal of notes. Consider bringing a small tape recorder so that you can tape the interview. If you do so, make sure your subject knows that you are using it. Do not rely on the tape recorder to be your note taker! Use the tape only to check the accuracy of your notes later.

Incorporating Quotations in Your Personality Profile

Accuracy is not the only reason to record an interview. Another good reason to have a tape recording is to make it easier to include direct quotations in your essay.

There are two types of quotations: direct and indirect. Direct quotation entails copying down word for word exactly what a subject says. When you directly quote someone, you must be absolutely sure to copy *exactly* and to use quotation marks. Here are examples of direct quotations:

> John said, "Winning that first cross-country race made me so proud and excited that I couldn't wait to go at it again."
>
> "Knowing that my whole family—my mom, dad, sisters, and grandma—was there made the whole experience especially important," Sue added.

An indirect quotation also relates what someone said without using his or her exact words. In this case, do not use quotation marks.

> John said that he was so excited after winning the first race that he really looked forward to the next race.
>
> Sue said that knowing that her mother, father, sister, and grandmother were there to support her made the experience very special to her.

You will certainly use indirect quotation in your essay, but some direct quotations will probably help make your essay lively and interesting. Direct quotations will draw readers into your writing by letting them actually hear the person talking. Journalists generally go by this rule regarding when to directly quote: If your subject says something that sticks in your mind, or if he or she says something better than you could, you should quote this statement directly. You will need to complete the following activity during your interview if you do not bring a tape recorder. If you do tape the interview, you will then complete it after the interview.

Activity 1: Listening for Direct Quotations

Use your tape recording to list five interesting statements your subject made during your interview. If you do not plan to tape the interview, listen very carefully. When you hear a particularly interesting statement, ask your interviewee to repeat it, and copy it down word for word.

Activity 2: The Interview

Conduct your interview now. Divide the amount of time available in half. Allow half the time for you to interview, and the other half for your partner to interview you. You may find that your interview ends up being more of a discussion. This is fine as long as you both get all the information you need to write your personality profiles.

Your interview and collaboration do not have to end at the classroom door! If you feel comfortable doing so, exchange telephone numbers and/or e-mail addresses. You may even want to meet for coffee in the student union or go out to lunch together. Indeed, as you move along in the process of writing your personality profile, you may very well find yourself going back to your subject to clarify certain responses or to ask follow-up questions. Doing so will ensure that you will have the necessary details to make your personality profile truly interesting to read.

Step 2: Organizing Ideas

At this point, you have gathered a great deal of information from interviewing your subject. However, your notes are in no significant order. They are merely responses to individual questions. Sometimes interviews are printed as such. If you have read an interview in a newspaper or magazine, you have read the interviewer's question followed by the person's response. Then you have read the next question, followed by a response

An entire art movement, known as Impressionism, based itself on the premise that artists could paint just "an impression" of a scene or subject. As the viewer of an impressionist piece moves closer and closer to the canvas, the impression falls apart. The impressions in your essay, however, should become stronger and stronger as you supply specific and showing details.

Source: *Madame Alphonse Daudet, nee Julie Allard, (1844–1940) wife of the poet.* August Renoir. Erich Lessing/Art Resource, New York.

and so on. A personality profile essay, though, is quite different. You will want to avoid simply listing questions or the responses for that matter. In fact, you may want to now ignore your questions, and look only at the responses. Your mission is to craft this jumble of notes into an organized essay that expresses an individual's personality.

Consider for a moment the woman with the black belt in karate. Might her participation imply that she is competitive? Determined? Dedicated? Health-conscious? Any of these might be so, but at this point, it is difficult to say with any certainty at all. What we are considering here are various impressions of this woman. The problem is that we don't have enough facts or details to make a strong determination. In other words, it takes more than one piece of evidence to build a good case.

To organize your personality profile, you must start to synthesize, or tie together in some meaningful way, the information from your interview. In other words, you must draw some conclusions from all the details you have collected about your subject. You then need to be sure you have sufficient details to support those conclusions.

Two worksheets follow this paragraph. The first will help you begin to develop your ideas and draw some conclusions about your subject's personality. The second worksheet will help you organize those ideas. By the time you finish the second worksheet, you will probably have developed more than one impression of your interviewee and be well on your way toward organizing your essay.

Organizing the Personality Profile: Part One

Answer the following questions as completely as you can.

1. In general, how would you summarize the life that your subject has lived so far?

2. List a few specific examples that support your response to the first question.

3. What do the person's friendships and hobbies tell you about him or her?

4. Do you think the person has the appropriate characteristics for the career he or she has chosen? Why or why not?

5. Did you find any issue that your subject did not want to talk about? How did that affect your interview?

6. Did your subject particularly *want* to talk about any issue? What did that tell you?

7. Based on your interview, what predictions can you make for your subject's future? Where do you see the interviewee in five years?

   In ten years?

   In twenty years?

   In fifty years?

Organizing the Personality Profile: Part Two

Person profiled: _____

Overall impression(s)—limit 3 _____

List at least three facts that support each overall impression. These facts can include events in the person's life, descriptions of relationships, or whatever else you deem appropriate.

   Impression 1: _____

   Supporting Fact: _____

   _____

   Supporting Fact: _____

   _____

   Supporting Fact: _____

   _____

   Impression 2: _____

   Supporting Fact: _____

   _____

   Supporting Fact: _____

   _____

   Supporting Fact: _____

   _____

Impression 3: _____
  Supporting Fact: _____

_____

  Supporting Fact: _____

_____

  Supporting Fact: _____

———

At this point you are organized and nearly ready to begin a first draft. What sort of thesis statement might be appropriate for a personality profile? Consider the following ideas. First, look again at the impressions you are able to support with at least three (and perhaps more) facts. You have two options. The first is to tie all those impressions together into one **dominant impression** of the person.

For example, if your impressions are that the person is studious, good at time management, and a busy parent, then you might say that your dominant impression is that she is industrious. Thus, your thesis statement might be the following: "Overall, Jane Smith is an industrious person." Your other option is to list your impressions in the thesis statement. An example might be the following: "Juan Ramirez is a fun-loving young man who is, however, quite serious about his family and his education." This profile will support the three impressions—fun loving, family oriented, and studious—in the body of the essay. With a working thesis statement in mind (working means that you may still be tinkering with it later), you are ready to move on to writing the personality profile essay.

Step 3: Writing

Now think about how you might start your personality profile. How will you get your readers' attention? What background information would be helpful for readers to know before they get to the main part of the profile? Of all the information you collected, what might work particularly well in the introduction? Don't be discouraged if you don't have these answers all at once. You may need to rewrite the introduction several times. For many, if not most, writers, this is a normal part of the writing process. You may even decide to write the body first and the introduction later. Keep all your options open and feel free to experiment.

As you write the body of your essay, use the second worksheet you completed as your outline. If you took time to complete the worksheet in detail, and if you follow it, the body of your essay will be well organized. Be aware, though, that you will probably need to explain each of your supporting facts more fully than you did on the worksheet. If, for example, you describe a significant event such as earning a black belt in karate, be sure to include enough specific details so that readers can picture this event vividly. Furthermore, you will have to include transitional words so the paragraphs won't be choppy and hard to follow. You might use some of the following transitional words and phrases: *first, second, third, next, last, another, also, moreover, in addition, before, later, after.* Choose transitions that make sense in your essay. You do not need to limit yourself to these suggestions.

Before you write, it may be helpful to read some examples of finished essays. Here are some examples of personality profiles. Students produced the first two in response to this very assignment. The third example, "Unforgettable Albert Einstein," is by physicist Banesh Hoffmann, who, while describing Albert Einstein's personality, explains how he came to know the great scientist as a colleague and friend.

Student Model #1

Daring Danielle

By Jennifer Cardin

1   Danielle Denise Payne is the only child of Beverly and Mack Payne Jr. Although she was born in Oakland, Danielle was raised in Los Angeles and West Covina, California. Today at the age of 18 she lives in Atlanta. She enjoys outdoor activities and being with her friends. Danielle is overall an adventurous person.

2   Danielle is a major risk taker. She has bungy jumped two times in her life. The first time was in Fontana, California. She paid thirty-five dollars to jump out of a crane. Danielle describes this horrific experience as like being on a roller coaster, feeling completely helpless and out of control. Danielle remembers feeling as if she were going to die. She explained how she closed her eyes and just jumped! The next time Danielle bungy jumped was out of a hot air balloon. The person instructing her explained how the weight of her body would not pull the balloon down. With the cord tied around her ankles, her arms held out tight, and her eyes wide open, she took a deep breath and swan dived out of the basket. Danielle expressed these two courageous events as the "most adrenaline rushing experiences I have ever had!"

3   Danielle's love for traveling also makes her an adventurous person. In the 7th grade she visited many of the countries in Europe. In Paris, France, she was almost in a wreck that resulted from driving down a one way street. In Frankfurt, Germany, she attended a carnival that kicked off Octoberfest. The carnival had lots of music and rides for children. She walked along cobblestone streets and ate world famous Godiva chocolates in Brussels, Belgium. She took a cruise down a river and had to pay an elderly lady change to use a McDonald's restroom in Amsterdam, Holland. Danielle had the wonderful experience of witnessing the

construction of an underground rail system leading from London to France. While in London she also heard Big Ben strike its chimes.

4   Two years ago Danielle and her family visited Japan. There they attended a Raiders preseason football game. She visited historical spiritual gardens. Danielle spoke about the calmness and peacefulness of the gardens. She also visited a unique Buddhist temple. The temple had beautifully groomed trees and streams with decorative bridges all around.

5   The adventures of Danielle are many. She has lived in different cities and visited foreign countries. Her daring personality has taken her to great heights. She has jumped out of a balloon and off of a crane! Her love for new lands, cultures, and excitement makes it easy for Danielle to travel and explore. All of these qualities make Danielle a truly adventurous person!

Collaborative Activity

In small groups, discuss the following questions.

1. Give at least three examples that show Danielle as a "daring" or "adventurous" person.

2. Note the one use of dialogue in the profile. Does it help? Would it be helpful to have more dialogue?

3. What sort of traveling partner do you think Danielle would make? Why?

Student Model #2

Kelly's Personality Profile

By Rahel Gebremeskel

1   Kelly M. Benefield is the oldest child born into the Benefield family. She was born in Dayton, Ohio, in 1977. Today at age 21, she lives in Atlanta with her mother and a sister. Her hobbies are writing, shopping, eating, and traveling. Kelly is working on becoming a child psychiatrist. Kelly's main goal is to pursue her career and help others.

2   One of the major things Kelly wants to do when she graduates from college is to make a difference among children. In her childhood Kelly experienced hardships growing up. As a child, Kelly was living in an environment where she had many responsibilities and hardships. Kelly's mother is a strong and determined person, but during Kelly's childhood her mother had to decide between getting an education or raising her daughters. Kelly's mother chose to go back to school so that she could give a better life for her two daughters.

3   While her mother was going to school, Kelly was responsible for taking care of her little sister; besides baby sitting, Kelly had to attend school. She was doing well in school even though she didn't have a father to depend on. When she was a little girl, her father was sent to prison. Part of her childhood was taken away from her. She didn't experience a father figure, but she became a little girl who would overcome a rough time.

4   Kelly's difficult time has taught her much in life, and has taught her how to help others. She mentioned to me that she would like to travel around the world. Her first priority is to visit Africa and Haiti. She said, "One of the reasons I want to visit Africa is to educate young people and help them be aware of the deadly disease known as AIDS." This disease has infected 3.4 million people in South Africa because people are not educated about it. Kelly said, "If I could help one person who is infected with the HIV virus, then to me, I have helped a million people." Kelly's philosophy is, "Help others just as you would help yourself."

5   Kelly's compassion comes from her mother and grandmother, who are both loving and determined people. They have influenced Kelly's life, and most importantly, they love her. Kelly said, "When I was engaged, my mother and grandmother didn't approve because they have strong beliefs in getting an education first. I did not want to break up my engagement, but I did not want to dishonor my mother and grandmother. I knew that my mother and grandmother knew what was best for me, but I was blind to it. After five months my fiance broke up with me, but I was glad that he did because otherwise I wouldn't be in school right now. I am expanding my education so I can have a better life for myself and for my family in the future." She will always thank her mother and grandmother for their dedication and their belief in her.

6   During my interview with Kelly, I had the opportunity to ask her about how she views the world. For example, I asked her about technology and how she feels about working with people. She answered straightforwardly with lots of emotion, "I think the advance in technology is benefiting us, but it is destroying human beings' capacity." She thinks that technology is good for researching deadly diseases, but we as humans shouldn't depend more on technology. Kelly said, "We ought to depend more on ourselves because technology is taking away part of human beings' communication, like spending time with families and friends." When I asked Kelly how she feels working with people, she said, "I like to work with children, but not with adults. The reason I don't like to work with adults is they are self-centered, rude, and, most importantly, they behave with improper conduct." She explained to me that the world is a nefarious place to live because adults don't have compassion and courtesy towards human beings and animals.

7   Kelly believes that family comes before anything. Even though she came from a dysfunctional family, she has developed a strong value in the family. Kelly said, "To me families are the most precious gift from God." One question I asked Kelly was how she would raise her own family. She

said, "I would raise my child the way my mother raised me, but not without a father or being overprotective. She wants to give her child the opportunity to discover who she or he is, and, most importantly, Kelly wants to give her child the chance to explore the world.

8   Kelly will be working on her career, and she is trying to accomplish the goal she has set, which is making a difference for children. I am glad I met Kelly and had a chance to write her personality profile. She is a wonderful, loving, intelligent, and extraordinary person; also, with her loving heart she is the best sort of friend one can have.

Collaborative Activity

In small groups, discuss the following questions.

1. Is the thesis for this profile directly stated or more indirectly implied? In your words, what is the thesis?

2. Why do you think Kelly's choice of being a child psychiatrist is appropriate or inappropriate for her?

3. What do Kelly's other goals (such as promoting AIDS education) make you think of her?

4. Why do you think Kelly says that working with children pleases her more than working with adults? Do you agree? Why or why not?

Professional Model

Unforgettable Albert Einstein

by Banesh Hoffmann

1   He was one of the greatest scientists the world has ever known, yet if I had to convey the essence of Albert Einstein in a single word, I would choose *simplicity*. Perhaps an anecdote will help. Once, caught in a downpour, he took off his hat and held it under his coat. Asked why, he explained, with admirable logic, that the rain would damage the hat, but his hair would be none the worse for its wetting. This knack for going instinctively to the heart of a matter was the secret of his major scientific discoveries—this and his extraordinary feeling for beauty.

2   I first met Albert Einstein in 1935, at the famous Institute for Advanced Study in Princeton, N.J. He had been among the first to be invited to the Institute, and was offered *carte blanche* as to salary. To the director's dismay, Einstein asked for an impossible sum: it was far too *small*. The director had to plead with him to accept a larger salary.

3   I was in awe of Einstein, and hesitated before approaching him about some ideas I had been working on. When I finally knocked on his door, a gentle voice said, "Come"—with a rising inflection that made the single word both a welcome and question. I entered his office and found him seated at the table, calculating and smoking his pipe. Dressed in ill-fitting clothes, his hair characteristically awry, he smiled a warm welcome. His utter naturalness at once set me at ease.

4   As I began to explain my ideas, he asked me to write the equations on the blackboard so he could see how they developed. Then came the staggering—and altogether endearing—request: "Please go slowly. I do not understand things quickly." This from Einstein! He said it gently, and I laughed. From then on, all vestiges of fear were gone.

5   Einstein was born in 1879 in the German city of Ulm. He had been no infant prodigy; indeed, he was so late in learning to speak that his parents feared he was a dullard. In school, though his teachers saw no special talent in him, the signs were already there. He taught himself calculus, for example, and his teachers seemed a little afraid of him because he asked questions they could not answer. At the age of 16, he asked himself whether a light wave would seem stationary if one ran abreast of it. From that innocent question would arise, ten years later, his theory of relativity.

6   Einstein failed his entrance examinations at the Swiss Federal Polytechnic School, in Zurich, but was admitted a year later. There he went beyond his regular work to study the masterworks of physics on his own. Rejected when he applied for academic positions, he ultimately found work, in 1902, as a patent examiner in Berne, and there in 1905 his genius burst into fabulous flower.

7   Among the extraordinary things he produced in that memorable year were his theory of relativity, with its famous offshoot, $E = mc^2$ (energy equals mass times the speed of light squared), and his quantum theory of light. These two theories were not only revolutionary, but seemingly contradictory: the former was intimately linked to the theory that light consists of waves, while the latter said it consists somehow of particles. Yet this unknown young man boldly proposed both at once—and he was right in both cases, though how he could have been is far too complex a story to tell here.

8   Collaborating with Einstein was an unforgettable experience. In 1937, the Polish physicist Leopold Infeld and I asked if we could work with him. He was pleased with the proposal, since he had an idea about gravitation waiting to be worked out in detail. Thus we got to know not merely the man and the friend, but also the professional.

9   The intensity and depth of his concentration were fantastic. When battling a recalcitrant problem, he worried it as an animal worries its prey. Often, when we found ourselves up against a seemingly insuperable difficulty, he would stand up, put his pipe on the table, and say in his quaint English, "I will a little tink" (he could not pronounce the

"th"). Then he would pace up and down, twirling a lock of his long, graying hair around his forefinger.

10   A dreamy, faraway and yet inward look would come over his face. There was no appearance of concentration, no furrowing of the brow— only a placid inner communion. The minutes would pass, and then suddenly Einstein would stop pacing as his face relaxed into a gentle smile. He had found the solution to the problem. Sometimes it was so simple that Infeld and I could have kicked ourselves for not having thought of it. But the magic had been performed invisibly in the depths of Einstein's mind, by a process we could not fathom.

11   Although Einstein felt no need for religious ritual and belonged to no formal religious group, he was the most deeply religious man I have known. He once said to me, "Ideas come from God," and one could hear the capital "G" in the reverence with which he pronounced the word. On the marble fireplace in the mathematics building at Princeton University is carved, in the original German, what one might call his scientific credo: "God is subtle, but he is not malicious." By this Einstein meant that scientists could expect to find their task difficult, but not hopeless: the Universe was a Universe of law, and God was not confusing us with deliberate paradoxes and contradictions.

12   Einstein was an accomplished amateur musician. We used to play duets, he on the violin, I at the piano. One day he surprised me by saying Mozart was the greatest composer of all. Beethoven "created" his music, but the music of Mozart was of such purity and beauty one felt he had merely "found" it—that it had always existed as part of the inner beauty of the Universe, waiting to be revealed.

13   It was this very Mozartean simplicity that most characterized Einstein's methods. His 1905 theory of relativity, for example, was built on just two simple assumptions. One is the so-called principle of relativity, which means, roughly speaking, that we cannot tell whether we are at rest or moving smoothly. The other assumption is that the speed of light is the same no matter what the speed of the object that produces it. You can see how reasonable this is if you think of agitating a stick in a lake to create waves. Whether you wiggle the stick from a stationary pier, or from a rushing speedboat, the waves, once generated, are on their own, and their speed has nothing to do with that of the stick.

14   Each of these assumptions, by itself, was so plausible as to seem primitively obvious. But together they were in such violent conflict that a lesser man would have dropped one or the other and fled in panic. Einstein daringly kept both—and by so doing he revolutionized physics. For he demonstrated they could after all, exist peacefully side by side, provided we gave up cherished beliefs about the nature of time.

15   Science is like a house of cards, with concepts like time and space at the lowest level. Tampering with time brought most of the house tumbling down, and it was this that made Einstein's work so important— and controversial. At a conference in Princeton in honor of his 70th

birthday, one of the speakers, a Nobel Prize-winner, tried to convey the magical quality of Einstein's achievement. Words failed him, and with a shrug of helplessness he pointed to his wristwatch, and said in tones of awed amazement, "It all came from this." His very ineloquence made this the most eloquent tribute I have heard to Einstein's genius.

16   We think of Einstein as one concerned only with the deepest aspects of science. But he saw scientific principles in everyday things to which most of us would give barely a second thought. He once asked me if I had ever wondered why a man's feet will sink into either dry or completely submerged sand, while sand that is merely damp provides a firm surface. When I could not answer, he offered a simple explanation.

17   It depends, he pointed out, on *surface tension*, the elastic-skin effect of a liquid surface. This is what holds a drop together, or causes two small raindrops on a windowpane to pull into one big drop the moment their surfaces touch.

18   When sand is damp, Einstein explained, there are tiny amounts of water between grains. The surface tensions of these tiny amounts of water pull all the grains together, and friction then makes them hard to budge. When the sand is dry, there is obviously no water between grains. If the sand is fully immersed, there is water between grains, but no water *surface* to pull them together.

19   This is not as important as relativity: yet there is no telling what seeming trifle will lead an Einstein to a major discovery. And the puzzle of the sand does give us an inkling of the power and elegance of his mind.

20   Einstein's work, performed quietly with pencil and paper, seemed remote from the turmoil of everyday life: But his ideas were so revolutionary they caused violent controversy and irrational anger. Indeed, in order to be able to award him a belated Nobel Prize, the selection committee had to avoid mentioning relativity, and pretend the prize was awarded primarily for his work on the quantum theory.

21   Political events upset the serenity of his life even more. When the Nazis came to power in Germany, his theories were officially declared false because they had been formulated by a Jew. His property was confiscated, and it is said a price was put on his head.

22   When scientists in the United States, fearful that the Nazis might develop an atomic bomb, sought to alert American authorities to the danger, they were scarcely heeded. In desperation, they drafted a letter which Einstein signed and sent directly to President Roosevelt. It was this act that led to the fateful decision to go all-out on the production of an atomic bomb—an endeavor in which Einstein took no active part. When he heard of the agony and destruction that his $E = mc^2$ had wrought, he was dismayed beyond measure, and from then on there was a look of ineffable sadness in his eyes.

23   There was something elusively whimsical about Einstein. It is illustrated by my favorite anecdote about him. In his first year in Prince-

ton, on Christmas Eve, so the story goes, some children sang carols outside his house. Having finished, they knocked on his door and explained they were collecting money to buy Christmas presents. Einstein listened, then said, "Wait a moment." He put on his scarf and overcoat, and took his violin from its case. Then, joining the children as they went from door to door, he accompanied their singing of "Silent Night" on his violin.

24   How shall I sum up what it meant to have known Einstein and his works? Like the Nobel Prize-winner who pointed helplessly at his watch, I can find no adequate words. It was akin to the revelation of great art that lets one see what was formerly hidden. And when, for example, I walk on the sand of a lonely beach, I am reminded of his ceaseless search for cosmic simplicity—and the scene takes on a deeper, sadder beauty.

Questions

1. What is Banesh Hoffmann's overall impression of Albert Einstein?
2. Hoffmann gives many excellent examples to support his impression. List three such examples.
3. Why do you think Hoffmann included the story about the sand?
4. What were Einstein's religious views?
5. How does Hoffmann begin his essay? Does this introduction get your attention?
6. How does Hoffmann conclude his essay?

Step 4: Revising

You have now produced a rough draft of your personality profile. Read your essay several times. Read it aloud to yourself. What are the strengths of your essay? How can you build on those strengths? What are the weaknesses? What can you do to improve your essay?

Revision is an opportunity to rethink and resee your essay. It is also, of course, an opportunity to improve structure and organization and fix mistakes in grammar and punctuation. But first make sure your facts are accurate, beginning with spelling your subject's name correctly.

Activity: Checking for Factual Accuracy

Get back together with your interview partner, and exchange rough drafts. Read over the essays, and point out anything that is factually incorrect to your partner.

Now that you know your facts are accurate, continue revising your draft. Use the following guidelines as you look for ways to improve your personality profile.

✏ A Checklist: Revising the Personality Profile

Seeing the Structure

1. What is the dominant impression or impressions of the person? Can you locate a thesis statement? Copy it in the space below.

2. For each impression, list at least three supporting details or examples.

3. Does the introduction make you want to read the essay? Why or why not? If not, give a suggestion for ways to improve the introduction.

4. Does the essay use direct quotations? If so, list two or three examples below.

5. Does the essay use indirect quotations? If so, list two or three examples below.

6. What is the best part of the essay and why?

Seeing Polish

1. Are spelling errors present?

2. Are there grammatical mistakes such as fragments, fused sentences, or subject-verb agreement errors?

3. Are punctuation marks used correctly?

4. Are words used correctly?

Collaborative Activity: Revising

Swap papers with someone other than your interview partner. Use the revision checklist again, but this time consider your classmate's essay, and write down your responses. Any verbal responses should be in addition to your written replies. Give the filled out form to your partner to aid him or her in revising the personality profile.

Grammar and Usage: Sentence Review

Examine the following sentences from "Daring Danielle" and "Kelly's Personality Profile." How are they similar and yet different?

1. Kelly M. Benefield is the oldest child born into the Benefield family.
2. Kelly's mother is a strong and determined person, but during Kelly's childhood her mother had to decide between getting an education or raising her daughters.
3. Although she was born in Oakland, Danielle was raised in Los Angeles and West Covina, California.
4. While her mother was going to school, Kelly was responsible for taking care of her little sister; besides baby-sitting, Kelly had to attend school.

After observing the four sentences, you will probably first realize that each is a sentence; that is, each contains at least one true blue verb in an independent clause. In fact, the first sentence contains exactly one independent clause and nothing else. This sentence is a **simple sentence.** The second sentence contains two independent clauses joined by a FANBOYS word or coordinating conjunction, so it is a **compound sentence.** It would also be a compound sentence if the clauses were combined by a lawyer word or conjunctive adverb.

Because the third sentence contains a dependent clause followed by an independent clause, the sentence has a comma in the middle, and we can say that it begins with a yellow light or subordinating conjunction and is a **complex sentence.** Finally, the fourth sentence contains two independent clauses combined by a lawyer word or conjunctive adverb, *and* it has a dependent clause with a yellow light or subordinating conjunction at the beginning. Since these two combinations make the final sentence both compound and complex, we call it a **compound-complex sentence.**

Because not everything that looks like a sentence is a sentence, you should benefit from the following review. Remember that if a construction begins with a capital letter and ends with a period but is *not* a sentence, it is a fragment. It may be a fragment for one of two reasons: it has no verb, or it is a dependent clause.

Likewise, a construction that begins with a capital letter and ends with a period may be flawed because it contains two independent clauses that have not been combined properly. If the two independent clauses are combined by no punctuation at all, we call the construction a **fused sentence.** On the other hand, if the two independent clauses are joined only by a comma, we call the construction a **comma splice.**

As you complete the following exercise, you will receive a review of verbs, clauses, dependent versus independent clauses, sentences, fragments, fused sentences, and comma splices—all of the concepts we have covered to this point. Perhaps you will find it helpful to tear out the exercise and have it, along with your lists of combiners, beside you whenever you write an essay or letter.

Exercise 1

Underline each independent clause and circle each dependent clause in the constructions below. Some constructions have no clauses.

1. By now everyone should be learning how to recognize a sentence.

2. You should begin by looking for the true blue verb.

3. If a construction has no true blue verb, then you do not have a clause; therefore, you have no sentence.

4. After you locate a true blue verb, you should next search for yellow lights or subordinating conjunctions.

5. Because a yellow light makes a clause dependent.

6. Yellow lights or subordinators are fine if another clause in the sentence doesn't have a yellow light.

7. We call a clause with no subordinators an independent clause.

8. In order to have a sentence, a minimum of one independent clause.

9. To repeat, a verb means that we have a clause.

10. Don't let a verbal trick you into thinking that you have a true blue verb.

11. Recognizing verbals and dependent clauses will help keep you from writing fragments, but your work does not end there.

12. Avoiding comma splices and fused sentences.

13. "Comma splice" means two sentences joined by a comma.

14. A fused sentence has the same error without the comma.

15. You want to have a good sentence; consequently, remember to count the independent clauses.

16. If your construction has even one independent clause, even ten dependent clauses won't make it a comma splice or fused sentence.

17. Combine two independent clauses with a comma and FANBOYS word or coordinating conjunction, and you will do well.

18. FANBOYS are good clause combiners; on the other hand, a lawyer word (conjunctive adverb) with a semicolon and a comma offers variety.

19. But the lawyer word without the semicolon or the comma without the FANBOYS word creates a comma splice.

20. All this information is a lot to remember, I hope I can keep it straight!

━━━━━━

Did you locate the three fragments and the one comma splice in the constructions in this exercise? If so, you are well on your way to avoiding serious sentence errors.

Exercise 2

Go back over the sixteen good sentences, and decide whether each is simple, compound, complex, or compound-complex.

━━━━━━

Using sentence variety will greatly help keep your own essay fresh and interesting, as you will see when you try it!

Exercise 3

Write a paragraph at least ten sentences in length, introducing yourself to someone whom you have never before met. Be sure your paragraph includes at least one of every sentence type: simple, compound, complex, and compound-complex.

━━━━━━

Chapter

How To: Illustrating a Real Process

Do you consider yourself an **expert?** Expert at what? you may well ask. Think about it for a moment. All of us, whether we have worked for a major corporation for twenty years or whether we have babysat our neighbor's child exactly two times, have probably developed a certain level of expertise at one or more tasks.

Maybe you know exactly how to scrub for surgery. Or perhaps you could tell even the most underqualified shade tree mechanics how to change the oil in their car. Then, again, you may have discovered the perfect recipe for Mongolian beef. Finally, you may have developed an absolutely spray-proof technique for changing an infant's diaper.

In any of these examples, you have become an expert at something. True, your expertise may or may not result in an appearance on local television where you share your knowledge with an audience of thousands. Nor can we promise you that an attorney will call you as an expert witness in a high-stakes trial. Still, the combination of your experience and your skill almost certainly makes you an expert at one or more activities.

Your major assignment for this paper will be to write a **how-to** essay. To begin, you will need to find a subject where you are enough of an expert to write the essay accurately and completely. Then, you will need to determine an audience for your essay, namely someone—preferably someone you know—who needs to learn how to do the activity. The finished product will offer a rationale for the essay, instructions for the process, and a conclusion that may very well explain what the audience will have gained from learning the skill or activity.

How-To Writing in Our Real Lives

Have you ever purchased a birthday or holiday present that, the box explains, requires "minor assembly"? Even if not, you will probably appreciate the scenario that follows. A father buys his child a bicycle for

Christmas. Seeing the "minor assembly" requirement, the father discreetly hides the box until late Christmas Eve, when he tugs the box beneath the tree, opens, it, and prepares to assemble a shiny new bicycle as the perfect present for his four-year-old.

Confident but weary, the father pulls the pieces from the boxes. His confidence begins to flag as he sees that there are more pieces and little plastic envelopes filled with pieces than he has imagined. He can hardly imagine where every piece will fit, but he does not despair—at least not yet. He keeps digging in the box, and then he finds what he wants: instructions. To his horror, however, the instructions are written in a language which the father does not speak. Looking more closely, he sees that the English translation is on the back, but the situation is scarcely better.

First of all, the instructions detail 32 steps to assembling the bicycle. Even worse, they require more tools than the father owns. Worst of all, the English translation appears to have been made by the same person who wrote the foreign language version on the other side, and it is almost impossible to follow unless and until the father can untangle such items as "The insertion of the flange into the small cap A will occur after the seat clamp is properly situated in the seat clamp post."

With every store closed, the father desperately calls the toll-free number at the bottom of the instructions. After receiving many busy signals, he finally finds a friendly customer service representative who talks him through assembling the bicycle. His child's Christmas is saved. Exhausted, the father collapses into bed, promising himself that next year he will pay the assembly charge, no matter how expensive, rather than put himself through this ordeal again.

If you have ever bought a bicycle, tricycle, swing set, or car stereo for a child or a friend and decided to assemble or install it at the last minute yourself, you understand that the example of the father and the bicycle is only slightly exaggerated (and may end too happily, at that!). Every set of directions you have ever encountered—whether they involve assembling something, cooking a delicious dish, or even finding a friend's house—is essentially a how-to paper. Unfortunately, this sort of writing often brings out the very worst language skills many people possess. Fortunately for you, however, developing the how-to techniques contained in this chapter and focusing on the uses of the communication triangle and models as presented here will help you approach your how-to assignment with confidence and skill.

Communication Triangle for the How-To Essay

Writing your personal how-to essay involves actively using two of the angles on the communication triangle. First comes the "it" angle. Your subject, or whatever skill or activity you choose to write about, is the "it" for your essay. If your essay is to successfully inform readers, you must demonstrate mastery of the subject itself, and you must present the subject accurately and completely.

Equally important in the how-to essay is the "you" angle of the communication triangle. In fact, the example of instructions to assemble a bicycle fails as a process essay because it does not take audience into consideration at all. It is written to fulfill the requirement of including instructions in the box without ever taking into consideration the way a real person who does not spend several hours per day contemplating bicycle assembly would respond when confronted with such a poorly written and technical piece of prose. For you to write a good process essay, you must consider the "you" of your essay almost from the very beginning. You will need to develop empathy, the ability to put yourself in the place of your audience, and imagine how these people will feel as they read what you have written. The combination of "it" accuracy and "you" awareness is what makes any good how-to essay succeed.

The Assignment: Explaining a Process

Aim or Purpose: Informative and Persuasive

Audience: Someone who wants to learn a particular skill

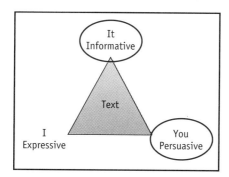

Step 1: Gathering Ideas

Freewriting

Your first step in producing your how-to essay is finding a subject. You will begin searching for a subject by writing a focused freewrite. Write for ten minutes, beginning with the words "I am pretty good or very good at. . . ."

Remember the simple rules for freewriting. The main rule is that you do not stop for any reason. If you make a mistake, leave it for now; you can go back and correct it later. If you have nothing to say, simply write "I have nothing to say" or something equally meaningless until you **do** have something to say. Do not stop until you have written for ten full minutes on the topic "I am pretty good or very good at. . . ."

Now that you have written for ten minutes, what do you find? Do you see before you a brief discussion of several abilities that you possess? Or have you focused on one or two abilities in which you are particularly expert? Or are you blocked for now and find that you need to take a brief break from the assignment and return later, when you hope to have more ideas for the topic?

In either case, as soon as you are ready, determine a list of two to five skills, activities, or abilities that you believe you have mastered well enough to explain to someone. Then, in your notebook, record this list.

At this point, you should have a good working list of potential topics for your how-to essay. You are now ready to turn your attention to determining an audience for your work. Think about people you know, and begin matching them against the topics you have listed. Whom do you know who is particularly weak at something you do especially well? Would it be to the other person's advantage to learn from you, and if so, how and why?

With these thoughts in mind, you are ready to write a second freewrite based upon the first one (or any subsequent freewrites you have already written). This time, stay away from the pronoun *I*. Instead, think of another real person or people who could be reading your work, and begin by writing "_____ (fill in the name) needs to learn to _____ (fill in the activity)." For ten full minutes, explain the task to the audience. If you are unable to complete the process in a ten-minute freewrite, do another freewrite as needed.

Collaborative Activity: Group Brainstorming

In a small group of three or four, discuss your lists of topics and potential audiences. As you listen to your peers, ask yourself several important questions. Moreover, be quick to ask these same questions or other questions of your own devising as you and your classmates discuss topics and audiences.

1. If I don't already know how, would I like to learn more about this activity? Why or why not?

2. Does my classmate seem to be enough of an expert to write about the activity? Why or why not?

3. Is the activity one that can be contained in a relatively short essay? Why or why not?

4. Does the activity sound like one that can be broken into clear steps and explained as such? Why or why not?

5. Does the audience (or do the audiences) selected by my classmates seem appropriate or inappropriate?

Feel free to make any changes that seem warranted based upon your group conversations. Your discussions with classmates will help steer you away from truly difficult topics and audiences and toward especially rewarding ones. When you are satisfied that your freewritings and collaborative work have resulted in a good topic and an appropriate audience, you will have successfully completed the first major step in writing a good how-to essay.

Step 2: Organizing Ideas

Focusing: Determining the Key Steps

If you were telling a friend how to make a peanut butter and jelly sandwich, would you use exactly the same steps as you would use if providing an English-speaking Martian the same directions? Almost certainly not. For one, you could assume that your friend would know to remove the tie back or plastic clip from the loaf of bread before reaching into the bag and selecting two slices. You could not make the same assumption about the Martian. Likewise, you could assume that your friend would know how to unscrew the lid from the jar of peanut butter. But could you assume the same about the Martian? Again, you could not. Therefore, you would find it necessary to break the task into many more and smaller steps for the Martian than you would for your friend.

As you can see, then, the concept of **key steps,** like many other elements of this essay, is driven by your audience. To help keep yourself focused, complete an updated version of the sentence that began one of your freewrites in Step 1:

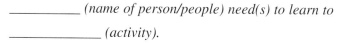

_____ *(name of person/people) need(s) to learn to*

_____ *(activity).*

You will next list the key scenes in completing the activity, but first you need to imagine that you are the audience you have in mind. What do you (meaning your audience) know ahead of time? What will be a key step, and what will be a waste of your time? What information, if omitted, will leave you completely unable to follow the rest of the directions?

With both the complete process and your audience in mind, list the key steps involved in finishing the activity successfully. Include nothing that insults your audience's intelligence. Omit nothing that, by its absence, would leave your audience confused and unable to follow the rest of the directions. List your steps in chronological order, from first to last. If you find that you accidentally put steps out of order, you may rewrite or number the steps as needed. At all times, remember that your list of steps should be accurate, in order, and complete.

Use of Division/Classification

Now that you have listed the key steps in your process, do you find that certain steps are related? For example, say that you are writing about how to wash a dog. It is quite possible that some key steps would involve gathering the items to use, others would involve getting the dog lathered up and washed, and others would involve getting her rinsed and dried. Other possibilities exist as well. Even so, chances are that any complete list of steps involving a process you understand well would suggest some groupings of key steps because you have come to think of the process this way yourself. When you actually write the essay, these groups of steps may become individual paragraphs or sections within your paper. As an aid to organization, review your list. Whenever consecutive steps seem related to each other and would seem to fit well in a paragraph or section of the essay, put a symbol such as a star, a square, a circle, or a rectangle next to them. This brief classification/division activity may be a real time-saver as you formally organize your work.

Activity: Drawing the Key Steps

Continue to put yourself into the position of your audience. Imagine now that you, as your audience, are actually following the steps you have listed above. Try to picture yourself putting the directions to work to fulfill a task. When several pictures have become vivid in your mind, draw out the moments that you think best typify the experience. It does not matter if your drawings are crude and end up looking more like a child's drawings than actual photographs! Try to keep photographic images in your mind as you draw, however. They will help you to organize more effectively.

Activity: Employing Sensory Details to Make the Key Steps Effective

Review your list of key steps. As you do so, ask yourself what in particular your reader should be able to **see, hear, smell, taste,** or **touch/feel** while completing this step. List appropriate details. List these five types of sensory details in your notebook now.

Use of Chart Outlining

One last organizational technique that may help you put your essay together is a chart outline. Very often organizations use charts to illustrate the chain of command. Likewise, scientists use charts to show the way that event follows event in a sequence. You can use a chart, as well, in your how-to essay.

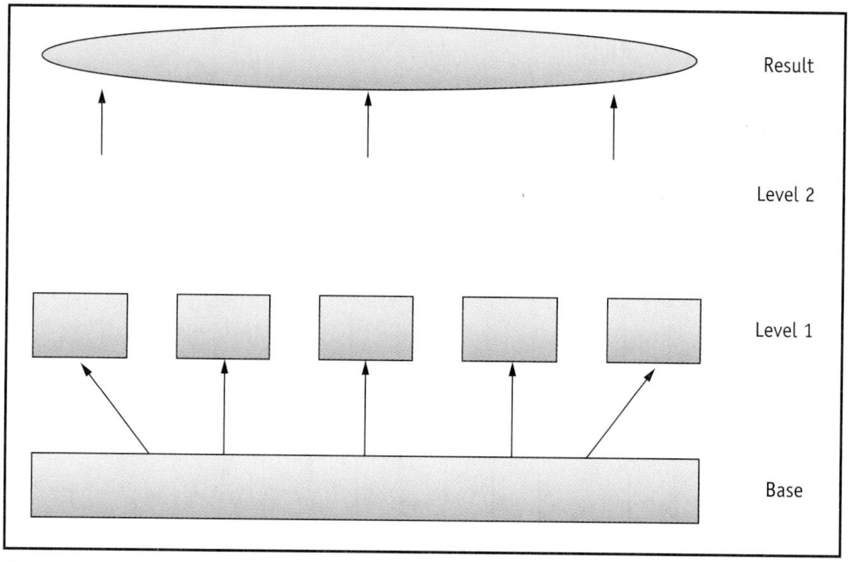

Figure 7.1 Chart Outline for How-To Essay

In the flowchart that follows, fill in the base with the topic—the activity you will be discussing in your essay. In the boxes above, list up to five major components of the work. You need not fill in all five boxes. You will find the division/classification activity helpful here if you want to have a number of major components smaller than the actual number of steps involved. Remember that steps often go together to make up a significant portion of the overall process. At the top, write in the desired result, whether it be a changed tire, a baked cake, an installed water heater, a quilted bedspread, or (as we shall soon see) a decorative aquarium.

Step 3: Writing

Part One: Student and Professional Models

You are about to read an essay, Pamela Ringberg's "Setting up an Aquarium," that was written in response to the assignment you have in this chapter. Ringberg chose a topic from her own experience and, thinking that virtually anyone can enjoy having an attractive aquarium for its beauty and stress relief, she wrote her essay for a very general audience. Read the essay, and then answer the questions that follow.

Setting Up an Aquarium

By Pam Ringberg

1   Have you ever wanted a fish aquarium and didn't know where to start? An aquarium can be an asset to your home as well as a benefit to your

children. Yes, you too can set up an aquarium with the following five quick and easy steps.

2   Before purchasing an aquarium, you will need to decide what size aquarium you want. The space you have available in your home to accommodate the aquarium and the amount of money you are willing to spend are two of the factors you need to consider. I recommend that you compare prices before actually purchasing the aquarium. For example, my friend Crystal wanted a twenty gallon starter kit aquarium, so we went to Walmart. We were able to find the aquarium that she wanted for a reasonable price, $74.96. The starter kit included a florescent hood, power filter, thermometer, heater, food, dechlorinator, a fish net, and a step-by-step instruction booklet.

3   You also need to purchase aquarium gravel. Since Crystal purchased a twenty gallon aquarium, she will need to buy twenty pounds of gravel. When you are adding gravel to your aquarium, please keep in mind that it is always a pound per gallon. Now you are ready to begin setting up your aquarium.

4   The first step is to wash the gravel thoroughly, so you can eliminate any chances of cloudiness that may occur. Please don't get discouraged if you experience any cloudiness; simply drain the water from the aquarium and rinse the gravel again.

5   Step two, when filling your aquarium with water, you need to add the dechlorinator to eliminate the chlorine from the water. You will generally add a teaspoon per ten gallons.

6   The third step is to place the power filter on the back of your aquarium. Before plugging the power filter in, make sure you fill the filter half way with water. If you do not add the water, there is a possibility you might burn out the motor in your filter system. After plugging your filter system in, place the filter cartridge into your power filter. Every two weeks you will need to take the cartridge out and rinse it off. You can reuse it, but I do recommend changing it with a new one every five to six weeks.

7   The fourth step entails fastening the heater on the back of the aquarium. Make sure that you do not over tighten it. A fire hazard is a possibility if it occurs. After you plug the heater in, you must keep an eye on the temperature over the next few days. You want the temperature to be between 74 to 78 degrees.

8   If your aquarium exceeds 80 degrees, do not panic. All you will need to do is adjust the gauge a little bit. If you would rather have cold water fish, such as goldfish, it is not necessary to place the heater on.

9   The fifth step is placing the hood on the aquarium. Crystal's starter kit came with a florescent hood. This hood has great features. It doesn't heat the water like an incandescent hood, and it accents all the beautiful colors in the fish.

10   Now that your aquarium is set up, you will need to wait five to seven days before introducing fish to it. The reason you need to wait is to make sure that everything is stabilized. The ratio of time before

putting fish into the aquarium varies. For example, if you have a ten gallon tank, you would want to wait two to three days. For a fity-five gallon tank, you would want to wait ten to twelve days, and so on.

11   I hope you will enjoy your fish aquarium as much as I enjoy mine. By following the five quick and easy steps I have listed, you are on you way to having an aquarium that your entire family can enjoy. If you should have any problems or questions while you are setting up your aquarium, do not hesitate to call a pet store for assistance.

Collaborative Exercise: Discussion Questions

In small groups, discuss the following questions. After you have satisfactorily reached individual and group answers to all the questions, compare your observations with those of the other groups in your class.

1. Does Ringberg seem to be enough of an expert to have written the essay on this topic? Why or why not?

2. Does Ringberg write in such a way as to show "you" awareness and keep your attention? Why or why not?

3. Why do you think Ringberg mentions her friend Crystal several times in the essay? What effect do these references have?

4. Where do you see evidence that Ringberg has grouped some of her steps together into paragraphs or sections of her essay? Do her groupings seem effective? Why or why not?

5. Does Ringberg leave you more interested in obtaining an aquarium than you were before, less interested, or about as interested? Explain.

A second model for you to consider is selected from Bonnie Friedman's *Writing Past Dark*, which promises in its subtitle to discuss "Envy, Fear, Distraction, and other Dilemmas—in the Writer's Life." The following selection from Friedman's highly personal book discusses the how-to's and pitfalls of writing in a particular collaborative environment, the writing workshop.

From *Writing Past Dark*

By Bonnie Friedman

1   How we learn is what we learn.

2   While the private act of the writing program may or may not be writing, the defining weekly ritual is public scrutiny. It doesn't matter whether it's your work that's up for discussion or someone else's: what is heard is criticism, what is said is criticism, until, for many, as they sit before their typewriters at home, what occupies their minds is criticism, criticism devouring their latent words.

3   Eudora Welty says, "I believe if I stopped to wonder what So-and-so would think, or what I'd feel like if this were read by a stranger, I would be paralyzed." And Joan Didion says, "When I first started to write pieces, I would try to write to a reader other than myself. I always failed. I would freeze up."

4   Yet at the Workshop we were trained to wonder all about So-and-so; we learned to write always to a reader other than ourselves. Once a week for two years we sat across a table with a Xeroxed story between us. It was tempting to write stories like a suit of armor; hollow, but impervious to attack.

5   And yet many of us became writers at Iowa. It was here that we noticed the nature of words.

6   It is possible to write for many years and never notice. It is possible to write so much one's page swarms, and still not detect how an individual word behaves. Writing school changes that. It taps its pencil against each particular word and says, "See this." Focusing on particular words can feel niggling. It can feel pedantic, even willfully obtuse—as if the viewer insisted on standing too close to a pointillist canvas and then complained that all she saw was dots. Where are the promised sunbathers, the river, the boats? Well, if you'll just take a step back, if you'll just squint. *Squint? Step back?* The audience stares, granite-faced. No, the text must convey itself from here. When I read, I read one word at a time.

7   So, faced with a table of granite readers, you look at your words again. The same scene might be described in another way entirely. You might ax all the adjectives, like chipping barnacles from the sleek prow of a ship. You might shift the whole thing into interior monologue and allow adjectives to bloom like cabbage roses, saturating the telling with the deep color of emotion. If you can change anything, you can change everything. A gulf appears; you have lived on a fault line and never noticed it. Now it has broken open, leaving you over here, and what you wrote over there. Forever after, this is how it shall be.

8   No longer can you assume, as I did, that the way you feel writing something will be pretty much the way a person will feel reading it. I used to go to a diner under the Number 1 elevated train, and order a grilled corn muffin and jelly, and many cups of coffee, and I wrote in a sort of pounding exaltation. I assumed my readers would experience a similar thrill. The method was to get very, very excited. The story was just the conduit to convey this excitement. The writing was the same as my jumpy fingers, or the train racheting overhead and making my heart vibrate.

9   Writing school detached the words from the vibration. I saw that the inchoate mood and the particular words—the heart's rattle and the lines of prose—may approach each other more and more closely, but they will never merge. You may fling a million strings of words, and lace them tight, and still there is a gap.

10   And then, astonished, you see something else: the reader isn't granite. It is words themselves that are stony. A sort of gritty earth-

bound gravity inheres in them. It is they who are stubborn, not the reader. The reader *does* squint, *does* step back and approach and turn things every which way trying to discern the depicted shape. The reader wants a good story. It is words themselves that are reluctant to cooperate.

11   The workshop does have a treasure to bestow. It teaches a new way of seeing. This is a loss of innocence that opens the way to all the pleasures of consciousness. It is often beautiful to revise, to enrich one's story and focus it more clearly. Moments spring to sharp life that before lay blurry. The real purpose of the story may now reveal itself. One increases the chances for a story's success.

12   Yet learning to write hurt me. I had to give up a sense of natural unity with my writing—of the rightness of my intuitive way. I recall the sensation that a certain story of mine had atomized. All its parts were sprayed out in various directions and hung, unrelated to one another and divorced from me. How far away they looked! Losing a sense of the instinctive aptness of one's words is a form of exile. My anger at writing school is in part due to this necessary loss, and to that extent my anger is misplaced.

Collaborative Exercise: Discussion Questions

In small groups, discuss each of the following questions about Friedman's essay. When you have finished all the questions, compare your observations with those made by the other groups in your class.

1. When Friedman says, "Yet at the Workshop we were trained to wonder all about So-and-so," what implication do her words have upon the how-to essay that you will write for this chapter?

2. What does Friedman mean when she says, "It is possible to write for many years and never notice"?

3. In your how-to essay, what strategies may you employ to ensure that, to use Friedman's words, your "reader *does* squint, *does* step back and approach and turn things every which way trying to discern the depicted shape"?

4. To what extent, like Friedman, must you give up "the rightness of [your] intuitive way" for your how-to essay to be effective? In what ways does this realization on your part reflect an awareness of the communication triangle?

5. Aside from blindly approving everything your classmates write, how can you work to lessen the anger at the collaborative approach that Friedman feels but acknowledges is "misplaced"?

Part Two: Writing the How-To Essay

You are now almost prepared to begin writing your how-to essay. For this particular essay, however, some cautionary notes and advice may merit your special attention.

First of all, the beginning is absolutely crucial to this essay's success. Remember that from the very first word, you are addressing a specific audience, not just Welty or Friedman's "So-and-so." As you begin, ask yourself what your audience would like to see at the beginning of an essay explaining how to do something. Consider beginning with a leading question: "Have you ever wished that you could improve the way your bedroom looks by installing a wallpaper border?" Or you could also begin with a telling scenario: "You have decided to invite some coworkers over for dinner, but you have a very strict budget. For under ten dollars, you need to prepare a meal for yourself and two guests that will make you look like a more than competent host and chef." In either case, your introduction will go on to offer a thesis that takes the audience toward success in the activity.

Another important issue in the how-to essay follows from the need for a strong beginning. Because you are writing to persuade an audience, perhaps even an audience of one, that they can do something, it is often important to use two little words—**you can**—to make your introduction work. You also must persuade the audience that the task at hand involves steps and, hopefully, that those steps will be easy if the audience follows your simple-to-read instructions. If you do not use these exact words, you absolutely should use a tone that reflects them. An introduction that begins with the wrong anecdote and tone can make your how-to essay useless. For example: "You are riding along on a rainy evening when you hear the familiar whap, whap, whap of rubber hitting asphalt. As you inspect your automobile, you find the expected flat tire on the front passenger's side. Proceed with extreme caution. Failure to properly use the equipment provided for changing a flat may result in severe injury, even death." Who in the world would ever read those words in an automobile owner's manual without a quickening of the pulse, rising blood pressure, and a strong urge to sit down on the side of the road and cry?

Another issue to consider is peculiar to the how-to essay. Because directions (especially recipes) are not always written in complete sentences, how-to essays sometimes tend to use what we have labeled "Tarzan language." Tarzan language is a variety of English that leaves out words like *a, an,* and *the.* "Insert screw into casing and rotate clockwise until screw is secure" is a prime example of Tarzan language. As you are writing, and especially as you proofread, try to eliminate all traces of Tarzan language from your essay.

Finally, students often ask about transitions and the number of body paragraphs in the how-to essay. How, you may wonder, do you move from step to step, and what is a good number of paragraphs to have in the body of your essay? The answers to both questions are determined by the nature of the essay and the subject matter. Because the how-to essay is like the narrative in that it moves in chronological order, **time order** transitions such as *first, next, then, when,* and *finally* usually work very well. In addition, the number of paragraphs depends largely upon the number of steps or number of combined sets of steps you derived during Step 2 of this chapter. Allow this number to drive the number of body paragraphs you write, with two caveats: absolutely avoid any long paragraphs that a reader would have difficulty following, and try to make certain each paragraph contains a minimum of two sentences. If your first draft reveals difficulties in this area, you may address them during revision.

Now write your how-to essay. Frequently refer to your chart outline, your freewritings, your responses to the models, your drawings, your list of sensory details, and any other materials you gathered as you prepared this essay.

Step 4: Revising

Revising for Structure

Collaborative Exercise: Essay Exchange

As soon as you have completed and proofread your essay, arrange a swap with one or more classmates so that every person has someone else's essay to read. Now take the essay written by your classmate, and read over it carefully. As you do, list each key step on a separate 3 × 5 index card, and number the cards. The steps should appear in the same order on your index cards as they do in the essay; if they do not, either you have misunderstood the steps, or there is a flaw in the presentation. In either case, the author needs to learn of the problem and possibly take steps to correct it.

For each step, ask yourself the following questions:

1. Is the step clear?

2. Is the step complete?

3. Can I actually imagine myself completing this step, especially if I don't already know how to perform the activity? On the card, draw a caption, even a stick figure of yourself carrying out the step.

4. Is the step presented so that I have to dig it out of a paragraph, or does it stand alone? If it occurs in the same paragraph as another step, are the steps separated by a transition, and is the transition clear?

5. Are there any steps that occupy separate paragraphs in the essay but would be more effective if combined into one paragraph because they are so closely related? What would be a good way to combine them? Suggest a transition within the proposed new paragraph.

Record your answers to these questions on separate index cards or another sheet of paper, and return all the materials to the author. Or, if time permits, return only the essay to the author, and have another student repeat the process regarding the essay you just reviewed while you review a new essay yourself. Remember that you cannot receive too many people's opinions about your essay! Also, remember to be honest but to phrase your replies in such a way as to promote a positive experience, not the anger Friedman experienced in her Iowa workshops.

When you and your classmates are finished, you should receive your original essay and at least one full set of responses to it. Consider those responses as you begin revising your essay structurally. Take any signs of reader confusion seriously because these signs may very well tell you that your how-to essay, as written, has problems with vagueness or disorganization. Carefully work to eliminate those problems. Afterward, become your own "collaborative" reader, or find a friend or classmate to review the essay on your own time.

Revising for Polish

Read your essay from beginning to end. As you do so, ask yourself, "Is what I am saying reader friendly?" In other words, does every paragraph, every sentence, even every word speak directly to your readers? Revise any paragraph, sentence, or word that does not address your readers clearly and directly. Also, examine microscopically for Tarzan language, and clean it up entirely. Then review for grammar and mechanics. You may find it helpful to focus on sentence variety, a technique that helps sustain interest throughout your essay.

Grammar and Usage: Sentence Variety

Directions: Using some of the suggested combiners and some you already know or find in Chapter 4, combine each of the following sets of sentences into one grammatical sentence. Find at least two correct ways to combine each set. Retain the original meaning, but add, subtract, or move words as you see fit. Be careful to avoid fragments, comma splices, and fused sentences (see Chapter 6).

1. Spring break is coming soon, and   Use *and* and *because* plus
   I can't wait, *because*   two combiners that you select.
   I am going to the beach.

2. I am watching TV, *however*,   Use *however* and *for* plus two
   I don't like this movie, *for*   combiners that you select.
   This movie is dumb.

3. Dictionaries are reliable, *and*
   I always keep one on me; *furthermore,*
   Everyone needs a dictionary.

   Use *and* and *furthermore* plus two combiners that you select.

after 4. I came home from school,
   I ate supper; *then,*
   I went to bed.

   Use *after* and *then* plus two combiners that you select.

When 5. I went to work,
   I did a good job, *so*
   I received a raise.

   Use *when* and *so* plus two combiners that you select.

6. The dog ran over the cat, *and*
   The cat played dead; *however,*
   The dog was too smart.

   Use *and* and *however* plus any other grammatically correct method.

7. Marley is standing on my paper, *and*
   Marley is playing; *furthermore,*
   I don't want to play.

   Use *furthermore* plus any other correct method you prefer.

8. I like to go to school, *because*
   I want to be educated; *in addition,*
   Learning is fun.

   Include *because* in at least one of the combinations you create.

Since 9. The woman screamed,
   The killer ran; *then,*
   Someone called the police.

   Use any combiners that are grammatically correct in this and all the remaining combinations.

10. Jason likes California, *and*
    Jason likes to swim, *because*
    Jason enjoys being on the beach.

11. The electricity went off last night; *therefore,*
    My alarm did not go off; *consequently,*
    I was late for school.

12. Nashrin had a long drive home, *and*
    Nashrin was traveling in 5:00 traffic; *thus,*
    Nashrin missed her dinner date.

13. John went to the store, *and*
    John bought $20 worth of groceries; *however,*
    John forgot to buy soap.

14. My car was dirty, *so*
    I washed my car; *as a result,*
    Now my car is clean.

15. Math is different, *but*
    Math is not so difficult; *nonetheless,*
    Math can be fun; *however,*
    Math is a challenge.

Exchanging Combined Sentences

In groups of three to five, compare your sentence combinations with those of your classmates. You should note a wide variety of answers in addition to those suggested for items 1–8. Correct any combinations that introduce fragments, comma splices, and fused sentences or that inadvertently change the meaning of the sentences. What does the wide variety of "good" answers tell you about the choices available to us as writers? How will using such variety make your writing more effective?

8

"In the Space Provided": Writing Essay Exams

How Do You Prepare for Essay Exams?

Benjamin Franklin said that the only two certainties in life are death and taxes. In college, virtually the only two certainties are that most of the offices on campus will come to know you by your identification number rather than your name and that you will take essay examinations! Often students face essay exams with fear, but such an attitude is at best somewhat mistaken and at worst utterly counterproductive. The fact is that you will continue to take essay exams. You may even face one at the end of this course.

Preparation for essay exams varies widely from course to course. If you are preparing for an essay exam in a history, psychology, biology, or political science course, your preparation will involve studying course content. You'll have your textbook, your lecture and study notes, and possibly other materials to help you cram as many ideas as possible into your head. You will certainly want to have a format for presenting those ideas to make you appear as informed and as organized as possible.

This last fact applies as well to essay exams that occur over unannounced topics with no explicit way (i.e., no textbook or notes) to prepare for the topic. Writing competency exams is an example. While you will not have a textbook to study or myriad facts to worry about remembering, you will still need to develop formatting options that will present your writing in the most favorable light.

And so we come to the purpose of this chapter. You already know that *what* you say is often no more important than *how* you say it. Even if your ideas are wonderful, they may be so disorganized or underdeveloped that a reader—in this case the professor grading your essay—may not be able to see just how good they are. The reason for disorganization or underdevelopment is often, quite understandably, the time constraints imposed by the essay exam format. Fortunately, instruction and practice can and will give you ways to ensure that your ideas are organized and show development. By following the advice and examining the student models in this chapter, you will learn to write effective essay exams.

Essay Exams and the Communication Triangle

Essay exams provide an almost pure example of "it" based writing, with "it" being the subject chosen by your professor or the examining committee. For a history, psychology, biology, or political science exam, the "it" will be the chapters and notes that you have carefully prepared for examination day. On the other hand, essay exams over unannounced topics will require an "it" that you invent largely from your own experiences and observations. Many topics will not ask you to use much "I" writing in an essay exam. Typically, the audience or the "you" of your essay does not extend beyond your professor or the committee responsible for grading your work.

The Assignment: An Essay Exam

Aim or Purpose: Informative

Audience: Your professor or examining committee

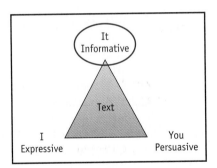

Step 1: Choosing from More than One Topic

Since this textbook is geared toward a writing course, the examples in this chapter will illustrate an essay over an unannounced topic, meaning that you must supply the ideas and examples from your imagination. The steps involved will carry over easily into essays where the subject matter is dictated by the course you have taken and the sources you have had available to you. Regarding unannounced topics, let us first consider an instance where you must choose between two topics.

Consider the two following examples:

What is your most prized possession, and why?

Discuss some of the reasons American teens use illegal drugs.

If you had to choose between these two topics, which would you choose, and why? One excellent way to choose between two diverse topics is to ask yourself briefly, "Which of these topics do I know the most about? Which of these topics will let me have the larger number of ideas to discuss?"

The answers to these two questions will be largely personal. If you just spent the night before the exam snuggled up next to the teddy bear your grandmother gave you when you were four, you will very likely tilt toward the prized possession topic. If, on the other hand, you had a long conversation that night with a teenaged friend or relative who has been battling a cocaine habit for several months, you may find yourself having much more to say about the illegal drug topic. Of course, rarely will your experiences and observations so clearly lead you to one topic over another, but you generally will find one topic that more readily uses your expertise.

The important consideration at this point is to reach your decision rather quickly. The chapters in this book have, thus far, presented writing as a process with an emphasis on extensive revisions to make a composition better. Timed writing does not afford you such opportunities. You need to give the topics reasonably thorough consideration; at the same time, however, you must be decisive, and you must rapidly begin to act upon your decisions.

Step 2: Generating and Organizing Ideas

The Topical Cluster

Let us say that you have chosen the topic "Discuss some of the reasons American teens use illegal drugs." Examine the topic closely to see if you can locate the key words that are likely to appear first in your thesis and later throughout your essay. To find these key words, ask yourself, "What will my essay be about?" In this case, your essay will be about the reasons American teens use illegal drugs. Hence, you have located the key words from the topic. To generate the topical cluster, write the key words in the middle of a piece of paper, as illustrated below. Then draw a circle (or ellipse) around the key words, and draw a series of lines that emanate from the circle. On as many of the lines as possible, write a response to the key words in the circle. Do not censor yourself at this point; list every idea that comes to mind, whether it seems really strong or only minimally so. The example in Figure 8.1 shows what a topical cluster should look like after you have completed these steps.

One advantage of the topical cluster as performed so far is that it allows you to generate a lot of ideas very quickly. As of now, however, those ideas reflect no organization. You could not simply sit down and write your essay based on what you have. Still, you have made an important beginning, and the next step will begin to shape your ideas into an essay.

Examine the ideas you have drawn on the lines. Do you see relationships among some of them? Do certain ideas seem very similar to each other, so similar in fact that they would fit neatly into a paragraph

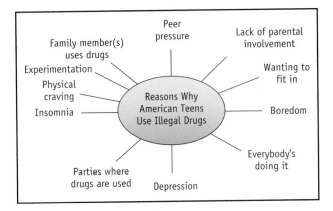

Figure 8.1 Example #1 of a Topical Cluster

together? Note, for example, the ideas "peer pressure," "wanting to fit in," and "everybody's doing it." These ideas express very similar but not identical concepts. They all illustrate ways that the desire for *popularity* can influence a teen to use illegal drugs.

Once you have made this determination, you have completed an important step in organizing your timed essay. In fact, you have largely generated the information for one of the body paragraphs. At this moment, you can't be certain where exactly in the body of your essay this paragraph will occur, but you do want to mark it for future reference. Try selecting a neutral marker—for example, a geometrical shape such as a circle, triangle, star, square, or rectangle—to enclose each of these related items on the topical cluster. Let's use the triangle for now. Then, off to the right of the cluster, write the word *popularity,* surrounded by the triangle. The example in Figure 8.2 shows the way your topical cluster and legend will now look.

Continue in this fashion until you have devised approximately three or four sets of related items. Each time you compile such a set, use another neutral geometrical symbol to mark it, and put the key descriptive word, such as *physical reasons* or *recreation* to the right, and mark them with the symbol. Add new items to your cluster as needed, and delete those that do not seem to fit.

When you have finished organizing your cluster and grouping items according to key words, ask yourself which of the groups of items is most important to your discussion and which is least important. For example, you could decide that popularity is the most important reason teens abuse drugs and recreation the least important. You will discuss the least important material first and the most important material last. The reason for putting the material in this order is that you want your essay to show stronger content with each new paragraph. Save your best point for last because readers usually remember best what they read last. Moreover, the reason that you have used neutral geometrical shapes so far is that you do not

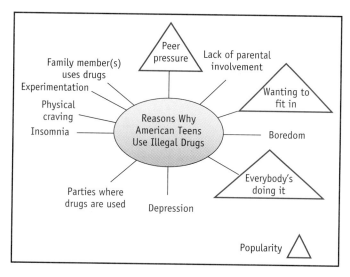

Figure 8.2 Example #2 of a Topical Cluster

want to have prejudiced your thinking by automatically labeling a particular item as first and another as third. Base that decision upon importance, not the mere order in which items occur to you.

After you have ranked your items in order of importance, number them in inverse order next to the key words. In other words, if you have three proposed body paragraphs, put the number 1 next to the least important (such as *recreation*), 2 next to the second most important (such as *physical reasons*), and 3 next to the most important (such as *popularity*). You will write your body paragraphs in this order. Of course, your rankings of the relative importance of the three items may differ utterly from the rankings we have assigned here.

When you have reached this point in your topical cluster, you are almost ready to begin writing your essay. In fact, you could go ahead and write your body paragraphs with little additional preparation. The primary remaining task is to generate an introduction with a thesis. We will discuss this matter in the next section of the chapter. For now, consider the example in Figure 8.3 of a completed topical cluster as an example of an outline for a timed essay exam.

Generating and Organizing Ideas by Outline

Consider each of the following possible topics for a timed essay:

1. What are some of the reasons American teens use illegal drugs?
2. Discuss some of the reasons American teens use illegal drugs.
3. reasons American teens use illegal drugs

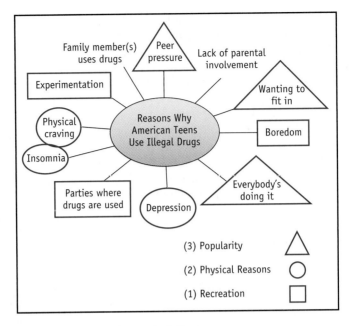

Figure 8.3 Example #3 of a Topical Cluster

Even a brief glance should reveal to you that the three topics are really the same. One expresses the topic in question format, the second offers the topic in an imperative sentence with the verb *discuss,* and the third gives only the key words without bothering with sentence structure. On timed competency exams, you could see the topic expressed in any of these three ways.

If you choose to generate and organize your ideas by outline, your first step after viewing the topic will be to generate a thesis statement. This task is actually quite easy as long as you remember one simple rule: most of the words for your thesis statement are already contained in the topic. In fact, you can use every word in the third expression of the topic as you generate your thesis. It, like the other two, focuses on the topic of American teens' illegal drug use and indicates that your essay will consist of reasons for this activity. By turning these key words into a declarative sentence (as opposed to the imperative sentence in topic number 2), you will have a good working thesis.

Remember the difference between an imperative sentence and a declarative one? An imperative sentence gives a command. A declarative sentence, on the other hand, makes a statement, such as a thesis statement. If we turn the imperative sentence in number two or the interrogative sentence in number one into a declarative sentence, we come up with something like "American teens abuse drugs for a variety of reasons." This sentence is not particularly fancy, but as a working thesis sentence, it will do just fine. It will also allow us to organize by outline or to go back to the topical cluster in the previous example and plug in a working thesis.

Outlines can be organized in different ways. At their most formal, they can use Roman numerals and capital letters. Not too many students use rigidly formal outlines in preparing timed essay exams. A less formal way of outlining is a **jotlist brainstorm.** In compiling such a brainstorm, you look at your thesis, "American teens abuse drugs for a variety of reasons," and ask yourself a simple question: "What are the **main** reasons American teens use these drugs?" After contemplating for a minute or two, you begin writing the reasons that you consider most important.

Your deliberations could lead you to develop any of a number of major reasons American teens use drugs. For the purposes of this exercise, however, say that the three you settle upon are the same as those in the topical cluster: *recreation, physical reasons,* and *popularity.* Proceed, then, to list each of these three categories of reasons across the top of your page as follows:

recreation   **physical reasons**   **popularity**

Next, begin to compile a list of examples to support each reason in the space beneath the category. An example will look something like this:

recreation	**physical reasons**	**popularity**
experimentation	insomnia	peer pressure
parties with drugs	physical craving	wanting to fit in
boredom	depression	everybody's doing it

The list will quickly give you a way of gathering all the information that you will need for the body paragraphs of your essay. With the list before you, your next task is to prioritize the categories from most to least important. As with the topical cluster, you will write about your most important category last and your least important category first. In fact, you have undoubtedly noticed by now that both of the methods detailed so far would produce exactly the same body paragraphs. However, depending upon whether you work better by having something in front of you visually or abstractly floating around in your head, you will have a choice regarding how to proceed.

Step 3: Writing the Introduction

Just as you have options regarding how to generate and organize ideas for your essay efficiently and quickly, you also have options for the introduction. One effective technique for introductions is to begin with the thesis statement and then enumerate each of the supporting points. Such an introduction for our essay on teens and drugs would contain exactly four sentences and would read approximately this way:

American teens abuse drugs for a variety of reasons. Some teens turn to illegal drug use because they find it fun and recreational. Still other teens find that they must use such drugs because they have developed addictions or other physical needs for the drugs. Most importantly, however, American teens use illegal drugs because these youths desire popularity.

As you practice for timed essay exams, you may find this quick, direct way of presenting introductions helpful.

You probably know, however, that the very easiest is often the least appealing. For example, combining sentences with FANBOYS or coordinating conjunctions is a very easy way to work on comma splices and fused sentences, but who wants to read an essay that contains an almost endless series of compound sentences? The same applies to the introduction illustrated above; while quick and easy to write, it tends to be monotonous and uninspiring.

Perhaps a better option for the introduction to a timed writing is the funnel introduction presented in Chapter 3. The funnel introduction begins with an attention-getter and puts the thesis at the end of the paragraph. Three excellent varieties of attention-getters are the leading question, the quotation, and the anecdote.

Activity: Attention-Getters

Try to develop at least two examples of each of the three techniques for writing attention-getters for the timed essay exam that will discuss teen use of illegal drugs. An example of a leading question might be, "Is teenagers' use of drugs an epidemic without a cure?" An example of a quotation might be, "Losers are users and users are losers."

Collaborative Activity: Comparing Attention-Getters

In small groups, compare the introduction attention-getters that you have developed with some of your classmates.

———

You may encounter leading questions like "Why do so many teens use drugs?" or "Is illegal drug use among teens going to ruin a generation of young Americans?" Some good quotations would include the following: "When the people behind the United Negro College Fund coined the phrase 'A mind is a terrible thing to waste,' they must have been thinking about teen drug use" or "Just say 'No' " followed by a brief explanation. An anecdote could talk about a hypothetical youth who is leading a fairly typical teenaged existence until he begins experimenting with drugs to become popular and have fun, only to discover the physical, financial, and emotional effects the substances have upon him. Attention-getters, by design, should be imaginative and interesting to read. Be creative!

Step 4: Transitions

If you have used either of the techniques presented in this chapter, you have designed your body paragraphs before your introduction or conclusion or even before you have thought about transitions between paragraphs. You do not want to neglect this important element in producing essays that flow smoothly from point to point and paragraph to paragraph.

Both transitions between and within paragraphs will help make your essay readable. For transitions within paragraphs, chronological or time order words can be helpful, along with contrasting words when you present information that contradicts what you just said. Within paragraphs, *first, next, then,* and *when* can be most helpful, as can *on the other hand, on the contrary,* and *in contrast.*

In writing transitions between paragraphs, some writers like to signal a transition at the end of a given body paragraph. For example, a writer may conclude her first body paragraph about teens and drugs by writing, "But while recreation is a key reason teens abuse illegal drugs, physical reasons are even more important to consider." This writer may then begin her next paragraph with a topic sentence on physical reasons, and readers will have been prepared for this transition. Another writer, on the other hand, may choose to put the transition at the beginning of the second body paragraph. He may conclude the paragraph on recreation and then begin his next paragraph, "Teens also abuse illegal drugs due to physical reasons." Here, *also* has served as the key transition word. Other examples that could work here include *another, in addition,* and *finally.*

The transitional devices suggested both between and within paragraphs are by no means complete. Feel free to experiment with techniques that work for you. Remember that the key goal is always to make your essay exam flow as smoothly as possible.

Step 5: Concluding

Writing a conclusion to a timed essay exam poses a special challenge. In all probability, you have used all the material you had in the introduction and body paragraphs, so a conclusion, if not carefully crafted, could be redundant. In fact, a conclusion does consist, in part, of a restatement of the preceding paragraphs. Such a conclusion on teens and drugs could begin,

> *As this essay has shown, teens abuse illegal drugs for a variety of reasons. Some do so for recreational reasons, others for physical reasons, and still others in the quest for popularity.*

These sentences are only part of the conclusion, however. In order to be effective, a conclusion needs to do more than summarize; indeed, it actually needs to conclude the essay. Here are two ways:

1. Offer a solution.
2. Make a prediction.

In other words, one good way to conclude an essay, especially one that addresses what is clearly a problem is to offer a way to solve the problem or dilemma. A student could write,

In order to curb this potentially disastrous problem of teen drug use, we must focus our resources on education and prevention. We need police officers and counselors in the schools and in centers. Only then may we begin to reduce the epidemic that teen drug use has become.

Equally as effective may be a prediction, which may be worded positively, such as in this example:

Recent prevention efforts have begun to make a dent in teen drug use, and it is to be hoped that by the time the next generation comes along, this problem will have lessened considerably.

Or the conclusion could sound a cautionary note:

Unless we work to reduce teen drug use soon, we risk turning our entire country over to a generation of stoned-out zombies, a risk we dare not take.

Again, as with the other elements of the timed essay examination, practice will help to make you more proficient. If you know that you need to take a timed essay exam to pass the English course in which you are using this book, it may be of great advantage to you to ask your teacher or the tutors in your learning support center to offer you topics for practice and review.

Pacing Yourself

In any timed writing situation, you are not in control of the time. Therefore, you will need to pace yourself carefully so that you will have the best chance at finishing the essay and having time to perform at least some proofreading and revision. Learn through practice how best to divide your time. One option is to divide your time into percentages, generally along the following guidelines:

20 percent to choose the topic and plan the essay (including topical cluster or jotlist brainstorm)

10 percent to write the introduction

40 percent to write the body paragraphs

10 percent to write the conclusion

20 percent to proofread and revise

Adjust these guidelines as your personal and collegiate needs dictate.

Student Model #1

The following essay was written by a student responding to the topic "the best friend I ever had." The student had 90 minutes to write the essay as a requirement for passing her English class. First, examine the topical cluster in Figure 8.4 that she developed to begin organizing. Then read the essay, and answer the questions that follow.

My Best Friend

By Barbara Willkomm

1 It was the second semester of my junior year in high school when I met Jon Wyatt. Jon and I started talking during the first day of class and have not stopped. Throughout the time that we have known each other, we have experienced a lot. Jon Wyatt is the best friend I've ever had. He is helpful, fun to be around, and very caring.

2 Jon has always helped me out in many ways. He will help me with my homework whenever I ask. Also, he always seems to give me the best advice. The things I really love that he does are those things he will do without asking. If he thinks my room is getting messy, he is the first person to clean it up. Jon is also a great cook. My favorite dish for him to make me is a grilled cheese sandwich. I know that isn't too difficult to cook, but he makes them extra special.

3 Jon and I have been a lot of places together. During the weekends we will just sit around and think of something new to do. We always seem to have loads of fun together. We can always make each other laugh. One of our favorite places to go is Panama City, Florida. We have been there four times. A wonderful quality Jon has is that he likes to shop. We have a blast picking out clothes and other items for each other. My favorite gift he has bought me is the ring I wear every day.

4 Lastly, the most meaningful characteristic about Jon is the way he is so caring. He loves to take care of me when I am sick. He will just sit beside me and rub my back. Jon always shows up with a rose, balloon, or a sweet card. If I am ever down, he knows exactly what to do that will cheer me up. I think it is so sweet that he cares so much about how I feel. He even asks for my guidance on every issue.

5 In conclusion, there are many events that have caused Jon to become my best friend. Jon is the one person I can tell anything. I

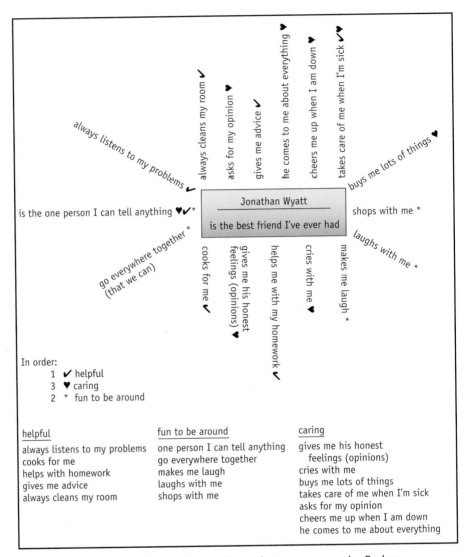

Figure 8.4 Topical cluster for sample student essay exam by Barbara Willkomm

know he is always there for me. Best of all, I know Jon and I will continue to grow closer as time goes on.

Collaborative Activity: Discussion Questions

In small groups, discuss the following questions.

1. What is the thesis for "My best friend"? Why is it effective or ineffective where it is?

2. Why do you think the author has directly stated her supporting points in her introduction? How is she able to maintain control over her essay by doing so?

3. What are at least three examples about Jon that help him stick in your mind?

4. Is the conclusion effective? Why or why not?

5. Where do you see evidence in the essay that Barbara was writing under a strict time limit and may not have been able to say everything she wanted to say? Is the essay strong enough anyway? Why or why not?

Revising

In writing a timed essay exam, you will almost certainly have little or no time to revise for structure. In fact, you may not even have time to copy your essay over. This fact makes it crucial to spend your time wisely organizing and developing. Hence, in revising timed essay exams, you will almost always have to focus on polish revision. Here is a checklist to help revise for polish.

1. Is my introduction clear AND interesting? Could I add a sentence or word anywhere to make it more so?

2. Do I use clear transitions between and within paragraphs? Where might I strengthen my transitions by adding a word, phrase, or sentence?

3. Have I avoided major sentence errors such as splices, fused sentences, and fragments? When I have combined sentences, have I used the proper punctuation?

4. Have I used at least one sentence with a lawyer word or conjunctive adverb as the combiner and correct punctuation? (Hint: the ability to use these combiners correctly often impresses teachers!)

5. Do the subjects and verbs of my clauses agree?

6. Have I consistently employed the same verb tense? If I have shifted tenses, have I had good reason for doing so?

7. Can I justify every comma, apostrophe, or semicolon that I have used? Do I need to add quotation marks for direct quotations?

8. Have I taken the time to review at least most of the words that I was uncertain about how to spell?

9. Does the ending of my paper do more than just summarize the thesis?

You may find other questions to help you review. For now, practicing with these should help you write successful timed essay exams.

Student Model #2

This student essay was written in response to the topic "the learning experiences young people encounter on a first job." Interestingly, this student organized the essay entirely in his head! Nevertheless, he passed the essay and the class. Examine the essay and then the questions that follow.

Skills for the Real World

By Jason Gilmore

1   When I turned 14, I received my first "real" job working at Wendy's on Jimmy Smith Blvd. I was nervous because I never was exposed to earning money from a company. My first day was horrible. I destroyed orders, dropped fries all over the floor, and demolished the rotation of the burgers as they cooked. However, I learned many skills such as good customer service, promptness with no failure to check schedules without excuses, and hard work.

2   Customer service at Wendy's meant giving customers a reason why they should stop and eat there. I had to cooperate with the customers and follow the "the customer is always right" policy. Wendy's taught me how to control my temper and easily take control of terrible situations without raising my voice. This skill is useful for the real working world. Many occupations are more flexible with workers they find well balanced and positive to work with. This example is one of the many experiences young people encounter on their first job.

3   Promptness is critical when working for a company that is productive and needs employees to be responding to their customers' needs. Many young employees find themselves in trouble regarding promptness. I learned a valuable lesson the first time I was late for my first job. To the employees, time is money, and if an employee is not on time, then money is wasted. Here is an example of what not to do.

4   It was a late afternoon. I thought I had to work from 3:00 to 9:00, so I did a few things around the house before I went. Suddenly, the phone rang. It was my boss telling me that my schedule required me to come in at 2:30 and I needed to take my job seriously because he could easily find someone else to replace me. I didn't know what to say. I then realized that I incorrectly looked at my schedule. I told him this, and all he said was, "Don't give me any excuses." The lesson from this incident may be to make sure you look at your schedule properly; however, when they wrote me up, the referral said "late to work." This meant that the boss didn't care whether or not I looked at the schedule the wrong way. In his eyes, I was late, period. The lesson may even be "Do not make excuses" because they don't get you anywhere but deeper in a hole.

5   Also, hard work is best work. When a boss sees an employee doing hard work, it makes the boss more appreciative of his worker and the

worker more valuable. Many times, if an employee is a hard worker but doesn't quite have all the skills required, the boss may look past the worker's ineptitude and interpret his/her hard work as ambition. Hard work is very important in the working field. It is the most important skill needed for the real world. It's critical to have good customer service and promptness; on the other hand, without hard work, how can one grasp good customer service and promptness without the passion for working at it?

6   If you work hard, naturally those skills will come. I learned how employers are more respectful to hard workers on my first job. You earn respect through hard work. For example, when I first started working, the boss had one kid he always picked on. He would call him lazy and say he acted like Frosty Gump because the worker was so slow with the Frosty machine. As I saw that, I was determined I wouldn't have that reputation. I was going to be well respected. In the real world, employers don't tolerate lazy employees. That example of the boy would not have been tolerated in a higher position. This is what I encountered at my first job.

7   All in all, many young people experience different learning incidents when encountering a first job, such as good customer service, promptness with no failure to check schedules and no excuses, and hard work. Many workers take these techniques and put them to good use. Others don't. If you have a job and give good customer service, are prompt without failure to check schedules, don't make excuses, and work hard, I'm sure you will have a long lasting occupation and a preparation for the "real world."

Collaborative Activity: Discussion Questions

In small groups, discuss the following questions.

1. Where is the thesis statement in "Skills for the Real World"? Is it appropriate there? Why or why not?

2. Where are the supporting points first stated? Why are they effective or ineffective there?

3. Where do we see really strong details in the essay? Cite at least five.

4. Where do we see evidence that a topical cluster or jotlist brainstorm would have made Jason Gilmore's organization clearer and easier to follow?

5. What are some ways that Jason Gilmore could have said as much while writing less?

6. Why is the conclusion of "Skills for the Real World" effective or ineffective?

Collaborative Activity: Example of Essay Topics

This chapter has helped you prepare for the competency exams that are common in English classes and as graduation requirements. Of course, you write extemporaneous essays in other college classes and in the real world. Bring to class two or three examples of essay questions from another class you are currently taking or have taken in the past. You might, for example, consider a history, psychology, sociology, business, political science, art, or science class. Or predict an essay question you might be asked on a test when you take such a class in the future. Compare your essay topics with those of two or three of your classmates. Do you find a great variety of types of questions?

Grammar and Usage: Emergency Repairs on Timed Essay Exams and Other Essays

Topic One: How do I check for fragments? To check for fragments, you may use the true blue verb test to identify a clause followed by the yellow light/subordinating conjunction test to make certain that you have at least one independent clause. Or you may practice what we like to call *fore and aft editing*.

Fore and aft editing means that you physically block out everything *before* and *after* the "sentence" in question. This way, you isolate it from the rest of the essay. If it seems to make sense by itself, with no attention paid to the sentences fore and aft, it probably is a sentence.

You may also test for a sentence by isolating the sentence and inserting the words "I believe that" in front of it. Again, if it makes sense this way, it probably is a sentence.

Topic Two: How do I check for comma splices and fused sentences? Use fore and aft editing for this problem, too. Isolate the "sentence" in question. Then, count the independent clauses. If you have more than one independent clause, make sure that it is combined in some way that is stronger than just a comma. A comma and a FANBOYS word (coordinating conjunction) may combine two sentences, and a semicolon and comma with a lawyer word (conjunctive adverb or transitional phrase) may do the same job nicely.

Topic Three: How do I know whether to use a semicolon before a lawyer word (conjunctive adverb or transitional phrase)? Again fore and aft editing will help you. This time, block out everything before and after the lawyer word. If all the words that come *after* the lawyer word sound like a sentence, you need to punctuate it with a semicolon fore and a comma aft. If not, treat the lawyer word as an interrupter, and punctuate it with commas fore and aft.

Topic Four: How do I know whether to use a comma before a FANBOYS word (coordinating conjunction)? If the words *before* the FANBOYS word are a sentence and the words *after* the FANBOYS word are both sentences, use the comma. If the FANBOYS word joins at least three items in a list, use commas after each item except the last.

Topic Five: What are some words to avoid in my essay? The word *thing* is almost never a good word to use in an essay. What is a thing? Also, you should be careful when using the word *this*. For an improved sentence, try substituting a concrete noun (that is, something you can actually see in your mind's eye) for each *thing,* and do likewise after each use of *this*. This tactic (see?) will make your essay clearer and will point you toward better showing details.

Topic Six: When should I use *who* or *whom* and *that*? First of all, *that* always refers to animals or objects, never to people. "A person that" is never the best way to express the idea; "A person who" is. If you have trouble choosing between *who* and *whom,* try substituting *he* or *she*. After all, *who, he,* and *she* are all Subjective or Nominative Pronouns while *whom, him,* and *her* are all Objective pronouns. This substitution may not make complete sense, but the one that makes better sense is usually right.

Topic Seven: How do I know whether to use a comma after the introduction to a sentence? Pages and pages have been written on this topic in grammar workbook after grammar workbook, but in an emergency, your best bet is to rely on the following: read the sentence aloud, and if you pause after the introductory element, place a comma there. If you do not pause, don't put a comma there. Generally you will not pause before verbs, so a sentence like "Winning the lottery, has always been my goal" has an unneeded comma, even if you feel the urge to pause after *lottery*. Also, when the word after the pause is a FANBOYS word, see Topic Four.

Topic Eight: How do I choose between *to* and *too*? The standard rule is that *too* always means "very" or "also," as in "I was too tired to water my garden" (very tired, indeed) or "Eli was tired, *too*" (also). If for some reason you have difficulty making this determination, try the *"tuh"* test. If the to/too can be pronounced *"tuh,"* as in "together" or "today," use *to*. If the to/too cannot be pronounced *"tuh,"* use *too*. For example, consider the sentence "Kinga is going to/too win a medal, to/too." In the first instance, we may say that "Kinga is going 'tuh' win a medal," so the proper form is *to*. We cannot, however, say that "Kinga is going to win a medal, 'tuh,'" so the proper form is *too*.

Topic Nine: How do I avoid overrelying on *which*? If you find yourself writing sentences that read "Agatha picks at her teeth with her fingernails, which annoys me," you will probably sense that you want to develop a better habit. A much better way to handle this sort of sentence is to replace *which* with *a _____ that*. Use a specific noun to fill in the blank. In other words, a revised version of the example would read "Agatha picks at her teeth with her fingernails, a habit that annoys me." As you can see, the second sentence is much clearer.

Topic Ten: What do I do if I am a weak speller but may use my dictionary only at the end of the time given?   One habit that students find helpful in dealing with sloppy spelling but limited dictionary access is to put a mark such as a small circle above each word that they think they may have misspelled. Of course, this technique will not help you very much if you think you may have misspelled *every* word!

If you have twenty or so words (just to pick a number) that puzzle you, place that small dot or circle above each. Then, when you are allowed to use your dictionary, begin with the first dotted word, and verify its spelling in your dictionary. Proceed in order. Draw a neat line through each dot or circle as you feel more confident about your spelling.

One good reason to use this particular technique is that it may allow you to build goodwill with your readers. For example, if you read a paper with ten misspelled words in the first half, with all of them corrected and corrections noted, while ten misspelled words remained in the second half, what might you assume? There is a very good chance that you would assume the writer simply ran out of time and would have corrected *all* the misspellings if given a little more time. This presumption could very well work in the writer's favor as a professor or a committee assigns the essay a grade.

You will probably come up with more "emergency" questions regarding your essays, but your instructor will be the best source for answers pertaining to them. For now, you have a list that discusses ten areas that cause major problems for students and that, hopefully, offers some practical solutions that you may use. As you begin writing practice timed essays, try applying these "rules." Also record any others that occur to you or your classmates. The more you practice, the more familiarity you will develop, and this familiarity may very well be what separates an unsuccessful essay from a successful one or a somewhat successful essay from a very successful essay.

A Real Persuasive Letter: The Job Application Letter

U nless we win an enormous jackpot from the lottery or a long-lost relative dies and bequeaths us a fortune, all of us will need to work at careers in order to survive. Careers today often require much stronger writing skills than they did a few decades ago. Fortunately, this new emphasis on workplace literacy gives those of us who prepare an opportunity to "sell" ourselves by showing off our skills. For many careers, the first time we turn our writing skills to the profession will occur when we write a letter of application.

Communication Triangle for Job Application Letter

A job application letter, like virtually any letter, has a specific audience, the recipient. Because the letter targets an individual audience, it is a pure example of "you" based writing. Before you write the letter assignment for this chapter, you will engage in a series of activities culminating with your selecting the actual recipient for your letter. To write a successful letter, you will need to know or make well-educated guesses about what this person wants to read.

> The Assignment: Writing a Job Application Letter
>
> Aim or Purpose: Persuasive
>
> Audience: Someone who is in a position to hire

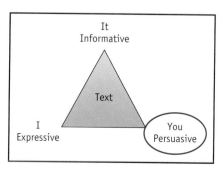

Part One: Researching a Career

Step 1: Visiting a College Career and Counseling Center

Perhaps you have known for several years what you want to be when you "grow up." Perhaps, on the other hand, you are like the majority of college students who change majors several times before they graduate and then change careers at least once after they graduate. In either case, one or more visits to your college career and counseling center may be help you to gain some important insights into a prospective career or careers.

If you are a student at a large university, your career and counseling center may occupy an entire building and may conduct workshops on résumé writing, interviewing, and even using the World Wide Web for career research. If you attend a smaller school, the career and counseling center may be less comprehensive. In this latter case, you may have more success visiting a state or county employment agency. More than likely, however, your college has at least some fairly good resources for performing a career search—if you use them wisely.

The obvious first step is to locate your college's career and counseling center. You may have received information about it in your orientation packet at your school. If not, your teacher or advisor should be able to help you find it. Once you know where the career and counseling center is located, you are ready to investigate the best ways to use it.

Various counseling facilities operate differently, so you should now learn the "rules" regarding what your college offers. Do counselors accept walk-ins? Do they require appointments? Is an orientation to the facility a mandatory activity before talking to counselors? Phone or visit your center with these questions in mind. It may be that you will be able to see someone right away. Do not be surprised, however, if the first person who greets you sets up an appointment for a later date and/or for an orientation workshop.

Ask questions about the resources and activities available to students. Often a counseling center will have a computer instrument, such as the Myers-Briggs Type Indicator (MBTI, a personality assessment), or a booklet like the Self-Directed Career Search (SDCS) to help start your research. While no such instrument is an infallible evaluation of what you should do with your career, the Myers-Briggs may give you some very helpful information about yourself, including confirmations of traits you have long understood. If the counselor asks you to use one or more such instruments, enjoy the opportunity. After all, psychometricians and other professionals often charge clients hundreds of dollars per hour to administer similar instruments!

Once you have taken the MBTI, the SDCS, or whatever other assessments the counselor recommends, sit down to discuss the results and ask questions of your own. If some of the results seem unclear, ask the counselor to help you interpret them. If your results seem radically different from what you expected, consider what this fact may mean. For example, the MBTI may describe you as an extrovert and may give you a list of careers that involve working with groups of people while the career you had in mind may call for much more solitary time. An extrovert who wants to be a computer programmer would seem to offer such an instance. This information does not mean that you should give up on your goal of becoming a computer programmer; however, it may well mean that you should look for a job in an office that allows you to work extensively with other programmers and/or that you should plan to have an active social life away from work.

You may decide to return and employ the instrument a second time, just to account for variances in mood. After you have performed a number of activities that you or, ideally, you and your counselor both consider appropriate, make a short list of careers that seem suited for you. Ask the counselor for any available handouts regarding these careers. At a minimum, this first step should result in your having at least a rough idea of one or more careers that seem to suit your skills, aptitudes, and temperament. You may also have made a professional connection with your tutor that will serve you well later on in your academic career, particularly as you approach graduation.

Step 2: Interviewing a Practitioner

As you well know, no test taken in a purely academic environment will give you everything you need to know about a career. Such knowledge comes only with years of experience. Fortunately, you may "borrow" at least some of the necessary information by interviewing a person who is currently a practitioner in the field that interests you. If you are interested in pediatric medicine, a pediatrician will be an obvious and useful source. The same applies to a diesel mechanic if that career appeals to you. By locating and interviewing the practitioner, you may save yourself hours, weeks, even months of lessons learned the hard way later on.

If you want to become a cosmetologist and your next door neighbor and best friend owns a salon, this step will seem very easy to you. If you want to become a meteorologist and the only meteorologists who are familiar to you are the ones you see on television, this task will appear more daunting. In any event, however, you don't want to dash off, pen in hand, ready to conduct your interview until you have engaged in proper preparation.

For openers, what do you want to ask the practitioner? An obvious question for many will be "How much money do you make?" Unfortunately, unless you happen to be *really* good friends with the interviewee, this question will probably be considered rude and will ruin the tone of your interview. That doesn't mean you can't indirectly ask it. If you know that your subject has taught history for ten years and has a masters degree in the subject, you may come around to asking, "After a decade or so in the field and a graduate degree, what sort of salary may I come to expect?" Chances are that the answer you receive will be at least a close approximation of your interviewee's salary. This question will seem much more reasonable than its alternative, however, because you will have used more tact.

Some people are shy about interviewing other people, especially those whom they don't know very well and when they know that certain questions (such as those related to salary) are taboo. Take heart from one piece of advice that is demonstrated very often and very well: except for certain extremely personal subject matter, most people love to talk about themselves. Most people also are at least reasonably comfortable in their jobs and will more likely than not be pleasantly surprised that another person wants to hear about the work they do. Consider this notion as you prepare a list of "user-friendly" questions to pose to your practitioner.

Activity: Develop a List of Questions

In your notebook, list no fewer than ten questions a practitioner could answer in such a way as to help you decide whether a particular career is for you and, if so, what are some good pieces of knowledge to have in pursuing it. Compose your questions with tact in mind and also with the certainty of knowing that most people will be glad to share most information with you. As a matter of fact, the person who would have to kill you if she revealed the specifics of her career is largely a myth invented by fiction writers!

————————

Now that you have this list, take a few minutes to review it. Are there any glaring omissions, questions that you absolutely must ask for your interview to be successful? Have you included any questions that, on second thought, might be too personal or seem too nosy to elicit good responses? Err on the side of caution in this area. Finally, if your subject answered all of your questions in some detail, would that give you enough information to form a fairly clear mental picture of what the career looks and sounds like? Revise your list as you see fit.

Collaborative Activity: Sharing Lists of Questions

Working with a small group (three to five) of your classmates, compare lists of questions. Although you may all be pursuing different careers, certain basic questions will be appropriate for any of several careers. As always, be willing to steal or have questions stolen from you. Time spent developing your list fully now may save you the time and inconvenience of endless follow-up interviews later. And while people generally do enjoy talking about themselves, they may well tire of talking over and over to the same person! Use your classmates as a sounding board for all of your questions, and add, subtract, or otherwise revise so as to develop the best list possible.

———

Now that you have developed what you hope will be a comprehensive list of questions, the time has come to choose a subject. If you are the student whose best friend and neighbor owns the salon you'd like to buy in five years, your choice of subjects is rather obvious. For most people, such will not be the case. In any event, begin with your and your family's friends and neighbors. Contacts that you have already established—your eighth grade math teacher, your internist, the manager of your favorite grocery store—are usually your best subjects if your chosen career is, respectively, middle school teaching, internal medicine, or retail management.

If you cannot select a subject so quickly, use other sources. The Yellow Pages of the phone book list services by occupation. Maybe you'll recognize one of the names listed for your prospective career. If not, people's general willingness to talk about themselves will still persuade many people you "cold call" to open up to you—once they know for certain that you do not intend to sell them anything! Certain career schools (such as those for cosmetologists or morticians) and certain government services employ professionals (such as meteorologists) who will have both the knowledge and, most likely, the willingness to discuss their career with you. If all else fails, go on the World Wide Web, and look for professionals in your field, be it horticulture or psychiatry. Many professionals or businesses have web pages with links that allow you to e-mail your "requests" (in this case, your questions). However you manage to do it, find a professional, and find a way to interview that person. If you are completely stumped, ask your instructor for help.

You will want to remember a few pointers as you set up the personal, telephone, or on-line interview. First, respect the professional's time and willingness to help you by working around his or her schedule. Second, come well prepared, with politely worded questions that help you gain the information you want. Third, be flexible; if your interviewee takes a question and goes into an area of discussion you hadn't previously considered but that may be very helpful, quickly adapt your questions to gain the additional information your subject is offering. Fourth, take good notes, but don't keep your nose buried in your notebook; people like eye contact. Fifth, before you begin the formal interview, ask your subject's permission to tape or video record the session, and supply your own equipment (including batteries). If your subject declines, take especially good notes. Sixth, at the end of the interview, ask your professional if she or he would mind being contacted at a later date (specify a range) for a follow-up after you digest the information you have received this day. And seventh and most important, relax and enjoy the interview. Your cheery mood will help put your subject at ease and will enable you both to function at your absolute best. Besides, this assignment should be fun for both of you. Keep it that way.

After you have conducted your interview and any necessary follow-up conversations, you should now know a great deal more about the career than you did when you first walked in to your college's career and counseling center some time back. Now you are ready to go to the library!

Step 3: Library Research

To this point, you have learned some general information about your aptitude for various careers and some very specific information about an individual's career. The next step is to visit your college's or your community's library and discover the information contained there.

Individually, with a few friends from class, or (if your instructor so arranges it) as a class, go to your college's or community's library. If your instructor has arranged a tour, you will simply follow along with the directions given. If you go alone or with just a few classmates, you may find the library a daunting place. One excellent way to remove some of the fear and begin your work productively is to approach a reference librarian. These are the librarians who usually work behind a clearly marked desk or counter and are extremely knowledgeable about the books that are used so often that no one is allowed to check them out.

A reference librarian can help you locate career information in many sources. These include the government, encyclopedias, and reference materials that describe specific careers. He or she will also know how to use the *Reader's Guide,* an exhaustive list of articles from popular periodicals over a given time period. Finally, if your library has good computer resources, the reference librarian will show you the electronic catalogue, various databases, and a variety of on-line publications or reproductions.

Topics that you will want to research during your visit to the library vary. You may want to learn about salaries in your career both in your hometown and in other places around the country. On the other hand, you may want to find out whether your chosen career is considered a "hot" field for the next decade. Additionally, you may want to compare job prospects in the field from region to region or even around the world. Your choice of topics for this library research is basically between you and your instructor. Remember that at all times you are primarily interested in information that will help you learn as much as possible about the career and how to "sell" yourself as a candidate for it.

Before leaving the library, you will need to locate one resource in hard copy (as opposed to exclusively on-line) and reproduce it. It may be a chart, an extended definition, or an article. You may originally find it online, but if you do, you must also find it in a physical periodical in the library. If you cannot find the article physically in the library and if time permits, request that the library obtain a copy from another library via interlibrary loan. The reference librarian should be able to tell you how long this process will take.

Step 4: Locate On-Line a Job in Your Career

If you have ever used the World Wide Web, you know how much fun it can be. With a computer, a modem, and a phone or network, you have millions of pages of information literally at your fingertips. You also have millions of jobs at the same place. For example, using your computer, a friend's, or one made available by your college, log on, and enter *www.yahoo.com* in the space provided for web addresses. Then, click on the word "job," and follow a series of links until you reach a page called "YAHOO! Employment." In May of 2000, this page's link for "Job Search" said "1,000,000+ jobs nationwide." That means that this one search engine alone had information on over a million jobs! For a more specific search, at the page *www.yahoo.com,* type in the name of the career you are pursuing, a plus sign, and the word "jobs." Leave no spaces: for example, pharmacist+jobs. Although you won't find a million openings for pharmacists, you will find more than enough to whet your interest.

Here are several other web addresses that have connections to jobs:

www.ajb.dni.us/ (America's Job Bank)—nearly 1.5 million jobs in May 2000

www.monster.com/—over 380,000 jobs in May 2000

www.HeadHunter.net/—over 190,000 jobs in May 2000

www.excite.com/

www.lycos.com/

www.hotbot.com/

Many corporations and trade associations also post job openings on their web sites.

Depending on which web page you visit, you will find a variety of job-related services (résumé writing, relocation, interview techniques, negotiating, franchising, etc.) that can help you be professionally successful. You may want to save (or "bookmark") some of the pages and links for later reference. In the meantime, you have one very specific assignment for Step 4: locate a *real* job that is currently open in the field you have chosen for yourself.

Use your imagination, and be creative. Have you often dreamed of living in Hawaii, Italy, or Montana? Find a real job that is currently accepting applications and that is located in your dream spot. Or do you actually happen to be searching for a job right now in your own hometown and would love to find out where your skills and the position are a perfect fit? Then use every search engine until you find just what you want, or at least something very close. Remember: there are literally millions of real jobs listed on the World Wide Web, and if you are diligent, you should find one that really appeals to you. When you have done so, you will be ready for this chapter's main assignment: the persuasive job application letter.

Part Two: Writing the Persuasive Job Application Letter

Three Ways to Persuade: Ethos, Logos, and Pathos

As we have noted, the job application letter is an example of persuasive, or "you" based, writing because it carries the fundamental question, "Won't you please hire me?" Ironically, although you select your prospective job by using a very modern technology, the World Wide Web, you will craft your letter applying for it using strategies that are millennia old. In fact, the rhetorical strategies *ethos, logos,* and *pathos* go back to Aristotle, a philosopher, critic, educator, and rhetorician who lived in Ancient Greece over 2,000 years ago. Aristotle developed these strategies primarily for use in oral discourse, but they have proven just as effective in writing. You'll see.

First, let's examine what each of these words means in terms of the letter you are about to write. **Ethos,** a term which resembles the modern English word *ethics,* refers to the character of the writer or speaker. In making an effective speech, an Ancient Greek orator wanted his audience to see him as a morally upright person; likewise, you wish to present yourself as having the ethics to be a conscientious employee. You will not want to develop ethos by sounding boastful; as a matter of fact, a boast such as "You will be very lucky to get a person like me to work for your company" not only establishes bad ethos, but it has an unintended double meaning that makes its writer sound lazy as well.

Good ethos usually comes from simple statements about your work ethic, your commitment to being on time, and your willingness to do whatever is proper to present yourself and your employer positively. Of course, this fact does not mean that you list in your letter every time you helped rake a neighbor's leaves, nor does it mean that being a good person alone will qualify you to be a day-care manager. Hence, once you have established your ethos, you must move on to give a strong logos.

If **logos** reminds you of *logic,* you have made a wise deduction. And, in fact, a persuasive letter is an example of *deductive* rather than *inductive* writing. Using inductive thinking, you look at a person, experience, or idea in a variety of ways before you decide what you want to say about it. You were behaving inductively when you walked into your college's career and counseling center with an open mind about what the assessments or interviews might tell you. Deductive logic begins with your mind already made up about a fact ("I want this job") and depends upon a rhetorical device known as a **syllogism,** which consists of three parts—a major premise, a minor premise, and a conclusion—to make your case. Consider the following syllogism proposed by Aristotle:

Major premise: All men are mortal.
Minor premise: Socrates is a man.
Conclusion: Socrates is mortal.

Just as the Ancient Greek *rhetor* used syllogisms to make his point, you will do likewise in your letter. Your working syllogism will, no doubt, resemble this one:

Major premise: A credible applicant for your job will have certain attributes.
Minor premise: I possess those attributes.
Conclusion: Therefore, I am a credible candidate.

As long as you have the logos to back up the minor premise, you will have a good syllogism (and, perhaps, a good chance at the job).

As you can see, logos refers to the reasoning in an argument. The major premise is usually taken for granted, but the minor premise must be proven. In this case, you must establish the facts or qualifications that make you a credible candidate for the career. If you happen to be a good person who has also taken coursework in early childhood education, worked as an aide in a day-care center, and moved up recently to assistant manager, these facts would be part of the good logos you would present in your letter.

A Word about Logos and Logical Fallacies. It is very easy, especially if you happen to listen to a lot of political dialogue, to make logical fallacies that severely undermine the logos of your work. Three of the most common fallacies are the *argumentum ad populum,* the *argumentum ad hominen,* and the *hasty generalization.* Before we proceed beyond logos, it is important for you to take a quick look at each of these fallacies and learn to avoid them in your letter.

What strikes you as not quite right about each of the following assertions?

1. I have worked hard to overcome my birth into poverty, and I will do an excellent job as accounts manager for you.
2. My boss at my last job will undoubtedly give me a bad recommendation, but he is just a jerk.
3. My evaluations as a stock clerk were excellent for three consecutive years; therefore, I am ideally suited for retail management.

The problem with the logos in the first statement is that there isn't any. While we all admire a person who works hard to overcome poverty, that doesn't necessarily make us want to put the person in charge of managing accounts. The person in this statement appeals entirely to ethos, suggesting that he or she is a good person indeed, but saying nothing about qualifications to manage money. This statement is an example of the *argumentum ad populum* (literally, argument to the people) as often occurs in political commercials like "Wayne Gage is an excellent husband and father. Vote for him for senate."

The second statement contains some logos, but it is really bad logos. It may sometimes be important to point out that you will be receiving a negative review from a previous employer and why. Prior immaturity on your part, a personality conflict, and, yes, even an irascible employer are all potential reasons. However, the person who wrote this assertion made no effort to argue that the negative evaluation was unmerited; instead, the writer attacked the personality and the ethics of the previous employer. This is an example of the *argumentum ad hominem* (literally, argument against the man), which you can expect to see any even numbered November, in something like "Wayne Gage used marijuana once as a teen. The man is utterly unethical and unfit for office."

The third statement is troubling for another reason. It starts off with logos, and good logos at that; three consecutive excellent evaluations speak to the person's professional competence and do so in a factual manner. The problem is that the fact given here (the evaluations) does not quite support the conclusion drawn (qualifications for retail management). It is entirely possible that the writer truly is an excellent stock clerk because of a meticulous attention to the most tedious detail, strong hand-eye coordination, and the ability to work very well in solitary endeavors. None of these characteristics (except possibly attention to detail) is important in retail management, where a person must make quick decisions, work primarily using her brain, and work surrounded by people. In fact, the person has mentioned none of the qualifications associated with management but has instead concluded hastily that skill at one retail job will inevitably lead to skill at another retail job. We call this fallacy *hasty generalization*.

Now let's improve each of the three fallacious statements given:

1. Although I was born into poverty, I worked very hard unloading trucks at night to put my way through school, and I am prepared to work very hard as a shipping clerk for your firm.

2. One of my former employers may give me a negative evaluation. Please consider that evaluation in context with the positive evaluations I received from other employers and the documented fact that I twice requested transfers to a different supervisor before leaving that company.

3. I have received excellent evaluations for three years as a stock clerk. Now, with your permission, I would like to begin training

to operate the cash register with an eye toward demonstrating my "people" skills and possibly moving toward management.

Perhaps you will agree that each statement is much stronger and demonstrates better logos the second time around.

The Final Ingredient: Pathos. As you have seen, a good ethos and a logos that avoids logical fallacies are crucial in writing a persuasive job application letter, but they alone may not be enough to get you the job. Your reader may think, "Gee, what a nice person" and "Hey, this person has some good qualifications," but you want your reader to do more than that. You want your reader to invite you for an interview, which you hope will lead to your reader actually hiring you for the job. For this reason, it is also necessary to use an appropriate amount of pathos in the letter. **Pathos** does not translate as easily into English as ethos or logos, but the word *passion* is a fairly close cognate. Pathos means that you want to arouse the passions of the reader, here possibly a human resources manager, sufficiently that the person picks up the phone, calls you, arranges the interview, and begins thinking in terms of the salary and benefits package to offer you.

You appeal to pathos by making the audience believe, in his or her gut, that something good will happen to that employer or that the employer will have made a noble decision by pursuing your possible employment. Although you may be thinking, "Please hire me," you don't say so in exactly those words because to do so would be to grovel, and that would constitute bad pathos. Good pathos requires that you show that you want the job and will make it well worth the employer's while to hire you.

Getting Started on a Résumé

Before you begin writing the persuasive job application letter, you need to make one very important decision. Perhaps your instructor's specific assignment will make this decision for you, but you need to decide whether or not you will actually mail the application letter. If that is the case, you will need to write a formal résumé, and it will need to be meticulously accurate in terms of past and present achievements, with the only reference to the future given in the job you seek. This letter will focus on who you are, what you have accomplished, and why you should stand out among all the applicants for a particular position.

On the other hand, you may be satisfied with your current working situation and may choose to write the letter applying for a job for which you hope the degree and experiences you have not yet gained will eventually qualify you. In that case, it would be wise to date the letter far enough in the future to give yourself time to have met certain goals (a degree, certification, work experience, etc.) along the way. You will also need to suspend your disbelief slightly in assuming that the job will still be available then!

Whichever decision you or your instructor makes, at least a mock résumé will help you gather specific ideas. If you do not intend to mail your letter, your mock résumé may be in the form of a jot list of accomplishments that you reasonably hope to have achieved by the time you would mail such a letter. You should know the best qualifications for the job from reading the ad but especially from visiting your college's career and counseling center, going to the library, and most of all, interviewing a practitioner.

It is very important, however, to draw a distinction between empty boasts of impossible achievements and realistic goals that you will set for yourself over the next two, five, or ten years. In fact, one of the reasons for doing this research is to help you plan out what you hope to accomplish over such a period of time. If, for example, you learn that admission to medical school requires at least a 3.6 grade point average, you should not only write that figure in your mock résumé, but you should also set it as a target for the rest of your college career. Likewise, if you learn that people who spend a semester doing a co-op in a computer field are much more likely to get the good jobs than people who do not, you will want to begin scheduling the term when you will have the best opportunity to pursue such an opportunity. Use your mock résumé to set realistic goals for yourself over the remainder of your college experience, and consider posting this "Goals 4 years from now" list next to your desk where you do your homework.

You will do wisely to divide your résumé into labeled sections, such as education, experience, references, personal, etc. Examples of résumés should be available in your college's library or career and counseling center. If you actually mail your letter and apply for a job, you will need to use résumé writing software, résumé advice from your college's career and counseling center or an Internet site, or a source recommended by your instructor. If you do not plan to mail the letter, you may leave your résumé in mock form. Certain items that you absolutely must include are your full name, address, a convenient phone number to reach you (and preferably not your pager!), and your e-mail address (if applicable).

Activity: Mock Résumé

On a sheet or two of notebook or legal paper, create a mock résumé.

Next you will find three letters written by students responding to this assignment. The students who wrote their letters to employers in New Jersey and California did not mail their letters; on the other hand, the student who wrote about an FBI internship did. Two students wrote their mock résumés and their letters to discuss only the accomplishments they had made at the time they wrote the letters while the other projected about one year into the future. In other words, the logos of two letters consists of goals accomplished, not set for the future, while the other does include future goals. Two of the students, Kari Beaty and Travis Williams, wrote their letters as teenaged students who had graduated from high school less than a year earlier. The other student, Peggy Kistler, was a 30-something returning student. We have changed the students' addresses and other geographically identifying information to protect their privacy. As you read each letter, focus on the ways it appeals to ethos, logos, and pathos. Then prepare to answer the questions that follow.

Student Model #1: Kari Beaty

March 17, 1999

Kari Beaty
1800 Sky Drive
Anytown, US 11111

TP (Cyber-recruiter)
The Wella Corporation
12 Mercedes Drive
Montvale, NJ 07645

Dear TP (Cyber-recruiter),

I am responding with regard to the Customer Service Coordinator position listed on the Internet. I am very interested in this position and would like to take this opportunity to provide you with my qualifications.

In 1998, I graduated from South County High School with a College Prep Gold Seal. Maintaining a 3.0 or above GPA for two years of high school enabled me to join the Beta Club. For three years I was part of the JV and Varsity squads of the Cheerleading team. While cheering, two years in a row, I was voted "Most Valuable." During my sophomore through senior years, I was selected for Who's Who of America's high school students. I was also part of the DECA club while I was a senior. During my senior year I left school at 11:20 every day to go to work.

Presently, I am working for a prestigious hair salon called Salon 248. I have been working here for approximately eight months as an apprentice to the hair stylists and also as a receptionist. I began the apprenticeship with the desire of becoming as knowledgeable of this industry as possible. Through this I have learned a lot about communication and many interpersonal skills. Currently I am also attending America Community College with the goal of earning a degree in Business.

I am planning on being in New Jersey the week of April 3, 1999. If at all possible, I would like to set up an interview. You may contact me at (555) 555-1212 at any time. Thank you for your time.

Respectfully,

[signed]

Kari Beaty

As listed with hotjobs.com:

The Wella Corporation
Customer Service Coordinator (Part-Time)
#Cust. Service
03/12/1999
Part-Time Position, Flexible Hours!
Montvale, NJ

Job Description:

- *In this position you will provide proper service to customers, consumers and employees.*
- *Ensure timely processing of orders, debits, credits, returns and inquiries.*
- *Tentative schedule is Monday–Friday, 10:00 am to 2:30 pm, with a 1/2 hour for lunch.*

Requirements:

To qualify, you must have 3–5 years of order entry/customer service experience. Strong communication/interpersonal skills. The ability to excel in our fast-paced environment. Strong computer skills. SAP knowledge a plus!

Company Background:

*Wella is a Worldwide leader in the **Professional Haircolor, Permanent Wave and Haircare** Industry, selling in over 140 countries around the world. The Wella Corporation is a $2 billion worldwide leader in hair-care products and cosmetics with headquarters in Germany, with over 16,000 employees in more than 100 countries.*

Only Qualified Applicants Will Be Contacted.

Environment/Benefits:

Wella offers a competitive salary and excellent benefits package, along with growth potential . . . Our corporate culture is relaxed, yet fast-paced.

Looking good means good-looking hair.

JOIN OUR TEAM!
If you want to be a part of the excitement at WELLA, you can apply for this position via Hotjobs, or mail your résumé and cover letter to TP(Cyber-recruiter):
12 Mercedes Drive
Montvale, NJ
07645.
Please specify hotjobs job code above.
Wella Corporation is an Equal Opportunity Employer. M/F/D/V.

Now look at the way Peggy Kistler "applied" for a different job.

Student Model #2: Peggy Kistler

March 13, 2001

Peggy Kistler
300 Marianne Circle
Anytown, US 11111
Kistler@noserver.com
(555) 555-1212

County of San Bernardino
Human Resources Department
157 West Fifth St.
San Bernardino, CA 92415

Dear Human Resources Manager:

I am writing to apply for your Social Worker 1 position advertised on *www.headhunter.net*. With thorough college training in behavioral and related studies, varied social service experience, and proven ability to work efficiently, I believe I could be an asset to your staff.

To prepare adequately for a social worker career, I have completed 30 semester hours of humanities and social sciences at the University of America, with a grade point average of 3.8 (on a 4-point scale). I studied four foreign language courses in Spanish and Russian. In addition to the humanities and social science courses, I have also completed two computer courses that will be useful to your company. My studies in speech and communication enable me to present clearly the reports and social services you require for this position.

Since your department specializes in adult services and children services, I believe I could be of special benefit to you because of my interest and work in this area. At age 19 I was preparing food baskets for geriatrics who could not manage on their own. My responsibilities included organizing the appropriate foods, keeping equipment records, reporting allergies and diabetes, and delivering food baskets. After my two children started school, I became actively involved in the PTA, Girl Scouts, and coaching my son's softball team. In September of 1995, I joined a core group for the Children's Aid Society Foundation. My responsibilities included raising funds for activities and counseling children who have been neglected or physically or sexually abused.

I am currently employed at Helpful Treatment Facility as a youth counselor (supervisor). I direct and supervise 25 staff members who provide educational guidance procedures and techniques to improve quality of services.

Serving as head counselor of the family support group required honesty, personal conviction, and a strong desire to help people. These qualities will be an important part of my code of ethics and public relations. By referring to my current employer and references, you will be able to form a more complete idea of my personality.

Will you please contact me at the above address to name a time when I may come, at your convenience, to talk with you about being your staff social worker? I am usually home after 5:30 p.m. each weekday.

Respectfully,

[signed]

Peggy Kistler

Enc. Employer, Volunteer work, and Personal References

Note: The enclosures have been omitted as they do not significantly affect the letter's content.

As posted on HeadHunter.net:

Social Worker I

Details	
Description:	Work for the Department of Aging and Adult Services or Children's Services. Evaluate the social, physical and mental functioning of clients; determine eligibility and social service needs; provide ongoing case management; and maintain records and reports. Travel throughout the county is required. Bi-lingual and older adults are encouraged to apply. A written test will be given on March 25, 1999.
Requirements:	Requirements: 30 sem. units of completed college coursework in a behavioral or social science AND 1 yr of experience interviewing clients to assess human service needs and explaining social service rules and policies. Applicants may substitute an additional 15 sem. units of qualifying coursework for the required experience. Application must be made by completing an Original County Application. Résumés will NOT be accepted as a substitute. Deadline: March 1, 1999. Apply to: County of San Bernardino, Human Resources Department, 157 West Fifth St, San Bernardino CA 92415. Telephone: 909-387-8304 or visit Web site at http://www.co.san-bernardino.ca.us
Required Education:	None
Required Experience:	Rookie
Required Travel:	Up to 25%
Job Type:	Employee-Full Time
Location:	US-CA-San Bernardino
Relocation Covered:	No

Compensation	
Base Pay:	$27,300–$34,900/Year
Other:	health insurance and retirement plans
Contact	
Company:	County of San Bernardino
Email:	Send An Email
Name:	
Phone:	
Fax:	
Contact Type:	Employer/Company
Reference ID:	RJ99146
Miscellaneous	
Categories:	Bilingual, Counseling, Social Services
Last Change:	1999/02/12 12:34:02

Finally, let's take a look at the letter that was actually mailed, Travis Williams' application to participate in an FBI internship program.

Student Model #3: Travis Williams

Travis Austin Williams
980 Student Boulevard Apt. 1321
Anytown, USA 10011

Federal Bureau of Investigation
Suite 400
2635 Century Parkway, Northeast
Atlanta, GA 30345

Dear Department of Human Resources,

As a result of reviewing your web site at *www.fbi.com,* I became very interested in your position of special agent in the field of anti-terrorism. From the information that I have obtained, this area of law enforcement holds great appeal to me. Although I am not at this time qualified (by reason of age and education), I hope you will be so kind as to assist me with my endeavor.

I am very interested in your internship program. I understand this involves three months of summer work, shadowing a current agent in the field. I believe I meet all the qualifications. Having maintained at least a 3.0 GPA during both high school and college, I believe I have the mental capability necessary to fulfill the responsibilities and duties associated with the intern program.

My previous employment experience has exposed me to several areas of working with and supervising others. I enjoy being a team player as well as being a team leader. The first two months I was employed at

Corky's BBQ restaurant, I was employee of the month. After three months, I was in charge of training new employees as well as performing supervisory duties.

At Aeropostale, a clothing retail outlet, I was originally a sales person part-time for two years. After exploring other avenues of part-time employment, I returned to Aeropostale and shortly thereafter was promoted to the position of key-holder (a person who has opening and closing responsibilities and a set of keys to the store). After approximately three months, I was promoted to assistant manager. The position of assistant manager involves performing all the duties and responsibilities relating to store operations including handling money, deposits, record keeping, inventory control, and general management functions.

Employment with the FBI holds great interest for me. I strongly desire to become a special agent once I have reached the appropriate age and education levels. For now, I want to obtain acceptance into the internship program, either this summer or next. My current supervisor informs me that I will be granted leave without pay for the period of the intern program. The leave of absence would allow me to participate and then return to my studies and work responsibilities here in Anytown.

Any assistance you might be able to provide me or additional information that would help me in this endeavor would be greatly appreciated. Thank you for your time and consideration in this matter.

Sincerely,

[signed]

Travis Austin Williams

[FBI Field Offices Addresses & Telephone Numbers]
56 locations in major U.S. cities and Puerto Rico
Revised 10/20/98

Retrieve Alphabetically by City
[A] [B] [C] [D] [E] [H] [I] [J] [K] [L] [M] [N] [O] [P] [R] [S] [T] [W]

Some of our Field Offices have Home Pages. You'll find the links to these Home Pages on the "CITY" name.

A
Federal Bureau of Investigation
Suite 502, James T. Foley Bldg.
445 Broadway
Albany, New York 12207
(518) 465-7551

Federal Bureau of Investigation
Suite 300
415 Silver Avenue, Southwest
Albuquerque, New Mexico 87102
(505) 224-2000

Federal Bureau of Investigation
101 East Sixth Avenue
Anchorage, Alaska 99501
(907) 258-5322

Federal Bureau of Investigation
Suite 400
2635 Century Parkway, Northeast
Atlanta, Georgia 30345
(404) 679-9000

B [Arrow]
Federal Bureau of Investigation
7142 Ambassador Road
Baltimore, Maryland 21244-2754
(410) 265-8080

Federal Bureau of Investigation
Room 1400
2121 8th. Avenue N.
Birmingham, Alabama 35203
(205) 326-6166

Federal Bureau of Investigation
Suite 600
One Center Plaza
Boston, Massachusetts 02108
(617) 742-5533

[FBI Seal]
Special Agent
Employment
Support Employment
Honors Internship
Benefits

FBI Divisions &
Offices

Vacancies

FBI Employment
Home Page

[Honors Internship]

[Navigation Links]

[Qualifications]

Each summer, a special group of outstanding undergraduate and graduate students are selected to participate in the FBI Honors Internship Program in Washington, D.C. The Program offers students an exciting insider's view to FBI operations and provides an opportunity to explore the many career opportunities within the Bureau. At the same time, the Program is designed to enhance the FBI's visibility and recruitment efforts at colleges and universities throughout the United States.

[Honors Intern]

FBI Home Page

QUALIFICATIONS

Honors Internship

Qualifications

Application
Requirements

Application Time
Frame

Selection Process

Things You
Should Know

Due to the very selective and highly competitive nature of the Honors Internship Program, a limited number of internships are awarded each summer. Only individuals possessing strong academic credentials, outstanding character, a high degree of motivation, and the ability to represent the FBI upon returning to campus will be selected. In order to be considered, individuals must meet the following qualifications:

* Undergraduate students should be enrolled in their junior year at the time they apply to the Program.
* Graduate-level students must be enrolled in a college or university and attending full time.
* Students must be returning to their campus following the Program.
* Students must have a cumulative grade point average of 3.0 or above.
* All candidates must be United States citizens.

Collaborative Activity: Letter Evaluations

1. In groups of three to five, discuss and list at least three ways that each writer appeals to ethos, three ways that each writer appeals to logos, and three ways each appeals to pathos.

2. Do you think that all three writers have adequately presented themselves as ethical people? What might they do to improve in this area?

3. Do you think that each writer has given sufficient reasons to interview and possibly hire him or her? What additional information would be useful?

4. Do you think that each writer has given the reader a reason, in her or his gut, to pursue the application? What would improve this area for each?

5. Do the style and language make you want to know more about Kari, Peggy, and/or Travis? Why or why not? What else might each say, or how might she or he say it to draw you in more fully?

As you write your own persuasive job application letter, use the respective strengths and weakness of the letters written by Kari Beaty, Peggy Kistler, and Travis Williams to guide you toward your best possible work. When you have finished your first draft, give it to two or more classmates to review with you. Focus your review on ethos, logos, and pathos. Where does grammatical correctness belong in this discussion? Why?

Grammar and Usage: Verb Tenses

We often need to be very precise about the time when actions happen. Just imagine lawyers, judges, and litigants trying to sort out "what happened on the evening of July 15?" if we had no way of clarifying which completed action happened before another completed action. In the following example, the past progressive (was walking) and past perfect (had eaten) tenses allow us to express information precisely:

On July 15 at nine p.m., I was walking to the restaurant where I had eaten dinner.

As you read the following examples from this chapter, note just how precise writers can be if they understand the various verb tenses. Consider, also, how the meanings might change, were the authors to use a different tense.

1. I **am** very interested in your internship program. (current action— present tense)

2. After three months, I **was** in charge of training new employees as well as performing supervisory duties. (completed action—past tense)

3. These qualities **will be** an important part of my code of ethics and public relations. (action will occur—future tense)

4. I **am responding** with regard to the Customer Service Coordinator position listed on the Internet. (continuing current action—present progressive tense)

5. I **have been working** here for approximately eight months as an apprentice to the hair stylists and also as a receptionist. (action began in the past, is still occurring, and is continuing—present perfect progressive tense)

The Present, Past, and Future Tenses. The following chart shows the basic past, present, and future tenses.

1. Use present tense for action that is currently happening, or that happens habitually or regularly.

I wash my clothes. (happens regularly)
My brother lives here. (current action)

2. Use past tense for action that has happened and is now over or complete. Most verbs (regular verbs) form their past tense by adding *–d* or *–ed*.

   I washed my clothes yesterday.
   My brother lived here.

3. Use future tense for action that is yet to happen. In general, form the future tense by combining *will* with the present form of the verb.

   I will wash my clothes Tuesday.
   My brother will live here.

Past	Present	Future
I worked	I work	I will work
you worked	you work	you will work
he, she, it worked	he, she, it works	he, she, it will work
we worked	we work	we will work
you worked	you work	you will work
they worked	they work	he, she, it will work

The Perfect Tenses. The next chart shows the past, present, and future perfect tenses. Make these forms by using the helpers *had, has,* and *have* with the past participle of the verb. Add *–d* or *–ed* to the present tense form of the verb to create the past participles of most (regular) verbs.

1. Use present perfect tense for an action that began in the past and continues into the present.

   I have washed clothes all day. (started in the past and continues)
   My brother has lived in Omaha for three years. (lived there in the past and still does)

2. Use past perfect tense for actions in the past that came before another action in the past.

   I walked my dog down the street where I had walked her the day before.
   My brother had lived in Europe before he moved to Omaha.

3. Use future perfect tense for action in the future that will happen before another event in the future.

   I will have passed this class by the time I graduate.
   My brother will have lived in Omaha for 10 years in May.

Past perfect	**Present perfect**	**Future perfect**
I had worked	I have worked	I will have worked
you had worked	you have worked	you will have worked
he, she, it had worked	he, she, it has worked	he, she, it will have worked
we had worked	we have worked	we will have worked
you had worked	you have worked	you will have worked
they had worked	they have worked	they will have worked

The Progressive Tenses. This final chart shows the past, present, and future progressive tenses. Use the progressive tenses to tell about an action occurring in a particular moment in time or to describe a continuing action. To make the progressive tenses, combine a form of the verb *to be* with a present participle (created by adding –*ing* to the verb).

I am writing you a letter now. (present progressive)
I was writing you a letter when you walked in. (past progressive)
I will be writing you a letter while I watch TV. (future progressive)

Past progressive	**Present progressive**	**Future progressive**
I was working	I am working	I will be working
you were working	you are working	you will be working
he, she, it was working	he, she, it is working	he, she, it will be working
we were working	we are working	we will be working
you were working	you are working	you will be working
they were working	they are working	they will be working

Note: The perfect tenses can combine with the progressive tenses to create a past perfect progressive, a present perfect progressive, and a future perfect progressive.

By the time I got my glasses, I had been seeing poorly for many years. (past perfect progressive)
My sister has been seeing the same doctor as me. (present perfect progressive)

Two Cautionary Notes

1. Many verbs are irregular, which means that they don't form their tenses the way most verbs do. The most irregular verb in the English language is *to be,* which is irregular in both the present and past tenses:

Some Forms of "to be"

Present tense	*Past tense*
I am	I was
You are	You were
He, she, it is	He, she, it was
We are	We were
You are	You were
They are	They were

Many other verbs do not form the past tense by adding *–d* or *–ed.* Some of these verbs are *buy (bought), bring (brought), dig (dug), leave (left), break (broke), draw (drew),* and *write (wrote).*

2. You should try to be consistent and keep to one tense unless there is a good reason to shift a verb to a different tense. Unnecessary (and generally unnoticed by the writer) shifts in tense (starting out in present tense and suddenly shifting to past, for example) may cause annoyance and possibly confusion in your readers. Of course, sometimes you may need to discuss something that happened at another time, and in such cases, changing that particular verb to a different tense is totally warranted.

Exercise 1

Directions: Combine each group of sentences into one complete sentence without any mistakes in verb tense. **Note:** You may have to change some of the tenses or even add words to clarify when actions are happening. Be creative with this one!

1. John and Bob went to the baseball game.
   John and Bob sit in the stands.
   Bob caught a foul ball.

2. I study all night.
   I took a math test the next day.
   I receive an A.

3. I am loving cats.
   I am loving dogs.
   I hate snakes.

4. It was raining outside.
   I do not have an umbrella.
   I get wet while walking to my car.

5. Josh has bought a new car.
   Josh washes the new car.
   It is raining on the new car.

6. The sloth was slow.
   The sloth had three toes.
   The sloth had been climbing up a tree.

7. My car had broke down.
   I had my car towed to the shop.
   I will pay the mechanic.

8. We had planted a tree.
   We watched the tree grow.
   The tree fell during a storm.

9. I should stay home today.
   I don't feel good today.
   I can't wait to get home.

10. Dad will be working with computers.
    Dad will be interrupted.
    Dad had been angry.

Exercise 2

Read over one or two essays you have written, and find two or three examples of shifts in verb tense. What is the reason for each shift? If there is no reason to change tense, then you have found an error!

Be a Critic: Writing a Restaurant Review

What Is a Critic or Critique?

Maybe it's a romantic dinner. Maybe it's lunch with a few friends, fellow students, or coworkers. Maybe it's just a day to avoid hot stoves and dirty dishes. Either way, most of us eat away from home more than our great-grandparents ever would have imagined.

Whenever we decide to eat out, we have a dizzying array of choices: Fast food? Italian, Chinese, or Mexican? Steak? Barbecue? Deli? Vegetarian? Check the local Yellow Pages, and chances are you'll find restaurants and cafeterias that you never even knew existed. To stay in business, each of these establishments must appeal to some group of customers.

Once you decide what kind of food you want to eat, you're ready to head out, aren't you? Not exactly. Let's say you come in from softball practice and decide that you really have a taste for a thick, juicy steak. Sam's Steak Shack may be just the place for you—if Sam happens to have his grill fired up at 3 P.M. on Saturdays. The alternative—Elegant Eats, the steak house that is closest to your home—requires semiformal attire. Would that be a good place for you, a sweaty teammate, and her four-year-old child to dine today? Before you go anywhere, you need to decide whether you want to dress up, where you can find a babysitter on short notice and whether your friend really wants to pay for one, and whether you want to drive 30 minutes to Sam's place. So you call Sam's, only to find that he shuts down on Saturdays from 2:30 until 5 P.M. Then you realize that this time you'll have to compromise your taste for steak by indulging yourself, your friend, and the screaming, hungry child on fast-food hamburgers. Meanwhile, you contemplate dinner reservations next Saturday at Elegant Eats.

This scenario is a reminder that we often must consider several factors when we decide to eat out. Not only must we decide what we want to eat, but we must also ask ourselves what we want to wear, how far we want to drive, and whom we will take with us. Then we will need to make sure that a restaurant we may want to visit is open when we want to go there and whether or not it requires reservations. And if the friend we want to take with us has never eaten at this particular place, she may need some additional information before she can decide to visit it.

As you can see, we need some information before eating out, especially when we try a new restaurant. One place we find such information is in restaurant reviews, which we can find in newspapers and magazines. As you work through this chapter, you will become a real dining critic as you perform real-life research in a real restaurant and produce a real restaurant review.

Keep in mind that *reviewer* and *critic* mean nearly the same thing, and *review* and *critique* mean nearly the same thing. In everyday usage, when we say "Don't criticize me," we mean "Don't speak negatively about me." But the word *criticize* has a broader definition that may include pointing out positive as well as negative characteristics. In this sense, *to criticize* means *to evaluate*. As a dining critic, you will inform your readers about a restaurant; then, you will either recommend or not recommend this restaurant to your readers.

Communication Triangle for a Restaurant Review

From the previous sentence, you may by now have inferred that reviews have a dual purpose: they are at once informative and persuasive. Let's review for a moment. Remember, one angle of the writing triangle represents expressive, or "I"-based writing. When we write expressively, we write with the primary purpose of presenting ourselves or our feelings. Frequently, our audience is ourselves as well. An example of pure expressive writing would be a diary or journal entry. Another angle represents informative, or "it"-based writing. When we write informatively, we write with the primary purpose of making sure we pass some information along to our readers. An example of pure informative writing would be a list of events. The last angle, then, represents persuasive or "you"-based writing. Our primary purpose when writing persuasively is to convince our readers to believe what we believe and/or to act the way we would like them to act. In your restaurant review, you will tell about a restaurant of your choosing (inform), and you will recommend that your audience try this restaurant or not try it (persuade).

The Assignment: Reviewing a Restaurant

Aim or Purpose: Informative and Persuasive

Audience: A specific target audience of your choosing

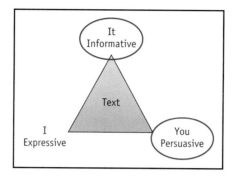

Step 1: Gathering Ideas

Brainstorming

Remember that brainstorming is one of several techniques we have discussed that may help you get started on any writing project. When we brainstorm, we simply list everything that comes to mind on any given topic. We do not allow ourselves to be concerned with quality at this point—whether or not, for example, the ideas are any good. We just want to come up with as big a list as possible.

Activity: Brainstorming

1. In a group of three or four, brainstorm a list of characteristics of a positive dining experience.

2. Now brainstorm the qualities of a negative dining experience.

3. From these two lists develop a large list of qualities diners look for when eating out. Some possibilities might be clean silverware or prompt service.

If you haven't already done so, it is now time to choose a particular restaurant; furthermore, if it is a chain, choose one particular location. You must also decide on a target audience. In other words, narrow your audience to a specific group. Will you be writing to college students like your classmates? Will you write for people with children? Will you write with senior citizens in mind? What type of audience will you keep in mind as you gather information and write your restaurant review? Finally, choose a time to visit the restaurant and collect notes. Before you go any further, complete the following:

Name of restaurant: _____

My target audience: _____

When I will visit: _____

Activity: A Target Audience

Look back over your list from the third brainstorming activity. Which of the qualities you listed would your target audience particularly care about? Which qualities would not be important to your target audience? Cross out those qualities that would not be important.

▬▬▬

From the remaining items on your list, you can now develop a criteria sheet that you will use to gather specific information when you go to the restaurant. Here is an example of a criteria sheet. You may use ours or adapt your own, freely adding or subtracting as you see fit.

🗀 Worksheet: for Restaurant Review

1. Write the address of your restaurant.
2. What does the restaurant look like?
3. How many customers can the restaurant serve at one time?
4. When is the restaurant most crowded? Least crowded?
5. Describe the restaurant's furnishings, including tables, chairs, wall hangings, and any memorabilia.
6. How much privacy does the restaurant offer? Is this level of privacy suitable for your audience?
7. Describe the restaurant's lighting and overall ambiance.
8. Describe the noise level in the restaurant. Would the noise level be appropriate for your audience?
9. Comment on cleanliness in the restaurant. Include tables, floors, bathrooms, and so on.
10. On your visit, did you enjoy prompt service? Did you enjoy polite service?
11. Where is the restaurant located? Would your audience find it easy or difficult to locate the restaurant? How could you best give directions?
12. Describe the restaurant's parking arrangements. Would they be suitable for your audience?
13. Does the restaurant limit itself to a particular variety of food (such as Italian, Chinese, or Mexican)? Is its menu eclectic? Would its offerings be adequate for your audience?
14. What food items would you recommend, and why? Which items would you not recommend, and why?
15. How much does food cost at the restaurant? Give specific prices.

Now visit the restaurant, and don't forget to take along your criteria worksheet, a couple of blank pages in case you need more room for notes, and a couple of pens. Do not try to rely on your memory. Take down as much specific information as you can. Observe carefully and look for very specific details. Remember that sensory details will let readers "get into" your review. Be sure to make note of what you see, hear, feel, taste, and smell, as you will need these details to make your review interesting for your reader. Look at the following examples of weak versus strong details.

Weak Detail	*Strong Detail*
Dirty	Three bugs crawling on the wall (see)
	Hand sticks to salt shaker (feel)
Loud	Metallica and AC/DC blaring from juke box (hear)
Smells good	The aroma of meat roasting on mesquite coals made my stomach growl as I approached.
Tastes good	Bread pudding had a melt-in-your-mouth richness

If you dress up a bit and carry a briefcase, they may even think you are working for the local newspaper! So consider potentially superior service a possible benefit of doing this assignment.

Step 2: Organizing Ideas

Focusing

After you return from your outing, look over your notes. Hopefully, you have much more information than you can possibly use in your review. As always, the next task is to decide which details you should include and which you may leave out. In other words, you must focus on what is most important to your audience.

Activity: Focusing by Drawing Details

From your notes, choose five details about the restaurant that you believe your audience would find particularly significant. An example might be that you saw spots on the knife and on the spoon. No matter how well, draw pictures of these five details you noticed on your visit to the restaurant. Then show your pictures to a classmate, and ask him or her to give you a "word picture" to match what he or she sees. Write down some of the key words you hear, and use them in your review.

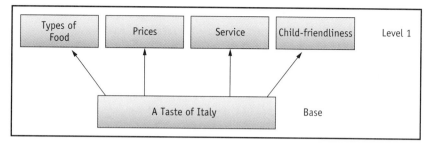

Figure 10.1 Beginning a Chart Outline for a Restaurant Review

Chart Outlining

One way to organize your details is by using a chart outline. Begin a chart outline by drawing one big rectangle near the bottom of the page. Then write your topic inside this rectangle. Next draw three arrows up from the rectangle leading to more rectangles (or squares, if you prefer). Inside these next rectangles, write down only the most important three to five qualities of dining for your target audience. This is Level One of your outline, which breaks down your topic into subtopics. You will have to make some choices here. For example, you may choose types of food, prices, service, and child-friendliness as qualities most important to a family with children under the age of 10 (see Figure 10.1).

Now you know your restaurant review will be well organized because you know what point you will discuss and support in each of four body paragraphs (or sections). You will also list the main points left to right in the order that you will discuss them in the body of the review. In this case, you may decide to save the quality of "child-friendliness" for last because it could be the most important point for an audience of parents dining out with children under age 10.

Now are you ready to begin writing? First of all, try to include the specific details you focused on in the previous activity. Then review the details you noted during your restaurant visit, and add those that are both appropriate and specific. See Figure 10.2 for an example.

As you might have guessed, you may even continue a chart outline to a Level Three. Above "pizza," for example, you might list vegetable toppings, meat toppings, and specialty pizzas. Above pasta you could list spaghetti, lasagne, ziti, and tortellini. Just as you had to decide which qualities of many are most important to your audience, you also decide how far to expand your chart outline.

Organizing by Using Narration

A second option is to organize your essay in narrative or story form. In other words, consider writing your restaurant review as a story that begins

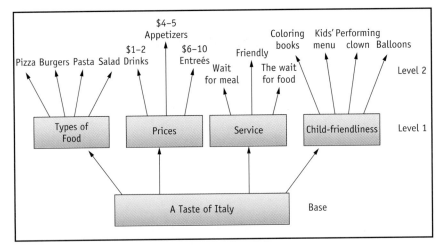

Figure 10.2 Adding Detail to a Chart Outline for a Restaurant Review

as you arrive at the restaurant and ends when you leave. If you choose to write your review this way, you will use chronological order. Along the way, be sure to include the information that is of key importance to your target audience.

Activity: Studying Real Restaurant Reviews

Clip two restaurant reviews from newspapers or magazines, and bring them to your next class meeting. The newspapers in most major metropolitan areas feature restaurant reviews on the weekends. In groups of three or four, share these reviews and decide how they are organized.

Step 3: Writing

Writing from a Chart Outline

You are organized and ready to write a restaurant review. Remember that your job is, first, to inform your audience about a restaurant and, second, to recommend whether or not your audience should invest time and money in the place. If you organize from a chart outline, you will focus on a particular quality in each body paragraph. One student, Kyrie Mendonca, used the chart outline method and produced the following restaurant review.

Student Model #1

Restaurant Review

By Kyrie Mendonca

1   Steer House Steakhouse is a great restaurant for dating couples. The amount of parking is very sufficient. I recommend the Timmersville location off Timmersville Hwy. Southbend Mall is just around the corner. The environment offers some privacy, and the noise level is not too loud. The best time to go is Sunday through Thursday before 7 p.m.

2   Steer House offers a variety of foods such as shrimp, chicken, burgers and salmon. The restaurant also has a wide variety of appetizers and drinks. It costs about $40–$45 for a full meal for two. I recommend the shrimp platter for $12.99 or the 16 oz. steak for $16.99. Both of these orders come with a salad, vegetables and baked potato. Frozen mixed drinks are about $4–$5 each. The prices are not outrageously high.

3   Furthermore, the bathrooms, tables, and floors were exceptionally clean. The waitress smiled often, and always asked, "Can I get anything else?" This was great service, for the restaurant was closing in about an hour. The environment had soft lighting and a low noise level. A variety of music played in the background. The restaurant also had TVs so the customers could watch the baseball game. There is a non-smoking section available too.

4   In addition, the décor of Steer House is attractive. The restaurant has a western theme. Many areas have wooden carvings of cowboys and Indians. The curtains have cows printed on them. The wooden floors match the wooden tabletops. In another area, fish hang from the ceiling. This restaurant also has many pictures of farm animals hanging on the walls.

5   Finally, Steer House is a great place for a dinner date. All the different scenery opens ideas for conversation. The food definitely is tasty. Prices are reasonable for two people. After dinner a couple could sit at the bar. They could watch the game and have a drink. This is a way to get to know one another better. I recommend this restaurant to anyone going on a date. It is a fun place to eat.

Writing with a Narrative Structure

A second option is to use a narrative or story form. Here is an example of a restaurant review, written by a professional journalist, a food critic, who uses narrative or story form to organize his ideas.

Professional Model

Ah! Asian
Crossroads Flavors Are a Wonder

By John Kessler
The Atlanta Journal-Constitution *Friday, June 19, 1998*

1   I don't remember a lot about my trip to Penang, the Malaysian island famous for its resorts. I remember the stomach-churning ferry trip over the Strait of Malacca. And I remember then immediately embarking on an hour-long taxi ride from hell, over winding dirt roads at an insane speed, during which time the driver introduced me to durian. You know durian? It's a pulpy yellow tropical fruit notorious for its stench. The cabbie had warm and sticky chunks of it he retrieved from the trunk.

2   Green for days after my high-speed durian encounter, I had no interest in the exotic food everyone else was eating. The only dish I could face was "chicken rice": wonderful, elemental pieces of marinated chicken served cold with a mound of seasoned rice and a little pot of spicy-sweet chili sauce. No suspect fruit. No gushy texture. Perfect.

3   I was thrilled to discover chicken rice again at Penang Malaysian Cuisine, a popular new Buford Highway spot. Then again, I was thrilled to try all the other dishes I missed in Malaysia. This crossroads cuisine—in which Chinese, Thai, Indian and native Malay dishes vie for attention—fills Penang's menu with a mind-boggling selection. You can start with Indian roti pancakes, Malaysian pickled vegetables with peanut sauce or duck web in spicy Thai sauce. Then move on to an entrée of Cantonese rice porridge with pork and preserved egg, barbecue fish in banana leaf or Singapore-style fried noodles.

4   Penang is the first outpost of a New York-area chain owned by the Cheah family, with two more scheduled for Washington and Chicago. The Cheahs have a smart formula that goes beyond the 150-item menu. They outfit the restaurant as a hip-tacky tropical beach that will put you in mind of Trader Vic's. You walk through a pitched bamboo roof, past the open kitchen where a chef stretches roti dough to impossible thinness and into a dining room set with plastic banana trees and walls covered with seaside murals. Blond hardwood floors and matching tables keep things from getting too goofy, as do the sleek waitresses in black leotards with colorful sashes around their waists.

5   Service appears to be the weak link of the concept, judging by the Chamblee staff. One time I had to get up and hunt down a server after a pregnant wait. Another time a waitress came to the table chewing something, didn't write down a thing and then screwed up the order. They bring the food at an awkward pace, and they hurry off before you can say a word.

6   Granted, they're busy. Word went out fast on Penang, and a mixed crowd of Asians and Westerners generally throngs the room waiting for tables. People here laugh loudly and chow down intently, and the energy feels palpable. This good vibe makes up for the chilly reception.

7   Every table apparently starts with an order or three of canai roti, those house-specialty pancakes with a side chicken curry dip. It's a texture thing, with all gradations of soft to crisp represented in the translucent folds of dough. Others in the know get a platter of achat, the sweet-spicy pickled veggies with a drizzle of peanut sauce. Or the shrimp puffs: minced shrimp wrapped in bacon and fried so perfectly you'd think there was a Southern grandma in the kitchen.

8   The skinny beef satays are fine, but the "satay tofu" is a revelation—crisp, hot wedges stuffed with cool, crunchy sprouts and cucumber and smeared with thick peanut sauce.

9   Since much of this food comes from a street-stall tradition, there are a number of "rice dishes" designed to provide a full meal on one plate. Nasi lemak pairs mild coconut rice with heartily spiced chicken curry (look for the whole cloves and cardamom pods), tiny anchovies tossed with onions in a sweet-sour-spicy tamarind sauce, a hard-boiled egg and refreshing chunks of unwaxed cucumber. Too weird? Then try my favorite Hainanese chicken rice.

10   There are also showy centerpiece entrees, such as a beautiful red snapper fried whole, slathered with spicy shrimp paste and wrapped in banana leaves. Beef rendang, the famous coconut curry that cooks so long the meat absorbs the sauce, should share the limelight. But Penang's version wastes a lot of cloves, cinnamon and time on gristly pieces of meat. Eight hours in the pot, and you still can't chew it.

11   Nor did I care for the coconut curry soup, a whole lot of noodles in a sharp, one-note broth. I much preferred the fine Cantonese-style clear soup, in which Chinese broccoli and innumerable pork-and-shrimp wontons float.

12   The key to successful ordering at Penang is this: Never stop exploring and don't overlook the dishes that seem too boring or too strange. Then you'd miss the desserts. The peanut pancake folds a roti over and over a filling of honey-sweet ground peanuts and ends up tasting like a divine Bit-O-Honey bar.

13   The ice kacang is a huge mound of shaved ice drizzled with rose syrup and coconut milk. As you dig deeper, you find many weirdnesses buried in the bottom: Kidney beans, corn, palm seeds and blobs of grass jelly. Yes, it's a bit like someone dumped a Sno-Kone over vegetarian chili. But I liked it.

14   As long as I stay away from durian, I think I like everything Malaysian.

**PENANG
MALAYSIAN CUISINE
OVERALL RATING: B**

- **Food:** B+

- **Service:** C

- **Atmosphere:** B

- **Address, phone:** 4897 Buford Highway, Suite 113, Chamblee. 770-220-0308.

- **Hours:** 11 a.m.–2 a.m. Mondays–Fridays; 10 a.m.–2 a.m. Saturdays–Sundays.

- **Price range:** Appetizers, $2.50–$7.95; entreés, $4.75–$17.95.

- **Credit cards:** Visa and MasterCard.

- **Recommended dishes:** Canai roti, satay tofu, shrimp puff, achat, nasi lemak, sambal ikan bilis, pangan ikan, peanut pancake, ice kacang.

- **Wine list:** A few bottled beers.

- **Reservations:** Yes.

- **Kids:** Not a problem.

- **Parking:** In lot.

- **Handicap access:** Full.

- **Smoking policy:** Separate smoking section.

- **Noise level:** High.

- **Takeout:** Yes.

Notice the boxed information published with Kessler's review. Critics frequently put additional information into a chart alongside or following their reviews. You may also want to include such a chart.

Now here is a restaurant review written by a student who has modeled her essay on one similar to the review you just read. She also uses a narrative pattern in relating a rather "hair-raising" experience at a local pizza establishment.

Student Model #2

Enrico's Pizza Palace Is Fit for a King. . . .
Not!

By Judy McQueen

1   Enrico's Pizza Palace Pizza has always been my favorite pizza, and still is. To me, Domino's, Little Caesar's, and Hungry Howie's could not compare to Enrico's thick crust, savory sauce pan pizzas. While Domino's and Little Caesar's offer only carry-out service, you have the option to eat in at Enrico's as well as to carry it out.

2   Several months ago during our hustle bustle baseball schedule, my family, another couple, and their son were very hungry, had no time to cook, and decided to have a scrumptious, mouth watering pizza. We chose Enrico's Pizza Palace because it was just minutes from our location.

3   On this weekend night, the restaurant, which holds a maximum of eighty people before being considered a fire hazard, was packed. As we patiently waited on the stick-to-your-legs, red vinyl covered bench seats, watching young kids playing video games while the juke box blared, our friendly waitress was ready to seat us for what ended up being an evening we will never forget.

4   It was not hard to decide what we wanted since my family is very fussy. I like my pizza with all the veggies, but, to make everyone happy, we ordered our usual: a large thick crust, deep pan pizza with extra sauce, thinly sliced mushrooms, spicy pepperoni, and ground beef.

5   As we sat conversing back and forth, our waitress finally delivered our steaming, cheese and sauce smothered pizza to our table. We had not discovered yet that we had an extra topping. As I took the wooden handled spatula to cut into the first piece of pizza, I spotted that extra ingredient. With a look of confusion on my face, I noticed short, curly, black hairs within the layers of our toppings. The only person I know who sheds while eating is my hairy father, but he was not dining with us that evening. I kindly asked the waitress (whose name I cannot remember) to look and see what I had discovered. An expression of shock was on her face, and she said we would have a fresh pizza right away. In the meantime, our friends were devouring their steaming hot, thin and crispy, hairless pizza, while we stared, foaming at the mouth.

6   Sitting patiently again, I saw something moving out of the corner of my eye. I ignored the thought and blamed my imagination on my hunger pains. There it was again! I saw something move rapidly across the smooth surface of the windowsill. This time I was not the only one who noticed. Our company and our children all saw what I saw. We were being invaded by a brazen roach. This roach was unreasonably determined. It

would race back and forth and would not leave. We had this bug's table, and this critter wanted us out. My husband Jimmy picked up a table knife and crushed the pesty bug in between the windowsill and the white, brick ledge where we could see this bug's essential contents. Our lady friend, Rosie, placed her napkin over her mouth, gagging and heaving, so I decided to stuff my small white napkin into the crevice covering this unpleasant sight. By this time the table was in an uproar, but my family was hungry, and we had not received our hairless pizza yet. We decided not to let one little bug bother us; however, we did have to calm Rosie down.

7   Our waitress finally brought our pizza to our table just the way we liked it. While eating, my daughter Jennifer kept thinking about the bug. She told me repeatedly that she felt that bugs were all over her. I told her in not a very sweet manner to please be quiet and just eat. She wiggled and squirmed, and when she looked down a roach was crawling up her leg. She screamed a high pitched shrill that would make one's hair stand on end. This time, a different roach decided to join us. Jennifer jumped to her feet slapping the bug off her leg. We all decided that enough was enough and it was time to go.

8   While handing our bill to the manager, he asked us how our meal was. I sarcastically explained to him that, except for the hair in our pizza and the roaches we had to beat away with our silverware, everything was great. What more could a family of four ask for? He apologized and generously took three dollars off our tab. What a joke! I think I need say no more. But if you are in for a night of entertainment, or better yet, would like to get rid of your mother-in-law, then for certain, Enrico's will make it great!

The author, Judy McQueen, makes her thesis, or main point, very clear by including vivid sensory details that let us see, hear, taste and smell. In fact, at times we see, hear, taste, or smell a bit more than we would like! Although her review of this particular location is very negative, she does begin by saying that Enrico's pizza is still her favorite pizza.

As you read earlier, you may want to write up a chart for additional information. The author of our student essay included a separate page providing some information which did not fit well in the review, but which she felt was, nonetheless, important. On this separate page she provided the address of this restaurant, the hours, the setting, her recommendations from the menu, the price range, a kid's menu, reservation information, wheelchair access, smoking/nonsmoking information, and parking. She also noted that there are other locations of this chain where she would return.

Last she developed a "roach rating" system for evaluating this particular restaurant and experience:

Five, the worst, means the restaurant is infested, and the next time I go in a roach may be wearing an apron ready to take my order.

Four means there are bugs, but if that's okay with someone, then it's okay.

Three means not too bad, maybe just a part of a critter in the food.

Two means if it cannot be seen, don't complain.

And, last but not least, **one** means the one bug you see could have come in with someone.

Accordingly, she assigned Enrico's Pizza Palace a rating of

Step 4: Revising

You have arrived at the revision stage of the writing process. Remember that revising means reseeing, so you'll want to try to see your written draft as clearly as possible. As we discussed in previous chapters, you'll want to make your writing as distant as possible in order to see it most clearly. Try a few of the techniques listed in Chapter 4 such as reading your essay out loud or reviewing each paragraph separately and backwards, beginning with the final paragraph. Also consider, but do not limit yourself to the following points as you look for ways you can improve your restaurant review.

✐ Checklist: Revising the Restaurant Review

Seeing the Structure

1. Does the review have an introduction, a body, and a conclusion?
2. What is the thesis of the review? Is it stated directly? If so, where?

3. Does the body of the review support the thesis? If so, how?
4. Are the body paragraphs supported with specific details? Give examples.
5. Is the review organized? Does it use a narrative organization? Is it organized by categories?
6. Does the review clearly identify and locate the restaurant?
7. Are food items identified clearly? Give examples.

Seeing Polish

1. Is everything spelled correctly?
2. Are there grammatical mistakes such as fragments, fused sentences, subject-verb agreement errors?
3. Are there mistakes using punctuation marks such as periods, commas, question marks, and so on?
4. Are all words used correctly?

Collaborative Activity: Revising

In groups of three, take turns reading restaurant reviews out loud. Then swap papers. Use the revision checklist again, but this time consider your classmate's paper, and write down your responses. Swap papers again and repeat. Finally, give each of the other authors your written responses to their reviews.

Grammar and Usage: Commas

If you have difficulty using commas in your writing, you may very well suffer from one of two comma "syndromes": the "Yahtzee" disease or the "when in doubt, leave it out, and I'm always in doubt" malady. Writers afflicted with the Yahtzee disease believe that a good composition should have commas in it somewhere. Since, however, these writers don't know exactly where the commas belong, they shake them up in a cup and sprinkle them—Yahtzee fashion—across their compositions. On the other hand, students whose comma instruction has consisted mainly of "when in doubt, leave it out" almost always find themselves doubting whether or not to use a comma; therefore, they almost always avoid commas, hoping they will thereby avoid mistakes.

A better "rule" to follow regarding comma use is the following: understand clauses, and justify each comma accordingly. The "when in doubt, leave it out" writers have accidentally stumbled into one truth about commas, namely that you must always justify why you have used one. However, finding the individual instances when a comma is necessary isn't nearly as hard as either these people or the Yahtzee folks would have you believe.

Examine the use of commas in the following sentences from John Kessler's review.

> They bring the food at an awkward pace, and they hurry off before you can say a word.
>
> Since much of this food comes from a street-stall tradition, there are a number of "rice dishes" designed to provide a full meal on one plate.
>
> As you dig deeper, you find many weirdnesses buried in the bottom: Kidney beans, corn, palm seeds and blobs of grass jelly.
>
> Beef rendang, the famous coconut curry that cooks so long the meat absorbs the sauce, should share the limelight.
>
> Granted, they're busy.

Also, consider these examples from Judy McQueen's essay.

> The only person I know who sheds while eating is my hairy father, but he was not dining with us that evening.
>
> As I took the wooden handled spatula to cut into the first piece of pizza, I spotted that extra ingredient.
>
> My husband Jimmy picked up a table knife and crushed the pesty bug in between the windowsill and the white, brick ledge where we could see this bug's essential contents.
>
> We decided not to let one little bug bother us; however, we did have to calm Rosie down.

Remember that in all cases, you must *justify* the use of a comma. How might Kessler and McQueen justify each of the commas they have used? Do the comma rules below contain some answers?

1. Generally use a comma before a coordinating conjunction (FANBOYS word) combining two sentences.

2. If a sentence begins with a clause or phrase that starts with a subordinator (yellow light) or preposition, use a comma *after* that clause or phrase. (If the introductory phrase or clause is short, though, the comma may not be necessary.)

3. Whenever a sentence contains a list of at least three anything combined with a coordinator (FANBOYS word), put a comma after each item except the one after the coordinator. Exception: in journalistic writing, the last comma is omitted.

4. Whenever you use two consecutive adjectives or adverbs to describe something and *do not* combine those two words with a coordinator (FANBOYS word), put a comma between them if you sense a pause there.

5. Two sentences joined by a conjunctive adverb or transitional phrase (lawyer word) require a comma after the combiner as well as a semicolon before it.

6. Certain set expression, such as place names (Seattle, Washington) and dates (January 23, 1999), require commas between items.

7. A sentence that contains a word, phrase, or clause that interrupts the smooth flow of the sentence often requires a comma.

8. Sometimes you need to use a comma to help a reader avoid confusion. If you reread a passage and believe that it is worded clearly but needs a special pause for clarity, try a comma. Note: these commas should be the exception, not the rule.

Now let's use the list above to justify the commas used by Kessler and McQueen.

The first sentence taken from each essay uses a comma because it joins two sentences using a coordinating conjunction, or FANBOYS word. Kessler's is *and,* McQueen's *but.* Sometimes when the two sentences joined are very short, you may omit this comma, and journalists often omit it in any event; nevertheless, most of your college instructors will expect you to use this comma.

They bring the food at an awkward pace, and they hurry off before you can say a word.

The only person I know who sheds while eating is my hairy father, but he was not dining with us that evening.

Likewise, the second sentence taken from each essay begins with a subordinating conjunction, or yellow light. You may remember that sometimes words used as subordinators, such as *after* and *until,* may also be used as prepositions. That distinction is unimportant here. Whether Kessler's *since* or McQueen's *as* functions as clause connector or preposition, it still requires a comma since it occurs at the beginning of the sentence.

> *Since much of this food comes from a street-stall tradition, there are a number of "rice dishes" designed to provide a full meal on one plate.*

> *As I took the wooden handled spatula to cut into the first piece of pizza, I spotted that extra ingredient.*

The third sentence from Kessler illustrates rule 3. Everything after the colon is part of a list. Since Kessler is a journalist, he has not used a comma before *and* in this list. Most style guides for academic and published writing call for this "serial comma."

> *As you dig deeper, you find many weirdnesses buried in the bottom: Kidney beans, corn, palm seeds and blobs of grass jelly.*

McQueen's third sentence illustrates rule 4. The words *white* and *brick* both describe the *ledge*. Although it is not always the case that an author uses a comma between two adjectives when one is a color, McQueen decided that a comma would be helpful here, and we agree.

> *My husband Jimmy picked up a table knife and crushed the pesty bug in between the windowsill and the white, brick ledge where we could see this bug's essential contents.*

The final sentence from McQueen contains a conjunctive adverb (lawyer word), *however,* used to combine two sentences. Therefore, a comma is necessary *after* the combiner.

> *We decided not to let one little bug bother us; however, we did have to calm Rosie down.*

In his fourth sentence, Kessler mentions a dish, beef rendang, that most of his audience has probably never encountered. Thus, just as we did in the previous sentence, he interrupts the flow of his sentence to provide important information. In his sentence and in ours, you could omit the material between the two commas and still have a sentence. The sentence simply wouldn't tell you as much. Note that Kessler and we have put commas both before and after the interrupters.

> *Beef rendang, the famous coconut curry that cooks so long the meat absorbs the sauce, should share the limelight.*

Finally, Kessler's last sentence packs a lot of information into three simple words.

Granted, they're busy.

The word *granted* clearly makes sense in the context of the sentence, but try reading the sentence without a comma: Granted they're busy. Kessler has employed this comma because he thinks it makes the sentence easier to read. Whenever you see a similar situation arise, use a necessary comma, but remember the earlier warning: these commas are the exception, not the rule.

Exercise 1

Directions: Insert commas as needed in the following sentences.

1. I am exhausted so I am going to bed.

2. When you have finished using the computer, you must remember to save your work.

3. Eating fried chicken is bad for his cholesterol; however Ralph truly loves the taste of a crispy crust.

4. After we all went home we found the spaghetti and heated it up.

5. The team was leading the division; nevertheless they traded for another pitcher.

6. My neighbors' ferret sometimes thinks she is ours not theirs.

7. Fall Semester classes begin on August 24 2001.

8. The Unknown Soldier lies buried in Washington D.C.

9. A complete gourmet dinner consists of appetizer, soup, salad, main course, and dessert.

10. Satay which usually includes meat and a peanut sauce is a popular Thai dish.

11. John Gotti was known as the "Dapper Don" because he wore expensive well-tailored suits.

12. When you proofread always look carefully at verbs; otherwise your writing may not interest the reader as much as you would like.

13. Roaches in a restaurant are disgusting and restaurants with roaches probably don't do a lot of business for long.

14. Since Roberta had served our organization for many years we elected her President a richly deserved honor.

15. A Yahtzee cup holds dice well but you shouldn't put your commas in it!

Exercise 2

Look over a paragraph you have previously written, and circle all the commas. What was the reason for each one? If you cannot justify a comma, it is probably unnecessary.

Be a Critic: Writing a Book Review

Why Write a Book Review?

You are late to class or work on a Friday morning. You have brushed your teeth, showered, and prepared to dress for your day. You wonder how cold it is outside, so you grab the remote control and click on one of the morning news shows, which shows your local temperature at the bottom of the screen. As you reach into your closet, you hear a friendly voice telling you about the latest movie starring Julia Roberts. As you dress, the reviewer tells you a bit about what happens in this film, who stars in it with Julia Roberts, and why you should go see it tonight.

Most of us are familiar with such a scenario. Perhaps you have even seen whole television shows dedicated to film reviews. You are probably familiar with other types of reviews as well. You may have read, for example, book reviews, theatre reviews, restaurant reviews, art show reviews, and record reviews. You may have seen various types of reviews published in the Food, Art, or Leisure sections of your local newspaper. In addition, magazines frequently publish reviews of all sorts. Your college's newspaper probably publishes reviews.

Most of us have a limited amount of money to spend, and all of us have a limited number of hours in our days. Yet we are bombarded with a seemingly endless number of records to buy, films to see, books to read, and restaurants to visit, especially if we live or work in a mid-size or large town or city. And even in areas with fewer people, there are generally still more options than we can personally explore, especially with the advent of the Internet and the mind-staggering amount of information available on the World Wide Web. With a large array of choices before us, we depend on reviewers for help. Reviews, then, help us decide when, where, and how to spend our energy, our time, and our hard-earned money.

As you proceed through this chapter, you will write a review of a novel. Many people who write book reviews are professional journalists

213

although people in many different professions, including teachers, businesspeople, and chefs, may be asked to review new books. As a book reviewer, your job will consist of two parts. First, you must tell your audience what the book you read is about. You will give your readers a "taste" of the book, preferably without giving the plot twists away. In doing so you will tell about significant ideas in the book and certain key events. You may choose to include important characters and discuss their significance as well. Second, you will let your readers know whether or not you think they should take the time to read the book. And you will support this recommendation with specific reasons.

(Note: For an alternate assignment, see "Writing a Movie Review" in the Additional Writing Assignments section.)

Communication Triangle for the Book Review

Writing a book review involves focusing on both the "it" and the "you" angles of the communication triangle. The subject or "it" is the book you or your instructor chooses for you to read and review. You must inform your audience about this book. You will be equally focused, however, on the "you" angle as you persuade your audience to read or not read this particular book.

The Assignment: Writing a Book Review

Aim or Purpose: Informative and Persuasive

Audience: Someone who has not yet read this book

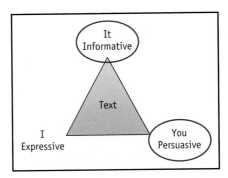

Step 1: Gathering Ideas

Choosing and Reading a Book

The first item of business in writing a book review is, of course, reading the book. At a newspaper, the editor will frequently assign reporters to read and write reviews of new books. Likewise, your instructor may assign you a book to review. He or she may even choose to assign the same book to your entire class. On the other hand, your instructor may give you the option of choosing your own book to review. Although reviews are most often published when a book is new, or when a book is updated in a new edition, you need not limit yourself to new books for this assignment.

Consider, but do not limit yourself to, this list of novels as you make your selection.

I Know Why the Caged Bird Sings by Maya Angelou

The Grapes of Wrath by John Steinbeck

Of Mice and Men by John Steinbeck

The Prince of Tides by Pat Conroy

Ordinary People by Judith Guest

The Joy-Luck Club by Amy Tan

The Hundred Secret Senses by Amy Tan

Song of Solomon by Toni Morrison

Beloved by Toni Morrison

Dinner at the Homesick Restaurant by Anne Tyler

Breathing Lessons by Anne Tyler

Your Blues Ain't Like Mine by Bebe Moore Campbell

A Separate Peace by John Knowles

Concentrating and Questioning

Have you ever read a couple of pages and said to yourself, "What did I just read?" Nearly everyone at one time or another has had this somewhat uncomfortable and frustrating experience. Don't feel bad if this experience is your most common experience. Reading takes practice like anything else. To avoid the problem of not remembering, learn to read actively. First, you need to be able to focus and concentrate while you are reading. Second, try to involve yourself in what you are reading.

Focusing can be difficult. Try to find a quiet space. If you live in a dorm, this may mean going to a study room, out to a quiet spot under a tree, or to a library. If you live at home with two toddlers who demand your attention, finding time and space will probably be even more difficult. Carry your book with you so that you can read at the doctor's office, while you wait to pick up your younger brother or child from school, or whenever you find some free time. Also, avoid reading in bed if you tend to fall asleep on top of your book! Many people read in bed specifically because they want to fall asleep! If they really want to read longer than ten or fifteen minutes, they often need to get out of bed.

The next challenge is to become involved as you read. One way to get used to this type of reading is by making notes in your book. There are many ways to do so, and we will discuss two. The first task is an important yet incredibly simple way to be involved. It is to create a list of characters on the inside front cover of your book. As you read, just add each and every character to the list. Another good way to become involved in what you are reading is by asking questions. At times during your reading of the book, you may not be sure what is happening in your book. This may be a problem, especially at the beginning. Our first response is to reread. Try this, but after reading a few pages two or three times, just go ahead. Don't feel that not understanding everything means you are a failure. Skilled readers learn to "go with the flow" and read on. You may find that things start to make sense later on.

Whenever you do not understand what is going on, write a question mark in the margin of your book and fold down that page, or jot down that page number on the back inside cover. These are exactly the items you should bring up in class. Then, when you read to the end of each chapter (or, if the chapters are very long, every 20 pages or so), write down two to four questions about what you just read. You may very well be able to answer these questions yourself. If you can't, then you will have these questions to ask in your next class meeting. Never be wary of asking these questions at your next class. Your doing so will show that you are studious and involved. Your classmates or instructor just may be able to answer the questions you develop, especially if several or all of you are reviewing the same book. Or they may very well lead your class to explore significant topics in discussions. Either way, you can may add an important contribution to class discussions.

Discussing

Class discussion will probably be an important part of your book review assignment. Be ready to contribute, and listen carefully to your classmates as they offer their opinions and interpretations. Try to relate what each of them says to your experience reading and to your book. If others are reading the same book as you, compare comments and questions frequently. Much of the enjoyment in reading comes from discussing, learning, and sharing with others. As you share more, you will find that you enjoy the reading more. The following worksheet contains discussion questions. Discussion questions do not necessarily have a right or wrong answer. They may be asking for your opinion. Be aware, though, that whenever you express an opinion, you will have to support it with specific examples from your novel. Discussion questions are frequently intended to lead to some disagreements among people who are reading the same book. They are supposed to evoke discussion!

📂 Worksheet: Discussion Questions for Novels

1. What is the significance of the title of the book?

2. Are there any symbols in the book? (A symbol is an object that has a special meaning.) Explain the importance of these symbolic elements.

3. What are the important themes in the book? (A theme is similar to a main idea.)

4. Who is the main character or characters, and what obstacles do they face in the book?

5. What is the setting, and what role does it play?

6. Choose three minor characters, and explain their importance to the main character or to the book itself.

7. Did any of the characters do anything that surprised you? Explain.

8. Do any characters change during the course of the book? Give two examples, and explain how these characters change.

9. Does the ending resolve conflicts or answer any questions? Explain.

10. Did the ending of the book surprise you in any way? Explain.

Writing Letters to Gather Your Thoughts

When we talk about characters in a book, we often speak of them as if they were real and alive. To understand a novel and its characters and themes better, it may be helpful to consider why the characters act as they do. In other words, it may help to consider their motivations. Writing a letter to a character may help you generate more ideas about the novel.

Activity: Writing a Letter to a Character

Choose either the main character or an important character in the book, and pretend this person is alive so you can contact him or her. Write a letter of approximately 300 words to this person explaining why you approve or don't approve of his or her actions in the novel. Try to use specific examples from the book as you make your points. You may assume that you have never met before, or may assume any relationship that you desire (i.e., distant relative of yours, friend, colleague.) Be creative and have fun with this assignment.

After you finish the book, try your hand at writing a letter to the author.

Activity: Writing a Letter to the Author

In about 300 words, write a letter to the author of the book. Feel free to say anything you like in your letter, but support your points with examples from the novel. You may want to express your opinions about the book. You may want to ask questions.

Step 2: Organizing Ideas

Focusing: Determining Key Events

A piece of writing that is as long as a novel contains a great deal of information. Your novel probably contains numerous characters and events. You should already have a complete list of characters in the front cover of your book. Now let's consider all those events that make up the plot of the novel. To understand the book and write a good book review, you will need to sort through all these events and determine which are very important, which are somewhat important, and which are relatively unimportant. If several of you have read the same novel, complete this activity as a group or in small groups. If you are the only one in your class reading a particular novel, complete the following activity yourself.

Individual or Collaborative Activity: Determining Key Events

List all the events you can remember from the novel in order as well as you can remember. Then take out the book, and use it as you add to your list. When you finish, read over your exhaustive list to make sure the events are in the order in which they occurred in the novel. When you have a complete list, cross through with one line those events that are least important to the main character. Then, from the events left on your list, put a check mark next to those that are most important to the main character. You may have no more than four events checked when you finish. If you check more than four events, cross out those that are less important until you have only four checked events left. These are the events that you believe to be most important to the main character.

———————

Completing the Form for the Book Review

You have now spent a good deal of time reading and thinking about a novel. You have read the novel, proposed questions about the novel, answered questions, discussed the novel, made a thorough lists of characters and events, and determined which events are the most important. You have also written letters to a character and to the author. You should feel confident that you have gathered many ideas and collected a great deal of information. Do not worry if you still have unanswered questions. If a novel left us nothing to think about, we probably would not appreciate it very much.

Your next step is to determine what exactly you want to say in your book review. Remember, as a reviewer you have two primary goals. The first goal is to let your reader know something about the book. The second goal is to recommend or not recommend it and give reasons for your opinions. Complete the following worksheet in as much detail as you can. For the first question do not respond with a name. Think more about issues like "family," "freedom," "identifying oneself," or "growing up." Your response to the second question, "What is the main idea?" may start with "The main idea of the novel is. . . ." You then complete the sentence. Your responses to the first two questions will probably be related. For example, if we say a novel is about freedom, then we might say the main idea of the book is that we must fight for freedom in all cases no matter what the cost. Take some time as you fill out the form as it will become the basis for your essay.

📁 Worksheet: Form for the Book Review

I. What is this book about? In other words, what is the topic of the book? (Answer in one or two words.)

II. What is the main idea of this book? (Answer in a complete sentence.)

III. List five events from the story (in order) that support your main idea from #II.

1.

2.

3.

4.

5.

IV. How does the book end? (Answer in a short paragraph)

V. What do you think was the author's purpose in writing this book? In other words, why do you suppose he or she chose to tell this particular story? (Answer in one to three sentences.)

VI. What is your opinion of this book? You must give several reasons for your assessment. (Answer in at least one paragraph.)

Step 3: Writing

You are now ready to write a rough draft of your book review. As you write, keep your book open to your responses on the Form for the Book Review Worksheet. You may write a positive review in which you recommend the book or a negative review in which you do not recommend it. Or you may write a mixed review in which you acknowledge both positive and negative attributes of the novel. You should, however, ultimately come down on one side or the other. Keep in mind, also, that the more mixed a review is, the harder it will probably be to write it. You will also need to remember to include transitions in your review so that the ideas will connect smoothly. This will probably be especially important as you discuss key events in the book. Use transitions like *first, next, second, third, later, meanwhile, before, after,* and *finally* within paragraphs.

Before you begin, write down a working thesis statement. Working means that you may go back and reword this statement later on as you write or as you are looking specifically to revise the essay. For a thesis statement you have a few options. You might, for example, briefly state whether or not you are recommending the novel and why. Your thesis statement might be a statement of the novel's main idea. Or the thesis statement might discuss the author's purpose in writing the novel.

Here are three examples of book reviews. Students authored the first two examples; a literature professor wrote the third. Notice how the authors Candace Harris, Christian Elliott, and James Polk tell us what the book is about, explain key events and how these events support their assertions, and discuss their recommendations about the book. You will also note that Harris and Elliott are reviewing the same book, Ernest Gaines' *The Autobiography of Miss Jane Pittman.* Both of these reviews are strong in different ways. After reading these examples and answering the questions that follow, write a rough draft of your book review.

Student Model #1

Book Review of *The Autobiography of Miss Jane Pittman*

By Candace Harris

1   "'You little wench, didn't you hear me calling you?' she said. I raised my head high and looked her straight in the face and said: 'You called me Ticey. My name ain't no Ticey no more, it's Miss Jane Brown. And Mr. Brown say catch him and tell him if you don't like it.'"

2   The quotation above comes from a very compelling two hundred and fifty-nine page novel, *The Autobiography of Miss Jane Pittman,* written by Ernest Gaines. In the above quotation, her mistress strikes her continuously asking her what she said her name was. Again and again Miss Jane answers, "Jane Brown." Clearly, this novel is about the life of a very courageous and strong willed woman by the name of Miss Jane Pittman, who lives to be approximately 110 years old, and she tells a wonderful story of her quest for Ohio. Ernest Gaines' purpose in this novel, designed to look like an autobiography, is to educate many about slavery and the fight for freedom up until the 1960s.

3   As the novel opens up, the slaves including the feisty Jane Brown learn of their freedom. As a result, she sets her goals on reaching Ohio, where Corporal Brown lives, the Yankee soldier who gave her the name Jane Brown. On her journey, she unexpectedly gets the responsibility of motherhood at the age of approximately ten or eleven years old. Because of the turning of events, Miss Jane realizes she has to be strong, for slavery is over but racism still exists, and she is all alone to raise a boy of about age five.

4   As Miss Jane Pittman continues her search for Ohio, she comes along many detours. She moves from plantation to plantation struggling to survive. During this time, anyone who stands up for what is right gets shot right down. Because of these actions, Miss Pittman sees many die, even those close to her. She never breaks down, but instead gets stronger and more determined. When the people around her are

getting into religion, she stays back. She says she doesn't have to be in church to give thanks to the Lord. The people think her a sinner for listening to baseball instead of being at the church. Miss Jane Pittman doesn't care a bit. Only when she is ready, then does she join the church, but even then she makes no secret that she still loves and watches baseball. Miss Jane Pittman is her own person, and she isn't afraid to let people know.

5   As the novel unfolds, Miss Jane Pittman is forced to make one of the biggest decisions of her life. If she stands up and fights for what is right, she may die like the others. If she does not stand up and fight, all the pain, suffering, and loss she has endured will have been for nothing, and the people will not understand the message that Gaines has been trying to relay.

6   In conclusion, I must say this novel is one of the best yet about slavery and the South. It tells of the travels of an extraordinary woman who is both strong and courageous. I truly believe this novel is for blacks, whites, mixed races, and all other races. Ernest Gaines achieves his purpose in educating people about slavery. Many people hear about what slavery was like in the South, but this novel actually puts the reader right there in Louisiana on the plantation with Miss Jane Pittman. You might ask, "Does Miss Jane Pittman get to Ohio?" or "Does Miss Jane Pittman ever find Corporal Brown?" or "Does she stand up and die?" or "Does she do nothing?" The only way to find the answers to these questions is to read *The Autobiography of Miss Jane Pittman*.

Now here's another review of the same novel.

Student Model #2

Book Review of *The Autobiography of Miss Jane Pittman*

By Christian Elliott

1   Ernest J. Gaines's *The Autobiography of Miss Jane Pittman* is an inspiring novel consisting of two hundred and fifty-nine pages. The novel is about a one hundred and ten year old woman, Jane, who is born during slavery and dies in the early 1960s, during the Civil Rights movement. *The Autobiography of Miss Jane Pittman* describes a woman's courageous battles and struggles through hardships. The novel shows how hardships can make people stronger inside and able to stand up for human rights and reach a destination whether it is physical or emotional. The purpose of Gaines's novel is to educate everyone about the hardships that many African Americans had to live through.

2   The novel opens by exploring Jane's childhood as a slave. Her slave name is Ticey until a Yankee soldier, by the name of Corporal Brown, renames her. Jane is so proud of her new name; it makes her feel important. When her mistress finds out about her new name, she beats her.

When Jane says, "My mistress got tired beating me and told my master to beat me some . . . I was already bleeding," she tells of the hardships she goes through for standing up for herself.

3   When Big Laura is murdered by the Patrollers, Jane says, "I didn't cry, I couldn't cry. I had seen so much beating and suffering; I had heard about so much cruelty in those 'leven or twelve years of my life I hardly knowed how to cry." In this statement Jane says that all the conflicts she has seen in her life have made her stronger. The fact that Jane then chooses to take care of Big Laura's son, Ned, when she herself is just a kid, shows a struggle in responsibility which leads to making her a stronger, more mature person overall.

4   With each death, Jane seems to become a stronger person. When the love of her life, Joe, dies, Jane says part of her went with him to his grave. The death of her boy, Ned, shows how her struggles make her a stronger person. Jane knows he is dead before word gets around; however, she does not start crying like the rest of the people in town. Jane calmly gets on her horse and drives to Ned's place; when she is alone with him, she talks to him as if he were still alive.

5   In the beginning of the novel, when Jane first hears of freedom, she sets out for Ohio to find Corporal Brown. However, as the novel progresses, it is apparent that Ohio is no longer a physical destination but an emotional journey. As the novel closes, it is visible how years of hardship and struggles have made Jane able to stand up for her people. The reader can then decide whether Jane ever reaches Ohio.

6   The tone of *The Autobiography of Miss Jane Pittman* is personal and informative as it tells of Jane's journeys. The tone is also touching during times of despair. The novel tends to draw the reader into Jane's life and gives a sense of empathy. *The Autobiography of Miss Jane Pittman* is a wonderful novel that makes the reader want to go back in time and stop slavery. I believe that even prejudiced people would lend their hearts out to Jane and the other slaves. For a book that is truly inspiring, I highly recommend Gaines's *The Autobiography of Miss Jane Pittman*.

Collaborative Activity: Evaluating Book Reviews

In small groups, discuss the following questions.

1. Although each introduction is very different, each is effective in its own way. What makes it so?

2. What does each introduction assert is the main idea behind the book?

3. List the key events the authors mention in common in their reviews.

4. List the key events that one review mentions but the other does not.

5. What reasons do the reviewers give for recommending that we read this book?

6. From reading the two reviews, what may we infer about Ohio?

7. How does each review reveal familiarity with the book review worksheet that you have been assigned to use in writing your own review?

Professional Model

The final book review model for you to examine is a professional review
that James Polk wrote of *Big Fish*. Examine the review, and answer the
questions that follow.

Dog Comes in a Bar
A son tries to get to know his dying father,
who hides behind a facade of jokes.

BIG FISH
A Novel of Mythic Proportions
By Daniel Wallace
180 pp, Chapel Hill, N.C.:
Algonquin Books of Chapel Hill.
$17.95.

By James Polk

1   Like many sons, William Bloom doesn't really know his father. For years,
any attempt to probe beneath the senior Bloom's surfaces have been
met by a stream of tired jokes of the dog-walks-into-the-bar variety. For
years, none of that mattered much. But now Edward Bloom is dying:
suddenly it matters a great deal.

2   William's increasingly desperate attempts to draw his father out, to
make contact with the man during this "journey to the end of his life,"
are only met by more old jokes. So what does he do? Within his own
imagining, he makes Edward into a myth, a quietly heroic figure standing astride the lives of all who know him. Even to those who merely
brush against him, in passing he becomes a benevolent colossus—a
truly Big Fish.

3   In his son's construction, the father's story becomes Homeric. In
one episode, a catfish as big as a man drags him through a community
of dead souls at the bottom of a lake. As a youth leaving home in rural
Alabama, Edward successfully makes it through a sort of purgatory of
lost dreams, where the grand ideas of countless others have crumbled
against the easy temptations of the familiar.

4   He tames a giant "as tall as any two men, as wide as any three and
as strong as any ten." He performs tasks that, although not exactly Her-
culean, have perhaps more resonance in the modern world—cleaning
out a veterinarian's kennels, selling a girdle to an impossible customer
at a department store, rescuing a child from the jaws of a massive
dog—because he knows he must "perform many great labors before he
assumed his rightful place." At least his rightful place in his son's eyes.

5   Moving smoothly from unlikely triumph to unlikely triumph (early on, he comes up with the phrase "Buy one, get one free"; later, he purchases an entire town), this invented Edward Bloom grows tall in his son's reckoning, but the reality of the man remains as elusive as ever. "How I wish I knew him better," laments William, even as the hero of his imagining assumes ever grander stature, "how I wish we'd had a life together, wishing my father wasn't such a complete and utter goddamn mystery to me."

6   In this first novel, Daniel Wallace begins with a nearly exhausted topic from men's groups everywhere (guys can't share emotions or boil water). He adds legends and folk tales from the Southern backwoods, throws in a smattering of Greek myth and attaches a few of his own inventions. Applying all of these to a life that might have been—for all we really know—quite ordinary has resulted in a story that is both comic and poignant.

7   While at times "Big Fish" is a bit too cute, with some exaggerations simply too excessive and others slightly off the point, most of it strikes the right notes. By the end, the figure that William's imagination creates somehow encompasses the actual man even while transcending the Edward Bloom who endures the bumps and bruises of the everyday.

8   That, after all, is a nice encapsulation of the complexity with which many sons view their fathers. They begin as mythical creatures, the first adult male the child encounters, moral and physical giants who can do no wrong. The flaws come later, as the son begins to glimpse the imperfections. In this novel, however the son chooses to go back before the flaws, to embrace and enlarge the myth. As he does, swimming upstream under water (to use one of the author's recurring metaphors), William is able to reach past the funny stories and the evasions to grasp at the humanity underneath.

9   But what of the father? Sadly, even after all of William's efforts, and even though the novel ends on a note of mutual regard, Edward's understanding of his son falls short, recalling the punch line to one of his more familiar jokes:

10   Meeting Jesus at the gates of heaven, an old man tells the story of his wondrous son. Christ embraces him and exclaims, "Father, father!"

11   "Pinocchio?" asks the bewildered old man.

James Polk teaches literature at Marist College in Poughkeepsie, N.Y.

Questions

1. What does James Polk say is the main idea of *Big Fish*?
2. Who are the major characters in the book?
3. List some of the examples James Polk included in his review of the novel.
4. Does the author recommend this novel? For what reasons?

Step 4: Revising

You should now have completed a rough draft of your book review. You will now revise your review to improve both structure and polish. First, you will look at the structure of your essay in pairs.

Collaborative Activity: Revising the Book Review

You will need one partner for this activity. Swap book reviews, and fill out the following evaluation form worksheet about your partner's essay. Then give each other your written responses.

🗁 Worksheet: Evaluation Form for the Book Review

Read over your partner's review, and respond to the following questions:

1. Did he or she summarize the work?

   If so, identify

   a. the topic

   b. the main idea

2. Does he or she make reference to some of the specific details (facts or events) in the work? What are they?

3. Does your partner personally react to the text?

   If so, how would you characterize that reaction?

4. Does your partner say anything about his or her process of reading this novel? If so, what?

5. Please make at least one suggestion to help your partner improve his or her review. Every writer *can* improve!

Finally, before considering your review complete, you should check the polish. Here is a short checklist that should help you locate polish errors. A helpful proofreading hint is to read over your book review several times, looking for a particular type of mistake each time. You will probably be more successful taking this approach than trying to look for all types of polish mistakes at once!

1. Can you find any grammatical errors such as fragments, fused sentences, comma splices, or verb mistakes?

2. Can you find any punctuation errors in using periods, commas, semicolons, or apostrophes, for example?

3. Can you locate any words that are spelled wrong?

4. Can you find instances in which you used the wrong word?

Grammar and Usage: Other Punctuation

In a sense, punctuation marks are to readers what street signs and traffic lights are to drivers. Just imagine leaving your home, getting into a car, and driving out onto a familiar street—only since you were last outside, someone has switched around all the street signs. Stop signs, yield signs, many signs are out of place. Furthermore, the streetlights are malfunctioning. Some are red that should be green; some are yellow that should be red. You can probably imagine what a scene of chaos and confusion would ensue.

Likewise, and thankfully on a less dangerous scale, you run the risk of irritating, confusing, or at worst losing your readers if you give them inappropriate or incorrect signals as they read your essay. For example, the comma (covered in Chapter 10) tells readers to slow down while a semicolon tells them to slow down and pause even longer. A period means to pause longer still. Other punctuation marks, like apostrophes, help readers understand important relationships between items in your sentence.

Periods, Question Marks, and Exclamation Points. You are probably quite familiar with these punctuation marks, which we use to end sentences. Use a period to end a sentence that makes a statement or issues a command. Use a question mark to end a sentence that poses a direct question. Finally, use an exclamation point only to show great surprise or very strong feeling. Use exclamation points sparingly. If you use them too often, they will not be effective at all.

Jamie is valedictorian of her class.
Take your seats now.

Is Jamie valedictorian of her class?
May I take my seat now?

Note: Use a period, not a question mark, to end a sentence that asks a question indirectly.

We asked if Jamie is valedictorian of her class.
I wanted to know when I could take my seat.

Wow! Jamie is valedictorian!
We won the national championship!

Semicolons. Here are three ways to use semicolons.

1. Use a semicolon to join two sentences that are closely related.

Your friends just left for the picnic; you can catch them if you hurry.

2. Use a semicolon before a conjunctive adverb (lawyer word) that connects two sentences.

Most young children enjoy swimming; however, most don't like very cold water.

3. Use a semicolon to separate items in a series or list if those items already include commas.

Please remember to bring the picnic basket, silverware, and napkins; the bread, the sliced turkey, and mayonnaise; and the cake, chocolate cookies, and ice cream.

Colons. Use a colon at the end of a statement when a list, a quotation, a word you want to emphasize, or a clarification or explanation follows the statement.

To make a peanut butter and jelly sandwich you will need the following ingredients: two slices of bread, a jar of peanut butter, and your favorite jelly or jam.

My mother hushed us all when she announced her news: "I'm pregnant again!"

In winter I can partake in one of my favorite activities: ice-skating.

Professor Greene clearly takes his job seriously: he answers our questions completely, he returns essays promptly, and he reads journals to stay knowledgeable in his field.

Apostrophes. Use an apostrophe to make a contraction or to show ownership or possession.

Apostrophes are abbreviations. As you read the examples, notice that in every case, the apostrophe tells us that letters (contractions) or a word (possessives) is missing.

Contractions:

I *will not* go to see that film.   I *won't* go to see that film
Johnny *does not* know how to read.   Johnny *doesn't* know how to read.
I *am waiting* for you.   *I'm* waiting for you.

Note: Be aware that when you use contractions, your writing will sound less formal.

Ownership:

That is the house *of* my father.	That is my father*'s* house.
The food *of* the puppy spilled.	The puppy*'s* food spilled
The clothes *of* my parents are	My parents*'* clothes are
in the closet.	in the closet.
The food *of* the puppies spilled.	The puppies*'* food spilled.

Centuries ago, English speakers used "of" to show ownership. That is why each of the first examples above sounds rather old-fashioned. Then, English speakers developed the *'s* as an abbreviation. Notice that *'s* takes the place of the word *of* in showing ownership.

You have probably noticed, though, that although we add *'s* to most words to show ownership, in the case of *parents, puppies,* and any other plural word, we add only the apostrophe. If we try to add *'s* to these plurals, we will end up with *parents's* and *puppies's,* which are tough to pronounce!

Other Issues Involving Apostrophes

1. In addition to ownership, we sometimes also use apostrophes to show a close relationship, as in the following examples:

   The book's pages were yellow and musty.
   The television's signal grew weaker and weaker.

   The "of test" still works: *the pages of the book, the signal of the television.*

2. As stated earlier, add only an apostrophe to plural words that end in *s,* but add *'s* to *singular words ending in s.*

   Charles's homework rests on your desk.
   Make sure the stylus's point stays sharp.

3. The possessive pronouns (*it, its, me, mine, your, yours, his, her, hers, our, ours, their, theirs*) also show ownership. Do not confuse the contraction *it's* with the possessive pronoun *its.* If you can rephrase the sentence and say "it is," then you want the contraction; otherwise you want the possessive.

   It's cold today. (It is cold today)
   The mouse ate its cheese.

4. Use apostrophes only to show ownership; don't confuse possession with simple plural nouns. Use the "of test." If you can't rephrase the sentence using *of,* then you do not want an apostrophe. The following are simply plural nouns; they do not show any ownership.

My four cats run circles around me.
The trucks backed out of the driveway.

Quotation Marks. Use quotation marks for direct quotation, to tell exactly what someone said or wrote. Do not use quotation marks for indirect quotations.

Direct quotations:

Mary shouted, "Look out below!" as she leaped from the ledge.
"Do you want breakfast yet?" my mother asked.
"Never try to kid a kidder," my Uncle Louie always said.
William Shakespeare first wrote, "To be or not to be."

Indirect quotations:

My mother asked us if we wanted breakfast yet.
Uncle Louie always told us not to try to kid him.

Other Issues Involving Quotation Marks

1. Use quotation marks around titles of songs, newspaper and magazine articles, chapters in books, short stories, essays, poems, and particular episodes of television shows.

2. Commas and periods go inside quotation marks. Colons and semicolons go outside quotation marks. Question marks may go inside or outside quotation marks, depending on whether the whole sentence or just the quoted part asks a question.

   Who just asked, "Do we need a new milk pitcher"?
   Upon his arrival, John asked, "Who cooks supper around here?"

Dashes. Use dashes, like exclamation points, very infrequently. Many times, when writers use dashes, they could just as well or better use a comma or a colon. Here, however, is an example of proper use of the dash. In this case, we use dashes to set off a series that breaks into the flow of the sentence.

My three best friends—Sandy, Sam, and Amber—all live on Baxter Street.

Exercise 1

Directions: Rewrite the following sentences. Insert punctuation wherever necessary, and correct any punctuation mistakes.

1. Joe said that "we should cook our own meals."

2. Every tackle box needs certain items lures, fishing line, hooks, and sinkers.

3. If you see trash, pick it up, furthermore, put it in a trash can.

4. This monkeys banana looks smashed to me.

5. Its another rainy day, let's go inside.

6. The vicious dog chewed a hole right through it's leash.

7. My favorite foods pizza, spaghetti, and burritos are all available at Tito's Restaurant.

8. My three cat's leashes are soaking wet; they dragged them all through a puddle.

9. I do believe in magic, said the little boy after the magic show.

10. John and Becky fell in love, however, they chose not to marry until after college.

Exercise 2: Collaborative Activity

Write a paragraph describing a member of your family other than yourself. Make sure you include at least one direct quotation, and also use at least one apostrophe and a semicolon. When you finish, proofread it carefully for correct punctuation. Then swap papers with a classmate, and check your classmate's punctuation.

Chapter

Academic Writing

You have probably already discovered that one huge difference between high school and college is the amount of reading that you are required to do. Professors often use the rule of thumb that you should expect approximately two hours of work outside class for every hour that you spend in class, and you may already have learned that sometimes this number errs on the conservative side! Rather than assigning and then "spoon feeding" readings the way your high school teachers may have done, college professors generally assign a certain number of chapters and then expect you to show up fully prepared to discuss, debate, and even write about the ideas in the chapters. This chapter will help you develop the necessary skills for writing about texts, also known as *academic writing*.

Academic Writing and the Communication Triangle

As you know, James Kinneavy's communication triangle contains "I" based writing, or expressive writing; "you" based writing, or persuasive writing; and "it" based writing, or informative writing. A triangle, however, does not just consist of its three angles. There is also the flat space in between the angles. In terms of the communication triangle, Kinneavy assigns this space to the type of writing known as literary writing. We call this flat space text-based writing, or academic writing. The fact that academic writing covers the entire triangle demonstrates that it is not restricted; in fact, academic writing can express, inform, and/or persuade. Whenever you write to explain, interpret, criticize, attack, defend, or do anything other than merely summarize a piece of writing, you are engaging in academic writing.

Assignment: Writing about a Text

Aim or Purpose: Varies

Audience: as small as one professor or as broad as an entire community of scholars

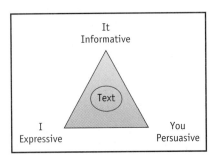

The first step, then, in academic writing is reading. You want to make certain that you have a relatively full understanding of the text in question before you begin to interpret it. Over your years of reading, you have undoubtedly developed a variety of strategies that you use to read and understand a work. If you are less than certain about your own strategies, you may want to review Chapter 7 on summarizing an essay or article in this book. Then, when you feel ready, read the selection below. Feel free to make notes, underline, highlight, or otherwise mark the text in ways that will help you. The selection is from a college history text called *The American People: Creating a Nation and a Society, Volume 1 to 1877,* by Nash and Jeffrey.

The People of America Before Columbus[*]

Edited by Gary B. Nash and Julie Roy Jeffrey

1   Thousands of years before the European voyages of discovery, the history of humankind in North America began. Nomadic bands from Siberia, hunting big game animals such as bison, caribou, and reindeer, began to migrate across a land bridge connecting northeastern Asia with Alaska. Geologists believe that this land bridge, perhaps 600 miles wide, existed most recently between 25,000 and 14,000 years ago, when massive glaciers locked up much of the earth's moisture and left part of the Bering Sea floor exposed. Ice-free passage through Canada was possible only briefly at the beginning and end of this period, however. At other times, melting glaciers flooded the land bridge and blocked foot traffic to Alaska. Paleoanthropologists remain divided on

[*]Excerpt from *The American People: Creating a Nation and a Society, Volume 1 to 1877,* New York: Longman, 1997.

the exact timing, but the main migration apparently occurred between 12,000 and 14,000 years ago, although possibly much earlier.

HUNTERS AND FARMERS

2   For thousands of years, these early hunters trekked southward and east-ward, following vegetation and game. In time, they reached the tip of South America and the eastern edge of North America, thousands of miles from their Asian homeland. Thus did people from the "Old World" discover the "New World" thousands of years before Columbus.

3   Archaeologists have excavated ancient sites of early life in the Americas, unearthing tools, ornaments, and skeletal remains that can be scientifically dated. In this way, they have tentatively reconstructed the dispersion of these first Americans over an immense land mass. Although much remains unknown, this archaeological evidence sug-gests that as centuries passed and population increased, the earliest

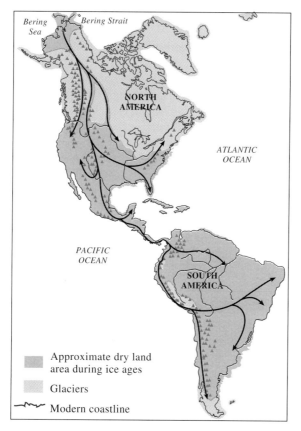

Migration Routes from Asia to the Americas
The arrows indicate the general flow of migrating societies over thousands of years before Europeans reached the Americas. Based on archaeological evidence, these migra-tory patterns are necessarily tentative.

inhabitants evolved into separate cultures, organizing life and adjusting to a variety of environments in distinct ways. Europeans who rediscovered the New World thousands of years later would indiscriminately lump together the myriad societies they found. But by the 1500s, the "Indians" of the Americas were enormously diverse in the size and complexity of their societies, the languages they spoke, and their forms of social organization.

4   Archaeologists and anthropologists have charted several phases of "Native American" history. A long Beringian epoch ended about 14,000 years ago. From that time, a rich archaeological record indicates that the hunters had developed a new technology. Big-game hunters now flaked hard stones into spear points and chose "kill sites" where they slew whole herds of Pleistocene mammals. This more reliable food source allowed population growth, and nomadism began to give way to settled habitations or local migration within limited territories.

5   In another phase of evolution, the Archaic era, from about 10,000 to 2,500 years ago, great geological changes brought further adaptations to the land. As the massive glaciers of the Ice Age slowly retreated, a warming trend deprived vast areas from Utah to the highlands of Central America of sufficient water and turned them from grasslands into desert. The Pleistocene mammals were weakened by more arid conditions, but human populations ably adapted. They learned to exploit new sources of food, especially plant life. In time, a second technological break-through, the "agricultural revolution," occurred.

6   We have sometimes imagined that these early people lived in a primordial paradise where they lived in harmony with their surroundings. But recent archaeological evidence points to examples of environmental devastation that severely damaged the biodiversity of the Americas. The first wave of intruders coming across the Bering land bridge found a wilderness teeming with so-called megafauna: saber-toothed tigers, woolly mammoths, gigantic ground sloths, huge bison, and monstrous bear. But by about 10,000 years ago, these animals were almost extinct. Many anthropologists believe that native hunters engaged in "Pleistocene overkill" of the giant species. However, a massive shift of climate that deprived the huge beasts of their grazing environment was also a cause.

7   The depletion of the megafauna left the hemisphere with a much restricted catalogue of animals. Left behind were large animals such as elk, buffalo, bears, and moose. But the extinction of the huge beasts forced people to prey on new sources of food such as turkeys, ducks, and guinea pigs. Their reduced food supply may have gradually reduced their population.

8   Over many centuries in the Americas, salinization and deforestation put the environment under additional stress. For example, in what is today central Arizona, the Hohokam civilization collapsed hundreds

of years ago, much like that in ancient Mesopotamia, when the irrigation system became too salty to support agriculture. At Arizona's Chaco Canyon, the fast-growing Anasazi denuded a magnificently forested region in their search for firewood and building materials. This, in turn, led to the erosion of rich soil that impoverished the region for the Anasazi.

9   When Native Americans learned to domesticate plant life, they began the long process of transforming their relationship to the physical world. Learning how to plant, cultivate, and harvest created a new relationship to natural forces that before had been ungovernable. Anthropologists believe that this process began independently in widely separated parts of the world—Africa, Asia, Europe, and the Americas—about 7,000 to 9,000 years ago. Though agriculture developed very slowly, everywhere it eventually brought dramatic changes in human societies.

10   Over the millennia, humans progressed from doorside planting of a few wild seeds to systematic clearing and planting of bean and maize fields. As the production of domesticated plant food ended dependence on gathering wild plants and pursuing game, settled village life began to replace nomadic existence. The increase in food supply brought about by agriculture triggered other major changes. As more ample food fueled population growth, large groups split off to form separate societies. Greater social and political complexity developed because not everyone was needed as before to secure the society's food supply. Men cleared the land and hunted game, and women planted, cultivated, and harvested crops. Many societies empowered religious figures, who organized the common followers, directed their work, and exacted tribute as well as worship from them. In return, the community trusted them to ward off hostile forces.

11   Everywhere in the Americas, regional trading networks formed. Along trade routes carrying commodities such as salt, obsidian rock for projectile points, and copper for jewelry also traveled technology, religious ideas, and agricultural practices. By the end of the Archaic period, about 500 B.C. (to use the Christian European method of dating), hundreds of independent kin-based groups, like people in other parts of the world, had learned to exploit the resources of their particular area and to trade with other groups in their region.

NATIVE AMERICANS IN 1600

12   The last epoch of pre-Columbian development, the post-Archaic phase, occurred during the 2,000 years before contact with Europeans. It involved a complex process of growth and environmental adaptation among many distinct societies—and crisis in some of them. In the American Southwest, for example, the ancestors of the present-day Hopi and Zuni developed carefully planned villages composed of large

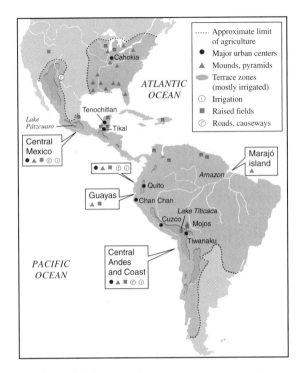

Pre-Columbian Societies of the Americas
Once described as nomadic hunter-gatherers, indigenous peoples in the Americas were agriculturalists and urban dwellers in many areas and populated the land as densely as did others in many other parts of the world.

terraced multistoried buildings, each with many rooms. By the time the Spanish arrived in the 1540s, the indigenous Pueblo people were using irrigation canals, dams, and hillside terracing to bring water to their arid maize fields. In their agricultural techniques, their skill in ceramics, their use of woven textiles for clothing, and their village life, Pueblo society resembled that of peasant communities in many parts of Europe and Asia.

13   Far to the east were the mound-building societies of the Mississippi and Ohio valleys. When European settlers first crossed the Appalachian Mountains a century and a half after arriving on the continent, they were amazed to find hundreds of ceremonial mounds, some of them 70 feet high, and gigantic sculptured earthworks in geometric designs or in the shapes of huge humans, birds, or writhing serpents. Believing all "Indians" to be forest primitives, they reasoned that these were the remains of an ancient civilization that had found its way to North America—perhaps Phoenicians, survivors of the sunken island of Atlantis, or the Lost Tribes of Israel spoken of in European mythology.

14   The mound-building societies of the Ohio valley declined many centuries before Europeans reached the continent, perhaps because of attacks from other tribes or severe climatic changes that undermined agriculture. But about A.D. 600, another mound-building culture, based on intensive cultivation of beans, maize, and squash, began to flourish in the Mississippi valley. Its center, a city of perhaps 40,000, stood near present-day St. Louis. Great ceremonial plazas, flanked by a temple that rose in four terraces to a height of 100 feet, marked this first metropolis in America. This was the urban center of a far-flung Mississippi culture that radiated out to encompass hundreds of villages from Wisconsin to Louisiana and from Oklahoma to Tennessee.

15   While the mound-building cultures of the continental heartlands mysteriously declined, their influence had already passed eastward to transform the woodlands societies along the Atlantic coastal plain. The numerous small tribes that settled from Nova Scotia to Florida never equaled the larger societies of the midcontinent in earthwork sculpture, architectural design, or development of large-scale agriculture. But they were far from the "savages" that the first European explorers described. They had added limited agriculture to their skill in exploiting natural plants for food, medicine, dyes, and flavoring and had developed food procurement strategies that used all the resources around them—cleared land, forests, streams, shore, and ocean.

16   Most of the eastern woodlands tribes lived in waterside villages. Locating their fields of maize near fishing grounds, they often migrated seasonally between inland and coastal village sites or situated themselves astride two ecological zones. In the Northeast, their birchbark canoes, light enough to be carried by a single man, gave them a means of trading and communicating over immense territories. In the Southeast, population was denser and social and political organization more elaborate.

17   As European exploration of the Americas drew near, the continent north of the Rio Grande contained at least 3 to 4 million people, of whom perhaps 500,000 lived along the eastern coastal plain and in the piedmont region accessible to the early European settlers. Though estimates vary widely, perhaps 40 to 60 million people lived in the entire hemisphere when Europeans first arrived. This contrasted with some 70 to 90 million in Europe about 1500 and about 50 to 70 million in Africa. The colonizers were not coming to a "virgin wilderness," as they often described it, but to a land inhabited for thousands of years by people whose village existence in many ways resembled that of the arriving Europeans.

18   In some important ways, however, Indian culture also differed from that of Europeans. Horses, for example, were not available to the native peoples of the New World as they developed their methods of farming, transportation, and warfare. Without draft animals such as the horse or ox, they had not developed wheeled vehicles or, for that matter, the

One of the hundreds of symbolic mounds built by people of the Hopewell culture; this one, in the shape of a serpent, is near present-day Cincinnati. (National Museum of the American Indian, New York)

potter's wheel, which also uses the wheel-and-axle principle. Many inventions—such as the technology for smelting iron, which had diffused widely in the Old World—had not crossed the ocean barrier to reach the New World. The opposite was also true: Valuable New World crops, such as corn and potatoes, which had been developed by Indian agriculturists, were unknown in the Old World before Columbus.

Questions. Now that you have read the history text, consider the following questions:

1. When did people first begin to arrive in what we now call America? What allowed them to do so?
2. Into what chronological divisions do Nash and Jeffrey divide the earliest Americans? What bases do they use for these divisions?
3. What were some of the technological breakthroughs of the "Indians"?
4. What was the situation involving Native Americans in the United States in 1600?
5. What did the text tell you about this continent's pre-European inhabitants that surprised you or contradicted information you may have previously believed?

The first four questions essentially test your ability to understand the facts presented in the text. In answering them, you simply reduce and simplify the longer answers provided by Nash and Jeffrey. Question 5, however, is a more academic question. It challenges you to think. In order to answer question 5, you must first ask yourself, "What did I think the situation was in North America in 1600 before I read this selection?" You must then compare your original mental files with the information before you. Chances are that you found some contradictions. So not only has the section on "The People of America Before Columbus" taught you new information, but it has corrected old beliefs that you may have held.

Collaborative Activity: Interpreting and Discussing

In groups of three to five, discuss and take notes on the following question: Using Nash and Jeffrey as support, explain why the terms "New World" and "Old World" are far from ideal in describing the Europeans of the 1500s and 1600s and the people they encountered when they sailed to what is now the United States?

———

Chances are that your discussion led to some interesting, perhaps even heated exchanges. One by one, members of your group may have read short quotations from the text to support various claims. What is more, no amount of discussion may have led to unanimity of opinions. That is precisely one of the points about academic writing. Because academic writing is interpretive and because people bring different ideas, experiences, and beliefs to their interpretations, one *good* interpretation may be significantly different from another. This disagreement is not necessarily a sign that someone is right while someone else is wrong; rather, it probably indicates that there are several *good* ways (or, if you insist, *right* ways) to look at a subject and a text about it. This diversity of opinions, so long as those opinions are well reasoned and well supported, is something that academic writing and the modern college classroom celebrate.

Now you will read a completely different piece of academic writing. The following selection, taken from Wade and Tavris's *Psychology,* discusses a mental illness called schizophrenia.

Schizophrenia*

By Carole Wade and Carol Tavris

1   To be schizophrenic is best summed up in a repeating dream that I have had since childhood. In this dream I am lying on a beautiful sunlit

---

*Excerpt from *Psychology,* 5th ed. New York: Longman, 1998.

beach but my body is in pieces. This fact causes me no concern until I realize that the tide is coming in and that I am unable to gather the parts of my dismembered body together to run away. The tide gets closer and just when I am on the point of drowning I wake up screaming in panic. This to me is what schizophrenia feels like; being fragmented in one's personality and constantly afraid that the tide of illness will completely cover me (Quoted in Rollin, 1980).

2   In 1911, Swiss psychiatrist Eugen Bleuler coined the term **schizophrenia** to describe cases in which the personality loses its unity: words are split from meaning, actions from motives, perceptions from reality. Schizophrenia is not the same as "split" or "multiple personality." As the quotation illustrates, schizophrenia refers to a fragmented condition, not the coexistence of several different personalities. It is an example of a **psychosis,** a mental condition that involves distorted perceptions of reality and an inability to function in most aspects of life.

THE NATURE OF THE "SCHIZOPHRENIAS"

3   If depression is the common cold of psychological disorder, said psychiatrist Donald Klein (1980), schizophrenia is its cancer: a baffling and complex problem. Schizophrenia produces *active or positive symptoms* that involve an exaggeration or distortion of normal thinking processes and behavior, and more subtle *negative symptoms* that involve the loss of former traits and abilities. The most common active symptoms include the following:

4   1. *Bizarre delusions,* such as the belief that dogs are anthropologists from another planet, disguised as pets to infiltrate human families. Some people with schizophrenia have paranoid delusions, taking innocent events—a stranger's cough, a helicopter overhead—as evidence that the world is plotting against them. Some have "delusions of identity," believing that they are Moses, Jesus, Joan of Arc, or some other famous person.

5   2. *Hallucinations* that usually take the form of voices and consist of garbled, odd words; a running conversation in the head; or two or more voices conversing with each other. Unlike the hallucinations that might occur in a normal person on a drug high, schizophrenic hallucinations feel intensely real and believable to the sufferer (Bentall, 1990). Most are voices, but some are tactile (feeling insects crawling over the body) or visual (seeing Elizabeth Taylor in the mirror).

6   3. *Disorganized, incoherent speech* consisting of an illogical jumble of ideas and symbols, linked by meaningless rhyming words or by remote associations called *word salads.* A patient of Bleuler's wrote, "Olive oil is an Arabian liquor-sauce which the Afghans, Moors and Moslems use in ostrich farming. The Indian plantain tree is the whiskey of the Parsees and Arabs. Barley, rice and sugar cane called artichoke, grow remarkably well in India. The Brahmins live as castes in Baluchis-

tan. The Circassians occupy Manchuria and China. China is the Eldorado of the Pawnees" (Bleuler, 1911/1950). The story goes that the great novelist James Joyce once asked Carl Jung to explain the difference between Joyce's own stream-of-consciousness writing and the odd associations of his schizophrenic daughter. Jung supposedly replied, "You dive—she falls" (Wender & Klein, 1981).

7   4. *Grossly disorganized and inappropriate behavior* that may range from childlike silliness to unpredictable and violent agitation. The person may wear three overcoats and gloves on a hot day, start collecting garbage, or hoard scraps of food. Some people with schizophrenia completely withdraw into a private world, sitting for hours without moving, a condition called *catatonic stupor.* In *Autobiography of a Schizophrenic Girl,* Marguerite Sechehaye wrote, "A wall of brass separates me from everybody and everything. In the midst of desolation, in indescribable distress, in absolute solitude, I am terrifyingly alone."

8   Negative symptoms may appear months before these active ones and often persist when the active symptoms are in remission. Negative symptoms include loss of motivation; poverty of speech (making only brief, empty replies in conversation, because of diminished thought rather than an unwillingness to speak); and, most notably, *emotional flatness*—unresponsive facial expressions, poor eye contact, and diminished emotionality (see Figure on page 244). One man set fire to his house and then sat down calmly to watch TV.

9   Cases of schizophrenia vary in the severity and duration of symptoms. In some individuals, the symptoms appear abruptly and eventually disappear with the passage of time, with or without treatment. In others, the onset is more gradual and insidious. Friends and family report a slow change in personality. The person may stop working or bathing, become isolated and withdrawn, and start behaving in peculiar ways.

10   As for prognosis, again schizophrenia is unpredictable. Psychiatrists often speak of the "rule of thirds": Of all people diagnosed and hospitalized with schizophrenia, one-third will recover completely, one-third will improve significantly, and one-third will not get well. The more breakdowns and relapses the individual has had, the poorer the chances for complete recovery (Eaton et al., 1992a, 1992b). Yet many people suffering from this illness learn to live with it, are able to work and have warm family relationships, and eventually outgrow their symptoms (Eaton et al., 1992b; Harding, Zubin, & Strauss, 1992).

11   The mystery of schizophrenia is that we could go on listing symptoms and variations all day and not finish. Some people with schizophrenia are almost completely impaired in all spheres; others do extremely well in certain areas. Some have normal moments of lucidity in otherwise withdrawn lives. One adolescent crouched in a rigid catatonic posture in front of a television for the month of October; later, he was able to report on all the highlights of the World Series he had seen. A middle-aged man, hospitalized for 20 years, believing he was a

Emotions and Schizophrenia

When people with schizophrenia are asked to draw pictures, their drawings are often distorted, lack color, include words, and reveal flat emotion. One patient was asked to copy a picture of flowers from a magazine (upper left). The initial result is shown upper right. The drawing on bottom right shows how much the patient improved after several months of treatment.

prophet of God and that monsters were coming out of the walls, was able to interrupt his ranting to play a good game of chess (Wender & Klein, 1981). People with brain damage usually cannot interrupt their madness to watch the World Series or play chess. How can those with schizophrenia do so?

NOTES

Bentall, R. P. (1990). The illusion of reality: A review and integration of psychological research on hallucinations. *Psychological Bulletin, 107,* 82–95.

Bleuler, Eugen (1911/1950). *Dementia praecox or the group of schizophrenias.* New York: International Universities Press.

Eaton, William W., Bilker, Warren, Haro, Joseph M., Herrman, Helen, et al. (1992a). Long-term course of hospitalization for schizophrenia: II. Change with passage of time. *Schizophrenia Bulletin, 18,* 229–241.

Eaton, William W., Mortensen, Preben B., Herrman, Helen, Freeman, Hugh, et al. (1992b). Long-term course of hospitalization for schizophrenia: I. Risk for rehospitalization. *Schizophrenia Bulletin, 18,* 217–228.

Harding, Courtenay M., Zubin, Joseph, & Strauss, John S. (1992). Chronicity in schizophrenia: Revisited. *British Journal of Psychiatry, 161* (Suppl. 18), 27–37.

Klein, Donald F. (1980). Psychosocial treatment of schizophrenia, or psychosocial help for people with schizophrenia? *Schizophrenia Bulletin, 6,* 122–130.

Wender, Paul H., & Klein, Donald F. (1981). *Mind, mood, and medicine: A guide to the new biopsychiatry.* New York: Farrar, Straus & Giroux.

Questions.   Briefly answer the following questions:

1. What are some of the characteristics of schizophrenia?
2. How does schizophrenia differ from "split personality"?
3. What is the prognosis for people with schizophrenia?
4. In what behavioral ways is schizophrenia different from brain damage?
5. What would lead you to believe that someone you knew or read about may have schizophrenia?

In these five questions, as in the five following the first reading, all but the last question ask you to locate and repeat information contained in the text. The fifth question, again, challenges you. Have you known people who walked along muttering incoherently to themselves? Have you encountered an individual who was convinced that the government or aliens had taken over his brain and implanted terrible messages there? How might you interpret "Schizophrenia" in such a way as to lead you to call a mental health crisis line and request help for someone who may have a terribly disabling disease?

Discuss "Schizophrenia," and list at least five specific behaviors that might lead you to suspect someone has schizophrenia.

Diversity of Literary Writing

Among all forms of writing, perhaps none generates, in turn, more academic writing than literary writing. To test this theory, visit any large university or city library and count the number of books and articles that you can locate on *Hamlet* alone. That is one play by one author, yet you probably could not live long enough to read what has already been written about it, let alone the additional books and articles that would come out while you were reading the previous ones.

Some people find this incredible diversity of opinion about literary works maddening; others find it fun. For your next assignment, you will read a literary work, a short story called "When Momma Crossed the Parking Lot to Pee" by Jack Riggs. When you finish reading this story, you will discuss it with your classmates and then write an essay on your choice of several topics that will require you to understand, interpret, and analyze the story as well as, in the case of one topic, synthesize the story with the reading by Wade and Tavris. But first read (and hopefully enjoy) "When Momma Crossed the Parking Lot to Pee."

When Momma Crossed the Parking Lot to Pee

By Jack Riggs

1   I once told my Momma I remembered being born. We were swinging on the porch in the evening in summer when light dulled even but did not disappear until nearly ten o'clock. The chains hanging from I-hooks suspended the swing, swayed it in silence broken only by the sound of the bugman spraying white clouds of DDT a block over on Vance Street. The air was hot. We sat rocking, attempting a breeze with folded sections of the afternoon paper and cardboard fans from Vance Funeral Home: *Eternal Peace, Its Breeze So Sweet* swished the air, moved it with a slightness that as much irritated as relieved.

2   We had just finished eating dinner, tomato sandwiches and cantaloupe, homemade sweet cucumber pickles and cold potato salad. Momma had served us each a second glass of iced tea and said, "Let's take it out on the porch and see if your father comes home." Slouched there in the swing, pushing with toes barely touching the gray painted porch floor, I had said with no great urgency, but with complete seri-

ousness, "Momma, I remember being born. I remember seeing the doctor's face. He smiled at me, then he whipped my butt."

3   Momma stopped the swing by pulling a leg out from under her and placing it on the floor beside my own which then hung in the air separated, floating. She said, "What made you say such a foolish thing? There is no way you could remember that, Raybert. Why your eyes weren't even fixed yet."

4   I looked at her and she at me. Flat light seeped beneath the canvass awnings skirting the front porch to wash her face incandescent. She was flushed, not with anger, but with heat. It always affected her in the middle part of summer, in July, flushing her face in its kindest attack, bringing out a burning, itchy rash when it wanted to test her spirit. That night on the porch, the irritation traveled somewhere in between the two extremes, her voice even, her eyes fixed on some distant point that as a child I could not see. Still my mother wanted to know how I had come up with such a tale. She held the swing steady as if the motionless moment would force me to come clean.

5   Momma said, "Where did you get such a story, Raybert?"

6   I told her, "I don't know, I just remembered it, that's all."

7   She looked out toward the sound of the bugman making his way around the far corner, heading up Williams Street, up toward our house. Her hair fell in strings around her cheeks, floated in disarray from failed attempts to pin it back with bobby pins. She stroked her neck rubbing beads of sweat smooth against her tortured skin. Momma said, "Well I guess you're just a Mister Know-it-all, aren't you?"

8   I didn't want to tell her I had stolen the words from my best friend, Palmer Conroy. We had been down by Finch Creek all day playing army in the woods, catching crawfish and salamanders, crawling through the caves that had been dug out from years of the Finch rising and overflowing its banks. We had been "one upping" each other all afternoon, daring and double daring, comparing muscles, and Indian leg wrestling, all of which I won. We took rides on the swing hanging over the Finch, attempting acrobatics, forcing each other to risk a little more with each turn.

9   In a moment of spectacular spontaneity, I had swung the Finch, let go in mid-air landing miraculously on the other side. It was then Palmer said it. He stood across from me, arms at his side, voice matter-of-fact as if he was telling me his name. *I remember being born,* he said.

10   The words put my world to spinning, made me want to say something with that kind of staying power, but I was empty as air. I sensed my own strengths—could run fast, ride my bike without hands. I could swim the length of the City Pool underwater, complete a one and a half somersault off the three-meter diving board. I could shoot a BB gun with great accuracy, having once when I was ten killed a bird, a small sparrow in a dogwood tree with one shot. I knew my world physically, but remained unfamiliar with the idea of my world as thought. This

pissed me off, so I re-crossed the Finch, hit Palmer in the face and ran home for supper.

11   Now I found myself stealing his words, floating them out into the evening heat as my own without a ready explanation for their meaning. The roar of the fog machine distracted, the DDT now in front of our house suffocated any chance of explanation from my lungs. I got up and lurched for my bike. It stood supported by the rod-iron railing along the cement front steps. My leap was as a cowboy jumping to his horse. I hit the seat pushing off with bare feet on cool grass. A small hill rolled our front yard down to the curbed street and gave me confidence enough to lie again, to sass my mother, "I know what I know, that's all I got to say to you."

12   Behind me, my mother's voice trailed a warning to stay out of the DDT, but I pretended not to hear. Her shrill annoyance disappeared, dissolved into the frog-throated noise of the fog machine, a grinding sound of chemicals being mixed and blown out into the atmosphere. The machine was tied down to the back of an old World War II Army jeep. The man driving wore a gas mask, heavy gloves and a yellow rain slicker as he drove up and down the neighborhood streets. Bug-eyed and profusely sweating, he yelled from beneath the rubberized mask to keep out of the sweetly poisonous cloud blowing thick from behind his seat.

13   Nevertheless, I dove into the wall of white where my eyes burned and the sweetness irritated my throat. Inside the cloud, the opaqueness turned into an oily blue hue as the smoke dissipated and was absorbed into the ground and trees and my body. At the end of our block, I leaned my bike into the corner taking the curve at full speed and flying down the Park Street hill. The hot air cleared except for the faint smell of diesel, and at the bottom of Park where Third Street intersected, I saw Lucky Luther stealing a stop sign. He had shimmied up the pole and was wrenching off the top bolt, the bottom already loose and dangling. He was racing, the bugman's cloud no longer hiding his theft. I skidded to a stop below the pole, leaving a thick black arc of tire rubber as my mark, and watched Lucky work the bolt. He sweated, his T-shirt wet against his back. The rust from the pole flaked onto his cutoff jeans while his legs gripped tightly, metal cutting deep indentations into his skin.

14   Lucky was always collecting things he wasn't supposed to have. A Yield sign and a Highway 52 marker were already on the wall of his basement bedroom. He stole the cap off a fire hydrant and pocketed an eight ball from the pool room at the YMCA. He had a drawer full of Pez dispensers, fake vomit, and Chinese handcuffs lifted from Briggs Hobby Shop. From his dad's Rexall, he stole condoms and cigarettes kept behind the counter, *Playboy* and *Mad* magazines from racks next to the cash register. He came from a good family, but that didn't appear to matter very much. Lucky was quickly becoming a juvenile delinquent. He seemed to aspire to it.

15   The sign broke free and fell to the ground slicing into the dirt and nearly taking off my right foot. Lucky shimmied down too quickly and scraped huge raspberries on the inside of both his thighs.

16   Lucky said, "S_ _ _ god almighty."

17   I said, "Hey Lucky. What's up?"

18   We both looked at the empty pole, thin and rusted, a little wobbly from Lucky's slide to the ground. He said, "That hurt like a m_ _ _ _ _ _-f_ _ _ _ _." He rubbed spit into the palms of his hands and gently touched his wounds, flinching when the cool saliva hit raw flesh. Lucky picked up the sign like it was a huge discus and flew it over into the tall grass of a vacant lot.

19   I said, "You could get put on probation for taking that sign."

20   Lucky said, "You got to get caught first. So shut up. I don't need no jinx messing things up. Want to kill a weed?"

21   I said, "Sure." We doubled on my spider bike, Lucky Luther balancing on the handlebars while I stood pumping the peddles hard. Below the city park was a small cluster of trees we called "the woods." It was an old picnic area cleared out for the city pool swimmers when the park was first constructed years ago. Now it was overgrown with vine and poison oak, the trail nothing more than a path wide enough for a boy's foot or bike tires to navigate. At the deepest point, one picnic table remained intact. It was the place where we came to smoke, to look at nudie magazines, and count the number of spent rubbers laying in the weeds and pine needles.

22   Lucky lit up then tossed me the pack of Salem menthols. The coolness with which the smoke went down gave me confidence. I felt as though I was Lucky's accomplice, that I had been there when he decided to shimmy up that pole to steal the stop sign. In my shame of feeling left out of something bigger than I could understand, I found a connection to Lucky. I imagined encouraging him to take the sign, offering the double dare he could not refuse. I felt I could be a delinquent too. I could run around stealing words as my own much in the same way Lucky stole material things. I could be an impostor, live with words and deeds devised by someone else and get away with it. In my mind, I had put my mother to shame and then split before she could call my bluff. I felt comfortable sitting on a picnic table shielded from a family who made Lucky seem to be the luckiest kid in the world. I blew out a thin white puff of smoke and then spit into the dirt below the table.

23   Lucky looked out toward the City Pool. He said, "When it gets dark, I'm going swimming."

24   The late sun, just dipping below the tree line shot orange sparks off the water and seemed to aim them into trees stilled by summer heat, burning the edges of the leaves, setting them on fire. I said, "Why don't you just go now?"

25   Lucky said, "S_ _ _, I ain't paying nobody to get wet. Besides, they'll throw you out for bouncing more than three times on the high dive. I need at least five to get where I'm going."

26   I said, "I did a one and a half in pike yesterday with one spring."

27   Lucky said, "Well then you win the prize."

28   I said, "Yea, what's that?"

29   Lucky said, "You get to kiss my a_ _."

30   I spit into the dirt again. "Okay," I said. "Smile and give me a hint."

31   Lucky looked at me like he was deciding whether or not there needed to be retaliation. I never fought with Lucky. We had been friends forever because he lived at the end of my block, but we were never close enough to come to blows. Lucky slipped off the picnic table and buried the cigarettes inside a tree stump, he said, "I ain't got time for your bulls_ _ _, Raybert. I got a great idea."

32   "What's that?"

33   Lucky said, "I'm taking a midnight swim."

34   I said, "Where?"

35   Lucky said, "Right down there, dumba_ _." He aimed his finger, his middle finger, at the city pool, squeezed his right eye shut to get a bead on his target with the left and then "Pow." Lucky Luther shot the bird at the pool.

36   I said, "You're crazy."

37   Lucky said, "You're crazy if you don't do it with me. There's a full moon tonight, Raybert. You can do your one and a half in pike right there in the silver light of the moon. You can dive through the Milky Way. You can shoot the moon to the man in the moon. Hell, you can get naked and piss in the pool for all I care."

38   I said, "You can bounce a thousand times on the high board."

39   Lucky said, "Hell, I'll bounce forever on that sucker." He wheezed hard, coughed like he had already been smoking for twenty years. "You got to do it Raybert or you ain't got a hair on your a_ _. Now give me some skin." He stuck his hand out for me to slap him five. The sun had gone, extinguishing the fire, leaving us in an idle light that dulled the senses and made the idea of sneaking out to swim in the City Pool a very real possibility.

40   Lucky Luther said, "Be right here at midnight. I like to have a smoke before I take my dip."

41   "But what if we get caught?" It was a possibility I could not escape.

42   Lucky said, "Look. I sleep in the basement and my parents don't give a s_ _ _. Your old man ain't ever there and your mother's crazy as a coot, so who's getting caught?"

43   It was the first time I had ever heard anyone call my mother such a name. Though she was peculiar at times and caused scenes out in public, I had never thought of her as crazy. Such a possibility struck a

blow that shook me to the core and once again rattled my sense of self and place. It kept me off balance just enough to feel nauseated, motion sick in a world where thoughts were still too invisible to be revealed to me.

44   I promised Lucky Luther I would meet him at midnight and left him where I had found him at Park and Third. I did not want to go home but did so in fear of my father's return and the punishment he would mete out for disobeying my mother's demand to stay out of the DDT. I told myself he would be home, that he was always there when I returned, that my mother would be sipping her iced tea while sitting on the porch swing, humming gently. I would not let my mother be crazy nor my father invisible. They would greet me; I would go to bed. In the morning I would wake up, my world intact, crystal clear, thoroughly revealed and understood.

45   I rode up Williams Street pushing hard against the pedals to make the hill. The street lights, frosted by the lingering DDT and July's humidity, dimmed into a softness accentuating the quiet a neighborhood comes to when it decides to rest for the night. On the front porch, the swing was empty and the sound of pans rattling in the kitchen told me my mother was not at rest but rather busy, preparing supper a second time, for my father who would not be coming home.

46   I did not want to go inside but knew my mother would need me, her condition flaring up, her need to go seeking my father's whereabouts nearly unbearable. Momma said, "I thought you'd never get here. Supper is ready, but we will wait for your father. If we starve to death, it will be his fault. That'll teach him, won't it?"

47   On the table, Momma had placed a platter full of broiled pork chops, mashed potatoes, fried okra, and collards. Iced tea was cooking on the stove, and glasses of ice water were sweating wet rings on the counter top. The kitchen was a hundred degrees even with the back door open and the attic fan on high. Momma lit the oven, a cherry pie waiting to be popped in.

48   I told Momma, I said, "We ate earlier."

49   She never looked up from the counter while she pinched the edges of the piecrust. "Don't be foolish, Raybert. Now go on the porch and look out for your father."

50   If it hadn't been eight o'clock at night, the meal would have been spectacular. But it *was* eight, and we had already had our dinner hours ago. I knew what was next, and so I went into my room to put on a T-shirt, my tennis shoes and socks. We sat together in the heat and dead air until something in my mother's head clicked. Her eyes cleared and her jaw set resolute at what she would have to do. The meal she cooked for my father was piled up and thrown into the garbage can out back. She grabbed her keys, and we hit the road in search of my father who she thought was off shacking up with some whore, but in reality at that

moment in time was resting on his cot in the backroom of the dry cleaning plant.

51   We headed out Highway 52 past the Donut Dinette and the bowling alley, the all night Kwik-Pik and Ferrell's bar-b-cue restaurant. These places seemed magical to me, parking lots bathed in neon and florescent light, people mingling, sitting on the hoods of their cars smoking cigarettes and drinking beer. They were living in a world I could only imagine, a world I dreamed of running away to as soon as I was old enough to drive.

52   My mother seemed more at ease traveling, and I imagined us on a road trip to the beach, nighttime driving, if we could have just kept going, kept pushing to the coast. But my mother wanted to catch my father. She wanted to prove her theory of his infidelity, and so we turned off Highway 52 onto a winding two-lane blacktop engulfed by Yadkin County darkness. We drove along through a land of junkyards and abandoned houses, wetland swamps and stubbled fields, past trailer parks and small shanty towns where bootleggers waited for those who didn't want to make the trip across the river to a wet county. We drove down dirt roads to shanties I never could have found in the daylight much less the pitch black my mother navigated through. We moved slowly as if she wanted to sneak up and surprise my father and those she was so certain gave him cover.

53   As we followed my mother's imaginary trail, the ease with which she drove would begin to tighten, twist into an unforgiving knot, and she would begin to spin conspiracy theories. "They know I'm coming," she would say. "They're helping him do this to me; they're watching out for him. I swear to God, I wouldn't spit on them if they were on fire." By the time we made our way back to town, the houses of friends and neighbors had unknowingly become part of the conspiracy. On our street alone, Momma spewed obscenities while honking the horn and driving up into the yards of our neighbors. She banged on doors of houses where people already were in bed asleep.

54   She confronted her best friend, Minnie Tamberlake, a woman who, while in Junior High, had gone to a dance with my father, two years before my mother met and fell in love with him. She had hated Minnie throughout high school, but they had later become best friends when they worked together at Cobb Mills. My father cleaned Minnie's laundry, delivered it when his hired help didn't show up for work, but my mother could not find it in her mind to understand this. It was fornication, it was betrayal, it was Sodom and Gomorra, and everyone involved would pay.

55   While my mother was inside Minnie's house screaming accusations, Mr. Timberlake came outside to the Buick where I waited. He was a small, thick man, tanned around the neck and arms, balding, a pooch sticking out that pushed his undershirt beyond his belt. He leaned into the window looking around as if he was thinking about buying the car. I said, "Is my daddy here?"

56   "No, Raybert. We were asleep. It's past eleven. We were asleep."

57   "Where's Momma?"

58   Mr. Timberlake took a deep breath and glanced back at the house. "She's talking to Minnie about where your father might be. Do you know where he is?"

59   I said, "Yes sir. He's at the dry cleaners."

60   "Did you tell your mother this?"

61   "Yes sir, twice."

62   Mr. Timberlake looked down to the ground outside the car door and then spit into the gravel. "You want to come in and stay here tonight?"

63   "No sir. I better stay with Momma."

64   He turned and walked away, his steps heavy in the darkness. Outside the door, Mr. Timberlake paused and listened as my mother and Minnie yelled at each other. When he disappeared inside, the shouting stopped. He brought my mother back to the car dragging her by the arm. She no longer yelled but was not very cooperative in leaving the yard. Mr. Timberlake opened the driver's side door and shoved her in, her head popping the top of the car's roof. It sounded like an egg cracking on the side of a pan, and Momma sat stunned for a moment.

65   Mr. Timberlake said, "Now Evelyn, the boy says Ray's at the cleaners. Do yourself a favor and go down there and look. Don't come back here tonight, do you understand?"

66   Momma sat there for a moment before she spoke, her jaw tightening, the muscles clinching like a fist. She never looked at Mr. Timberlake, just stared straight ahead as if she were already back on the road headed for her next stop. "Wayne Timberlake, don't think I don't know what you're doing. You keep Minnie away from my goddamned husband, or I'll splatter you both from here to kingdom come."

67   Mr. Timberlake looked over at me, his eyes sad and tired. This wasn't the first time my mother had threatened him. He said, "Don't let her come back, boy. She's a good friend when she's right. Go get your father; you find him, he could put a stop to this—" Before Mr. Timberlake could finish, Momma gunned the car forward, nearly running over his toes as tread marks ripped into soft fescue, cutting a deep gash across the front lawn.

68   We left the Timberlakes' house and drove up Williams Street past our own. The windows were dark, the house seemingly abandoned, and I felt for the first time in my life I was alone in a world that had no plan for me. I was here only to assist my parents as they destroyed themselves, and then I would live a long, hard, and lonely life. I could not see any significance to what we were doing. I only felt embarrassment and sadness for my mother who, as Lucky Luther had said, was crazy as a coot.

69   I wanted to help, I really did, and so I lied. I said to Momma, "Momma, he's at the dry cleaners. He called just before we left, while you were looking for your purse. He told us to come pick him up, that he was ready for supper."

70   Momma said, "Don't lie to me Raybert."

71   I said, "I ain't lying. He said come up there and pick him up. I just forgot to tell you. I think we ought to go by and see if he's still there."

72   Momma said, "He's gone, Raybert. He's long gone." In my mother's mind, the short circuit continued while we remained in pursuit of my father, looking through every dead-end Yadkin County had to offer along the darker side of its roads. I think sometime during our journey, I began to hope Momma was right. I wanted to believe that all she accused my father of was true. I wanted truth so we could go home, simple truth so all of this would be over and my mother would be normal again. We drove for hours and found nothing, my mother continuously refusing to drive by the dry cleaning plant. Upon my constant suggestion, she would say, "Save your breath, Raybert. I wouldn't go by that place if Jesus Himself was there saving souls," and off we would go in some dark and desperate direction, perhaps to a place we had visited earlier that night or into new and uncharted regions where I knew there could never be truth simple enough to set my mother free.

73   It was shortly after midnight when we ran out of gas at the corner of Hargrave Street and Ninth Avenue. The car sputtered and coughed, desperately lurched forward in an attempt to keep going before it died in the parking lot of the American Legion baseball field. This seemed to shock my mother, took her by surprise that the vehicle with which she could track my father was now failing to accomplish the mission. She sat in silence looking out over the deserted diamond illuminated softly by the full moon high in the night sky. She sighed and took her hands from the steering wheel. Momma said, "S_ _ _. I never saw this coming."

74   The loss of motion seemed to change her state of mind, ease her up on Daddy. We sat in the darkened car listening to the engine pop and tick as it began to settle down for the night. I thought about the time, how Lucky Luther would be expecting me to show up, and if I didn't he'd never let me live it down. His insults would cut deep. He'd call me a sissy, queerbait, butthole. He'd stop offering me cigarettes, and I would have to find the courage to buy my own, something I had yet to do.

75   Out on the baseball field an old stray dog was jumping high into the night air snapping at candle moths that had strayed from the security light dimly illuminating the stands behind the backstop. He ran after his own shadow, chased his tail, gnawed at his a_ _, and hiked his leg along a fence line holding the advertisements of local businesses. The mutt exhausted himself in play before collapsing along the warning track to breathe heavily and fall asleep on the cool red clay.

76   I said to Momma, "Can I have the dog?"

77   Momma looked at me like I was crazy.

78   I said, " I'd keep it fed. It could sleep in my room with me."

79   Momma said, "Dogs have fleas."

80   I said, "I'd keep it clean. I'd even pick off the ticks."

81   Momma looked at me for a long time, her eyes steeled and full of tears. In that brief moment I knew I would tell her everything, that even when I lied, I would always confess my guilt and ask her forgiveness. I told her then and there that Daddy had not called us to come get him. Momma said, "I knew that, Raybert."

82   I told her I had no idea about being born, that Palmer had said it and I had hit him in the face. Momma said, "It's all right to imagine things, son, but you apologize to Palmer next time you see him. He's your best friend this side of a brother."

83   I confessed that I was going to sneak out with Lucky Luther at midnight and go for a swim in the City Pool. Momma said, "That Lucky is sure headed for trouble. He reminds me of your father. You ought to stay away from boys like that. But I know you can't."

84   We sat in silence watching the dog out onto the baseball field. The stray lifted its head to bite at the empty air. It got up on all fours, circled three times to wind itself up into a furry ball, and then settled back down. Momma said, "Raybert, if things were different you could have a dog, but your Daddy, the way he is, well, I'm sorry—." Her voice trailed off almost inaudibly into a whisper, "I've got to go."

85   I said, "Maybe Daddy's at home."

86   "I've got to go pee over there in those trees. Will you be all right alone?"

87   I said, "Yes."

88   Momma said, "All right then." She got out of the car, the click of the door latch alerting the stray dog of an intruder. It rose quickly, tail tucked between its legs, and scurried off the clay track, yelping as it moved into the shadows of the visitor's dugout, its bark weak, an unconvincing threat. My mother walked across the parking lot, her sandals flip flapping in the silent night. She hummed a melody in a sweet voice I had never heard before, smooth and lovely. I watched her move, glide really, across the gravel. Her white halter-top shimmered in the moonlight. Her body, skin tanned by the darkness, seemed to absorb light and disappear, ghostlike into the shadows. She walked up to a line of trees just behind the outfield wall, turned and waved in a long arcing motion that had much greater permanence than a wave used when walking off to take a pee. Illuminated, transparent, my mother dipped beneath the limbs and was gone.

89   Sometime after, they found her walking along Highway 52, naked of all clothes except her bra and panties, and Aunt Iris came to take care of me. The city of Cobb decided to end the spraying of DDT throughout our neighborhoods. The bugman would no longer drive our streets poisoning anything that breathed, and I would never again ride my bike into the white clouds in defiance of my mother. Lucky Luther moved closer to his intended goal of becoming a true delinquent when he sniffed glue for the first time down in the woods at the picnic table.

We had been to a Pepsi Cola show that morning at the Carolina Theater and then next door into Briggs Hobby shop where he stole three tubes of plastic cement and a paper bag. In the woods, Lucky had squeezed an entire tube into the small brown bag, covering the bottom, filling the air with the sharp metallic sweetness of glue. He stuck his nose and mouth into the opening and inhaled the fumes until he could no longer see straight. Pulling his head out just long enough to empty his second tube, Lucky looked at me as if I were a stranger and wheezed, "Far out."

90   My father continued to be steady, staying at the cleaners, coming home periodically to check on me and make sure Aunt Iris had everything she needed. One night he came to see me, his huge figure dwarfing the small back room I used in summer for sleep. He sat down on the cot, the sweet smell of Jim Beam and burnt tobacco hovering. He looked at me and said, "Don't be thinking too hard about all this, Raybert. You're still young with chances for great things."

91   I said, "I think Momma's going to die?"

92   Daddy said, "No Raybert. What your momma's got won't kill her like that."

93   I said, "Will she ever be back?"

94   Daddy said, "Yes, when she's all right, when she's well."

95   "Will you ever come back to stay?"

96   Daddy said, "Raybert, I'm never too far gone. That's the best I can do right now." He then told me a story about a drunk who fought every evening out behind the dry cleaning plant. He said, "This old man was cut and bruised and scarred by a hard life. He had lost fingers and toes and teeth and hair; he drank hard and fought hard and beat younger men half his age. I'd always see this old man behind the cleaners fighting and clawing, biting and scratching at those who took him on. One day I asked him why he got himself into such a fix. The man told me he had committed murder somewhere in Mississippi, a black boy in the wrong place at the wrong time. He was legally out, had been acquitted, but he had done it; he guaranteed me that. He lied at his trial, and his friends had given him good alibis. The jury was lily white and didn't care for colored anyhow, so they let him off."

97   I said, "That ain't fair, is it?"

98   Daddy said, "No, it ain't. And the man knew it. The man said to me, he said, 'I fight to even the score. Every time they take a bite out of me, I'm giving it back to that boy I kilt. Pretty soon there won't be enough of me to go around anymore, but that's all right. I figured all this is my cross to bear. Now what's yours?'" My father stopped there and stood up. He looked at me as if I should have known the answer to the old man's question. And now as I remember the story, I think I always knew, for in my father's eyes I could see great suffering, I could see great life.

99   After he left my room, I took off all my clothes and crawled into bed. I broke down and cried and cried, naked and sweating in the heat

of a dying summer. I cried for no reason at all. I cried for everything I could never understand. I cried for the black boy dead at the hand of an angry white man and for my mother, whose life balanced precariously between sanity and insanity. My tears flowed for Lucky Luther, a delinquent on his way to oblivion, and for my father, a man who tried as hard as he could, but would never have enough. My tears soaked the pillow and then my sheets and mattress. They mixed with my sweat and grime and glued me to the bed so I could not move, I could not get away. I went to sleep and slept like a drunken sailor. I tossed and turned dreaming past my tortured sleep that I would wake up and do great things, know who I was and who I would be for the rest of my life. In my dreams, I found the answer to all the great pain in life. I slept hard and long and restlessly. I slept for a very long time.

Collaborative Activity: Discussion Questions

In groups of three to five, discuss each of the following questions. You do not have to agree with your partners. As you discuss, make frequent references to specific statements in the story. Then, in your notebook, write your *own* answer to each question after discussing the question in your group.

1. Describe the setting of the story. What clues point toward time and place?

2. What is DDT? How might the spraying of DDT be significant in this story?

3. How would you describe Raybert's relationships with his friends Palmer Conroy and Lucky Luther? Explain.

4. Why are Lucky and Raybert developing a connection with each other?

5. Why do you think Raybert runs away first from Palmer and later from Momma?

6. At the end of paragraph nine, the narrator says, "I knew my world physically, but remained unfamiliar with the idea of my world as thought." What might this mean?

7. Describe Raybert's relationship with each of his parents.

8. What unusual behaviors does Momma exhibit during the course of this story? Give several examples.

9. What is Mr. Timberlake's reaction to Momma's accusations? What is his reaction to Raybert?

10. At what points in the story does Momma exhibit a shift in her thinking and/or behavior?

11. Why does Raybert's father tell him the story about the old man who had gotten away with a murder?

12. Describe Raybert's state of mind at the end of the story.

▬▬▬▬▬

Of all the discussions you have had with peer groups, the debate over "When Momma Crossed the Road to Pee" may be the most animated yet. Each of us brings our own personal and cultural perspectives to reading and evaluating any work of literature, and this story, with its eccentric (even bewildering) title character is no exception. The only way to judge your evaluation or anyone else's is to see how well you support what you say using the story itself. Selected brief quotations and summaries of events you deem key will help you make your argument.

Assignment: Analysis of "When Momma Crossed the Parking Lot to Pee"

Write an essay of approximately 400 to 500 words in response to one of the three following topics. Be sure to include a thesis statement, and plan to make three or four main points in the body of your essay. Remember also to include selected quotations and explain how they support the assertions about the story. When you quote dialogue from the story, make certain to set it off by using double quotations: e.g., when told about the man's acquittal for a murder he committed, Raybert recalls, "I said, 'That ain't fair, is it?'" You will find other examples of direct discourse in the student models below. Use them as examples of successful responses to Topic 1 and Topic 2, not for imitative purposes.

1. Reread the selection, "Schizophrenia," from Wade and Tavris. Although you may lack the expertise to make a psychiatric diagnosis, you may still use Wade and Tavris as a prism for looking at Momma. In addition, you may want to locate additional information about schizophrenia on the World Wide Web. In what ways does Momma exhibit the characteristics of someone with schizophrenia?

2. What role does Lucky Luther play in the story? Why and how is he significant?

3. In what ways is "When Momma Crossed the Parking Lot to Pee" a story about coming of age and maturing? Discuss the ways the narrator, now a grown man recalling a childhood event, reflects on his process of growing and maturing. What does he begin to understand by the end of the story? What does he still have to learn?

▬▬▬▬▬

Student Model #1

Schizophrenia: Does Momma Have It?

By Helen M. Kruskamp

1   Schizophrenia is defined by Carole Wade and Carol Tavris as a psychosis that exhibits itself in delusions, including paranoia; hallucinations; and erratic behavior. Momma in "When Momma Crossed the Parking Lot to Pee," by Jack Riggs, displays several if not all of these symptoms. She is what most of us with no intense knowledge of this disease would call absolutely crazy.

2   Momma has severe delusions. She thinks that her husband is coming home, and when he does not, she believes that he is cheating on her with another woman and that complete strangers, along with her best friends, are in on it. In the story, Raybert says of Momma's state of mind, "By the time we made our way back to town, neighbors and friends had unknowingly become part of the conspiracy." When reading this story, I, at first, had a hard time deciding if I thought this was how Momma always was, or if it was only during extreme outbursts of her illness. However, after re-reading the story several times, I was able to conclude that Momma was most always a bit delusional, but not always totally out of control.

3   Momma behaved in several bizarre ways throughout the story. Sometimes she was loud and disruptive, while at other times she did quieter things such as cook a huge second dinner for her husband when she should have known perfectly well that he was not coming home. She would make storming rampages through her best friend Minnie's house, accusing Minnie of sleeping with her husband. You can tell from the dialogue in the story that this was a recurring event. Mr. Timberlake, Minnie's husband, said to Raybert, after dragging Momma out of his house and into her car, "'Don't let her come back, boy. She's a good friend when she's right. . . .'" His calmness in handling the situation shows that this is a problem he has dealt with before. Momma does other peculiar things, such as become perfectly calm for a moment, and she is able to carry on a seemingly normal conversation after having run around screaming and shouting all night.

4   When Momma becomes absorbed in her world of paranoia, it is easy to see that she is incapable of normal social interaction. She is convinced that everyone is plotting against her, and she cannot or will not accept reality. She is filled with rage and most definitely does not fit in to normal social standards. She blatantly rejects the truth that her husband is at the dry cleaning shop that he runs and is overwhelmed by the idea that he is cheating on her. Her feelings run wild, and her actions and speech are filled with rage and appalling threats. When Mr. Timberlake tells her that her husband is at the cleaners, she responds

with, "'Wayne Timberlake, don't think I don't know what you're doing. You keep Minnie away from my goddamned husband, or I'll splatter you both from here to kingdom come.'" She is absolutely out of control, and she is incapable of comprehending reality.

5   Momma, in my opinion, displays the symptoms of schizophrenia throughout the entire story with but a few moments of normalcy. She is absorbed in a world of untruths, paranoia, and overall sickness. She has no sense of the real world of social appropriateness. She is blatantly incapable of accepting simple truth and is terribly caught up in a disastrous world of her own.

Student Model #2

Why and How Is Lucky Luther Significant?

By Erik Miller

1   In Jack Riggs' story "When Momma Crossed the Parking Lot to Pee," the character Lucky Luther is static because throughout the story he does not change. When Lucky is first introduced, he is depicted as a thief, and at the end of the story, he is "becoming a true delinquent." In the story, Lucky never sees the error of his ways, and he probably never will. Lucky only has a minor role as a character in the story; however, he is very important to the story because of his significance to the main character, Raybert.

2   Raybert is a child, but he is going through the changes of adolescence, and he is confused about his role in life. He is depicted as "playing army in the woods, catching crawfish and salamanaders, . . . daring and double daring, comparing muscles, and Indian leg wrestling." All of these games are stereotypical boyish childhood acts, and Raybert is quite good at all of them. Raybert says that he "knew my world physically, but remained unfamiliar with the idea of my world as thought." Raybert is perplexed by his feelings of inadequacy on a mental level, as many adolescents are. When he tells his mother, "'I know what I know, that's all I got to say to you,'" he is using a typical response of many teens that lacks critical thinking on his part. Raybert also says that he "pretended not to hear her." If Raybert were more secure with his identity, he would be much less likely to act out in defiance of his mother.

3   When Raybert meets Lucky in the story, Raybert thinks that Lucky is the epitome of what he wants to be like. Raybert feels that "people mingling, sitting on the hood of their cars smoking cigarettes and drinking beer" is the level of life to which he wants to aspire, and Lucky represents those qualities to him. As do many adolescents, Raybert sees an older person, Lucky, as an escape to his "world I could only imagine, a world I dreamed of running away to as soon as I was old enough to drive." Raybert wants to be deemed cool by Lucky as a way of feel-

ing that he fits in with the older crowd and can "escape" his family problems.

4   Even though Lucky probably does not like Raybert as much as Raybert likes Lucky, Raybert still "found a connection to Lucky," and he "felt as though I was Lucky's accomplice." Raybert thinks that because Lucky does whatever he wants to do that Lucky is "the luckiest kid in the world"; however, many more mature people would say that Lucky is headed down a dead end road. Lucky tries to convince Raybert that if Raybert does not go swimming with him that Raybert is "'crazy'" for not doing it, and Lucky says, "'You got to do it Raybert, or you ain't got hair on your a_ _.'" Raybert still has a feeling that breaking the rules is not right, but he is forced to agree to the peer pressure because he needs to feel accepted by Lucky. If Raybert were slightly more mature himself, he would have denied Lucky's request.

5   When Raybert is stuck out all night with his mother, he comes to the realization that he has missed his appointment with Lucky, and the fear of not being accepted by Lucky makes him realize that Lucky does not care about him. Raybert believes that Lucky would "stop offering me cigarettes and I would have to find the courage to buy my own." This shows that Raybert feels that if he does not do what Lucky wants that Raybert risks losing Lucky's friendship. Raybert believes that Lucky will "call me a sissy, queerbait, butthole," and "his insults could cut deep" into Raybert's heart. Confused by his adolescent emotions, Raybert says, "[T]houghts were still too invisible to be revealed to me," and he is, therefore, unsure if he can be a strong person without Lucky.

6   By the end of the story, Raybert has realized that he does not need Lucky to find his place in life, and he even realizes that Lucky is really a loser. When Raybert sees Lucky sniffing glue, he sees Lucky in a different way than before. This revelation is important to Raybert because after that point Raybert can make his own choices and decisions. The Raybert who was in the beginning of the story is symbolically gone when he says, "I broke down and cried." Raybert says that he "cried for everything I could never understand"; this is a very mature act, and for the first time in the story, Raybert actually does understand something on a mature level. Raybert finally realizes that he does not understand certain things about life that some people may, but in knowing that, he can now grow intellectually and mature as a young adult.

7   Even though Lucky Luther's part as a character in the story is small, his role for Raybert's growth as a character is enormous. To Raybert, Lucky, in the beginning of the story, was everything that he looked up to, but Raybert realized that Lucky was not the type of person to be involved with. Lucky represents a symbolic jump from boyhood to adulthood for Raybert, and without Lucky's small part in the story, Raybert would never have been able to realize that he was capable of being a unique person on his own.

Collaborative Activity: Discussion and Comparison of Essays

In groups of three to five, compare your essay with those of some of your classmates. Also, compare your essay with the two student models. What makes each of the models successful? What might be done to improve each model? What might be done, as well, to improve your own essay? As you look at your classmates' work, try to find additional quotations or incidents in the story that would make their arguments stronger, too.

Grammar and Usage: Pronouns

*When **Native Americans** learned to domesticate plant life, **they** began the long process of transforming **their** relationship to the physical world.*

*A middle-aged **man,** hospitalized for 20 years, believing **he** was a prophet of God and that monsters were coming out of the walls, was able to interrupt **his** ranting to play a good game of chess.*

Pronouns are words that take the place of nouns. The word or phrase a pronoun replaces is called its **antecedent.** In the previous examples, the pronouns and antecedents are written in bold. Singular pronouns replace singular antecedents; plural pronouns replace plural antecedents. In addition, some pronouns (like *he, she, him,* and *her*) show gender (tell whether the person is male or female). Thus, we say pronouns must agree or match with their antecedents in terms of number (singular or plural) and gender (male or female).

There are many kinds of pronouns including relative pronouns (*which, that,* and *who,* for example), reflexive pronouns (*myself, himself, themselves*), indefinite pronouns (*each, every, some, all*), and the personal pronouns that you will find on the following chart. Personal pronouns identify the speaker or writer (first person), the audience (second person), or the person or thing spoken or written about (third person).

Personal Pronouns
Singular Pronouns

	Subjective Case	Objective Case	Possessive Case
First Person	I	me	my, mine
Second Person	you	you	your, yours
Third person	he, she, it	him, her, it	his, her, hers, its

Plural Pronouns			
	Subjective Case	Objective Case	Possessive Case
First Person	we	us	our, ours
Second Person	you	you	your, yours
Third Person	they	them	their, theirs

Writers choose a pronoun from a particular case depending on how the word will be used in a particular sentence. **Function** is what matters. If the pronoun will function as the *subject of a verb* or as a *subject complement,* then we must use a pronoun in its *subjective case.* A pronoun functioning as a subject of a verb answers the question, "Who or what did the action?" A pronoun functioning as a subject complement follows a form of "to be," (am, is, was), a linking verb (seems, looks), or a sensory verb (smells, tastes) and identifies the subject.

> *She* went to the movies. (subject of the verb *went*)
>
> It was *she* at the door. (subject complement)

On the other hand, if the pronoun will function as an **object** (*direct object, indirect object, objective of a preposition,* or *object of a verbal*), we must use a pronoun in its **objective case.** Pronouns that function as direct objects, in general, receive the action. Indirect objects usually answer the questions "For whom or for what" or "To whom or to what" was the action done? The object of a preposition follows a preposition. And the object of a verbal follows and completes the sense of a participle, gerund, or infinitive.

> Joey saw *them* at the mall. (direct object)
>
> I wrote *her* a letter (indirect object)
>
> Please cook a meal for *us.* (object of the preposition *for*)
>
> Just knowing *him* is a pleasure. (object of the verbal *knowing*)

Furthermore, if we want to show possession or ownership, we need a pronoun in its **possessive case.**

> The baby ate all *her* cereal. (the cereal of the baby)
>
> The dog brought *its* owner a red leash. (the owner of the dog)

To sum up, in addition to choosing a pronoun that agrees with its antecedent in gender and number, we need to be sure it is in the correct case, which depends on how it will function in the sentence.

Some Issues Involving Pronoun Agreement and Pronoun Case

1. The pronouns *everyone, each, everybody, anybody, anyone, either,* and *one* are always singular. Thus, when used as subjects, they always require a singular verb. In addition, when they become antecedents, the pronoun that takes their place must be singular.

Everyone finishes *their* work. (incorrect)

Everyone finishes *his or her* work. (correct)

> (*Note:* Using *he* to refer to both genders is generally no longer acceptable. Furthermore, *he or she* or *his or her* is preferable to *he/she* or *his/her.* But it is best, whenever possible, to use a plural antecedent. Instead of "Each student did his or her homework," "All the students did their homework" is much smoother.)

2. Do not add *self* to the possessive pronouns *their* or *his.*

They did it all by *theirself!* (incorrect)

They did it all by *themselves!* (correct)

My baby spilled soda on *hisself.* (incorrect)

My baby spilled soda on *himself.* (correct)

3. *Who* is subjective case; *whom* is for objective case.

That is the man *who* will teach your next class.

Who likes to read poems by Emily Dickinson?

Who is lying to *whom* around here?

4. Pronouns that are part of compound subjects follow the same rules for case as any pronoun.

Mary and *she* will be seeing the show tonight.

When you arrive, look immediately for Mary and *her.*

My friends and *they* are almost here.

Exercise 1

Directions: The following groups of sentences contain at least one mistake in pronoun agreement or case. Combine each group into one complete sentence without any pronoun errors.

1. Please give Pauley and he that note. [*him*]
   [*because*] That note comes from the principal. [*and*]
   It looks important.

2. Jane and them went to a movie. [*they*] [*and*]
   They nearly scared theirselves to death. [*themselves*]
   It was terrifying.

3. We heard a loud siren ten minutes into the lecture. [*;*]
   Everyone got up from their seats; however, [*his or her*]
   It was only a false alarm.

4. Me and my uncle like to shoot pool. [*My and I*]
   We like to rent movies, and
   We like to eat.

5. Sue takes we girls shopping. [*us*]
   We like big department stores.
   Us girls like to try on clothes.

6. The little boy looked at hisself in the mirror. [*himself*]
   He smiled at hisself. [*himself*]
   He liked who he saw. [*seen*]

7. I wrote this letter for whomever wants to read it. [*whoever*]
   I don't care who sees it.
   I could get in trouble.

8. Waiting for Mary and he is tiresome. [*him*]
   I wish they would hurry. [*them*]
   I want to go home.

9. Native Americans once lived here.
   Native Americans fished in this river.
   Native Americans built these mounds of earth theirselves. [*themselves*]

10. Everyone will do their own work. [*his or her*]
    No one will work collaboratively today.
    Everyone will take a test.

Exercise 2

Write a paragraph describing how to play the children's game called Ring Around the Rosy. When finished, circle all the pronouns you used in your paragraph.

An Essential College Essay: The Persuasive Research Paper

From the traditional freshman course often called "Comp 101" all the way through to doctoral dissertations, college students write research essays. The most common type, the persuasive research paper, will require you to identify, read, and cite a variety of sources in order to support an opinion that you will develop or that your professor will assign you. Some of the undergraduate classes that may require you to write a persuasive research paper are English, history, psychology, sociology, business, humanities, art, philosophy, film, and drama. Science classes also may require essays or reports that involve research.

In many ways, the persuasive research essay offers you, as a writer, certain advantages that other essays do not. For one, you will usually have longer to work on the research paper than, say, a narrative assignment. For another, your instructor will probably not direct you as to which position you should take on an issue (a notable exception being you and another student each taking the "pro" and "con" side of the same issue). Thus, you will have an opportunity to read the words of some real experts before you must formulate an opinion. Third and perhaps best of all, when you find especially helpful ideas and even specific phrases or sentences in the works of the experts, you may—indeed will—cite those phrases or sentences and use them to enhance your paper.

Students who develop competency, even mastery, of the skills to write good research papers are most likely to do well in upper division courses and in graduate school. What is more, as the workplace increasingly turns to long written proposals that frequently use sources (such as statistics, past performance figures, and experts' future projections), writers who can use research to "sell" their ideas gain a further advantage. The persuasive research paper is one of the most important types of writing that you will use through the rest of your academic career and, more and more likely, in your professional career as well.

Communication Triangle for the Persuasive Research Paper

Depending upon the way you look at it, a persuasive research paper may have one of three audiences. Suppose you are writing about health care costs for the elderly. You find a mountain of statistics that you believe will lead almost anyone to interpret as saying that rising health care costs pose a financial burden for senior citizens. You believe that a particular collaborative effort among insurance companies, state insurance commissioners, and drug companies will help to solve this problem.

One potential audience you may write to consists of people who feel the same way you do. They have educated themselves about the problem and may have decided, just as you have, that various involved parties must collaborate to remove a potentially devastating financial burden from the elderly. As these people read your essay, they will frequently nod in assent and may even murmur, "Yes, I think so myself." Wouldn't it be wonderful if you could always write for such an audience? Unfortunately, you will have no such audience for your persuasive research paper. These readers are already persuaded; to address them further amounts to "preaching to the choir."

Another audience disagrees with you. Some of these people believe that the problem of rising health care costs for seniors is so severe that virtually no action will correct it. They will see all efforts, including yours, as futile and will quickly read and then discard what you and your experts say. On the other hand, other people will disagree with you because they have considered the problem and decided that a different approach will solve it. They may resent your idea of including government officials in the solution. Or they may believe that insurance companies are doing enough already and that the burden lies on drug companies or the consumers themselves. Whatever their reasons, these people will respond to your work with comments of "No, no, no." Luckily for you, these readers are not your audience, either.

Finally, there are those readers who have not yet made up their minds. Perhaps they have seen a news report or read an article that has caused them to feel a vague sense of alarm about rising health care costs for the elderly, particularly as their parents or even they themselves grow older. Although they know a little about the problem, they have not thought their way through to a solution. They are interested, however, in what the experts have to say, and they may very well respond to a thoughtful, original presentation that includes a synthesis of much of the professional research out there. These readers are not naïve or gullible. In fact, they may even be quite skeptical, but they do have open minds. If you do a good job, you may reach them. They are your audience.

Of course, you know quite well that unless your paper eventually is published in a journal, a case study, or even a textbook like this one, your *real* audience is the instructor of your English, history, or art appreciation class. Likewise, unless you really work in the business world, your researched sales proposal will have as its *real* audience your finance professor. Understand, however, that these teachers have spent years learning to read student research with a sense of empathy. In other words, your English professors will understand the way a general audience might react to your papers and will read them accordingly. So as you write research papers, beginning with the one assigned in this chapter, remember to engage in what a poet once called the "willing suspension of disbelief" and write as if the professor really were that undecided individual discussed earlier. The results should make your suspension of your disbelief worthwhile.

The Assignment: Writing a Persuasive Research Paper

Aim or Purpose: Informative and Persuasive

Audience: Someone who is undecided about a particular issue

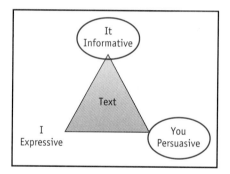

Step 1: Brainstorming a Topic

What inspires passion in you? Do you care deeply about teen pregnancy, the social factors that cause it, and ways to reduce its occurrence? Does the amount of violence in our popular culture disturb you? Are you fearful that government, in its zeal to reform and redress, often needlessly restricts and controls? Do you worry that the harm landfills and strip mining do to our environment endangers our children's and our children's children's futures?

On a piece of paper, briefly list several problems that you would like to see society or individuals solve. Try to stay away from problems so vast that only cooperation among all the peoples of the world could possibly solve them. In other words, a persuasive research essay about permanently ending all wars might be fun to write but would ultimately be likely to have little, if any effect. Similarly, do not write about a topic so restricted that a simple resolution by one person would effect your desired result. As much as you may want to write a paper persuading your eleven-year-old daughter or sister to put her laundry in the hamper, avoid the temptation. This topic is not broad enough.

So-called "hot button" social issues also pose special problems. Two topics, in particular, frequently produce unsuccessful persuasive research essays. The first and more serious is abortion. Most people already have their minds made up about abortion and are unlikely to be persuaded by a thousand new words pro or con. This statement is especially true when essays adopt a shrill "Abortion is murder and those who condone it permit murder" *or* an angry "My body is my own and no one can make me give birth if I choose not to" tone. Unfortunately, far too many essays on abortion read just this way. Imagine how off-putting such words are to the (rare) undecided reader out there.

The other topic that often produces persuasive research essays that, alas, are not very persuasive is the drinking age, especially when people between the ages of eighteen and twenty write about it. Most readers know that age eighteen meets or exceeds the legal age to marry, stand trial as an adult, vote, drive, serve on a jury, and register for the military draft! For various reasons, however, most adults over age twenty-one feel no pressing need to legalize drinking by those younger than they. Additionally, most essays on this topic tend to repeat the same litany you read two sentences ago.

None of this is to say that you absolutely should not write about abortion, the drinking age, or any other issue that matters to you. In fact, as you brainstorm, you may write down virtually anything you like. You will always have time to refine your list later. The better job you do, however, of generating topics that actually do lend themselves well to persuasive research papers, the less time you will spend needlessly repeating steps or conducting new research later. Consider the student and professional models in this chapter as you brainstorm. By the time you complete your brainstorm activity, try to limit yourself to two or three topics that you believe may lead to fruitful reading and research in the library or on the Internet.

Step 2: Researching a Topic— Locating Sources

From the rise of the modern public library until the very late 1900s, most people performed research by going to a public or school library. There, they checked out circulating books or read selected reference materials or periodicals housed in the library itself or ordered from another branch or system.

During the late 1990s, the rise of the Internet saw tremendous amounts of material put on-line. Although most books remained in traditional libraries, articles proliferated as fast as workers could type or scan them into databases. Suddenly, students living in Somalia could read a periodical published in England without having to wait weeks or months for a copy of the periodical to reach their local library.

More than likely, you will use a combination of library and Internet sources to conduct research for this paper. Indeed, you may find yourself conducting Internet research within the library itself, or at home while accessing the library's computers. This very recent boom in access to information offers tremendous opportunities to you, in addition to imposing some new requirements. We will discuss the requirements later.

First, however, you need to decide literally where you want to begin. If you have Internet access at home or in a classroom or dormitory, you may want to log on and begin researching your topic using any of a number of databases. If you lack easy Internet access (or possibly even if you have it), you may begin by visiting your campus or community library. Even a relatively brief scan of computer databases or library catalogs will often give you a pretty good idea about the amount of research that other people have already performed on your topic and on the amount of controversy it has generated. Both of these bits of information will help you tremendously.

When you go to a library, begin by looking in the library's catalog to see whether the library contains any book titles relevant to your subject. Larger libraries, such as university or major metropolitan libraries, are most likely to have material you will want. Even so, smaller libraries will often have computer access to the catalogs for larger systems and may allow you to order books via interlibrary loan. This service is a real boon—unless you procrastinate and render it worthless.

To facilitate this search, you absolutely will want to ask for assistance from the librarians. A major part of their job is helping people find books and helping people avoid some of the pitfalls that stand between them and books. For example, you may want to research teens who sniff glue, or "huff," and may not find much information when you type in "sniffing glue" as key words. The librarian may suggest a variety of other key words, such as "teenage drug abuse" or "inhalant abuse," to open new possibilities to you. An initial search that turns up no items at all may produce three or four books within a few minutes after you receive assistance from the resident expert, the librarian.

Select a reasonable number of books to check out, order, or (if they are marked "Reference") use in the library. A reasonable number means that you will have sufficient time to skim the less relevant parts of the book and read the more relevant parts before you have to begin writing your essay. For most authors of essays in the 1,000 word range, approximately three books should be a reasonable number. If your professor assigns a longer or shorter paper, adjust the number of books accordingly.

When you have located or ordered the books you will examine, move on to periodicals. Periodicals often have the advantage over books of being more timely. It usually takes several years for a book to move from conception to print. An article, on the other hand, will frequently appear in print months, or even weeks, after the author(s) begins work on it. On issues where policies, statistics, and other important facts change, this timeliness is a major asset.

Many sources are available to help you find good periodical articles. A trusty old source is the *Reader's Guide to Periodicals,* which focuses primarily on popular periodicals and is available both on-line and in hard copy. Other computer and text sources will help you find articles from periodicals that are less widely read but often more academically respected. Your instructor and your reference librarian can help you locate such sources.

Another way of locating both book and periodical sources may sound, at first, like cheating, but it is actually both legitimate and desirable. Any book or periodical that contains research itself will likely have a Works Cited section or a Bibliography. If you like the ideas contained in the book or the article, you may very well find yourself liking the ideas contained in the sources the author(s) of the book or article consulted. Feel free to seek out and read these sources yourself. Perhaps you will find additional information not cited in your source but that pertains directly to the topic you are researching. In this case, the sources you use your library to locate help you in two ways: they contain useful information for you, and they point you to other sources of similar information.

As we mentioned earlier, many articles now exist on-line. This recent phenomenon gives you almost immediate access to articles that you otherwise would have waited days, weeks, or even months to view yourself. This fact alone constitutes a major benefit. Keep two points in mind, however, as you use articles that you locate on-line.

The first caveat about on-line articles is that an abstract for an article is *never* an acceptable substitute for the article. If you end up citing an abstract in your paper when, in fact, you have read only an on-line abstract, you are relying completely on someone else's honesty and, more important, accuracy in reporting what another person has said. Use on-line articles when and only when you gain access to the full text. Feel free, then, to take down all the information about the title, author, and publication source of the actual article. Then, check with your librarian or your library's serials or periodicals list to see whether your library already has the article in hard copy. On-line, abstracts and full-text articles will almost always be labeled as such, but still be careful.

Second and equally as important is the need to order a hard copy even of an article that you locate on-line. Let's say you find an article about whether or not children need fathers that takes the point of view that fathers are less necessary than most people in society generally think. Such an article may give you an intriguing, provocative source for a proposed essay on divorce's effect on relationships between children and fathers. Indeed, you will find exactly such an article later in this chapter.

Even so, finding the full-text article on-line and reading it are not exactly the same as reading the actual article. Often individuals who, like all of us, are prone to errors, type these articles into databases.

To cite a specific instance, the authors originally located the article "Kids Need 'Fathers' Like Fish Need Bicycles," which you will soon read, through an on-line database. Unfortunately, the last sentence of the first paragraph reads as follows: "By way of illustration, I will relate the story of raising my son ano me ways I see that his encounters with his father have shaped him." Ano me ways? Has Karla Mantilla, the author of the article, suddenly switched into a bizarre combination of Latin and English? Of course not. Instead, the person who typed in the sentence simply made two rather bad typographical errors. We were able to correct these typos by ordering the article from a university library and then using a photocopy of the original, not the version obtained on-line, in this textbook. You will be well advised to allow yourself the time to do likewise.

Step 3: Researching a Topic—Taking Notes

Once you have obtained several good sources that discuss your topic, you must decide how to employ them. Begin by developing good note-taking skills. A combination of jotting down facts, paraphrasing, and quoting directly will give you the materials to make the research part of your persuasive research paper strong.

Let us assume that you have before you a reference material or a periodical article (hard copy or on-line) that you cannot check out from the library. Let us also suppose that you do not relish the idea of endlessly feeding coins into a photocopier or paying virtually unlimited printing fees. You have both a high-tech and a low-tech option available to you at this point. The high-tech option is to obtain a portable scanner, which you can use to scan in as many pages as you need. Make certain, however, to include the publication data page of a book or any page that contains publication data for an article, or you will have to use valuable time to obtain this information (perhaps even relying on your mind's strained memory!) later. When you return to a computer at home or in your classroom, you may use your computer and printer to produce hard copies of the pages then. Make your personal notes in the margins, and use a highlighter to mark words, phrases, and sentences that you think are especially well written and pertinent. If you expect to make many hundreds of copies during your college career, the initial cost of a portable scanner can be a sound investment.

The low-tech option involves index cards and a pen or pencil (warning: pencils smudge). Take a pack of 3 × 5 index cards and a pack of 4 × 6 index cards along with your writing implement to the library. As you find information that you think you may be able to use in your essay, write it on the 4 × 6 index cards. Any time that you use an exact word or words from the essay, use quotation marks and put page numbers in parentheses immediately to the right of the direct quotations. If you restate an idea entirely in your own words, simply cite the page number. Determining the exact page number of an article that has been printed on-line can be next to impossible, so until you obtain the actual hard copy, record the paragraph number.

Do not try to save trees or money here by cramming a lot of ideas onto a single index card. In fact, it is best if you restrict yourself to a single idea per card. This way, as you add and delete ideas and especially as you arrange and rearrange the order in which you wish to state ideas, your task is as simple as producing, discarding, or reshuffling 4×6 index cards.

Of course, as you are using sources, you will also have thoughts of your own that are inspired by but not taken from your reading. Absolutely do not hesitate to write these ideas, individually, on your 4×6 index cards. These ideas may turn into the thesis statement or topic sentences or even the conclusion of the paper you will eventually write. Writing them down as they occur to you, even while you are conducting research, eliminates the risk that you will forget these important ideas before you sit down to "write" the paper. Notice that the word "write" appears in quotation marks here because taking notes in this way makes up a large part of writing the essay. Often entire research papers have come from wisely organized sets of note cards.

You will probably use fewer 3×5 index cards, but they are every bit as important as their larger counterparts. On a separate 3×5 index card, write down the title, author(s), place of publication, date of publication, pages, and other source information for each book, article, or other source you consult. If you find your material on-line, include as much of this information as possible as well as the URL (the website address, a long string of letters and characters that often begins "http://") and the date you accessed the source. These cards will produce the Works Cited sheet that will come at the very end of your essay. You will simply need to alphabetize the cards (by author's last name or title, whichever is appropriate) and copy the information in MLA (Modern Languages Association) or any other format your professor requires.

Of course, using index cards is merely one of several low-tech ways of taking notes and compiling sources. If you have another system that works for you, by all means stay with it. Always remember, though, to focus on completeness and accuracy. You will appreciate both these qualities, especially if you find yourself putting the finishing touches on your paper at 3 A.M. on the day it is due!

Often students have questions about quoting and paraphrasing. After instructors deliver frightening lectures about the consequences of plagiarism, or academic dishonesty, students can become terrified of committing this grave intellectual error and seeing their academic careers diminished or even ended as a result. You will need to worry very little if you follow some simple guidelines.

1. If a piece of information you find in your article is considered common knowledge, you need not cite it. The two most common examples of common knowledge that apply to research papers are information so widely known that virtually any educated person can be expected to know it (such as the fact that there are nine planets orbiting the sun) and material that may not be so universally known but can easily be obtained from a standard reference source (such as Dr. Martin Luther King's birthday, January 15). If you reasonably believe that information falls into either of these two categories of common knowledge, simply write it on your 4 × 6 index card, and treat it as if it were your own idea.

2. If a piece of information cannot fairly be classified as common knowledge but you have restated it *entirely* in your own words, consider it paraphrased. Paraphrased information does not call for quotation marks. In writing it on your index cards, simply include the author's (or authors') name and the page number. If you go on to use the material in your paper, give the author(s) credit by mentioning him/her/them (either in the text or in parentheses) and by citing the page number (always in parentheses). When two or three consecutive sentences in your essay come from the same page of the same source, you may simply write, at the end of the last sentence and in parentheses, "Preceding three sentences from Strunk 79." This way, the citations impede reading the paper as little as possible. Later in this chapter, you will encounter specific examples that show the use of paraphrasing both in general and within the context of actual students' persuasive research papers.

3. Whenever you use one or more words directly from the source, you *must* use quotation marks to show that you have done so. Use the exact words of the source only if you believe that the original source states the idea so well that you could not possibly expect to improve upon it. A judicious use of quotations improves any research essay, but quotations may be overdone. Other than using quotation marks, cite them on your note cards and in your essay the same way you cite paraphrased material.

In addition to these three rules, you should bear two others in mind at all times when you write the essay.

1. When in doubt, cite. You absolutely do not have to worry about being accused of plagiarizing material that you properly cite. It is always a good idea to err on the side of citing as opposed to not citing.

2. When in doubt, ask your professor. What is acceptable on Monday will still be acceptable on Tuesday. And if you are failing to cite when you should, it will be informative, not painful, to learn this information *before* you hand in the essay for a grade.

Step 4: Reviewing Examples of Potential Sources

The following essay, "Kids Need 'Fathers' Like Fish Need Bicycles," by Karla Mantilla, appeared in the periodical *Off Our Backs* in June 1998. Mantilla develops an argument about children and fathers based on her own experiences as a mother who separated from her husband and then observed the relationship between her husband and son.

Read Mantilla's essay carefully. While reading, take notes over ideas and facts that interest you. Use a combination of paraphrased material and appropriately noted direct quotations. To hone your skills for the library, use 4×6 index cards for these notes, and cite the page numbers from your textbook. Write "Mantilla as cited in Jones" on each card so that you will be able to determine later that you read Mantilla's essay in this textbook. You will learn more about how to cite a source that is reproduced in another source (an anthology, a case study, a collection of essays, etc.) later. Whenever Mantilla inspires you with your own original idea, write it down on its own 4×6 card. When you have finished, answer the questions that follow.

Kids Need "Fathers" Like Fish Need Bicycles

By Karla Mantilla

1   I am highly suspicious of the upsurge of praises of fatherhood and the necessity of kids to have a male role model. I come by this suspicion after much experience with my own two kids and their male role model, their father. By way of illustration, I will relate the story of raising my son and the ways I see that his encounters with his father have shaped him.

2   My son was a very difficult toddler and child, always stubborn as if his life depended on defying me. It was very trying for me and made me thoroughly doubt not only my ability to mother, but my very sense of what was good for people. I had thought that people were not born evil, and would respond well to kind treatment and positive human regard. But these things did not seem to work with my son. My then husband was more strict; he "knew" that my son was trying to get away with things and needed harsh discipline more than kind admonishment. At first I disagreed, but as my son continued to be hard to handle and stubborn, I became more inclined to doubt myself: maybe I was wrong and the only thing people respond to is discipline; maybe human relations are best conducted on the basis of power rather than mutuality; maybe boys are biologically unable to have the same kinds of relationships women shared. Try as I might to establish communication with my son, tucking him in at night and trying to talk to him about how he felt, being sure to nonjudgmentally listen to his thoughts and feel-

ings, he was steadfastly closed off to me, answering always "I don't want to talk about it." I felt helpless and at a loss. Perhaps boys do need a firmer hand than I thought.

3 When my son was 10 years old, my dissatisfaction with my husband became so severe that I made plans to leave him. By this time I had discovered that I could get far more emotional satisfaction relating to women. During the time I was finding a place to live and arranging a legal separation, I had a lot of worries about what this would do to my children and especially my son. I was not alone. Those who should have been my allies made no bones about telling me that I was a bad and selfish mother to break up my marriage; that it would be awful for my son especially. One of my sisters, a child psychologist, went on about how bad it would be for my son to be raised by such an ardent feminist. Another sister told my husband that he should try to get custody since I was such a manhater. My own lawyer regaled me with a litany of terrible things that my children would experience as a result of the divorce; severe drops in grades, behavior problems, nightmares, regressive behavior, etc. It was a difficult time compounded twentyfold by such friends and allies.

4 Of course I cared deeply about the well being of my children and the idea that what I was doing could harm them was horrible to me. Luckily I was enough of a feminist to doubt that these people were right. But the virtual mania about the horrors of divorce had begun to overtake the country and these people were responding to that. I wonder how many women are discouraged from leaving their husbands because of this children-need-their-father mania, staying for the sake of the children. I worry how many women doubt their own instincts in raising children because of the current hysteria over children needing fathers. And how many lesbians search for male role models for their children?

WHAT DID HAPPEN?

5 Only good. Contrary to my lawyer's dire predictions, my kids both maintained their straight A average (ok, a mother gets to brag once in a while), their behavior was fine and there were no regressions. But the most significant and surprising thing that happened was that my relationship with my son changed dramatically. About six months after leaving my husband, my son began to reveal his feelings to me for the first time in his life. When I would tuck him in at night, we began to have heart-to-heart talks which continue to this day (he is 13 now and it is uncommon indeed for closeness to increase rather than diminish at this age). He had always had a temper problem which he insisted was uncontrollable. It was agonizing to him that he had it and in fifth grade he even joined a school support group called "hotheads" for kids who were trying to control their tempers. After I separated from my husband, my son's temper began to abate, later to disappear entirely.

After one and a half years he began to tell me he loved me for the first time in his life. And after two years, he and I together began to see the damage that had been caused him by his male role model. His temper he had gotten directly from his dad, his stubborness as well. The more he was able to see these things, his disposition, mood and sociability dramatically improved.

6   His father is by everyone else's standards, a good father, involved with his kids, etc. All our mutual friends and neighbors showed their disapproval to me for leaving such a "good" man. One of my neighbors who was my friend and confidant for 10 years invited my ex-husband rather than me over for our first Thanksgiving apart. People who had been exclusively my friends suddenly began inviting him over to their parties. Everyone felt so sorry for him. What a nice guy he was. But this paragon of fatherhood was ruining his son's happiness. When I would get the kids after being with their father, my son would act horribly for the first day. He would tantrum, cry and complain that he wanted to die. It took my partner to point out to me, as doubtful I was of myself and my worldview by this time, that my son was in great pain and was acting badly because of it. When I began to examine this idea I found that my ex-husband's temper, his need to win, his inability to listen, his belief that his son was "trying to get away with things," his "discipline," his favoring of our daughter over our son were tormenting my son. (Not surprisingly, my daughter was not the target of his fits of temper and discipline; she was pampered and catered to by him.)

BUT ISN'T DIVORCE BAD FOR KIDS?

7   No. I don't think kids care so much who their parents are sleeping with as how well they are treated by the human beings male or female, who raise and nurture them. I think that my divorce, surprisingly even to me, turned out to be one of the best things that could have happened to my kids, especially my son. His chance to live in a home where different values, in fact traditionally feminine values, prevailed, proved to be nurturing for him. My kids got a chance to see their mother, away from a situation where I was devalued and sneered at, in an environment where kindness is a strength rather than a weakness, where listening to each other is positive and not the mark of a loser, where admitting you are wrong is respected rather than pounced on. Having two environments gave them a chance to see clearly the differences between the two worldviews and I hope will enable them to choose the one with which they are most comfortable, or the aspects of each which suit them the best.

DON'T KIDS BENEFIT FROM HAVING TWO PARENTS IN THE SAME HOME?

8   Not necessarily. In my case, my husband's devaluing of my way of being in the world robbed my kids of seeing my worldview as a

respectable and valid life choice. The major benefits I can see to the overrated two-parent family are material and practical: it is so much harder to not have someone to share the considerable responsibilities of raising children.

DON'T KIDS NEED FATHERS OR MALE ROLE MODELS?

9   I cannot emphasize enough what an absurd idea this is. Do we harp on female role models? What we need are good examples of humane values transmitted to our children, period. I submit that men tend to emphasize values such as discipline, power, control, stoicism, and independence. Sure, there can be some good from these things but they are mostly damaging to kids and other living things. They certainly made my son suffer an isolated and tortured existence until he began to see that there was a way out of the trap of masculinity.

ARE MOTHERS ALONE INADEQUATE?

10   No. Any human being who teaches their children how to be humane, mostly through treating them kindly and with humanity is all a child really needs. I wonder how many of the problems of "children of divorce" are caused by their exposure to stepfathers or other men introduced as "male role models." The other cause of such problems I believe to be the result of the impoverishment of women upon becoming divorced. And this impoverishment can be one of time rather than money. After a divorce, overburdened mothers are often overstressed and less able to spend time raising their children according to their values. When you are tired, worried about money and overburdened with work, you don't always set the best example and you don't always treat your children as well as you'd like.

THE CYCLE OF PATRIARCHY—FROM FATHER TO SON

11   What happened to my son is not an isolated family constellation. It is a pattern I have seen over and over with so many of my married friends. Their children act badly because of the harsh treatment by their fathers. Then because the mother sees the children act so badly, they believe that maybe the father is correct in his view that children need such discipline and their ability as mothers and commitment to more humane values become undermined. I have a friend who feels so overwhelmed by the behavior problems of her son that she has come to believe that her husband is right that he needs a firmer hand. She even told me that her husband is so much better with the boy than she is. When I asked her what she meant by "better," she replied that he obeys his father better than her.

CHILDREN ACT BAD WHEN THEY FEEL BAD

12   When I worked at an abused women's shelter, one consistent phenomenon I saw was that children who had behaved well at home out of fear of their abusive father would act like holy terrors at the shelter once they were no longer under the reign of terror of their home. Many

of the mothers felt inadequate, that they could not control their children, and several suggested going back to their husbands because the
kids acted better there. Maybe their husbands were right after all, he
was better with the kids than the mothers were.

13   But these kids acted badly because they were acting out—they
were in pain and once in a safe space were finally free to express it with
the parent with whom they felt safer. Curiously, kids often act worse
with the *better* parent, the one with whom they feel more secure will
accept them and help them heal from their pain. It is actually more
hopeful for such a child to act badly than to be cowed into submission.
(Ironically, their acting worse around the mother is touted as evidence
by many fathers that she is too soft on the kids and they need his
firmer hand.)

HOW GOOD MOTHERS COME TO FEEL INADEQUATE

14   But since the treatment of harsh disciplinarian fathers, particularly
of sons, is seen as a good thing, mothers cannot explain to themselves
why their boys act so bad. They conclude, much like I did, that they are
too soft, that feminine values are inadequate to the task of raising
boys, that their husband is right that boys need discipline, that maybe,
after all, it is biological. But the reason the boys begin acting badly is
the emotional pain inflicted on them by a harsh father who imposes his
will without regard for the child's experience, and without mutual
respect and good will. So the cycle begins: boy misbehaves in a way
typical to all children; father comes down hard on the boy, laying down
the law early; boy feels hurt and cries; father becomes angered at the
boy's expression of weakness and acts more harshly. This scenario happens over and over, until the boy learns that adults do not care how he
feels, that showing feelings is weak and leads to more severe punishment, that people cannot be trusted to show mercy, and the best thing
to do is to close off from people altogether. But the pain and loneli-
ness drive him to act out occasionally which triggers a new round of
harsh discipline.

15   I have seen this pattern over and over again with so many of my
friends who are married to men. The cycle becomes complete when
the mother, seeing the bad behavior of her children, assumes that
she is not adequate to the task of raising the children alone and
becomes more yielding to her husband's insistence that what they
need is the firmness only a father can provide. I see so many kind-
hearted caring mothers overrun by their husband's Machiavellian view
of child rearing who abandon their children out of their own self-
doubt. No, the propaganda that children, especially boys, need
fathers I think has contributed incalcuably to the misery of children
all over the world.

WHAT CHILDREN DO NEED

16   Children are just like us: they need caring, communication and connection with those around them. These qualities *can* be shown to children by anyone—parent, aunt, neighbor, friend—male or female—but these qualities have been most often embraced by women. I do not want to be misunderstood as saying that women are always better parents than men—indeed some mothers are appallingly lacking in warmth, nurturance and caring, and many mothers are abusive, and these mothers are as bad for children as bad fathers are. However to the extent that women have tended to value kindness and nurturance more than men, they are better parents. It is the *qualities* of kindness and nurturance, that matter most of all—the genitalia of the caretaker have nothing to do with it whatsoever. Contrary to all the pro-father rhetoric of late, to the extent that we value fathers precisely for their "discipline" and "toughening up" qualities, we create children (especially boys) who are less empathic and caring. If we want kinder, gentler (and less violent) adults, we need to focus on kinder, gentler parenting.

Collaborative Activity

In small groups, answer each of the following questions.

1. What was Mantilla's opinion about the relationship between fathers and sons before her divorce? What was the primary source of this opinion?

2. On what basis does Mantilla argue that the changes on her son were "[o]nly good" after her divorce?

3. Why does Mantilla use the question/answer method during the middle sections of her essay? Do you find her answer persuasive? Why or why not?

4. Why do you think Mantilla's sister called her a "manhater"? Do you agree or disagree with this assessment? Why?

Now we will take a look at the effect of divorce upon father and child relationships from another perspective. The following are several pages excerpted from *Surviving the Breakup: How Children and Parents Cope with Divorce*, by Judith S. Wallerstein and Joan B. Kelly. This 1996 volume reflects the cumulative results of more than two decades of research that Wallerstein has conducted on the subject of divorce. Read Wallerstein and Kelly. Just as you did with Mantilla's essay, practice taking notes on 4 × 6 index cards. Once again, use paraphrases and quotations, and record your original observations as they occur to you. Then answer the questions that follow.

Why Are Visits So Hard?*

By Judith Wallerstein and Joan B. Kelly

1   With the marital separation, father and child both face an abrupt discontinuity in the form of their daily contact. Suddenly, they must adapt their mutual feelings and needs to the narrow confines of the visit. During the years that follow, the father-child relationship rests entirely on what can be compressed into the new and limited form. The difficulties inherent in his compressed funneling process have been insufficiently appreciated. And if anything the courts, and the embattled partners and their respective attorneys, have directed their efforts to imposing restrictions and strict conditions which further encumber a relationship which under the best of circumstances is fragile and needs encouragement.

2   The parent who moves out of the household begins a new role for which there is no dress rehearsal and no script. A visiting relationship between parent and child is strange by its very nature. The daily events which structured the parent-child relationship have vanished. The roles are awkward and new, no longer defined by sharing meals or family tasks. Neither child nor parent fully shares the life of the other, nor is fully absent.

3   The part-time parent and the part-time child often begin with a bewildering sense of no place to go and no idea of what to do together. The relationship is from the outset beset by practical problems: by the presence of children of different ages and colliding interests; by the absence of the mother who had often served as an interpreter of the children's needs. To many fathers these practical problems seemed at first insurmountable. What to do with young children still in need of actual nurturing care? Or with older children who appeared to need continual stimulation and entertainment in order to control their restlessness? Some confused men changed their entire routine for the children's visits, others changed nothing at all, and still others, equally perplexed, expected the children to take full responsibility for the agenda. "I feel like a camp director," said one exhausted father.

4   The broad parameters of the new role are unclear. To what extent is the visiting father a guest, a favorite uncle, or a parent? More explicitly, to what extent does the visiting parent continue to take responsibility for setting behavioral and moral standards? To what extent does he register approval or disapproval, or enforce discipline or even homework, and how can he do so without the built-in safeguards and bed-

---

*Excerpt from *Surviving the Breakup: How Children and Parents Cope with Divorce* (Basic Books, 1996).

time rituals of intact family life which lessen disappointment, soften anger, and provide safe channels for alleviating the inevitable conflicts and frustrations of the relationships? Hurt feelings are more likely to continue and misunderstandings are more likely to remain unclarified. Men who were used to commanding their children experienced a new sense of impotence and frustration. All of these complexities combined to keep the father's sense of who he is now unsettled and unsettling.

5   The sense of time as a component of the parent-child relationship has also changed. For parents and children who share the repeated tasks of daily living together, time is part of the unobtrusive background of family life and provides a steady, muted rhythm which by its very unobtrusiveness conveys the comforting notion that the present will endure. For the visiting parent and child, time is a jarring presence. The constraints of time and space may impose a severe burden or, in some instances, a welcome limit on the interactions of the relationship. But both parent and child must now find time for their meeting, and must part on time. Both meeting and parting have acquired new meanings and accompanying anxieties which may long endure.

6   Many other factors also generate stress and threaten this fragile relationship. Children, as we have described already, take on special significance at this time: as economic or psychological burdens whose presence is resented; as important sources of self-esteem whose reassurance is sought and whose absence is feared; as friends and needed helpmates and even counselors during lonely, stressful decision-making times; as prizes to be fought over; as the only reliable allies in the marital battles. The complex dependence of adults on children for *their* self-esteem is especially apparent as fathers become vulnerable to their children in new ways that sometimes radically change the balance of the relationship.

7   One-half of the men were afraid of rejection by their children. They were worried about their children's disapproval and anger because of the divorce. Partly out of these and related concerns, at least one-third of the men were unusually generous to their children, plying them with special treats or money. Playing Santa Claus helped them with their discomfort about what to do and enabled them to deal with guilt about the divorce by making restitution with generous gifts. Their generosity also helped win the children's approval, cooperation, and eagerness for the next visit. This role strained the fathers financially and emotionally and, of course, often angered their divorcing wives.

8   There were many other problems. Men were uneasy about what to do with their lovers at visiting time. How would this affect both their children and the developing relationship with the woman? They did not know how to arrange for privacy in close quarters, and they often failed

abysmally to understand or to be aware of the consequences of their own behavior or to anticipate the children's response.

9   Mr. A. had a large waterbed in his apartment which he and his seven-year-old daughter shared during her weekend visits. Occasionally, when he invited a woman friend to join them he sent the child for the night to an adjoining room, replacing her with his friend. He was annoyed and mystified by the child's tearful protestations.

10   Visiting parents also found that the visit itself became an arena which readily evoked in both parents the ghosts of the failed marriage and the fantasies of what might have been. Raw feelings of both marital partners tend to be exacerbated by visits even when there is no actual contact between former spouses or when such contact is fleeting. The visit is an event continually available for the replay of anger, jealousy, love, mutual rejection, and longing between the divorcing adults. In addition, one-third of both parents in our group were in active competition for the affection and loyalty of their children. Unfortunately, therefore, each visit provided a potential second battleground or rendezvous that always involved the children; and although the majority of parents tried to honor the children's visiting time, even those who tried hard often failed. Two-thirds of the women were moderately or severely stressed during the father's visits in the first year following the separation, and the great majority of the men felt much the same. In fact only a small fraction, approximately one-fifth of the men, was not stressed by the visits during this early period.

11   The fighting between the parents occasionally reached pathological, even bizarre, intensity. One gently bred matron, for example, smeared dog feces on the face of her husband when he arrived to see his children. One father sought a court order requiring his former wife to make herself invisible when he came to the door. All in all, one-third of the children were consistently exposed to intense anger at visiting time. The tension generated by the parents burdened the visits and stressed them and the children. A preponderance of the visits ruined by parents in this way were visits with the older children. Younger children were more protected.

12   Perhaps half of the mothers valued the father's continued contact with his children, and protected the contact with care and consideration. One-fifth saw no value in this whatsoever and actively tried to sabotage the meetings by sending the children away just before the father's arrival, by insisting that the child was ill or had pressing homework to do, by making a scene, or by leaving the children with the husband and disappearing. In between was a large group of women who had many mixed feelings about the father's visits, resenting the father's excessive gift-giving and his freedom from domestic responsibilities. These irritations were expressed in their difficulties in accommodating the different schedules of the other parent to make the visit possible and to protect the child's access to both parents, in forgotten appointments, in insistence on rigid schedules for the visits, in refusal to per-

mit the visit if the father brought along an adult friend—in a thousand mischievous, mostly petty, devices designed to humiliate the visiting parent and to deprecate him in the eyes of his children.

13   Sometimes the child's anxiety at crossing the no-child's-land between father and mother spilled into the child's behavior. Exhausted by the ordeal of the crossing or saddened anew at the farewell to the father, children were cranky or poorly behaved after the visit, or they developed symptomatic behaviors in response to the anxiety and fear of angering one or the other parent. They felt that they were in jeopardy between two warring giants and they reacted accordingly.

14   Unfortunately, some angry women attempted to use the child's symptomatic behaviors as proof that the visits were detrimental to the child's welfare and should, therefore, be discontinued. Attorneys were called by aggrieved mothers who blamed their husband for the child's lapses, thus distressing the unhappy children even more.

15   The custodial parent's continued presence alone made her an available target for the child's unhappiness and resentment around the visit. Thus, for example, since she was available, whereas the visiting parent was present only intermittently, it was not unusual for children to behave splendidly with the visiting father and to return home cranky and petulant with their mothers. Their behavior often reflected their greater concern that their father might abandon them and their judgment that the custodial mother was more reliable. Mothers, however, rarely appreciated this and felt that they were being treated shabbily as compared with their husbands, who carried so much less responsibility in the care of the children. Not unexpectedly, they blamed the visit for the child's sulkiness or his different behavior upon return, and they threatened to discontinue the visitation.

16   Contrary to our expectations, parental friction at the time of the visit of the kind just described, although profoundly disturbing to the children, did not necessarily result in fewer visits. The mother's angry opposition strengthened the father's perseverance as often as it discouraged visiting. Friendliness between the parents and the mother's interest in maintaining the father's visits did, however, encourage visiting, and fathers who were encouraged to visit were more likely to continue to come regularly.

WHAT FACTORS CONTRIBUTE TO VISITING

17   These factors in the father's response to the divorce, which were reflected in the visiting patterns, were counterbalanced by the passionate, persistent yearning of the children, especially those below the age of nine, by the commitment of many fathers to their children, which held despite their fear of hurt and rejection, and by the interest of about half of the women in maintaining the visits. Thus, the visiting relationship which successfully outlived the marriage reflected not the relationships of the predivorce family primarily, but the father's motivation, the child's motivation, and the psychological capacity of

fathers, mothers, and children to adapt flexibly to the new conditions of the visiting relationship. Men who could bend to the complex logistics of the visiting; who could deal with the anger of the women and the capriciousness of the children without withdrawing; who could overcome their own depression, jealousy and guilt; who could involve the children in their planning; who could walk a middle ground between totally rearranging their schedule and not changing their schedule at all; and who felt less stressed and freer to parent, were predominantly among those who continued to visit regularly and frequently.

FATHERS WHO WELCOME LIMITS

18   Some fathers who regularly visited their children welcomed the limits of the postdivorce relationship, claiming it was easier to visit their children within a circumscribed period. In a number of families these limits enabled fathers to get to know their children better, to express greater affection, to concentrate on their parenting in ways not possible during the marriage when the children's needs were burdensome. We found this especially true among fathers of preschool children and adolescents.

19   Mr. B. was a critical, ill-tempered man during his marriage. At the time of the separation his adolescent daughter openly expressed her anger at him.

20   Following the divorce Mr. B. insisted on a rigid visiting schedule which his daughter resented, but with which she nevertheless complied. Away from home in a more relaxed setting and without the presence of the mother, father and daughter began to converse without rancor. Out of this association they gradually achieved a friendship. Four years later his daughter decided to follow her father's demanding professional career.

21   Tina said of her father, "He has a heart of gold, but he's impossible to live with, especially for me because I have a temper, too, and we fought all the time. As long as we don't live together we get along well."

OTHER FACTORS THAT CONTRIBUTE TO VISITING

22   The concern of men for the children left in the care and custody of depressed or psychologically troubled women led some to visit more frequently if the men were not overtaken by their own guilt. Fathers who were lonely, psychologically intact, and not depressed visited more. Fathers who were economically secure and educated visited more. Fathers whose children were not angry visited more. And fathers and families where the relationship between the parents had calmed down or was no longer marked by intense animosity tended to visit more, *although* the mother's negative attitude toward the visiting was a factor of *fading* significance over time.

23   Finally, it is reasonable to assume that the interventions of our project played a significant role in encouraging the fathers to visit

more frequently and in facilitating the development of better relationships with the children. As we learned subsequently, the interventions were influential far beyond our modest expectations. A striking discovery of the study was how fluid father-child relationships appeared immediately after the divorce when the new visiting relationship leaves behind its predivorce form, and how appreciative fathers are of advice at this crucial time. The relationship between visiting father and child is at its most malleable immediately after the father has moved out of the household and as the visiting pattern emerges. The foundations of the new visiting relationship are laid down during the immediate post-separation period. If weakened at this time, the relationship may be more difficult to restore. But visiting parent and child also have a second chance at this critical juncture, a chance to break free of past unhappy relations and establish a new bond between father and child.

Collaborative Activity

In small groups, discuss the following.

1. To what extent would you say that Wallerstein and Kelly agree with Mantilla, and to what extent would you say they disagree with her? Explain.

2. Do you believe that Wallerstein and Kelly make too many excuses for fathers who do not live with their children? Why or why not?

3. Do Wallerstein and Kelly's use of plurals ("fathers"), statistics ("one-third of the men"), and scientific sounding examples ("Mr. A") build or fail to build credibility for their arguments? Why?

4. Do you agree or disagree with the conclusion that divorced fathers and their children may move beyond "past unhappy relations" to a "new bond"? Explain, with examples.

Step 5: Reviewing Model Paraphrases and Quotations

You have read and discussed the Mantilla essay and the selections from Wallerstein and Kelly. Many of your ideas are now in your notes, either as discussion notes or on the 4 × 6 index cards you used when you originally read the sources, both, or some other note-taking format you prefer. But what do you do with the material you have gathered?

As you have read before and will read again, the persuasive research paper is *your* essay, with *your* ideas supported by other sources. Still, the need to incorporate sources properly is fundamental. Here are some examples of ways you would cite a source in your finished paper.

Paraphrase

Determining exactly how the absentee father functions in a divorced family is difficult, with possibilities ranging from intimate caregiver to occasional visitor (Wallerstein and Kelly 123).

Here the idea clearly comes from the paragraph in Wallerstein and Kelly that begins "The broad parameters," yet none of the language (except the very common word "father") is the same. Therefore, the citation is considered a paraphrase, and the authors' names and page number are listed in parentheses at the end of the paraphrase. Note that the period comes after the parentheses.

Paraphrase That Includes the Author's Name

According to Mantilla, her children continued to do very well academically after their parents' divorce (12).

In this case, there is no need to put Mantilla's name inside the parentheses, for her name is part of the sentence itself. The page number alone suffices.

Direct Quotation of a Single Word or Phrase

One divorced mother writes that her own sister called her a "manhater" (Mantilla 12).

This word is quoted directly because it so strongly expresses the idea that Mantilla (like her sister) was trying to express. It would be difficult to express it more simply than in the word originally used in the essay.

Direct Quotation of an Entire Sentence

Sometimes parent/child limits benefited both divorced father and their children. In fact, "In a number of families these limits enabled father to get to know their children better, to express greater affection, to concentrate on their parenting in ways not possible during the marriage when the children's needs were burdensome" (Wallerstein and Kelly 130).

This well-written sentence in Wallerstein and Kelly seems to warrant direct quotation in full. Having a quotation mark suddenly appear out of nowhere would look awkward, and so a tag such as "In fact," or "As Wallerstein and Kelly say" allows the sentence to flow grammatically. Of course, if the quotation began with the tag "As Wallerstein and Kelly say," the names would not be repeated in the parentheses.

Lengthy Direct Quotation. Mantilla offers an adamant response to the idea that boys need men to imitate or model:

> *I cannot emphasize enough what an absurd idea this is. Do we harp on female role models? What we need are good examples of humane values transmitted to our children, period. I submit that men tend to emphasize values such as discipline, power, control, stoicism, and independence. Sure, there can be some good from these things, but they are mostly damaging to kids (and other living things). They certainly made my son suffer an isolated and tortured existence until he began to see that there was a way out of the trap of masculinity. (Mantilla 13)*

In this case, Mantilla writes with such energy and insistence that it seems important to preserve her every word. Such instances will be rare in your persuasive research paper. When you do use an extended quotation that is more than four lines long, make it a **block quotation.** Block quotations are double-spaced, as are other quotations, but each line is indented on the left. Also, at the end of the quotation, note that the period comes at the end of the last sentence, before the parentheses containing the author's name and page number. Finally, you do not need to add quotation marks to block quotations. The block format serves the same function that quotation marks would.

A Quotation That Already Appears in Quotation Marks in Your Source

> *One child found that having an absentee father actually improved the parental relationship. She claimed, " 'As long as we don't live together we get along well' " (Wallerstein and Kelly 130).*

> *"All our mutual friends and neighbors showed their disapproval to me for leaving such a 'good' man" (Mantilla 12).*

In these two quotations, you will discover that the beginning and the end of each quotation is marked by quotation marks. Additionally, however, a single quotation mark appears after the first quotation mark in the citation from Wallerstein and Kelly, while a second single quotation mark appears before the second quotation mark. Moreover, the single word "good" appears inside single quotation marks in the citation from Mantilla.

The reason for these single quotation marks is simple. They set off material already in quotation marks in the original source. The double quotation marks show the material quoted from the source. Without the single quotation marks, the reader could not know which part of the work was in quotation marks in the original. Note that an entire quotation or a single word may be set off in this manner.

Step 6: Citing Sources

By now, you have used several 4 × 6 index cards or a method of your own choosing to record your observations, paraphrases, and quotations from Mantilla and Wallerstein and Kelly. If you have begun doing formal research on your own topic by now, you may also have a rapidly growing stack of index cards pertinent to your own paper. To this point, however, you have not filled out a 3 × 5 index card on either the Mantilla essay or the Wallerstein and Kelly book. The 3 × 5 cards that you have filled out for the other sources you have consulted probably contain a hodgepodge of information in no particular format, unless you have read ahead or consulted a format you previously used.

What follow are the 1998 revisions of MLA formats for some of the most common sources that you will use in writing your research paper. Use these formats on your 3 × 5 index cards and then again in your Works Cited sheet. In all likelihood, you will complete more index cards on sources than your Works Cited sheet will reflect. Why is this the case? The reason is simple. Understand that a Works Cited sheet is **not** the same as a bibliography. If you are compiling a bibliography on a subject, you will locate every source that you can find relevant to the subject and include it in your bibliography. An **annotated bibliography** also includes a short descriptive statement, usually between a sentence and a paragraph long, about each source.

A Works Cited sheet differs from a bibliography in that it contains only the sources that you actually cite (that is, paraphrase or quote) in the essay itself. No matter how good you may consider a book or article, it does not belong in your Works Cited sheet unless you have used it in your essay. For this reason, a Works Cited sheet will usually be quite a bit shorter than a bibliography.

Realize, too, that no brief section in a single chapter of a textbook can possibly include all the sources you may find in doing research. Although this chapter will show you how to develop proper citations for most, if not all of the sources that eventually end up in your Works Cited sheet, exceptions are certainly possible. In this case, ask your instructor for guidance. Also, once you know exactly which style your professor wants you to use (for example, APA, Turabian, or the MLA style used in this chapter), your reference librarian will undoubtedly be able to direct you to a style manual that will guide you to a proper citation. Along with the many blessings of the Internet, one of its difficulties has involved formats for citation. As quickly as the technology and the formats change, it becomes all the more important for you to make certain that you have the most recent manual for any given style.

Before you view formats for many of the types of sources you are likely to encounter, a word or two about acceptable versus unacceptable sources seems wise. You want to use research sources that are both accurate and appropriate. Some potential sources will meet one of these two tests, some both, and some neither. For example, the *World Book Encyclopedia* is a source that many college professors will tell you to avoid, preferring a more scholarly encyclopedia written for a more adult audience. This is not to say that a single word in the *World Book Encyclopedia* is inaccurate. Other sources may be written at such a level of abstraction as to be "over the heads" of a general audience who might read your essay. *Italian Language Studies of the Napoleonic Age* (a made-up periodical title) would be such a source.

Then, again, some sources are altogether unsuitable for persuasive research papers. You should absolutely avoid the grocery story check-out counter periodicals that recount tales of alien babies and visitations by Elvis Presley. Similarly, be careful with Internet research. Understand that almost anyone can and will put up a web site or post an Internet article making all sorts of claims. *Always* verify Internet information, either against a hard copy of the original (as discussed earlier) or with an expert, such as your professor, who can tell you (or find out for you) whether or not an Internet source is accurate and appropriate.

Now, here are some types of sources you are likely to encounter. Sometimes a single example will address two or three issues. Read carefully before seeking assistance.

Books

Book by One Author

Guterson, David. *Snow Falling on Cedars.* New York: Harcourt Brace, 1994.

Note the order in which items appear. The author's name is given, last name first. Then the title follows, underlined. You may also choose to use italics, which are usually interchangeable with underlining. Then you list the city where the book was published. If multiple cities are given, list the one closest to you. A shortened version of the publisher's name follows, and finally you give the date. If several dates are listed, use the most recent one.

Book by Two or Three Authors

Valeri-Gold, Maria, and Frank Pintozzi. *Taking Charge of Your Reading: Reading and Study Strategies for College Success.* New York: Addison Wesley Longman, 2000.

Here it is noteworthy to see the way the authors' names are handled. You cite the lead or first author's name the same way you would as if she were a single author. Then simply write out the second author's name as if you were signing your own name. If there is a third name, add a comma after the second name, and write the third name as you did the second.

Note also the hanging indention form. Works Cited look just the opposite of paragraphs. Whereas you indent the first line of a paragraph and begin all the other lines at the left margin, you do exactly the opposite on the Works Cited sheet.

Book by More than Three Authors

Book with More than One Volume

Book with More than One Edition

Divine, Robert A., et al. *America: Past and Present.* Vol. 1. 4th ed. New York: Longman, 1998.

This citation addresses several formatting issues. First of all, "et al" is a Latin abbreviation meaning "and others." As shown, it is appropriate whenever more than three authors collaborated on a source. The abbreviation "Vol. 1" tells that at least a second volume of this work exists and helps the reader avoid choosing the wrong volume, should he or she decide to read the original. Moreover, "4th ed." acknowledges that the work has already gone through three editions and that the fourth is cited in the essay. Finally, you will observe that when you have used a work consisting of both multiple volumes and multiple editions, the notice of multiple volumes comes first.

Book with Unknown Author
Let's Go. Central America. New York: St. Martin's Press, 1998.

When you have no author, simply use the title. In your actual essay, use the first word of the title (excluding a, an, the, and prepositions) in parentheses to connect the citation to the Works Cited sheet. The same applies to periodical articles with unknown authors and any other anonymous sources.

Book with an Editor and Author
Greene, Graham. *The Portable Graham Greene.* Ed. Philip Statford. New
    York: PenguinBooks, 1977.

Book Containing Collected Essays with an Editor
Williams, Mary E., ed. *The Family: Opposing Viewpoints.* San Diego:
    GreenhavenPress, 1998.

Anthology
Gilbert, Sandra M., and Susan Gubar. *The Norton Anthology of Literature
    by Women: The Traditions in English.* 2nd ed. New York: W.W.
    Norton, 1998.

A Work from an Anthology (a Collection of Works by Various Authors)
Truth, Sojourner. "Ain't I a Woman?" *The Norton Anthology of Literature
    by Women: The Traditions in English.* 2nd ed. Sandra M. Gilbert
    and Susan Gubar. New York: W.W. Norton, 1998. 370.

The author of the work is listed first and appears in parentheses in your essay. The number at the very end is the page number from the source where you found the work.

Encyclopedia Work in Multiple Volumes
"Caldwell, Erskine." *Academic American Encyclopedia.* 21 vols. Dan-
    bury, CT: Grolier, 1998.

This encyclopedia article is anonymous; hence, the citation begins with the title, and the word "Caldwell" in quotation marks would be used in the parentheses inside the paper.

Translation

Marquez, Gabriel Garcia. *Collected Novellas.* Trans. Gregory Rabassa and J.S. Bernstein. New York: HarperPerennial, 1991.

Government or Corporate Book or Pamphlet

United States Department of Labor. Bureau on Labor Statistics. *Occupational Outlook Handbook.* 1998–1999 ed. Washington: GPO, 1998.

Articles

Daily Newspaper

Steinberg, Jacques. "After Bitter Campus Battles, The 'Great Books' Rise Again. *New York Times* 18 Jan. 2000, late ed.: A1+.

The reference to A1+ indicates that this article begins on page 1 of section A and is continued elsewhere. Note the absence of punctuation between the name of the newspaper and the date, and also observe the European way of writing the date.

Weekly Newspaper or Magazine

Dunn, Janice. "The Name of the Father and the Making of a New American Family." *Rolling Stone* 3 Feb. 2000: 40–45.

Monthly Magazine or Scholarly Journal with Separate Pagination

Goldwasser, Joan. "Cash or Charge." *Kiplinger's Personal Finance Magazine.* Nov. 1999: 82–83.

Monthly Scholarly Journal with Continuous Pagination

Schlueter, June. "Rereading the Peacham Drawing." *Shakespeare Quarterly* 50 (1999): 171–84.

The number immediately following the journal's name is the volume number. The year appears inside parentheses. The specific issue for the year is unimportant since the journal uses continuous pagination throughout the year.

Letter to the Editor

Whyte, L.M. Letter. *Wall Street Journal* 20 Jan. 2000: A23.

Review

Kapur, Akash. "A Third Way for the Third World." Rev. of *Development As Freedom,* by Amartya Sen. *Atlantic Monthly* Nov. 1999: 124–29.

Nonprint Sources

Movie

American History X. Dir. Tony Kaye. New Line Productions, 1998.

Television or Radio Program

"Busted: America's War on Marijuana." *Frontline.* Narr. Will Lyman . Writ. Elena Mannes. Dir. Tim Manzini. PBS. WGBH. 28 Apr. 1998.

Interview
Vick, Anita. Personal interview. 24 Jan. 2000.

Lecture
Hathaway, Karry. "Race and Education." Class lecture. English 1101.
      Georgia Perimeter College, Lawrenceville. 24 Jan. 2000.

Electronic Sources

Since electronic sources, especially those obtained via the Internet, are put
up, taken down, and changed daily, gather as much information as you can
about any electronic source you use. Make certain to include the URL, or
web address as it is more commonly known, and the date you accessed the
source. Of course, you will want to include the usual title, author, date of
publication, etc., information.

A Personal or Professional Web Site
CPOG Web Page. Concerned Parents of Gwinnett. 29 Dec. 1999
      <www.cpog.org>.

Online Newspaper Article
"Exploring the Solar System." *New York Times on the Web.* 25 Jan. 2000.
      25 Jan. 2000 <http:www.nytimes.com/library/national/science/
      solar-main.html>.

Online Journal Article
Lewis, Michael, and Tabitha Soren. "Changing Tallulah." *Slate* 24 Jan.
      2000. 25 Jan. 2000 *<http://slate.msn.com/I*SeeFrance/entries/
      00-01-24_73614.asp>*.

Online Database Article
Stubbs, Dori. "The Right Clothes Are Just the First Step." *Seattle Times*
      18 Jan. 2000: F8. *Lexis-Nexis Academic Universe.* GALILEO.
      25 Jan. 2000 *<http://web.lexis-nexis.com/universe/
      docum. . .lzS&_e73e0209336f2ac53255be18914de39c>*.

As you can see, the original publication data comes first. The word
GALILEO is included because GALILEO is a subscription service used
here to access Lexis-Nexis.

Online Book
May, Sophie (pseudonym of Rebecca Sophia Clarke). *Little Prudy's Sis-
      ter Susy.* Chicago: 1864. 25 Jan. 2000 <wysiwyg://207/http://
      members.tripod.com/ddj9999/girlser/lpsuz1.html>.

Online Poem
Marvell, Andrew. "To His Coy Mistress." *Andrew Marvell (1621–1678).*
      28 Jan. 2000 <http://22.luminarium.org/sevenlit.marvell/
      coy.htm>.

E-mail

McMullen, Kendra. "Your Query." E-mail to Alexander Sommers. 11 Nov. 1999.

CD-ROM

Macbeth. Films for the Humanities and Sciences. CD-ROM. Cromwell Productions, 1997.

No city of publication was available for this CD-ROM. Had one been, it would have been cited immediately before the name of the producer.

Step 7: Reviewing Student Models

You are about to read two persuasive research papers written by first-semester college students. As you read the essays, examine the ways that the two students, Jim McPherson and Angel Jones, combine their own ideas with the ideas of other people who are experts in various fields. Pay close attention to material that is paraphrased and quoted directly. Here are ten questions to ask yourself as you read each paper.

1. Does the author state a clear thesis in the essay, and is the thesis in the author's own words?

2. Whenever the author makes a statement that is either not generally known or verifiable in a reliable research source, such as an encyclopedia, does the author cite the statement?

3. Does the author generally use paraphrases well and smoothly?

4. When the author uses direct quotations, are the quotations justified because the original author put the idea so well?

5. Do direct quotations grammatically fit into the author's own sentences or paragraphs?

6. Does every work paraphrased or quoted directly in the source have a corresponding entry, with the link clearly discernible, in the Works Cited sheet?

7. Does the author give reason to believe that he or she knows or has learned enough about the subject to be justified in discussing it?

8. Does the author use enough facts to be persuasive but not so many as to be redundant?

9. Would a reader who has not already reached a firm decision on the issue find the arguments in the essay persuasive?

10. Could the paper actually lead a previously undecided reader to go out and take some action based on what the essay says?

The first paper is Jim McPherson's "Recycling—Why Should I Care?" As you can guess from the title, the author's purpose is to persuade an undecided reader to begin recycling. Using the ten questions, read McPherson's paper. Then move on to the collaborative activity that follows.

Recycling—Why Should I Care?

Jim McPherson

Mr. Jones
English 1101
11 November 1999

1   A nineteenth century Indian chief once gave this warning to nearby settlers: "Continue to contaminate your bed and you will one night suffocate in your own waste" (Gay 92). This was his way of telling the settlers that if they did not respect the land, the land would not respect them. Although it's been nearly two hundred years since then, the wise chief's saying still holds true. Earth is our home, and if we ruin it, there's nowhere else to go. Although 63 percent of Americans consider themselves "environmentalists" (Fritsch A12), less than half the nation (including businesses) actually recycles. In fact, nineteen percent of Americans answered the question "Do you recycle" by asking another question—"Why should I?" (Lund chapter 10.4) The answer is simple. Recycling saves money, protects the environment, and ensures a beautiful planet for generations to come.

2   Recycling was the least of America's problems fifty years ago. Thinking of recycling bottles was absurd when the threat of nuclear winter was present. Now, however, the world's affairs are in a state of equilibrium, and America has begun to reassess its priorities. Nearly all state governments have made goals to improve their recycling rates within the next 10 years (Lund chapter 10.2). Perhaps it's time for *every* American to reassess his/her priorities just as these governments have done. With industry and population increasing every year, mankind is becoming more and more wasteful. In the other words, the longer we wait to recycle, the harder it's going to be to patch things up with the environment. Recycling is truly a snowball process; the sooner it starts, the easier it is to continue it. Therefore, recycling isn't always about immediate results. It's the beginning of a long process that will eventually save the Earth's environment.

3   Although the government has recently began putting forth efforts to improve America's environmental awareness, many misconceptions about recycling have come as a result of poor government involvement in the past. The fact that there are currently no sternly enforced federal laws regarding recycling often causes the following course of

thought: "If the government doesn't care, then why should I?" However, most of those who take this attitude don't know that there are
many interest groups and lobbyists in Washington D.C. that push for
mandatory recycling laws everyday. Just because there aren't any official recycling laws doesn't mean that recycling isn't at the top of the
issue lists for congressmen. For instance, the Government Accounting
Standards Board (GASB) has recently passed a new standard which
forces both state and local governments to report all environmental lia-
bility and cleanup costs (Sutherland paragraph 3). On the other hand,
there are numerous interest groups that impede the process of the government rather than accelerate it. "Greenscamming" groups who have
environment friendly names but do nothing more than harm the environment are causing setbacks in state and local legislation (Fritsch A1).
The government has the issue of recycling on its mind, yet real results
won't show until it's already too late. The time to act is now, and it all
starts with everybody taking individual responsibility instead of waiting for the government to do something.

4   The average person, when confronted with the thought of "recycling," feels inundated with responsibility, yet it's really not all that
hard to do. I myself started with crushing cans in the garage for a few
extra bucks. The same concept can be applied to much larger themes;
businesses, for example, can save a significant amount of money by
recycling. Every day, U.S. businesses use enough paper to encircle the
earth 20 times, and almost 70 percent of all office trash is recyclable
(Strong 65). Recycling materials is cheaper than paying a waste disposal service to pick them up. Businesses can save a lot of cash this
way, and, in turn, save the world some cash too. For example, enough
energy is saved by recycling a ton of paper to heat a house for six
months (Strong 66). Recycling, therefore, provides a cheap and effi-
cient way to dispose of waste materials.

5   An even more important incentive to recycle than money is the
preservation of the atmosphere. Although terms like "the greenhouse
effect" and "global warming" seem to many people as no more than
words on TV, they *do* have extreme importance. The average temperature of the earth has steadily risen over the last 60 years. It's no surprise, then, that the rise in temperature is directly correlated with the
rise of industry, automobiles, and population. One method of waste disposal that is more than likely responsible for the steady rise in global
climate is incineration. Incinerating waste produces pollutants such as
carbon dioxide, the main cause of ozone depletion. If the rate of pollution stays the same, the earth's average temperature is expected to
rise between two and nine degrees within the next half century (Rock
25). Recycling paper is one huge way to prevent air pollution. When
manufactured, recycled paper puts out 74 percent less pollution than
ordinary paper (Strong 66). The benefits of recycling, especially the
preservation of the atmosphere and the environment, are of significant

importance. Recycling requires minimal effort and produces huge results when everyone is responsible with his/her waste.

6   Personally, I don't recycle for any of the reasons mentioned above. I do it because I don't want my children growing up in anything less than a beautiful planet. Even though I'm seventeen, I care about the future. The thought of having my children or grandchildren not be able to go outside because it's 112 degrees saddens me, and I assume you feel the same way. Before you ask "Why should I recycle?" you should ask yourself "Why should my child grow up in a dump?" At the rate of nearly 200 million tons of waste per year, America is filling up fast (Lund chapter 10.2). If you don't recycle for yourself, then at least recycle for your children and your grandchildren. It's a small price to pay to ensure that they grow up in a beautiful environment.

7   As you can see, recycling is important for plenty of reasons. It saves money, prevents pollution, and provides a clean future environment for our posterity. With recycling, a small bit of effort goes a long way; it's one of the few areas where one individual *can* make a difference. *No one* can fathom what the world would be like in 100 years if recycling wasn't around. It's up to each and every citizen to do his/her part for the earth by recycling. Truly, the only answer I can give to the question "why should I recycle?" is this one: "because you can."

WORKS CITED

Fritsch, Jane. "Friend or Foe? Nature Groups Say Names Lie." *New York Times* 25 Mar. 1996: A1+.

Gay, Kathlyn. *Garbage and Recycling*. Hillside: Enslow Publishers Inc., 1991.

Lund, Herbert F., ed. *The McGraw-Hill Recycling Handbook*. New York: McGraw-Hill Inc., 1987.

Rock, Maxine. *The Automobile and the Environment*. New York: Chelsea House Publishers, 1992.

Strong, Debra L. *Recycling in America*. Santa-Barbara: ABC-CLIO, 1997.

Sutherland, Donald. "State, Local Governments Must Meet New Environmental Accounting Standard." ens.lycos.com. 22 Nov. 1999. <http://ens.lycos. com/ens/nov99/1999L-11-22-06.html>.

Collaborative Activity

In small groups, discuss each of the following questions.

1. Why do you think McPherson begins his essay by quoting a nineteenth century Indian chief? Does the quotation seem appropriate or inappropriate? Why?

2. Why does McPherson argue that recycling is more important now than it was half a century ago? Discuss why you find these reasons compelling or not.

3. How does McPherson balance governmental and individual action? Why could you argue that either can or cannot be effective?

4. Explain ways that the paper offers easy, practical ways to begin recycling. Would you consider doing them?

5. Although the essay is a persuasive research paper, it adopts an informal tone, with contractions such as "it's" and "don't." Do you find the contractions effective or ineffective? Explain.

6. In the context of the essay, discuss why you find " 'because you can' " an adequate or inadequate reason to recycle.

The second student paper will remind you somewhat of the Mantilla essay and the excerpts from Wallerstein and Kelly. Angel Jones, in "Mandatory Parent Education," discusses the issue of divorce and children and makes a proposal. Jones believes that any couple with children should have to take a course in parenting before they can receive a divorce. As you did with Jim McPherson's essay, read Angel Jones's with the ten general questions in mind. Then return to small groups for the ensuing collaborative activity.

Mandatory Parent Education

Angel Jones—English 1101

Persuasive/Research Essay

1   For the last hundred years of human existence, the definition of marriage has drastically changed. Once a definition colored with love and eternal commitment, marriage has become too casual and seems to have lost its sacred definition. The downward trend of marriages in the past twenty years is horribly disappointing. In fact, "by 1980, one in two marriages ended in divorce, as has been true of the nineties" (Young 176). The tragedy of this situation is the children who are thrown into the middle of the divorce. Unfortunately, the children of the divorcing parents are the real victims of divorce. Also, the number of children who must cope with their parents' divorce has risen. Now, "forty percent of kids in the United States will experience the divorce of their parents" ("Schools" 8). If we implement laws that would create a mandatory parent education course as a component to the divorce settlement, the separated parents would learn how to interact with their children throughout a stressful situation. These courses have been tested and have been proven effective; therefore, the legislation of the United States should enforce these classes on parenting after separation.

2   Parenting classes would help the children, the typical victims of divorce, through the divorce process. Commonly, the divorce overwhelms the parents and they often neglect the offspring that the two have

produced. In reaction to the lack of attention and the uncomfortable situation, children respond in various, yet distinct patterns. When the child becomes stressed by his or her parent's divorce, the most common reactions include depression, anxiety, withdrawal, or even disorientation (Samenow 129). Often, parent's stress becomes a catalyst to the child's stress. Recently, a report was released that concluded, ". . . 66% of parental interactions two months after divorce were characterized by conflict and anger" (Cummings 79). If over half of the married couples who are choosing to divorce one another are continuing to dispute after the marriage has ended, the children involved are therefore suffering before, during, and after the divorce procedure. The only way to end these disputes is knowledge and understanding. In mandatory parenting courses, newly divorced parents will learn to deal with their children's anxieties.

3   In some cases, children whose parents have divorced become rebellious and uncontrollable. In a case described in *Before It's Too Late,* a young boy named Paul chooses the wrong ways to deal with his parents' separation. He constantly neglects his schoolwork and frequently lies to both of his parents. In order to deal with their child, the parents, although now separated, placed Paul on restriction. The restriction does not last long, however, because both of Paul's parents worked to maintain a single-parenting lifestyle and, neither was at home to enforce Paul's restriction. Mr. Strong, Paul's father, attempted to monitor Paul's actions by calling the house frequently and trying to trap Paul in his lies. In reaction to her former husband's detective-like ways of enforcement, Ms. Strong became very upset. To extinguish this upsetting situation, the former Strong family (no pun intended) turned to counseling. The three had to learn to work as a team, with the framework built on communication between Paul's parents. This communication helped to stop Paul's lies to both his mother and to his father (Samenow 171). Typical in many situations involving divorce in the United States, counseling is beneficial to both the relationships between the mother and father and, more importantly, the relationship between parents and child. If a program was implemented in which counselors could be found and a list of available counseling programs was also listed, stress after divorce and parenting situations similar to the Strong family's could be reduced drastically.

4   With rates of divorce between parents increasing, education through counseling for these parents is an obvious solution. Family counselors who would be able to provide support throughout years ahead would lead the program. "[Counselors] can offer not just support, but good concrete suggestions about how to handle tough situations" (Wolf 48). Living in a society where conversations between parents and their children are very uncommon, counselors provide the push needed to initiate conversation between parents and their children about their concerns and opinions on not only the divorce, but general subjects as well. These advisors help parents, "to recognize their role in the child's difficulties and actively work toward reducing family conflict, [as well to] lessen the

child's feelings of pain and increase his or her feelings of wellness" (Young 111). Counselors have time and again proven their ability to help in cases of divorced parents. These counselors resolve problems throughout the family, not just those involving the parent and child.

5   Throughout the United States, laws enforcing post-divorce parenting programs have been tested and proven effective. One of the most popular programs is called the K.I.D.S. program (Kids In Divorce and Separation), which is used in areas such as British Columbia. This four-hour pilot course was developed to educate parents about the effects of conflict and separation/divorce on children, to change parents' behavior so that they can handle conflicts more constructively, and to provide parent education in a format that meets high standards for consumer satisfaction. The K.I.D.S. program consists of a pretest, an intervention program, posttest, and a follow-up questionnaire. The program has a very high satisfaction rate from the subjects who go through the class. I believe that a program similar to the K.I.D.S. program should be implemented throughout the United States. This pilot course's founders concluded:

> (a) The program effectively educated parents about the effects on children of interparental conflict and divorce, (b) participation decreased parents' perceived (or reported) engagement in negative conflict behaviors, and (c) parents were satisfied with the delivery, format, and materials of the program, and participants found the program useful. (Cummings 89)

All these characteristics are ideal for a program that could be used nationwide. If a program such as this one could become part of the divorce settlements throughout the nation, a drastic increase in the number of good parent/child relationships would occur.

7   Throughout the country, state and county legislations are beginning to require married couples with children who choose to divorce to attend and pass parenting education courses. "In [these courses], parents learn about communication and problem solving skills that will help them and their children work through their separation" (Thompson 1). These classes are beginning to be piloted throughout the world. In British Columbia, laws will require participation in a parenting after separation education program for separating parents. "In Cobb County, Georgia, an all-day [parenting education] program has reduced in-court custody litigation—a big baddie for kids—by 60 percent" ("Schools" 8). A similar program has been enforced statewide for Connecticut; and in Florida, a course for kids is additionally required. In Columbus, Ohio, any couple with children wishing to file for divorce must attend a parenting class within 45 days of court date, or else no approval is given ("Schools" 8). It has been proven throughout the country that these mandatory parent education programs are successful and very helpful. If these courses could be required nationwide, the lives of children of divorced parents could be easily improved and less stressful.

8   As we, citizens of the United States, approach the 21st century, we face the alarming reality that fifty percent, one out of every two marriages, will end in divorce. If we want to give birth and participate in raising a successful generation after us, we must provide children with seemingly steady and safe families in which to live. The only way to succeed at this is to offer good, responsible parenting to our children. After a divorce, this type of parenting tends to be hard or often impossible. With the help of divorced parenting classes, provided by the U.S. government, the quality of parenting could only increase. These programs have proven their value through the successes of the K.I.D.S. program and through their work in states and counties around the country. The classes seem to be an obvious choice to help raise children who have had to be in the middle of divorce. If we want to raise a successful generation to lead the country when we are gone, we must be successful parents, with or without a steady spouse.

WORKS CITED

Cummings, Mark E., and Kelly Shifflet. "A Program For Educating Parents About the Effects of Divorce and Conflict on Children: An Initial Evaluation." *Family Relations*. January 1999: 79.

Samenow, Stanton E. *Before It's Too Late*. New York: Random House, 1998.

"Schools for Splitsville." *Psychology Today*. Mar./Apr. 1995: 8.

Thompson, Kate. "Pilot Program Tests Mandatory Parent Education In Burnaby/New Westminster." *Ministry of the Attorney General*. 3 Feb. 1998: 1.

Wolf, Anthony E. *Why Did You Get a Divorce? And WHEN Can I Get a Hamster?* New York: The Noonday Press, 1998.

Young, Bettie B. *Stress and Your Child*. New York: Fawcett Columbine, 1995.

Collaborative Activity

In small groups, discuss the following questions over "Mandatory Parent Education."

1. Angel Jones' essay asserts and then seems to assume that children are the "victims" in most cases of divorce. Based on your reading of Mantilla and Wallerstein and Kelly and on your personal knowledge, do you accept this premise? Why or why not?

2. Do you agree that reducing, through education, the stress that the parents feel during a divorce could offer positive results for their children? Give reasons for your answer.

3. Please offer your own response to the paper's claim that open, effective communication can help resolve family problems, including those between parent and child.

4. What effect does the citing of instances such as British Columbia, Connecticut, and Florida have on making the mandatory class seem reasonable?

5. Do you think the people you have known who were divorced and/or who were the children of divorced parents may have benefited from a class such as the one Angel Jones discusses? Why or why not?

6. In what ways does the "Mandatory Parent Education" make you stop and think about your own current or future parenting skills?

Step 8: Composing the Persuasive Research Paper

Before you write the first word of your persuasive research essay, remind yourself exactly what you are writing. First and foremost, you are writing a paper, *your* paper, on a given subject and supporting your point of view (whether you have held the particular point of view for years or days). Second, you are using research *only* to the extent that it supports what you already want to say. Your stacks of index cards will offer great assistance throughout the process, but do not make the mistake of letting the experts you have chosen do all your talking. Retain your own voice and perspective. Even if you choose to begin with a quotation (as Jim McPherson did), make it one that works for you, and not the other way around.

In your class, you may or may not have written the Job Application Letter assigned in Chapter 9. Regardless, the section "Three Ways to Persuade: Ethos, Logos, and Pathos" contains information—much of it millennia old—that can help you begin writing. Remember that just as with any other essay, you want a good beginning (with a "hook" and a thesis), middle (with examples), and end (with conclusion). The appeals to *ethos, logos,* and *pathos* can help you establish each of these while simultaneously helping your essay to persuade an undecided reader.

There is, of course, no single correct way to go forward from here. You may walk around with your index cards in your pockets for a few days and craft paragraphs of your paper while showering or jogging. Then, again, you may sit down and produce draft after draft of your introduction or a particular body paragraph. The important idea here is to use the process you have developed over a lifetime of writing and especially while completing various assignments in this book and to write the best persuasive paper you can while doing so. Begin!

Step 9: Reviewing and Editing the Persuasive Research Paper

During "Step 7: Reviewing Student Models," you encountered ten good questions to use while reviewing any research paper. After you have completed a draft—be it the first or the sixth—of your research essay, put it aside for a while. Then try to put yourself into the position of your potential readers, including your professor. Read your essay as you believe someone else would, and devise answers to the ten questions in this section. Also, working in groups as you or your instructor selects, exchange papers with your classmates, and perform the same critical exercise. Whenever you are dissatisfied with the answers you develop or receive regarding your own essay, you will have identified likely opportunities to revise.

Because persuasive research papers are generally longer than the other essays you write in most college classes, you want to pay special attention to organization and to mechanics. The following questions will help you meet these goals.

1. Does each paragraph clearly link to the thesis statement? If not, why, and would the essay be more effective if it did?

2. Does each paragraph lead clearly to the next?

3. Are there any paragraphs in the essay that are too long to be considered a single unit or too short to stand alone? If so, how might this problem be resolved?

4. Have you spent a sufficient amount of time on each page, down to the last line, to proofread carefully for fragments, comma splices, subject-verb agreement, etc.? If not, would reading a page or two and then taking a short break before continuing make your proofreading more effective?

5. Does the paper sound good when read aloud? If not, what would make it sound better?

Grammar and Usage: Marking Quotations

Examine the following quotations.

Wallerstein and Kelly tell us that "[o]ne-half of the men were afraid of rejection by their children" (124).

According to Wallerstein and Kelly, "One-half of the men were afraid of rejection by their children" (124).

Wallerstein and Kelly summarize the issue as follows: "[o]ne-half of the men were afraid of rejection by their children" (124).

Only the second of these three quotations reproduces the material exactly as written by Wallerstein and Kelly. The first and third use brackets around the letter "o" because they change it to a lowercase letter in order to make it fit the grammar of the sentence. Why?

The first time the quotation is used, it is introduced by the word *that.* If you remember that the word *that* is often a subordinator, or *yellow light,* you can see why the words that follow it would not be a complete sentence and would not, therefore, begin with a capital letter.

Likewise, the third quotation divides the sentence into two parts, with a colon in between. You will likely use the colon more in your research paper than in any other form of writing. One way to tell yourself the time has come to use a colon is to try substituting a phrase such as *and it is, and they are,* or *and he/she is.* The colon tells you that important information is to follow, and substituting these words can be a helpful cue for it. However, you won't generally use a capital letter after a colon (except in your essay's title).

So why does the second quotation, unlike the first or third, maintain the exact appearance of the original? The answer lies, again, in the way the quotation is introduced. *According to Wallerstein and Kelly* is a prepositional phrase at the beginning of a sentence. Generally, you use a comma following such an introducer, and you do here. Then, the words that follow the comma need to be a complete sentence, or the entire construction is a fragment. Thus, whenever you introduce a quotation with a prompt such as *According to* or *As Simpson says* or simply *He writes,* follow the quotation with a capital letter. If the original source lacks the capital, use brackets to supply it.

And now here's one last quotation to examine.

Wallerstein and Kelly relate that "parental friction at the time of the visit . . . did not necessarily result in fewer visits."

Why does this quotation use three consecutive periods in the middle? Does the original source do so? The answer is no. These three periods, known as **ellipsis,** indicate that the person quoting Wallerstein and Kelly has seen fit to omit one or more words that occur between *visit* and *did.* The writer believes that the intervening word or words do not communicate crucial information and that the quotation is more effective when amended as shown. Use ellipses to keep your use of quotations tight and precise.

Exercise

Review your own persuasive research paper for your use of quotations. Note the ways you introduce each quotation. Does the succeeding punctuation or lack of punctuation match the introduction? Do all quotations "work" grammatically? Are there any places where you could use an ellipsis to be more precise? Are there any places where using an ellipsis changes what you mean to say?

Supplemental Readings

As you have accomplished various assignments in *College Writing: Keeping It Real,* you have used a variety of modes and methods to express, inform, persuade, or interpret. The same is true of the eight readings that follow. An eclectic collection, these readings come from the fields of journalism, literature, and politics. Some of the authors are members of Generation X while others have been dead for a century or more. We have chosen these eight readings to entertain you, to enlighten you, and even to provoke you. You may find yourself vigorously agreeing or disagreeing with the ideas, themes, and recommendations. In all cases, we hope you will not be bored.

If you have questions, comments, or suggestions for the supplemental readings in future editions of *College Writing: Keeping It Real,* write us at *ljones@gpc.peachnet.edu* or *ajones@gpc.peachnet.edu.* In the meantime, enjoy!

Selection 1

"Ahh!" (That's the wonderful sound of relief)

by Celestine Sibley

1   Two wonderful new words have been added to my vocabulary: Butt out. There are a few ways you can say them. A preemptory "Butt out!" might be considered rude and feelings-hurting. A gentler, thoughtful rendition of the words is the way my visiting daughter said them to me.

2   As I have mentioned before, we have a new baby in our family, the son of my eldest grandson, which makes him my great-grandchild. For some reason, I have been having my say about that child long before his birth.

3   I was afraid his parents might miss the opportunity to name him John for his father. It is one my favorite names, and I was, I know now, very persistent in urging it. His parents-to-be didn't tell me they had already decided on that name. They kept annoying me by advancing all kinds of names they knew I would abhor.

4   Finally, on the day of his birth, they confessed that all along they had intended for him to be named John—and as an added act guaranteed to delight me, they were going to call him Jack for my late husband.

5   My daughter, here to celebrate the birth of her first grandchild, said thoughtfully: "They just wanted you to butt out."

6   Of course, I should have learned. But the long-term meaning of the words was lost on me. I started butting in almost immediately. "Now about the christening. . ." I began.

7   They admitted they were already planning for that for a few months hence, at my church and theirs.

8   "Everybody will want to come," I pointed out. "So we should have a little family gathering afterward."

9   **My daughter said** she and her husband would surely come from Omaha and a party would be nice, but . . . She waited for the baby's mother to have a say. I didn't. I plunged right in. I thought of Sweet Apple, and then I thought of the work in both house and yard that that would entail. There are beautiful houses in Roswell opened for receptions of various kinds. Maybe we should investigate one of those.

10   The baby's mother and her mother-in-law didn't say much about it, so I switched to the christening dress. Do we have one in either family?

11   "I know long dresses aren't regarded as necessary anymore," I offered. "But they are traditional, and I always love it when a

baby at our church is all dressed in batiste and lace instead of those little short pants they put on boy infants nowadays. Their legs look scrawny until they are a couple of months older."

12   The baby's mother said she was thinking of having him christened in diaper and undershirt. I agreed that they look adorable anyhow, but . . .

13   My daughter admitted that there is a beautiful antique christening dress in the family, stowed away somewhere in tissue paper.

14   "Just the thing," I was about to say when my more tactful daughter said she would send it to Jack's parents and let them decide.

15   **Later, as we drove away,** she said quietly and persuasively, "I think we should butt out about the christening. It's their business, not ours."

     "Butt out?" I cried. "I don't want to. It's an ugly-sounding admonition anyhow. Butt out, for goodness' sake! When you know you're right about something, don't you think you should have a say?"

16   She shook her head. "It's none of our business. Whatever they decide will be fine with me."

17   I went home to pout, but we went to see the movie "Shall We Dance?" at the Garden Hills Cinema, and I was so pleasantly distracted by that, I forgot christening parties and christening dresses.

18   And later, after I'd had a nap, I realized that I had a sweeping sense of relief. I don't have to make decisions about anybody's life but my own (that's trouble enough).

19   I kind of like the sound of it now. Butt out.

Collaborative Activity

In small groups discuss the following questions.

1. What pattern of development does Sibley use to develop her point? Why is it effective or ineffective?

2. In your family, what role would a prospective great-grandparent play in the various ceremonies involved in welcoming a new child?

3. Do you accept Sibley's statement that her daughter's telling her to "butt out" was a kind thing to do? How would older members of your family respond to such a statement?

4. What are some specific activities your family or culture engages in to celebrate the arrival of a new baby? Do the generations agree, or is there intergenerational conflict? How do the answers given by the various members of your collaborative group differ, and what does that tell you?

Solo Activity #1

If possible, discuss your own birth with your parents or other family member. Or ask about the circumstances surrounding your adoption. Ask as many questions as you think necessary to learn the story behind your birth and also the various cultural rituals associated with your birth. Did your father pass out cigars? Was there a naming ceremony? Did relatives come from miles around? Consider which events surrounding your birth were medically necessary and which were matters of culture and habit. In what ways (e.g., handing out cigars) have traditions changed since you were alive? What does that tell you about the role of ritual in a new child's arrival?

Writing Assignment #1

Based on the information you learn, write a short essay based on the topic (not necessarily the title) "The Birth of a Child." Use your own childbirth, if possible, as material, and write an essay that gives descriptions, makes comparisons, or seeks to persuade.

Solo Activity #2

Look up your actual date of birth on a newspaper microfilm or on-line collection. What were the major stories of the day? How was the weather? What items were advertised for sale, and at what prices?

Writing Assignment #2

Write a brief descriptive essay giving a picture of the world on the day you were born. Note the changes and the similarities over time.

Selection 2

Sally, from *The House on Mango Street*

by Sandra Cisneros

Introduction: Born in 1954, Sandra Cisneros is one of the most widely admired Latino writers living and working in America today. Her 1984 book *The House on Mango Street* is frequently taught in collegiate and high school English classes around the country in both English and Spanish.

1   Sally is the girl with eyes like Egypt and nylons the color of smoke. The boys at school think she's beautiful because her hair is shiny black like raven feathers and when she laughs, she flicks her hair back like a satin shawl over her shoulders and laughs.

2   Her father says to be this beautiful is trouble. They are very strict in his religion. They are not supposed to dance. He remembers his sisters and is sad. Then she can't go out. Sally I mean.

3   Sally, who taught you to paint your eyes like Cleopatra? And if I roll the little brush with my tongue and chew it to a point and dip it in the muddy cake, the one in the little red box, will you teach me?

4   I like your black coat and those shoes you wear, where did you get them? My mother says to wear black so young is dangerous, but I want to buy shoes just like yours, like your black ones made out of suede, just like those. And one day, when my mother's in a good mood, maybe after my next birthday, I'm going to ask to buy the nylons too.

5   Cheryl, who is not your friend anymore, not since last Tuesday before Easter, not since the day you made her ear bleed, not since she called you that name and bit a hole in your arm and you looked as if you were going to cry and everyone was waiting and you didn't, you didn't, Sally, not since then, you don't have a best friend to lean against the schoolyard fence with, to laugh behind your hands at what the boys say. There is no one to lend you her hairbrush.

6   The stories the boys tell in the coatroom, they're not true. You lean against the schoolyard fence alone with your eyes closed as if no one was watching, as if no one could see you standing there, Sally. What do you think about when you close your eyes like that? And why do you always have to go straight home after school? You become a different Sally. You pull your skirt straight, you rub the blue paint off your eyelids. You don't laugh, Sally.

You look at your feet and walk fast to the house you can't come out from.

7   Sally, do you sometimes wish you didn't have to go home? Do you wish your feet would one day keep walking and take you far away from Mango Street, far away and maybe your feet would stop in front of a house, a nice one with flowers and big windows and steps for you to climb up two by two upstairs to where a room is waiting for you. And if you opened the little window latch and gave it a shove, the windows would swing open, all the sky would come in. There'd be no nosy neighbors watching, no motorcycles and cars, no sheets and towels and laundry. Only trees and more trees and plenty of blue sky. And you could laugh, Sally. You could go to sleep and wake up and never have to think who likes and doesn't like you. You could close your eyes and you wouldn't have to worry what people said because you never belonged here anyway and nobody could make you sad and nobody would think you're strange because you like to dream and dream. And no one could yell at you if they saw you out in the dark leaning against a car, leaning against somebody without someone thinking you are bad, without somebody saying it is wrong, without the whole world waiting for you to make a mistake when all you wanted, all you wanted, Sally, was to love and to love and to love, and no one could call that crazy.

WHAT SALLY SAID

8 He never hits me hard. She said her mama rubs lard on all the places where it hurts. Then at school she'd say she fell. That's where all the blue places come from. That's why her skin is always scarred.

9   But who believes her. A girl that big, a girl who comes in with her pretty face all beaten and black can't be falling off the stairs. He never hits me hard.

10   But Sally doesn't tell about that time he hit her with his hands just like a dog, she said, like if I was an animal. He thinks I'm going to run away like his sisters who made the family ashamed. Just because I'm a daughter, and then she doesn't say.

11   Sally was going to get permission to stay with us a little and one Thursday she came finally with a sack full of clothes and a paper bag of sweetbread her mama sent. And would've stayed too except when the dark came her father, whose eyes were little from crying, knocked on the door and said please come back, this is the last time. And she said Daddy and went home.

12   Then we didn't need to worry. Until one day Sally's father catches her talking to a boy and the next day she doesn't come to school. And the next. Until the way Sally tells it, he just went crazy, he just forgot he was her father between the buckle and the belt.

13   You're not my daughter, you're not my daughter. And then he broke into his hands.

LINOLEUM ROSES

14 Sally got married like we knew she would, young and not ready but married just the same. She met a marshmallow salesman at a school bazaar, and she married him in another state where it's legal to get married before eighth grade. She has her husband and her house now, her pillowcases and her plates. She says she's in love, but I think she did it to escape.

15 Sally says she likes being married because now she gets to buy her own things when her husband gives her money. She is happy, except sometimes her husband gets angry and once he broke the door where his foot went through, though most days he is okay. Except he won't let her talk on the telephone. And he doesn't let her look out the window. And he doesn't like her friends, so nobody gets to visit her unless he is working.

16 She sits at home because she is afraid to go outside without his permission. She looks at all the things they own: the towels and the toaster, the alarm clock and the drapes. She likes looking at the walls, at how neatly their corners meet, the linoleum roses on the floor, the ceiling smooth as wedding cake.

Collaborative Activity

In small groups, discuss the following questions.

1. Is Sally's beauty more a help or a hindrance to her? Explain.

2. Why is Sally's father so restrictive with her? Does he succeed in his goal? What evidence tells you why or why not?

3. In moving from her father's house to her husband's, has Sally obtained more or less freedom? Discuss in detail.

4. To what extent has Sally been able to make informed choices during her life? Why?

Solo Activity and Writing Assignment

Compare Sally's upbringing with your own and the one that you are giving or hope to give to your own child or children. What mistakes does Sally's father make that you believe you must avoid? What steps may you actively take to avoid those mistakes? Then, using description or persuasion, write a short essay on the topic "Bringing up a Child in the Twenty-First Century."

Selection 3

The Two, from *The Women of Brewster Place*

by Gloria Naylor

Introduction: Gloria Naylor's *The Women of Brewster Place* has, since its publication in 1982, been a widely admired depiction of the lives several African-American women lived in a run-down inner city apartment building. The novel has also been made into a movie starring Oprah Winfrey. About fifteen years after *The Women of Brewster Place,* Naylor wrote a sequel, *The Men of Brewster Place,* which is available in both book and unabridged audiocassette form.

1   At first they seemed like such nice girls. No one could remember exactly when they had moved into Brewster. It was earlier in the year before Ben was killed—of course, it had to be before Ben's death. But no one remembered if it was in the winter or spring of that year that the two had come. People often came and went on Brewster Place like a restless night's dream, moving in and out in the dark to avoid eviction notices or neighborhood bulletins about the dilapidated condition of their furnishings. So it wasn't until the two were clocked leaving in the mornings and returning in the evenings at regular intervals that it was quietly absorbed that they now claimed Brewster as home. And Brewster waited, cautiously prepared to claim them, because you never knew about young women, and obviously single at that. But when no wild music or drunken friends careened out of the corner building on weekends, and especially, when no slightly eager husbands were encouraged to linger around that first-floor apartment and run errands for them, a suspended sigh of relief floated around the two when they dumped their garbage, did their shopping, and headed for the morning bus.

2   The women of Brewster had readily accepted the lighter, skinny one. There wasn't much threat in her timid mincing walk and the slightly protruding teeth she seemed so eager to show everyone in her bell-like good mornings and evenings. Breaths were held a little longer in the direction of the short dark one—too pretty, and too much behind. And she insisted on wearing those thin Qiana dresses that the summer breeze molded against the maddening rhythm of the twenty pounds of rounded flesh that she swung steadily down the street. Through slitted eyes, the women watched their men

watching her pass, knowing the bastards were praying for a wind. But since she seemed oblivious to whether these supplications went answered, their sighs settled around her shoulders too. Nice girls.

3   And so no one even cared to remember exactly when they had moved into Brewster Place, until the rumor started. It had first spread through the block like a sour odor that's only faintly perceptible and easily ignored until it starts growing in strength from the dozen mouths it had been lying in, among clammy gums and scum-coated teeth. And then it was everywhere—lining the mouths and whitening the lips of everyone as they wrinkled up their noses at its pervading smell, unable to pinpoint the source or time of its initial arrival. Sophie could—she had been there.

4   It wasn't that the rumor had actually begun with Sophie. A rumor needs no true parent. It only needs a willing carrier, and it found one in Sophie. She had been there—on one of those August evenings when the sun's absence is a mockery because the heat leaves the air so heavy it presses the naked skin down on your body, to the point that a sheet becomes unbearable and sleep impossible. So most of Brewster was outside that night when the two had come in together, probably from one of those air-conditioned movies downtown, and had greeted the ones who were loitering around their building. And they had started up the steps when the skinny one tripped over a child's ball and the darker one had grabbed her by the arm and around the waist to break her fall. "Careful, don't wanna lose you now." And the two of them had laughed into each other's eyes and went into the building.

5   The smell had begun there. It outlined the image of the stumbling woman and the one who had broken her fall. Sophie and a few other women sniffed at the spot and then, perplexed, silently looked at each other. Where had they seen that before? They had often laughed and touched each other—held each other in joy or its dark twin—but where had they seen *that* before? It came to them as the scent drifted down the steps and entered their nostrils on the way to their inner mouths. They had seen that—done that—with their men. That shared moment of invisible communion reserved for two and hidden from the rest of the world behind laughter or tears or a touch. In the days before babies, miscarriages, and other broken dreams, after stolen caresses in barn stalls and cotton houses, after intimate walks from church and secret kisses with boys who were now long forgotten or permanently fixed in their lives—that was where. They could almost feel the odor moving about in their mouths, and they slowly knitted themselves together and let it out into the air like a yellow mist that began to cling to the bricks on Brewster.

6   So it got around that the two in 312 were *that* way. And they had seemed like such nice girls. Their regular exits and entrances to

the block were viewed with a jaundiced eye. The quiet that rested around their door on the weekends hinted of all sorts of secret rituals, and their friendly indifference to the men on the street was an insult to the women as a brazen flaunting of unnatural ways.

7   Since Sophie's apartment windows faced theirs from across the air shaft, she became the official watchman for the block, and her opinions were deferred to whenever the two came up in conversation. Sophie took her position seriously and was constantly alert for any telltale signs that might creep out around their drawn shades, across from which she kept a religious vigil. An entire week of drawn shades was evidence enough to send her flying around with reports that as soon as it got dark they pulled their shades down and put on the lights. Heads nodded in knowing unison—a definite sign. If doubt was voiced with a "But I pull my shades down at night too," a whispered "Yeah, but you're not *that* way" was argument enough to win them over.

8   Sophie watched the lighter one dumping their garbage, and she went outside and opened the lid. Her eyes darted over the crushed tin cans, vegetable peelings, and empty chocolate chip cookie boxes. What do they do with all them chocolate chip cookies? It was surely a sign, but it would take some time to figure that one out. She saw Ben go into their apartment, and she waited and blocked his path as he came out, carrying his toolbox.

9   "What ya see?" She grabbed his arm and whispered wetly in his face.

10   Ben stared at her squinted eyes and drooping lips and shook his head slowly. "Uh, uh, uh, it was terrible."

11   "Yeah?" She moved in a little closer.

12   "Worst busted faucet I seen in my whole life." He shook her hand off his arm and left her standing in the middle of the block.

13   "You old sop bucket," she muttered, as she went back up on her stoop. A broken faucet, huh? Why did they need to use so much water?

14   Sophie had plenty to report that day. Ben had said it was terrible in there. No, she didn't know exactly what he had seen, but you can imagine—and they did. Confronted with the difference that had been thrust into their predictable world, they reached into their imaginations and, using an ancient pattern, weaved themselves a reason for its existence. Out of necessity they stitched all of their secret fears and lingering childhood nightmares into this existence, because even though it was deceptive enough to try and look as they looked, talk as they talked, and do as they did, it had to have some hidden stain to invalidate it—it was impossible for them both to be right. So they leaned back, supported by the sheer

weight of their numbers and comforted by the woven barrier that kept them protected from the yellow mist that enshrouded the two as they came and went on Brewster Place.

Collaborative Activity

In small groups, discussion the following questions.

1. How have the longtime residents of Brewster Place established their own culture? Who would or would not be able to join this culture?

2. Although the story never explains what "*that* way" means, the meaning should be apparent to you by now. If it is not, discuss the term's meaning with the other members of your group. Does this difference merit the treatment that the two women receive? Why or why not?

3. Is there such a thing as a "straight culture" or a "gay culture"? If so, how do "The Two" meet or fail to meet either definition?

Solo Activity

In your own words, offer your opinion regarding sexual orientation. Is it a political concern? A moral one? A religious one? A purely personal matter?

Writing Assignment #1

In a short essay, describe the way you would feel as a resident of Brewster Place and as one of "The Two." As you write, see whether and to what extent empathy with your subjects affects the way you feel about the issue.

Writing Assignment #2

Read the rest of *The Women of Brewster Place* or rent the movie version. Discover what happens to "The Two" later on in the story. Does this treatment outrage you? Why? In a short essay, discuss the topic "Sexual Assault and Its Effects."

Selection 4

How to Lose It

by Elizabeth Wurtzel

> *Introduction:* After writing about music for *The New Yorker* during the early 1990s, Elizabeth Wurtzel produced a memoir called *Prozac Nation* when she was twenty-six years old. In *Prozac Nation*, Wurtzel described her long-time struggle against depression, her coincidentally having been one of the first Americans to take Prozac, and the effects that she believes Prozac has had upon American culture. *Prozac Nation* was one of the first best-sellers written by a so-called Generation X author.

1   If boys weren't confusing enough, drugs addled the situation even more. Ecstasy had not yet been scheduled by the DEA in any of the agency's illicit categories, so the little white capsules that looked like a vitamin supplement and felt like a nitroglycerin love-bomb going off in your cerebral cortex were still perfectly legal during my freshman year. I didn't like pot, I didn't like cocaine. I didn't like drinking—though I seemed to do all of them anyway—but ecstasy was sweet relief for me. On an X trip, I got to be away from myself for a little while.

2   Until it got out of hand. We started to do so much of it so often that around campus people began to refer to me, Ruby, and our other pal, Jordana, as the ecstasy goddesses. We walked up to people at parties whom we didn't know and told them how much we loved them. On ecstasy, we were best friends with everybody, we no longer felt the class distinctions that were all over Harvard, we no longer thought that we were poor and ugly. We could escape the wide gulf of circumstance that separated the three of us—with our overworked, overtired single mothers, with our scholarships and student loans—from the boys we seemed to keep hooking up with, the ones with last names like Cabot and Lowell and Greenough and Nobles. All of them seemed to have gone to Andover and Hotchkiss and were at Harvard as legacies, as "development cases"—the code phrase the admissions office used for the children of major-money donors—all of them substandard students who the school insisted take a year off before entering. Why all of us—we smart, urban Jewish girls who worked as waitresses and typists to earn tuition money—chose to take up with these guys for whom Cliffs Notes were invented is beyond me. But we did. It was pretty obvious that they just hung with us because they wanted a break from all the blonds who played field hockey and had names like Libby, the girls they'd known forever from summers in Maine

or NOLS courses or prep school. But why we allowed ourselves to be swayed by their money and their cocaine is still a mystery. Maybe I thought it was part of the Harvard experience.

3   Three days before winter break, I realize I have bottomed out when I wake up in Noah Biddle's room on a Sunday after an ecstasy trip the night before. Noah is the heir to a banking fortune, an Andover boy from Philadelphia's Main Line who is such a brat that when Harvard told him he had to take time off before entering as a freshman, he actually hired a consultant to plan the year for him. He does so much coke that I have started to wonder how he will look with a third nostril. I don't really like him much, but for some reason I will do anything to get him to like me, an impossible task because he just doesn't. I keep thinking that if I could only win Noah's love, I would finally feel as if I've actually arrived at Harvard, appended myself to someone so integral to the place that the minefields in my head would stop exploding at long last.

4   So here I am, lying nearly naked on the carpet in the common room of his suite, my head pillowed by a puddle of beer. Noah is next to me on the floor; we are wrapped in each other the way dried, harried flowers start sticking together after a week in a vase. In my parched exhaustion, I can just barely survey the debris of last night's mess: Since everyone smokes and chews gum with ecstasy, there are ashes and little sticky pink blobs attached to the coffee table and the floor; because everyone feels so agile on ecstasy when in fact they are extremely clumsy, there are spilled bottles and empty plastic cups. There are items of clothing everywhere, mostly mine. But I can't see a clock through the blur of my desiccated contact lenses, which I should have taken out hours before, and I need to know what time it is because my grandparents are supposed to visit and I've got to meet them at my room sometime before noon. When I finally can see my watch, can see that it's past 4:00 P.M., that they have probably come and gone, and that, besides, I've got a paper due tomorrow that I haven't even thought about yet, I feel a panic come over me that doesn't quite erupt because the residual effect of the ecstasy preempts it. But somewhere deep down inside, under all the anesthesia, I know I have really f_ _ _ _ _ up big-time. I know that nothing is as it should be, nothing is even the way I wish it would be, I've slept through my grandparents' visit, I might as well sleep through the rest of my life, and I am so horrified that I let out the loudest scream I've ever made.

5   Noah pops up, frightened of how frightened I am, tries to silence me, says people will think I'm being raped or murdered, but I can't stop screaming. He's petrified, he's wishing he'd never got mixed up with me, he's looking at me like I'm a tornado or a dust bowl that's

just outside his window and way beyond his control, and he's just praying that the damage will be minimal. I keep screaming. Being a veteran preppy stoner, Noah is so used to acid freak-outs in the middle of Grateful Dead shows that he knows how to cope, knows how to get into an adrenaline-induced dealing mode. He puts on his clothes, manages to get me into my clothes, covers my mouth with his hand as he picks me up and walks me out the door and over to the emergency room at University Health Services, me screaming all the way, all the way through the Yard and the snow and the freezing cold.

6   Noah leaves me there, leaves me with a nurse who shuffles me into an examining room. The nurse calls the psychiatrist on duty. She won't let me leave, even though I keep saying, I've got to see my grandparents, they're waiting for me, we have to get brunch, they're eighty years old, they drove up here from New York this morning. The nurse explains that it's too late anyway, that it's 5:00 in the evening. But I just keep saying, I've got to find my grandparents.

7   They ask me if I've done any drugs in the last twenty-four hours, and I say no. Then I say I guess I smoked some pot and snorted some coke, but that was just to make the ecstasy last longer. I also admit to them that I had some liquor, maybe a couple of sea breezes somewhere in there, too. And then the doctor asks if I have a substance-abuse problem and all I can do is laugh. I laugh really hard and really loud, a howling-hyena laugh, because what I'm thinking is how nice it would be if my problem were drugs, if my problem weren't my whole damn life and how little relief from it even drugs provide. I keep laughing, on and on, like a nut, until the doctor agrees to give me some Valium and keeps me half prone on the adjustable examining table until I calm down. Maybe an hour goes by. In its quiet, gentle way, the Valium flattens my hysteria into a mere lack of affect, and after many assurances that I will be just fine, really I will, the doctor sends me on my way, telling me to get some rest over winter vacation.

8   When I get back to my room, there are eight messages from my grandparents, calling from various points in Cambridge, the final one saying that they're leaving. My hallmates, who say they tried to call me all morning at Noah's but there was no answer, look at me like I'm a really bad person. Brittany says, *Maybe you should take some time off.* Jennifer says, *What's wrong with you? Everyone goes crazy sometimes, but how can you do this to your grandparents—they're these little people, they were so worried?* And all I can do is go into my room and crawl into bed.

9   When I wake up, after a Valium sleep that makes me think I'm turning into a creep like my dad, I call my political-philosophy section leader and tell him that I can't hand in the essay that's due tomorrow on time because I slipped on the ice and had a concussion. The girl who never once submitted a paper or an article a day

late, the girl who lived for the small amount of structure that dead-lines provide, seems to have decided that all that good stuff just doesn't matter anymore. That girl is gone. She is going home for winter break and never coming back.

10   The thing is, there was never any pleasure, no element of par-tying, in any of the drug use and abuse I was involved with. It was all so pathetic, so sad, so psychotic. I was loading myself with whatever available medication I could find, doing whatever I could to just get my head to shut off for a while. Maybe for Noah, who was pretty much a happy-go-lucky child of a happy home, coke and ecstasy were all about being party-hardy—I can remember his silly delight as he taught me how to do a bong hit, how to snort a line of cocaine without blowing the rest of the stuff off the mirror like in that scene in *Annie Hall*—but for me it was all just desperation. It wasn't just recreational drug use—I would find myself, whenever I was in anyone's home, going through the medicine cabinets, stealing whatever Xanax or Ata-van I could find, hoping to score the prescription narcotics like Percodan and codeine, usually prescribed following wisdom-tooth extraction or some other form of surgery. On Percodan, which is nothing less than an industrial-strength painkiller, I felt almost no pain. I would hoard those little tablets, save them up for a big pain emergency, and take them until nothing much mat-tered anymore.

11   Basically, drugs were no solution to any of my problems. I was a klutz with a joint in my hand, so inept at chemical self-destruction that I was often reminded of the story about Spin-oza trying to kill himself by drowning but failing because his foot got stuck in the dock. My God, how much I wanted just to be sane and calm on my own! I would have loved nothing bet-ter than to see my grandparents, to take them around Cam-bridge. I would have loved to take them to one of the cafés where I spent long, lazy hours reading and gossiping and drink-ing double espressos to stay awake. I would have loved to show them that I was all right after all, that their lonesome little grandchild who always seemed so bookish and morose had really turned out okay.

12   During my senior year of high school, my first cousin—one of their other grandchildren—had married a Wall Street tycoon, had celebrated with a huge wedding at Windows on the World, and had made the whole family so damn proud by making such a good match. I knew I would never do anything like that, I knew I was attracted mostly to hopeless hippies and other lost souls like me, but I wanted my grandparents to be impressed with the things I could do: I could write, I could study, I could get into Harvard. I

looked forward to their visit with about the same amount of glee that a former fat girl who has slimmed into a glamorous woman looks forward to her tenth-year high school reunion. Noah could have come to brunch with us—at least in my fantasy he would have—and even though he wasn't Jewish, he was a charming Pennsylvania Yankee (his sisters had made their society debuts all over the Northeast) and my grandparents would head back home to Long Island thinking what a stunning collegiate success I had been.

13   Instead, they were just worried, scared stiff, wondering what the hell had happened to their youngest grandchild, the one who used to come to their house every weekend and on every vacation when she was little because her mother worked and her father slept and there was no one to take care of her. They had practically raised me, and now they would wonder what had gone wrong. There was no way I could possibly explain to them that I was suffering from an acute depression, that it was so intense that even when I wanted to get out of my own head and attend to other people's needs—as I had so much wanted to do that day—I couldn't. I was consumed by depression and by the drugs I took to combat it, so there was nothing left of me, no remainder of the self that could please them even for a few hours. I was useless.

Collaborative Activity

In small groups, discuss the following questions.

1. Although this 1994 *Esquire* excerpt from the then forthcoming *Prozac Nation* is called "How to Lose It," do you consider the essay an example of the "how to" mode? Why or why not?

2. What attitude does Wurtzel seem to demonstrate toward drugs, legal and illegal? How does her attitude affect your reading of the essay or your attitude toward Wurtzel?

3. Do you think that the response of the clinicians at University Health Services is appropriate or inappropriate? Why or why not?

4. Would you consider the persona projected by Wurtzel in "How to Lose It" a typical Generation X person or not? Explain.

Solo Activity and Writing Assignment

Since the early 1980s, the United States has publicly been waging a "War on Drugs." At the same time, awareness and treatment of mental disorders such as depression has greatly improved, thanks in part to new medications such as Prozac, Paxil, and Zoloft. These new medications often help people, like

Elizabeth Wurtzel, who had previously been self-medicating through alcohol and illegal drugs. Read up on depression in a psychology textbook or by visiting the National Alliance for Mental Health's web page [www.nami.org], and write an essay on the topic "Treating Severe Depression."

Selection 5

An Interval

by David Foster Wallace

> *Introduction:* Just a few years older than Elizabeth Wurtzel, David Foster Wallace is one of the most provocative writers born in the 1960s. His 1,000+ page novel *Infinite Jest,* which also includes more than 100 pages of footnotes has been, variously, praised as a work of genius, derided as garbage, or utterly misunderstood by critics and readers. "An Interval" is set in a detox center and employs the language of twelve-step groups alongside Wallace's usual biting satire.

1   Both House Director Pat Montesian and Don Gately's A.A. sponsor like to remind him how the new Ennet House resident Geoffrey Day could be an invaluable teacher for him, Gately, as Staff.

2   "So then at forty-six years of age I came here to learn to live by clichés" is what Day says to Charlotte Treat right after Randy Lenz asked what time it was at 0825. "To turn my will and life over to the care of clichés. One day at a time. Easy does it. First things first. Ask for help. Thy will not mine be done. It works if you work it. Grow or go. Keep coming back."

3   Poor old Charlotte Treat, needle-pointing primly beside him on the old vinyl couch that just came from Goodwill, purses her lips. "You need to ask for some gratitude."

4   "Oh no but the point is that I've already been fortunate enough to *receive* gratitude." Day crosses one leg over the other in a way that inclines his whole little soft body toward her. "For which, believe you me, I'm grateful. I cultivate gratitude. That's part of the system of clichés I'm here to live by. An attitude of gratitude. A grateful drunk will never drink. I know the actual cliché is 'A grateful heart will never drink,' but since organs can't properly be said to imbibe and I'm still afflicted with just enough self-will to decline to live by utter non sequiturs, as opposed to just good old clichés, I'm taking the doubtless hazardous liberty of light amendment. Albeit grateful amendment, of course."

5   Charlotte Treat looks over to Gately for some sort of help or Staff enforcement of dogma. The poor b_ _ _ _ is clueless. All of them are clueless, still. Gately reminds himself that he too is probably still mostly clueless, even after all these hundreds of days. "I Didn't Know That I Didn't Know" is another of these slogans that look so shallow for a while and then all of a sudden drop off and deepen like the lobster waters off the North Shore. As Gately fidgets his way through daily A.M. meditation he always tries to remind himself daily that this is all an Ennet House residency is supposed to do: buy these poor yutzes some time, some thin pie slice of abstinent time, till they can start to get a whiff of what's true and deep, almost magic, under the shallow surface of what they're trying to do.

6   "I cultivate it assiduously, I do special gratitude exercises at night up there in the room. *Gratitude-ups,* you could call them. Ask Randy over there if I don't do them like clockwork. Diligently. Sedulously."

7   "Well it's true is all." Treat sniffs. "About gratitude."

8   Everybody else except Gately, who is lying on the old other couch opposite them, is ignoring this exchange, watching an old movie whose tracking is a little messed up so that staticky stripes eat at the picture's bottom and top. The Ennet House Director, Pat M., encourages new Staff to think of residents they'd like to bludgeon to death as teachers of patience, tolerance, self-discipline, and restraint. She can always tell when Gately's exercising tolerant restraint, because of the slight facial tic that betrays his effort of will, and makes it a point to praise his willingness to grow and change when the cheek starts to spasm.

9   Day isn't done. "One of these exercises is being grateful that life is so much *easier* now. I used sometimes to think. I used to think in long compound sentences with subordinate clauses and even the odd polysyllable. Now I find I needn't. Now I live by the dictates of macramé samplers ordered from the back-page ad of an old *Reader's Digest* or *Saturday Evening Post.* Easy Does It. Remember to Remember. But for the Grace of God. Turn It Over. Terse, hard-boiled. Good old Norman Rockwell-Paul Harvey wisdom. I walk around with my arms out straight in front of me and recite these clichés. In a monotone. No inflection necessary. Could that be one? Could that be added to the cliché pool? No inflection necessary? Too many syllables, probably."

10   Poor old Charlotte Treat, all of nine weeks clean, is looking primmer and primmer. She glances again over at Gately, lying on his back, taking up the living room's whole other sofa, one sneaker up on the sofa's square worn-fabric arm, his eyes almost closed. Only House Staff get to lie on the couches.

11   "Denial," Charlotte finally says, "is not a river in Egypt."

12   "Hows about the both of you shut the f_ _ _ up," says Emil Minty.

13   Geoffrey (not Geoff, Geoffrey) Day has been at Ennet House eight days. He came in from Roxbury's infamous Dimock Detox, where he was the only white person, which Gately bets must have been broadening for him. Day has a squished blank smeared flat face, one requiring great effort to like, and eyes that are just starting to lose the nictitated glaze of early sobriety. Gately tries to remind himself that Day is a newcomer and still very raw. A red-wine-and-Quaalude man who finally nodded out in late October and put his Saab through the window of a Malden sporting-goods store and then got out and proceeded to browse until Boston's fines came and got him. He'd taught something horses_ _ _ sounding like social historicity or historical sociality at some Jr. college up the Expressway in Medford and came in saying in his Intake interview that he also manned the helm of a scholarly quarterly. Word for word, the House Manager had said: "manned the helm" and "scholarly quarterly." His Intake indicated that Day'd been in and out of a blackout for most of the last several years, and his wiring is still as they say pretty frayed. His detox at Dimock, where they barely have the resources to slip you a Librium if you start to D.T., must have been real grim, because Geoffrey D. now alleges it never happened: his story is he just strolled into Ennet House on a lark one day from his home five-plus miles away in Malden and found the place too hilariously egregious to want to leave.

14   It's the newcomers with some education that are the worst, according to Staffer Eugenio M. They identify their whole selves with their head, and the Disease makes its command headquarters in the head. Day wears chinos of indeterminate hue, brown socks with black shoes, and shirts that the House Manager had described on the Intake form as "East-European-type turtleneck shirts." Day's now on the vinyl couch with Charlotte Treat after breakfast in the Ennet House living room with a few of the other residents who either aren't working or don't have to be at work early, and with Gately, who'd pulled a night shift down in the front office till 0400, then got temp-relieved by Johnette Foltz so he could go to work down at the Shattuck Shelter till 0700, and then came and hauled a_ _ back up and took back over so Johnette F. could go off to her N.A.-convention thing with a bunch of N.A. kids in what looked like a VW bus without a hood over the engine, and is now, Gately, covering Johnette's half of the day shift until somebody else gets here, and is trying to unclench and center himself inside by tracing the cracks in the paint of the living room ceiling with his eyes. Gately often feels a terrible sense of loss, narcotics-wise, in the A.M., still, even after all this drug-free time.

His A.A. sponsor over at the White Flag group says some people never get over the loss of what they'd thought was their one true best friend and lover, they just have to pray daily for acceptance and patience and the brass danglers to move forward through the grief and loss, to wait for time to harden the scab. The sponsor doesn't give Gately one bit of s_ _ _ for feeling bad: on the contrary, he commends Gately for his candor in breaking down and crying like a baby and finally telling him about it one A.M., the sense of terrible loss. It's a myth no one misses it. Their particular Substance. S_ _ _, you wouldn't need to give it up if you didn't miss it. You just have to Turn It Over, the emptiness and loss, Keep Coming, show up, pray, Ask for Help. Gately rubs his eye. Simple advice like this does seem like a lot of clichés—Day's right about how it seems. Yes, and if Geoffrey Day keeps on steering by the way things seem to him, he's a dead man sure. Gately's already watched dozens come through here and leave early and some of them die. If Day ever gets lucky and breaks down, finally, and comes to the office late at night to clutch at his pant cuff and blubber and beg for help, Gately'll get to tell Day that the clichéd directives of recovery are a lot more deep and hard to actually do. To try and live by instead of just say. But he'll only get to say it if Day comes and asks. Personally, Gately gives Day like a month at the outside before he's back tipping his hat to parking meters. Except who is Gately to judge who'll end up getting the Gift of the program v. who won't; he needs to remember. He tries to feel like Day is teaching him patience. It takes great patience and tolerance not to want to punt the guy out into Commonwealth Ave. and open up his bunk to somebody that really wants it, desperately, the Gift. Except who is Gately to think he can know who wants it and who doesn't, deep down. Gately's arm is behind his head, up against the sofa's other arm. The VCR is on to something violent Gately neither sees nor hears. He can sort of turn his attention on and off like a light. Even when he was a resident here, he'd had this pro housebreaker's ability to screen input, to do sensory triage. It was one reason he'd been able to stick out his nine residential months with twenty-one other newly detoxed housebreakers, hoods, whores, fired execs, subway musicians, beer-bloated construction workers, vagrants, cirrhotic car salesmen, bunko artists, mincing pillow biters, North End hard guys, Avon ladies, pimply kids with nose-rings, denial-ridden housewives and etc., all jonesing and head-gaming and desperate and grieving and basically whacked out and producing non-stopping output 24/7.

15   At some point in here Day says, "So bring on the lobotomist, bring him on I say!"

16   Except that Gately's counsellor when he was a resident here, Eugenio Martinez, one of the volunteer alumni counsellors, a one-

eared former boiler-room bunko man and now a cellular-phone retailer who'd gone through the House under the original pre-Pat founder and now had about like ten years clean, Eugenio M. had lovingly confronted Gately early on about his special burglar's selective attention and about how it could be dangerous, because how can you be sure it's you doing the input screening and not the Spider. Eugenio had called addiction the Spider instead of the Disease, and dispensed his advice in terms of like for example "Feeding the Spider" v. "Starving the Spider" and so on. He'd called Gately into the House Manager's back office and said what if screening his attention's input turned out to be Feeding the Spider and what about an experimental unscreening of input for a while. And Gately had said he'd do his best to try and had come back out and tried to watch a Celtics game while two resident pillow biters from off the Fenway were on the couch having this involved conversation about some third fag having to go in and get the skeleton of some kind of f_ _ _ _ _ _ rodent removed from inside his butth_ _ _ The unscreening experiment had lasted half an hour. This was right before Gately got his ninety-day chip and wasn't exactly wrapped real tight, still. Ennet House this year is nothing like the freak show it was when Gately went through. Gately has been Substance-free for four hundred and twenty-one days today.

17   Charlotte Treat, with her carefully made-up, ruined face, is watching the static-striped movie on the VCR while she needlepoints something. Conversation between her and Geoffrey D. has mercifully petered out. Day is scanning the room for somebody else to engage and piss off so he can prove to himself he doesn't fit in here and stay separated off isolated inside himself and maybe get them so pissed off there's a beef and he gets bounced out, Day, and it won't be his fault. You can almost hear the Spider of his Disease chewing away inside his head. Emil Minty, Randy Lenz, and Bruce Green are also in the room, sprawled in spring-shot chairs, lighting one gasper off the end of the last, their posture the don't f_ _ _-with-me slouch of the streets that here makes their bodies' texture somehow hard to distinguish from that of the chairs. Nell Gunther is sitting at the long table in the doorless dining room that opens out right off the old donated VCR and monitor's pine stand, whitening under her nails with a manicure pencil amid the remains of something she's eaten that involved serious syrup. Joe S. is also in there, *way* down by himself at the table's far end, trying to saw at a waffle with a knife and fork attached to the stumps of his wrists with Velcro bands. A long-ago former C.P.A., Joe Smith is forty-five and looks seventy, has almost all-white hair that's waxy and yellow from close-order

smoke, and finally got into Ennet House last month after a summer in the Cambridge City Shelter. Joe S. is making his fiftieth-odd stab at some kind of durable sobriety in A.A. Once devoutly R.C., he's had crippling trouble with Faith in a Loving God ever since the R.C. Church apparently granted his wife an annulment in '91 after fifteen years of marriage. Then for several years a rooming-house drunk, which in Gately's view is like one step up from a homeless-person-type drunk. Joe S. got jumped and rolled and beaten half to death in Cambridge in the storm on Xmas Eve of last year and left to freeze in an alley, and ended up losing his hands and feet. Whenever residents Doony Glynn and Wade McDade are together in a room and Joe S. comes teetering in on his blocky prosthetic shoes, G. and McD. will stand up and shout together: "Hail Joe, Asleep in the Snow!" Repeated threats of Restriction and worse have not broken them of this practice. Doony Glynn's also been observed telling Joe Smith things like that there's some new guy coming in and moving into the Disabled Room with Joe who's totally minus arms or legs or even a head and communicates by farting in Morse code. Which sally earned Glynn three days' Full House Restriction and a week's extra House Chore for what Johnette Foltz described in the Staff Log as "XSive Crulty." There is a vague intestinal moaning in Gately's right side. Watching Joe Smith smoke a Benson & Hedges by holding it between his stumps with his elbows out like a man with pruning shears is an adventure in f_ _ _ _ _ _ pathos, as far as Gately's concerned. And forget about what it's like trying to watch Joe S. try to light a match.

17   Gately, who's been on Live-In Staff here four months now, believes Charlotte Treat's devotion to needlepoint is suspect. All those needles. In and out of all that thin sterile-white cotton stretched drum-tight in its round frame. The needle makes a kind of thud and squeak when it goes in the cloth. It's not much like the soundless pop and slide of a real cook-and-shoot. But still. She takes such great care.

18   Gately wonders what color he'd call the ceiling if forced to call it a color. It's not beige and it's not gray. The brown-yellow tones are from high-tar gaspers; a pall hangs up near the ceiling even this early in the new sober day. Some of the drunks and trank-jockeys stay up most of the night, joggling their feet and chain-smoking, even though there's no movies or music allowed after midnight. Don G. has that odd House Staffer's knack, already, after four months, of seeing everything significant in both living and dining rooms without really looking. Emil Minty, a hard-core smack-addict punk here for reasons nobody can quite yet pin down, is in an old mustard-colored easy chair with his combat boots up on one of the standing ashtrays, which is tilting

not quite enough for Gately to tell him to watch out, please. Minty's orange Mohawk and the shaved skull around it are starting to grow out brown, which is just not a pleasant sight in the morning at all. The other ashtray on the floor by his chair is full of the ragged new moons of bitten nails, which has got to mean that Esther Thrale, who Gately ordered to bed at 0230, was back down here in the chair having at her nails again the second Gately left to go mop up s_ _ _ at the Shattuck Shelter. Another gurgle and abdominal chug. When he's up all night Gately's stomach gets all acidy and tight, from either the coffee, maybe, or just the staying up. Emil M.'s been sleeping in the streets since he was maybe sixteen, Gately can tell: he's got that sooty complexion homeless guys have where the soot has insinuated itself into the dermal layer. And the big-armed driver for Leisure Time Ice, the quiet kid, Bruce Green, a garbage-head all-Substance-type kid, maybe twenty-one, face very slightly smunched in on one side, wears sleeveless khaki shirts, used to live in a trailer in that apocalyptic Enfield trailer park out near Allston; Gately likes Green because he seems to have sense enough to keep his yap shut when he's got nothing important to say, which is basically all the time. The tattoo on the kid's right tricep is a spear-pierced heart over the hideous name *MILDRED BONK*, who Bruce G. told him was a ray of living light and a dead ringer for the late lead singer of The Fiends in Human Shape and his dead heart's one love ever, and who took their daughter and left him this summer for some guy who'd told her he ranched f_ _ _ _ _ _ longhorn cows east of Atlantic City, N.J. He's got, even by Ennet House standards, major-league sleep trouble, Green, and he and Gately play cribbage sometimes in the wee dead hours, a game Gately picked up in jail. Joe S. is now hunched in a meaty coughing fit, his elbows out and forehead purple. Gately can see everything without moving his eyes at all.

19   And then Lenz. Randy Lenz is a small-time organic-coke dealer who wears sport coats rolled up over his big forearms and is always checking his pulse on the inside of his wrists. It's come out that Lenz is of keen interest to both sides of the law; this past May he'd apparently all of a sudden lost all control and holed up in a Charlestown motel and freebased most of a whole hundred grams he'd been fronted by a suspiciously trusting Brazilian in what Lenz didn't know was supposed to have been a D.E.A. sting operation in the South End. Having screwed both sides in what Gately secretly views as a delicious f_ _ _up, Randy Lenz has, since May, been the most wanted he's probably ever been. He is seedily handsome in the way of pimps and low-level coke dealers, muscular in the way certain guys' muscles look muscular but can't really lift anything, with complexly gelled hair and the little bird-like head movements of the deeply vain. One forearm's hair

has a little hairless patch, which Gately knows all too well spells knife owner, and if there's one thing Gately's never been able to stomach it's a knife owner, little swaggery guys who always queer a square beef and come up off the ground with a blade so you have to get out to take it away from them. Lenz is teaching Gately a restrained compassion for people you pretty much want to beat up on sight. And it's obvious to everybody except Pat Montesian—whose odd gullibility in the presence of human sludge, though, Gately needs to try to remember, was one of the reasons why he himself had got into Ennet House—that Lenz is here mostly just to hide. He rarely leaves the House except under compulsion, avoids all windows, and travels nightly to the required A.A./N.A. meetings in a disguise that makes him look like Cesar Romero after a terrible accident; and then he always wants to walk home solo afterward, which is not encouraged. Lenz's leg never stops joggling; Day claims it joggles even worse in sleep. Lenz is seated low in the northeasternmost corner of an old fake-velour love seat that he's jammed in the northeasternmost corner of the living room. Randy Lenz has a strange compulsive need to be north of everything, and possibly even northeast of everything, and Gately has no clue what it's about but observes Lenz's position routinely for his own interest and files.

Second-month resident Charlotte Treat has violently red hair. As in hair the color of like a red crayon. She doesn't have to work the usual outside mental job, because she has some strain of the Virus or maybe A.R.C. Former prostitute, reformed. Why do prostitutes when they get straight always try and get so prim? It's like long-repressed librarian ambitions come flooding out. Charlotte T. has a cut-rate whore's hard, half-pretty face, her eyes lassoed with shadow around all four lids. Her also with a case of the dermal-layer sooty complexion. The thing about Treat is how her cheeks are deeply pitted in deep trenches that she packs with foundation and tries to cover over with blush, which along with the hair gives her the look of a mean clown. The ghastly wounds in her cheeks look for all the world like somebody got at her with a woodburning kit at some point in her career path. Gately would rather not know.

20   Don Gately is almost twenty-nine and sober and just huge. One shoulder blade and buttock pooch out over the side of a sofa that sags like a hammock. Lying there gurgling and inert with eyes half shut and a tolerant if ticcy smile. Gately looks less built than poured, with the smooth immovability of an Easter Island statue. It would be nice if intimidating size weren't one of the factors in a male graduate's getting offered the male Live-In Staff job here, but there you are. He has a massive square head made squarer-looking by the Prince Valiant-ish haircut he tries to maintain him-

self in the mirror, to save money. Room and board aside—plus of course the opportunity for Service—he makes very little money as an Ennet House Staffer, and is paying off restitution schedules in three different district courts. He has the fluttery white-eyed smile now of someone who's holding himself just over the level of doze. Pat Montesian isn't due in until 0900, and he can't go to sleep until she shows, because the House Manager has driven Jennifer Belbin to a court appearance downtown and Gately's the only Staffer here; Foltz, the other Live-In, is at a Narcotics Anonymous convention in Hartford for the long weekend. Gately personally is not hot on N.A.: so many relapses and unhumble returns, so many drug stories told with undisguised bulls_ _ _ pride, so little emphasis on Service or serious Message; all those people in leather and metal, preening. Rooms full of Randy Lenzes, all hugging each other, pretending they don't miss narcotics. Rampant vulnerable-newcomer f_ _ _ _ _ _. There's a difference between abstinence and recovery, Gately knows. Though who is Gately to judge what works for who. He just knows what seems like it works for him, today. A.A.'s tough Boston love, the White Flag group, old guys with suspendered bellies and white crewcuts and geologic amounts of sober time who'll take your big square head off if they sense you're getting complacent or chasing tail or forgetting that your life still hangs in the balance every f_ _ _ _ _ _ day. White Flag newcomers so crazed and sick they can't sit, and have to pace at the meeting's rear, like Gately when he first came. Retired old kindergarten teachers in polyresin slacks and a pincenez who bake cookies for the weekly meeting and relate from behind the podium how they used to blow bartenders at closing for just two more fingers in a paper cup to take home against the morning's needled light. Gately, albeit an oral-narcotics man from way back, has committed himself to A.A. He drank his fair share, too, he figures, after all.

21   House Director Pat M. is due in at 0900 and has application interviews with three people, 2 F and 1 M, who better be showing up soon; and Gately will get up and answer the door when they don't know enough to just come in and will say Welcome and get them a cup of coffee if he judges them able to hold it. He'll take them aside and tip them off to be sure to pet Pat M.'s dogs during the interview. The dogs'll be sprawled all over the front office, sides heaving, writhing and biting at themselves. He'll tell the applicants it's a proved fact that if Pat's dogs like you, you're in. Pat M. has directed Gately to tell applicants this, and then if they do actually pet the dogs—two hideous white golden retrievers with suppurating skin afflictions, plus one had grand-mal epilepsy—it'll betray a level of desperate willingness that Pat says is just about all she goes by, deciding.

22   A nameless cat oozes by on the broad windowsill above the back of the fabric couch. Animals here come and go. Graduates adopt them or they just disappear. Their fleas tend to remain. Gately's intestines gurgle. Boston's dawn this morning was chemically pink. The nail parings in the ashtray on the floor are, he sees, way too big to be fingernail bits. These bitten arcs are broad and thick and a deep autumnal yellow. They are not from finger. He swallows hard.

23   Gately'd tell Day how even if they are just clichés, clichés are: (a) soothing, and (b) proclaim a common sort of common sense, and (c) license the universal assent that drowns out silence. And fourth, silence is deadly, pure Spider-food, if you've got the Disease. The older White Flaggers say you can spell the Disease "disease," which sums the basic situation up nicely. Gately should probably also tell him that the only real ultimate relief from the Disease is God, as in finding and cultivating some kind of personally comfortable and worshipable Higher Power, but Gately still can't bring himself to say this kind of thing out loud. Pat has a meeting at the Bureau of Substance Abuse Services in Government Center at noon she needs to be reminded about, since she can't read her own handwriting. Gately envisions going around having to find out who's biting their f_ _ _ _ _ _ toenails in the living room and putting the disgusting toenail bits in the ashtray at like 0500. House Regs prohibit bare feet anyplace downstairs.

24   There's a pale-brown water stain on the ceiling over Day and Treat the exact shape of Florida. Randy Lenz has issues with Geoffrey Day because Day is educated and a teacher and mans a journal's helm. This threatens the self-concept of Lenz, who sees himself as a kind of hiply sexy artist-dash-intellectual. Small-time dealers never think of themselves as just small-time dealers. For Occupation on his Intake form Lenz had put "free lance writer." And he makes a big show of the fact he reads. For his first sober week here in August he'd sat all day smoking and joggling in the northeast corner of the living room, holding open a gigantic medical dictionary and pretending to be reading medical words until Glynn and McDade started busting his balls about never turning the page. At which juncture he quit reading and started talking, making everybody nostalgic for when he just read. Johnette F. had put in the September Log that Lenz would, quote, "get on your very last nerve," which Gately had underlined in a different-color ink. Plus Geoffrey D. has issues with Randy L., too. The dislike is mutual. There's a certain way they don't look at each other. And so now of course they're mashed in together in the tiny three-man bedroom, since last week three guys in one night missed curfew and came in without one normal-sized pupil between them and all refused Urines and got discharged on the spot, and so Day got moved up in his first week

from the five-man newcomers' room to the three-man. Seniority comes quick around here. Lenz and Day: a beef may be brewing. Day'll try to goad Lenz into a beef that'll be public enough so he doesn't get hurt but does get bounced out, and then he can leave treatment and go back to Chianti and ludes and make out like the relapse is Ennet House's and never have to confront himself or his Disease. To Gately, Geoffrey D. is like a wide-open textbook on the Disease. One of Gately's jobs is to keep an eye on what's possibly brewing among residents and let Pat or the House Manager know and to try to smooth things down in advance if possible.

25   The ceiling's color could be called dun, if forced. Someone has farted; no one knows just who, but this isn't like a normal adult place where everybody cooly pretends a fart didn't happen. Here everybody has to make their little comment.

26   Time is passing. Ennet House reeks of passing time. It is the humidity of early sobriety, hanging and palpable. You can hear ticking in clockless rooms here. Gately changes the angle of one sneaker, puts his other arm behind his head. His head has real weight and pressure. Randy Lenz's obsessive compulsions include the need to be north, a fear of disks, a tendency to take his own pulse, a pathological fear of every form of timepiece, and a constant need to know the time with great precision.

27   "Day man, you got the time maybe real quick?" Lenz. For the third time in half an hour. Patience, tolerance, reserve, compassion. Gately remembers his own first few straight months here: he'd felt the sharp edge of every second that went by. And the freak-show dreams. Nightmares beyond the worst D.T.s you'd ever heard of. One reason to have a night-shift Staffer down in the front office is so somebody's there for the residents to talk at when—not if, when—when the detox nightmares ratchet them out of twisted sheets at like 0300. Nightmares about relapsing and getting high, about not getting high but having everybody think you're high, about getting high with your alcoholic mom and then killing her with a baseball bat. Whipping it out for a court-ordered Urine and starting up and flames come shooting out. Getting high and bursting into flames. Having a water-spout shaped like an enormous syringe suck you up inside. A vehicle explodes in a bloom of enhanced flame on the VCR, its hood up like an old pop tab.

28   Day is making a broad gesture out of checking his wrist-watch. "Right around eight-thirty, fella."

29   Randy L.'s fine nostrils flair and whiten. He stares straight ahead, eyes narrowed, fingers on his wrist. Day purses his lips. Gately hangs his head over the arm of the sofa and regards Lenz upside down. "That look on your face there mean something there, Randy? Are you like communicating something with that look?"

30   "Does anybody maybe know the time a little more exactly is what I'm wondering, Don, since Day doesn't."

Gately checks his own cheap digital, head still hung over the sofa's arm. "I got eight-thirty-two and fourteen, fifteen, sixteen seconds, Randy."

31   "Thanks a lot D.G. man."

32   And now Day has that same flared narrow look for Lenz. "We've been over this, friend. Amigo. Sport. You do this all the time with me. Again I'll say it—I don't have a digital watch. This is a fine old antique watch. It points. A memento of vastly better days. It's not a digital watch. It's not a cesium-based atomic clock. It points, with hands. See, Spiro Agnew here has two little arms: they point, they suggest. It's not a f_ _ _ _ _ _ stopwatch for life. Lenz, get a watch. Am I right? Why don't you just get a watch, Lenz. Three people I happen to know of for a fact have offered to get you a watch and let you pay them back whenever you feel comfortable about poking your nose out and investigating the work-a-world. Get a watch. Obtain a watch. A fine, digital, incredibly *wide* watch, about five times the width of your wrist, so you have to hold it like a falconer, and it treats time like pi."

33   "Easy does it," Charlotte Treat half sings, not looking up from her needle and frame.

34   Day looks around at her. "I don't believe I was speaking to you in any way shape or form."

35   "Peace," Gately says softly, his head still hanging over. Joe Smith, upside-down, is having another coughing fit over in the dining room.

36   Lenz is staring blackly at Geoffrey Day. "If you're trying to f_ _ _ with me, brother." He shakes his fine shiny head. "Big mistake."

37   Day puts his hands up to his cheeks. "Ooh I'm all atremble. I can barely hold my arm steady to read my watch."

38   Lenz points his cigarette. "Big big big *real* big mistake."

39   Emil M.'s contorted way forward in his chair in the way of somebody communicating that he's trying to watch TV around a distraction. "Hows about I give you both a beating if you don't shut up."

40   A time-killing fantasy Gately has lately is in the middle of bulls_ _ _ squabbles like this he all of a sudden picks Geoffrey D. up bodily and swings him by his dress shoes and uses him as a bludgeon to beat Randy Lenz's overgroomed head in, freeing up two bunks at once. His progress consists of just entertaining such thoughts now instead of acting on them, which Pat M. reassures him is almost the same as patience. The Ennet House living room has no clock. Gately likes that his cheap watch counts off the sec-

onds: sometimes he just sits and watches the seconds on his big wrist tick digitally off, to remind himself that an interval of time is passing, will pass.

41   Day has crossed his legs and laced his hands over the knee, a posture they all know Lenz detests for some reason. "So let me get this straight. We're engaged in an argument about whether it's appropriate for you continually to harass innocent watch wearers for the exact time in lieu of buying your own watch, and you win the argument by claiming that my argument is an attempt to quote *f_ _ _* with you, and by threatening me with physical harm if I don't acquiesce to your argument. This, to you, is winning."

42   Lenz says, "I ain't got time for this s_ _ _."

43   Charlotte Treat slaps at her needle-point frame to indicate she's exasperated. "He didn't *threaten* you."

44   Emil Minty suddenly stands, making the ashtray topple. "I'm f_ _ _ _ _ _ serious."

45   Gately twists on the couch to catch Minty's eye. Past Minty, down at the dining-room table's end, Joe S. is still coughing, still hunched over, his face a dusky purple, and Nell Gunther is behind him pounding him on the back so hard that it keeps sending him forward over his ashtray, and he waves one stump vaguely over his shoulder to signal her to quit. Gately locks eyes with Minty until the kid sits back down, running a hand over his Mohawk and wearily asking when he can get the f_ _ _ out of here.

46   "I'm just trying to get clear on what's being said here," Day is saying.

47   Only a couple months ago Gately would have stood up and stood over Minty and physically intimidated him to get him to sit down. Charlotte T. is trying to catch Gately's eye as Lenz sits there joggling and telling Day all he's saying is Day better hope to Christ he doesn't make Lenz have to get up out of this chair right here. Minty is making no move to start cleaning up the ashtray's mess. Gately has no idea where he'll live or what he'll do when his term as Live-In Staff is over.

48   Day joggles his own foot and asks Gately for his feedback on what's transpiring here, whether Staff can confirm hearing a, how shall we say, he says, *menacing* aspect to Lenz's tone and/or content. Joe Smith's coughs have taken on your serious cougher's deep slow searching aspect, like he's trying to pronounce something.

49   "Easy *Does* It!" shrieks Treat, holding out her absurdly tiny needle, brandishing it.

50   "Peace on earth good will toward men," says Gately, back all the way on his back, smiling up at the cracked dun ceiling, not even a hint of a tic to betray anything but a tolerant willingness to

let it all pass, for the moment. To work itself out, seek its own level, settle, blow over. Die of neglect. He's pretty sure he knows who farted.

Collaborative Activity

In small groups, discuss the following questions.

1. Given what you know about his distant and recent past, is Don Gately a reliable narrator for this story? How does your perception of his reliability affect your reading?

2. Why does Gately believe Geoffrey Day is being so recalcitrant? Can you offer a better explanation for Day's sarcasm and anger?

3. What role does Charlotte Treat play in "An Interval"? In what ways may her name be said to be ironic?

4. As nearly as you can, trace the plot of "An Interval." What does this effort reveal?

5. Why has Wallace named the story "An Interval"? Whose "interval" is it?

6. Why do you believe Wallace concludes with the sentence "He's pretty sure he knows who farted"? Is that sentence an appropriate or an inappropriate ending for "An Interval"? Why or why not?

Solo Activity and Writing Assignment

Based on what you have seen on the news, encountered in fiction or movies such as *One Flew over the Cuckoo's Nest,* and heard from people you know, how accurately does Wallace portray life in a detox center? To help yourself answer this question, look for television or radio commercials advertising such a place, and phone it for information. When you believe you have enough information, write a short essay on the topic "Overcoming Addiction." You may use personal experience, if appropriate, and if such experience is not too personal to reveal.

Selection 6

To His Coy Mistress

by Andrew Marvell (1621–1678)

Introduction: Andrew Marvell lived over three hundred years ago, but some of the issues he raises in "To His Coy Mistress" are as current as barroom discussion all over the world today. Read his poem first for literal understanding and second for a specific comprehension of what exactly the male speaker is asking the female audience to do.

1   Had we but world enough and time
This coyness, Lady, were no crime.
We would sit down and think which way
To walk and pass our long love's day,
Thou by the Indian Ganges' side
Shouldst rubies find; I by the tide
Of Humber would complain. I would
Love you ten years before the Flood,
And you should, if you please, refuse
Till the conversion of the Jews.
My vegetable love should grow
Vaster than empires and more slow;
An hundred years should go to praise
Thine eyes and on thy forehead gaze;
Two hundred to adore each breast,
But thirty thousand to the rest;
An age at least to every part,
And the last age should show your heart.
For, Lady, you deserve this state,
Nor would I love at lower rate.

2   But at my back I always hear
Time's winged chariot hurrying near;
And yonder all before us lie
Deserts of vast eternity.
Thy beauty shall no more be found,
Nor, in thy marble vault, shall sound
My echoing song; then worms shall try
That long preserved virginity,
And your quaint honor turn to dust,
And into ashes all my lust:
The grave's a fine and private place,
But none, I think, do there embrace.

3   Now therefore, while the youthful hue
   Sits on thy skin like morning dew,
   And while thy willing soul transpires
   At every pore with instant fires,
   Now let us sport us while we may,
   And now like amorous birds of prey,
   Rather at once our time devour
   Than languish in his slow-chapped power.
   Let us roll all our strength and all
   Our sweetness up into one ball,
   And tear our pleasures with rough strife
   Thorough the iron gates of life:
   Thus, though we cannot make our sun
   Stand still, yet we will make him run.

Collaborative Activity

In small groups, discuss the following questions.

1. Why has Marvell broken the poem into three sections? In one sentence, try to state the main idea of each section.

2. What do the transition words "But" and "therefore" signal at the beginning of stanzas two and three?

3. The line of reasoning in "To His Coy Mistress" suggests that the reader is depending upon logos to make his case for him. How successful do you believe he is in doing so?

4. Specifically, what does the speaker mean when he mentions "worms" in stanza 2? Should he expect this image to help him achieve his goal?

Solo Activity and Writing Assignment

Seemingly for as long as there have been men and women, some men have resorted to various appeals in order to achieve sexual conquests. With your answers to the collaborative questions in mind, consider how successful or unsuccessful this appeal is likely to have been—in the 1600s or today. Then observe the couples you see at your college, in your town, and elsewhere, and write a short essay on the topic "Male Come-Ons: Sexual Harrassment or Harmless Flirting?"

Selection 7

The Gettysburg Address

by Abraham Lincoln

Introduction: Shortly after the battle of Gettysburg (July 1–3, 1863), the United States dedicated the battlefield as a national monument. It also was and is the cemetery for thousands of Union soldiers who died there. The dedication ceremony, in November 1863, featured one of the day's most prominent orators and also included some brief remarks from President Abraham Lincoln. Today Lincoln's great speech, which took only about two minutes to deliver, is considered one of the finest examples of oratory ever produced.

Four score and seven years ago our fathers brought forth on this continent a new nation, conceived in liberty and dedicated to the proposition that all men are created equal. Now we are engaged in a great civil war, testing whether that nation or any nation so conceived and so dedicated can long endure. We are met on a great battlefield of that war. We have come to dedicate a portion of that field as a final resting-place for those who here gave their lives that that nation might live. It is altogether fitting and proper that we should do this. But in a larger sense, we cannot dedicate, we cannot consecrate, we cannot hallow this ground. The brave men, living and dead who struggled here have consecrated it far above our poor power to add or detract. The world will little note nor long remember what we say here, but it can never forget what they did here. It is for us the living rather to be dedicated here to the unfinished work which they who fought here have thus far so nobly advanced. It is rather for us to be here dedicated to the great task remaining before us—that from these honored dead we take increased devotion to that cause for which they gave the last full measure of devotion—that we here highly resolve that these dead shall not have died in vain, that this nation under God shall have a new birth of freedom, and that government of the people, by the people, for the people shall not perish from the earth.

Collaborative Activity

In small groups, discuss the following questions.

1. Why does Lincoln begin with the words "Four score and seven years ago"? To what historical event is he specifically referring by using these words?

2. The language at the end of the first sentence may seem familiar to you. What is its original source? How is Lincoln establishing ethos by citing this source?

3. Given the fact that Lincoln was standing in a battlefield and speaking directly to the surviving family of the men buried there, why did he use a relatively brief logos section in his speech?

4. What point and what activity is Lincoln attempting to inspire in the final three sentences of the speech? In what ways are these sentences an appeal to pathos?

5. Would you say that today we are closer to or farther from "government of the people, by the people, for the people" than we were in Lincoln's day? Explain.

Solo Activity and Writing Assignment

A century after Lincoln gave his Gettysburg Address, Dr. Martin Luther King, Jr., stood at the Lincoln Memorial in Washington, D.C., and delivered a speech that cited both Lincoln and the Declaration of Independence, which Lincoln had cited. Many Americans consider the Declaration of Independence, the Gettysburg Address, and the "I Have a Dream" speech three of our most precious historical documents. Locate a copy of the Declaration of Independence in your library or on line. Also, locate Dr. King's speech. One good place to look for all of Dr. King's works is The Martin Luther King, Jr., Papers Project at Stanford University (*http://www.stanford.edu/group/King/*). This web site will link you to the "I Have a Dream" speech and many other important King documents. After you have made yourself familiar with the Declaration of Independence, the Gettysburg Address, and the "I Have a Dream" speech, write a short essay on the topic "Freedom in America." You will, of course, narrow this topic as you and your instructor see fit.

Selection 8

The Hate Epidemic

by David Leavitt

> *Introduction:* David Leavitt is the author, most recently, of "The Page Turner," a novel, and is editor with Mark Mitchell of the anthology "Pages Passed From Hand to Hand: The Hidden Tradition of Homosexual Literature in English From 1748 to 1914."

1   When I read the account of Matthew Shepard's murder, the words that I could not forget were those reportedly used by one of his killers after he and a companion had lured Mr. Shepard out of a Laramie, Wyo., tavern and into the pickup truck in which they would drive him to his place of execution: "Guess what? I'm not gay—and you just got jacked."

2   These words—odors from the abyss, as Forster might have put it—recalled others spoken by the narrator of Eudora Welty's 1963 story "Where Is the Voice Coming From?" which she wrote in a white heat after the assassination of the civil rights leader Medgar Evers. "Now I'm alive and you ain't," Evers's killer tells his dead victim in the story. "We ain't never now, never going to be equals, and you know why? One of us is dead."

3   Certain commonplaces cannot be restated enough: hatred of gay men in this country is an epidemic as pernicious as AIDS, and as unfathomable. Nor is any gay man untouched by this epidemic.

4   It haunts not only the drag queen who takes her life in her hands every time she steps onto the street, not only the middle-aged man who invites a stranger home with whom he has spoken on a phone sex line, not only the isolated college student in Wyoming longing for friendship and trusting in the overtures of moles from the Stasi of hate, but also the forward-thinking, well-adjusted, worldly homosexual man who imagines that in his urban corner of sanity and tolerance, in Greenwich Village or Los Angeles or London, he is somehow immune.

5   He is not immune—either from hatred or from the fear of hatred, which is in many ways even more destructive. Thus even though Mark Mitchell and I have lived together for almost seven years, even though when we stay at the homes of our enlightened parents we are treated by them no differently than, say, my brother and his wife, even though we share a house, a bed, a car and a bank account, when we walk together in any city we never hold hands—and not because we flinch at "public displays of affection" (as might my brother and his wife, for whom such decisions carry little weight) but because we are afraid of being killed.

6   No, gay killings are not everyday occurrences, any more than lynchings were ever a daily event in the South, but the fear colors everything—especially in a year when reported bias crimes against gay people in New York City have increased 81 percent.

7   Certain commonplaces cannot be restated enough. In the brutal con game to which Matthew Shepard fell prey, what was exploited was nothing less than a young man's trust and hope and eager longing, if not for love, then at least for friendship, for camaraderie.

8   In this game, kindness can be held out as bait; sex can be used as a lure. The payoff may be death, as it was for Matthew

Shepard, or it may be robbery or gay-bashing or merely unkind, ignorant words. But few of us walk away unscarred, if we are lucky enough to walk away at all.

9   For years AIDS conveniently helped the hate-mongerers do their job, by wiping out gay men in appalling numbers. But now, for the first time in more than a decade, AIDS deaths are down, and it seems as if ignorance is stepping in and picking up the slack.

10   "Shoot a gay or two," a piece of graffito in Laramie announced several years ago. I have seen—and become inured to—a blunter epithet, one that is found too often on bathroom walls and in university libraries: "Faggots die."

11   Die: That's really what it's all about, if for no other reason than that it is only when faggots die that their systematic persecution ever gets any attention.

12   In part this is our own fault. For instance, when I was robbed a few years ago in Paris by a man who invited me to his apartment building for "coffee," I never reported the incident to the police, or even spoke of it, out of shame. Nor, I suspect, would Matthew Shepard have gone to the police had he merely been beaten to a pulp. And if he had, would it have done any good?

13   Shoot a gay or two. Psychiatrists have long speculated that many killers of gay men are themselves repressed homosexuals, which is why, so often, they murder their victims after sex. For these attackers, the mere fact that another man desires them (not to mention the possibility that others might consider them to be gay) is seen as justification for an act of retaliatory violence.

14   This may have been what happened to my friend Lou Inturrisi, a journalist and travel writer, whose body was discovered last August on the floor of his apartment in Rome.

15   His skull had been bashed in; he had not, however, been robbed. His was one of a spate of gay killings in Italy in recent years, only one of which has been solved. In that case, the killer turned out to be a male prostitute.

16   There are many reasons a gay man would go home with a stranger. Perhaps because the thrill of danger excites him. Perhaps because he is naive. Perhaps because he does not know any better.

17   In the end, however, none of this excuses the person who kills—or those who blame the victim for his own murder, in much the same way that women are often blamed for having encouraged the men who raped them.

18   When I was Matthew Shepard's age, my greatest fear was AIDS, because I had no idea then how the virus was spread. Now, 16 years later, there is still no cure for AIDS, but there is prevention: we can instruct a Matthew Shepard in how to protect himself against infection by H.I.V. But could we instruct him in how to protect himself against hatred?

Collaborative Activity

In small groups, discuss the following questions.

1. What has inspired Leavitt to write this editorial, which appeared in *The New York Times?* Were you a professional writer, might you have been similarly inspired?

2. How does Leavitt strengthen his argument by comparing the Shepard case to a 1963 short story Eudora Welty wrote about a civil rights leader's murder?

3. What reason does Leavitt give for not holding his lover's hand even in large, "tolerant" places such as the Greenwich Village section of New York City?

4. What does Leavitt say has been the ultimate effect on him of reading, over and over again, graffitti such as "Faggots die" in place after place? What danger does this effect pose?

5. How does Leavitt say the gay male's fears have changed over the decade and one-half between his early twenties and Matthew Shepard's?

Solo Activity and Writing Assignment

Using the World Wide Web, research the Matthew Shepard case and its aftermath. Notice, in particular, that Shepard was singled out to be murdered specifically because he was a homosexual. After you have sufficiently studied the case, write a persuasive essay explaining why sexual orientation should or should not be included in hate crimes legislation. Carefully use ethos, logos, and pathos to build your case.

Additional Writing
Assignments

In this section, you will find four additional writing assignments: a problem-solution letter, a movie review, an essay defining a concept, and an essay that compares and/or contrasts two items. Although we will discuss these additional assignments in relatively brief terms, you will still find one or two model essays for each. Your instructor may choose to assign one or more of these writing assignments, or he or she may allow you to choose one or more that appeal to you.

1. Writing a Problem-Solution Letter

There's no doubt about it. Just when you think you have your life under control, some new problem arises. Perhaps your roommate starts paying the rent and utility bills late, or the landlord raises the rent for the second time this year. Maybe there is not enough student parking at your college, resulting in your occasionally being late to classes. Or you keep receiving incorrect bills from your insurance company. Maybe you discover you have been overcharged in bank fees. Furthermore, you can't help but notice the unsightly trash littering the streets and sidewalks in your neighborhood. Dealing with these types of problems is certainly a part of everyone's life; however, how you handle the problems and conflicts that befall you says a good deal about you as a person. Simply complaining, or even ranting and raving, usually won't get the problem solved. Very frequently, being able to state your case clearly and persuasively in writing will earn the attention you deserve and, hopefully, the results you desire in life.

For this assignment, you will write a business letter in hopes of solving a problem that currently annoys you. When deciding on a problem to write about, be sure to choose one that somebody is in a position to solve. In your letter, you will need to explain the problem clearly, propose a solution to it, and attempt to convince your reader to implement your solution. You will also need to find out who is in a position to act on your suggestions so that you will know exactly where and to whom you will send your letter.

The Problem-Solution Letter and the Communication Triangle

The Assignment: Problem-Solution Letter

The Purpose: Informative and Persuasive

Audience: A real person who is in a position to act on your proposed solution

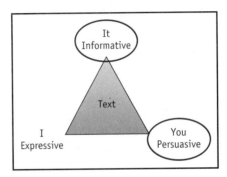

Organizing the Letter

In your letter, you will first need to convince your reader that a problem exists. Make sure you supply specific details and facts for evidence. Then you will outline your plan, your solution to the problem. Be very specific. How exactly will your solution be handled? Put yourself in your reader's place. What questions would you have about the proposal? Make sure your discussion of your proposed solution answers all the questions you can imagine your reader asking. If your plan is complicated—as a plan you have really thought through may well be—you may need to present it in steps or stages. Then try to conclude on a positive note (and possibly with a heightened appeal to emotion).

Make sure you use proper business letter format. If you are not sure about business format, use the upcoming example letter as a model. Of special importance, do send your letter to an individual by name, and find out how to spell that name correctly! Letters sent to "To Whom It May Concern" are not very effective and may very well never make it to the correct person. If you want to be taken seriously, do your research and find out the name of the person who is in the best position to act on your proposed solution.

Opposing Arguments

Whenever you write persuasively, you need to consider your opposition. In this case, think of all the reasons why the person to whom you are writing may not want to implement your plan. Be sure to consider issues of *time* and *money* especially. If it seems appropriate, bring up some of these counter arguments in your letter. You may refute them outright if you can show why they are not valid arguments, or you may explain that although a counter argument is a good one, the benefits of your proposal outweigh that possible disadvantage.

Ethos, Logos, and Pathos

You may want to review the discussion of ethos, logos, and pathos presented in Chapter 9, A Real Persuasive Letter: The Job Application Letter. Remember that if your ethos, the way you present yourself through your writing, is bad, then you will probably not be taken seriously. To build positive ethos, try not to come across as totally self-serving; it is always a plus to explain how your proposal would help others as well as yourself. No matter how strongly you may feel about your subject, do not lose your cool; although you do want to write forcefully, you do not want to come across as an out-of-control hothead! Pay particular attention to building good ethos at the beginning of your letter. And finally, make sure your grammar, punctuation, and spelling are correct. Polish errors like these also detract from your ethos.

As for logos and pathos, a balance of the two is quite effective. Your logos or logic of your plan is, of course, important. In this assignment, good logos depends greatly on how well you have thought through your proposal. Be sure to give it the time and attention it deserves; your audience will not consider it at all if it does not make good sense. Appealing to your reader's emotions, the persuasive appeal to pathos, may be appropriate. A heightened appeal to emotion is particularly useful in the conclusion (and sometimes as an attention-getter at the beginning) of this type of letter. However, you do not want to overdo the pathos, and good pathos will rarely make up for poor logos.

Read the following problem-solution letter. As you do, pay careful attention to Alice Gold's specific request and to the way she builds a case for it. Then, in small groups, answer the questions that follow.

A Model Problem-Solution Letter

Alice D. Gold
55 N. Wilson Rd.
Viva, MD 20003
February 27, 2000

Mr. Maurice Hobson
President of Reynolds Trucks
22 W. Phillips Ave.
Dublin, NM 10002
Dear Mr. Hobson:

My husband and I have been customers of Reynolds Trucks three times in the past six years. The first two times we were completely satisfied with our experiences. This last move, though, we were rudely shocked when we arrived to pick up our reserved truck on our moving day and were turned away with nothing.

I first reserved a 24-foot truck from a small Reynolds location in Hampton, MD, three weeks before our moving day. A week and a half later, I received a call from this location, notifying me that our truck had been released for a long distance move (mine was local). I was told that if I wanted a truck bigger than 15 feet (this was all that was left now), I should call a large Reynolds center. I then contacted the big Reynolds center on John Morgan Pkwy in Harrison, MD. I was told of no problems and that I should show up for my truck at about 8:30 on moving day—Saturday, January 29. The employee did tell me that the availability of utility dollies was on a first-come, first-served basis, but that at 8:30 everything should be fine.

On our moving day, my husband, my 8-month-old son, and I arrived at the John Morgan Pkwy Reynolds early—at 7:45. We had planned to return some unused boxes and get our truck. The single-file line was so long it was out the door! We were surprised, but realizing that many people move at the end of the month, we decided to make the best of a bad situation. The baby and I went home to finish packing and greet the friends arriving to help with our move.

After waiting about 1 1/2 hours, my husband was fourth in line. At that time a Reynolds employee announced that there were no more trucks to let out and that everyone should leave. When my husband told him we had already been charged and paid $80 deposit for a reservation, he said that it was not *his* fault that people did not return trucks on time. Overall, the employees were unhelpful and quite rude. We were left with no moving truck, people waiting to help us move, and my husband stranded with no way home. I could obtain no Reynolds truck in the entire metropolitan area that day. However, I did obtain a 15-foot truck from your competitor at no notice.

A few days later I returned the Reynolds boxes (there was no way to do so on that Saturday as there had been only one line for *all* customers). At that time I asked an employee to check to be sure my $80 charge had been cancelled from my credit card. As I had suspected, it had not been cancelled!

Overall, my husband and I have been extremely dissatisfied with our experience at Reynolds. Surely a reservation (and payment!) must mean something to your company. Because of Reynolds' irresponsible behavior, we had to move with a smaller truck that was more expensive than we had anticipated! Our Reynolds truck with mileage included was to cost us $67 plus $10 insurance plus $20 for two dozen furniture pads and $5 for a utility dolly for a total of $102. The competitor's truck cost $99.95 plus $17.15 for mileage charges plus $20 for two dozen furniture pads and $10 for a hand truck for a total of $162.10. I am not including the tax in any of these figures. We believe Reynolds is in general a fair company, and we believe in all fairness that Reynolds should refund us the difference in the cost of our move—a total of $60.10. I am including receipts from Reynolds and from your competitor as I am sure you will want to rectify this situation.

Sincerely,
Alice D. Gold
Alice D. Gold

Collaborative Activity

In small groups (three to five people), discuss the following questions.

1. Explain why you find Alice Gold's use of narrative structure effective or ineffective.

2. Why do you believe Gold does not include the point of view of someone who could potentially disagree with her request?

3. In what ways do details like the 8-month-old son build ethos? Is this detail strong or weak?

4. Where does the author most effectively use logos? Do you find her facts persuasive?

5. This letter by Alice Gold (not her real name) actually resulted in the trucking company crediting her account with approximately $30. Why do you think the company reached this decision?

The Problem-Solution Essay: Suggested Essay Topics

Consider the topics below. Use one of them, a topic of your own choosing, or a topic supplied by your instructor for your problem-resolution essay.

1. Problems at work

2. Problems at school

3. Problems with companies or organizations

4. Problems with specific rules or laws, lack of rules or laws, or lack of enforcement

5. Tenant/landlord problems

6. Problems with stores

Collaborative Activity: Editing Guide for the Problem-Solution Letter

After completing a rough draft of your problem-solution letter, swap papers with a partner, and fill out the following editing guide. Then give your written responses to the author of the letter.

Checklist: Editing Guide–Problem-Solution Letter

Editor's Name _____
Author's Name _____

1. Is a problem described? What is it?

2. Is the solution to the problem clearly described? What is it?

3. Does the author acknowledge and/or refute possible arguments against his or her proposal? What are some opposing arguments?

4. Does the writer build and maintain a good ethos? If no, what can he or she do to improve the ethos? If yes, what helps create the positive ethos?

5. Where does the author use pathos to persuade?

6. Where does the author use logos?

7. Is there a good balance of logos and pathos? If not, what could be done to make the letter more persuasive?

8. Do you see any grammatical, punctuation, or spelling errors? If yes, point them out to the author.

2. Writing a Movie Review

Writing a movie review shares many of the same characteristics as writing a restaurant review (Chapter 10) and a book review (Chapter 11). All reviewers—whether they review books, restaurants, concerts, theatre, or movies—must tell their readers a bit about the book, the restaurant, the concert, the play, or the movie, and they must give their recommendations. Furthermore, they must give *reasons* for their recommendation. The reader of a movie review, therefore, needs to know a bit about the film (but not everything!) and wants to know why you recommend it or don't recommend it in some detail. In other words, your movie review needs to supply some background information about the film, some summary, and your opinion with several reasons for that opinion.

The Movie Review and the Communication Triangle

The Assignment: Writing a Review of a Movie

The Purpose: Informative and Persuasive

The Audience: Someone who has not yet seen a particular film

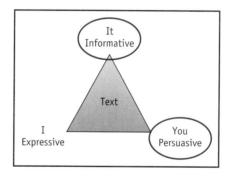

As you write your movie review, keep in mind that your readers have not seen the film. You will tell them enough about it that they can make an educated decision as to whether or not to see it. However, you will not want to give away so much of the plot that you spoil the film. Finally, you absolutely won't want to give away the ending, especially if it is surprising.

Your instructor may assign you a movie to review. If not, consider the following list of thought-provoking films:

American History X

Bullworth

The Shawshank Redemption

American Beauty

The Opposite of Sex
A Thousand Acres
Shakespeare in Love
My Own Private Idaho
Wag the Dog

Organizing a Movie Review

First of all, you will need to decide the details about the film to include in your review. Your decision will depend, at least in part, on your audience and partly on the film itself. You may, for instance, choose to discuss the themes in the film, the quality of the acting, the costumes, the lighting, the direction, special effects, or any of a number of other issues. Obviously, you could not and would not want to discuss every aspect of the movie. Nor would your readers need or want to know about every characteristic of the film. You should consider what stands out as most important in the particular film you review and what you think your particular audience would need and want to know.

There are various ways to organize a review. For example, you could organize your review this way:

Introduction
Summary of the film (excluding the ending!)
Your opinions and reasons
Your conclusion (in the form of a recommendation)

Or you could organize it this way:

Introduction
Discussion of important themes
Discussion of the quality of the acting
Discussion of the special effects employed in the movie
Your conclusion (in the form of a recommendation)

In this case, you would need to be sure that along the way you reveal enough about what happens in the film that your reader could intelligently decide whether or not he or she should take the time and spend the money to go see it or to rent it.

Discussing the Movie and Formulating Ideas

You will soon read two students' reviews of the movie *American History X*. But first here is a list of questions the students discussed in small groups and then as a class to help them gather and focus their thoughts about the film. If your instructor has given this assignment to you, he or she may provide a similar list of questions. If not, you may find it helpful to devise your own list of questions to help you develop your ideas.

Discussion Questions: American History X

1. Discuss some of the factors that led Derek to become a skinhead.
2. Why does the movie go to such pains to portray Derek as an intelligent person rather than an ignorant moron?
3. Why do you think the principal says about Danny, "I'm not ready to give up on this child"? Do you agree or disagree?
4. In what ways does the initial scene between Principal Sweeney and Danny foreshadow the ending of the movie?
5. Why do Derek's skinhead friends in prison turn so violently on him? What does this attack itself symbolize?
6. How do you find it significant that the only "friend" Derek makes in prison is a black man?
7. Discuss the immediate causes and the root causes behind Derek's decision to reform.
8. What does this film have to say about the effects of racism and hatred on the individual, the family, and society at large?
9. At the movie's end, what future do you see for the youth who has been fighting with Danny?
10. At the movie's end, what future do you see for Derek? Do you think Danny's report will have any effect on that future? If so, what?

Student Model Essays

Students Emily B. Patterson and Ben Thompson wrote the following reviews of *American History X*. After reading both essays, complete the activity that follows in small groups.

American History X

By Ben Thompson

1   *American History X,* the story of a young skinhead who lives by anger and violence, is an interesting film about the social effects of racism and indiscriminant hatred. The film opens with Derek Vinyard, our protagonist and tragic hero, in an act of consummation with his girlfriend when his younger brother, Danny, informs him of a larceny being perpetrated against his automobile by a black man. Derek, a skinhead not merely of words, but of action, feels that he most certainly must rectify this injustice and proceeds to eliminate any further threat posed by these miscreants by relieving them of their brain matter. While the murders were committed during defense of his property, due to the particular severity of his crime a jury sees fit to sentence Derek to jail for some period of time; he is paroled after three years. Next we see the younger Danny being chastised by his principal for turning in an essay

praising Hitler's *Mein Kampf* to his Jewish teacher. He is ordered to rewrite the paper, but this time the topic would be his brother's life and the events surrounding his incarceration.

2   The story unfolds along two lines. The present day where Danny is writing his new paper serves as a frame for the film. This part is portrayed chronologically and in color, following Derek's first two days out of prison. The past, Derek's story, is presented in black and white, perhaps to illustrate harsh emotions he felt during that time, or perhaps just to keep the viewer from being confused by rapid change in time. It is during these flashbacks that Derek's prison ordeal is revealed; his violation by other skinheads and his befriending of, oddly enough, a black man. In the present, Derek has to take care of some business from his past and confront some individuals who particularly caused him trouble. He tries to show his brother that the hatred really isn't worth it—it just leads to trouble . . . jail . . . death.

3   The primary goal of this film seems to be to analyze the social ramifications of these all-consuming racist beliefs, particularly the effect on the family, that basic building block of society. Derek's family is seen at dinner one evening—dinner at a nice semi-suburban two-story home with draperies and the like. Derek is enthusiastic about some of the things he is learning in a literature class, especially a book by a black man. His father thinks the curriculum of a literature class shouldn't be changed just to accommodate a black author, and he then makes some bigoted statements about blacks and admonishes Derek to be skeptical about things that promote blacks and minorities such as affirmative action. The point of this scene is, of course, to show where the seed of racism had been planted. Then Derek's father is killed fighting a fire at a crack house, presumably by a black man; the seed sprouts and begins to flower. For a lack of a father he turns to a skinhead group and becomes its leader, nay its avatar, the living embodiment of skinhead-ness. Through his charisma and the manipulations of an older more devious racist patrician, the skinheads grow in numbers in this Venice Beach town that has recently seen an increase in minorities and crime and displacement of white businesses. Before any race war occurs, Derek is jailed for his crime and transcends his position among the skinheads, becoming a martyr; his persona acts as a magnet attracting anyone with a racist thought. Derek's lack of a father is now transferred to Danny, and this cycle begins to continue again. Danny joins the skinheads to make his brother proud. The family is seen later living in a cramped apartment, possibly for lack of funds after losing a primary income earner, but also for demoralization after losing two dominant male figures to crime. The walls of Danny's room in this apartment are covered in Nazi paraphernalia—flags and propaganda posters—and his mother avoids the room. Derek realizes the havoc he has wrought and is convinced he must change his ways.

4   The film is enjoyable; it makes a credible attempt to expose the effects of hatred on one family and the community around them. How-

ever, some of the plot devices are hackneyed and entirely transparent; the hero undergoes a radical reformation after only three years in jail and his ward does the same in only two days, and the ending is certainly no surprise. The acting is competent, with one exception. I enjoy some of Edward Norton's movies, and his portrayal of a skinhead here certainly burns an image into the mind. Edward Furlong's performance is another matter entirely; here and in his only other major film, *The Terminator 2,* he seems very childish, and his acting is rather emotionless, totally unmemorable. The other players were fine, nothing outstanding but they don't detract from the picture. The most important reason to see this movie is the subject matter, and it does a good job of educating and entertaining at the same time.

American History X

By Emily B. Patterson

1   One would think that America as a more modern society is moving forward with the legalization of affirmative action, equal rights, and our government laws allowing immigrants and refugees to become U.S. citizens. However, *American History X* shows contemporary racism at its worst through the eyes of a young teenager, Daniel Vinyard (Edward Furlong). Furthermore, differences in skin color and cultural beliefs are the visual characteristics that have recently incited various hate crimes. Recent headlines of the Columbine High School shootings and murders are about race hatred. Laws that give non-white ethnic groups the rights to share in education and form businesses add a new frustration to middle class white America. *American History X* gives a strong theatrical view of how the teachings of parents and the laws of our government negatively affect, confuse, and frustrate the youth in today's society. This film demonstrates how the need for leadership and protection grouped with single parent homes and the desire for respect may lure today's youth to find refuge through gangs and hate groups. This film offers a lesson to be learned for both the young and the old.

2   The film is set in Venice Beach, California. Film writer David McKenna and film director Tony Kaye made this film easy to follow by using the character Daniel Vinyard as a narrrator through the course of the movie. The film also distinguishes the past and present events by using a black and white contrast for past events and color for present events. The film centers on the Vinyard brothers, Derek Vinyard (Edward Norton) and Daniel Vinyard, after and before the death of their father. Edward Norton does a fantastic job of bringing his character to life. In his 1996 thriller, *Primal Fear,* Norton portrays an innocent church boy who commits a hideous murder. In *American History X,* Norton's role as Derek is a realistic conception of modern day, middle class teens and young adults. Derek Vinyard is an intelligent, young man. As a result of life's tragedies, he becomes a skinhead, which lands him in prison for

the murder of two black males. Danny, as Derek's younger brother, though confused about the morals of white supremacy, believes in his brother and decides to follow these beliefs while Derek is in prison, believing that it will make his brother proud.

3   One of the most important attributes of the film is the characters who influence Derek and Danny to the roads of supremacy and reform. Dennis Vinyard (William Russ), the boys' father, voices opinions about the unfairness of affirmative action, social inequalities and the black race, sowing a seed of destruction that he does not live to know about. Equally important, Bob Sweeney (Avery Brooks) is a black, educated teacher, principal, and activist against race gangs. Sweeney takes on the role as Danny's history teacher, advising Danny to write an essay about Derek's life. Sweeney hopes that this project will shine a light in Danny's mind and assist him with the transition of reforming. Derek shares the dark side of his prison experiences with Danny and Sweeney and accepts help and advice from Sweeney, who encourages him to reform before he leaves the high walls of Chino Prison. Doris (Beverly D'Angelo) is a soft-spoken mother with unconditional love. However, she offers little communication or discipline. Lamont (Guy Torry) is a black prison inmate whom Derek is forced to work with in the laundry room; his role is significant in the film because he serves as a friend and protector to Derek. Cameron (Stacey Keach) plays the behind the scenes culprit who promotes the skinhead group.

4   *American History X* is a "must see" movie for today's parents, teens, and young adults of all ethnic groups. This film allows parents to form an understanding of the world our children are living in today. It shows parents and adults how their guidance and actions may cause our children's success or demise as they grow into their adult lives. This movie will have you sitting on the edge of your seat, from the beginning to the end of the film. It leaves viewers wondering "What's next?" "Who dies?" and "Why?" Derek and Daniel are two brothers who allow hatred and racism to rule their lives. *American History X* tells society that hatred and racism do not gain honor and respect: they can only lead their followers down a dark road of destruction.

Collaborative Activity

In small groups (three to five students), answer the following questions about Patterson's and Thompson's movie reviews.

1. Does each author tell you enough about the movie that you could decide whether or not you would like to see it? Why or why not?

2. What reasons does each give for recommending that you see this movie?

3. What aspects or qualities of the film does each author choose to discuss?

4. Do the authors present a balance of summary and opinion/reasons? Explain.

---

3. Defining a Concept

In everyday life, we define terms and explain concepts quite regularly. For instance, as you watch a World Series game, your mother overhears the announcer talking about the failed "squeeze play" and asks you what that means. On the other hand, perhaps a new coworker needs to know about the company's "fringe benefits policy." Then, again, on an outing to the circus, the ringmaster speaks of "trapeze artistry," and your 8-year-old companion asks you what that is. In fact, if your job requires you to train others or if you have children or spend time around a child, you no doubt define and explain concepts rather frequently.

Furthermore, definition plays an essential role in academic life. Every time you open a textbook, for just about any course, you will probably notice certain key terms typed in boldface print. Students quickly learn that these are words that they should understand and be able to explain; moreover, the wise student realizes that these are the terms most likely to show up on the next exam and on the final exam as well. These words often represent significant concepts in the body of the course material. For example, botany students had better understand and be able to define and explain the concept called *photosynthesis;* math students must do likewise with terms like *imaginary number* and *quadratic equation.* Literature students, on the other hand, must understand and may need to explain the use of *foreshadowing* in a short story or novel.

The Definition Essay and the Communication Triangle

The Assignment: Defining a Concept

Aim or Purpose: Informative

Audience: Someone who does not know about a concept, or someone who wants to understand more fully a particular concept

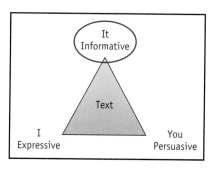

When you choose a topic for a definition essay, keep in mind that this assignment asks you to define a concept and that *concept* means nearly the same thing as *idea.* You may choose to define a concept about which the average reader may know little or nothing. An example might be defining *artificial intelligence* to people who understand little about how computers work. On the other hand, you may choose to define a common human emotion like *envy* or *compassion* that, while universal, is nonetheless quite complex.

Denotation and Connotation

Pretend a Martian, who landed in your backyard a few weeks ago, has become you newest friend. It is mid-November, and your new friend has heard much talk, especially on television and radio advertisements, of something called "Thanksgiving." How will you define the concept of what Thanksgiving is to your confused Martian friend?

You might begin with a **denotative definition** that may go something like this:

> *Thanksgiving, a holiday to give thanks and relive a feast celebrated by the native Americans and the pilgrim settlers at Plymouth, Massachusetts, is celebrated on the third Thursday in November.*

Denotative definitions are frequently referred to as "dictionary definitions." But in order to understand fully all that is meant by "Thanksgiving holiday," your Martian will need more information. What other associations do we make with the idea of Thanksgiving? The associations we have with a particular word or idea are the **connotations.** What, then, does the idea of Thanksgiving connote? What about turkey and dressing, cranberry sauce, and pumpkin pie? Do you think about parents, grandparents, aunts, uncles, cousins, and friends? How about all those football games? Now you might also mention those after–Thanksgiving Day Sales! For the Martian to understand what Thanksgiving truly means in America, you will have to provide both the denotative definition and many of the associated connotations. You will need to supply an **extended definition** to explain a relatively complex idea.

Organizing the Essay That Defines a Concept

How will you organize an extended definition? First of all, it is often a good idea to present the denotative definition in the introduction of the paper. Then you will have several options. One common way to proceed is to develop the body of your paper by giving examples. You might opt to break your subject down into parts, which is classification. You might even supply a narrative as an example or use contrast by explaining what your topic is not.

Two Student Models

Read the following two definition essays written by two different students. The first, by Jim McPherson, defines the concept of *intelligence.* McPherson uses classification and example to develop his essay. In the second essay, Lauren Gibson ponders the meaning of *happiness* in her own life. Read each essay, and then in small groups discuss the questions that follow.

Intelligence

By Jim McPherson

1   What is intelligence? It is sought after, it is valuable, and it is definitely essential for everyday life, but what does it *really* consist of? *Webster's Dictionary* defines intelligence as "the faculty of perceiving and comprehending meaning." This denotative definition does not give nearly enough insight into the mystery of intelligence. Psychologists constantly sit and ponder over its meaning. Often they come up with nothing at all. While intelligence cannot be perfectly defined, it *can* be broken down into key components. Three such components are the ability to reason, the ability to adapt, and the ability to perform tasks at accelerated rates.

2   Reasoning is the act of making decisions based on past knowledge and present thought. If a stove is hot, then a person can use logic to know that he shouldn't touch the stove. This decision is made using his prior knowledge. If a person were never told by someone that he could be burned, or if he had never been burned himself, then he would be unable to use reason or logic in his decision. However, such simple situations do not do justice to human intelligence. For example, a lab rat can deduce, through experience, that a certain lever will give it food, and another lever will give it a shock. Thus, using a primitive form of reasoning, the mouse can make the decision to push the food lever and avoid the shock. Therefore, because even the lowest of life forms can reason in some way, true intelligence must be measured by more than reasoning alone.

3   The ability to adapt to various situations is important when considering the definition of true intelligence. Consider the mouse from the sample above: if the functions of the levers were reversed, the mouse would not adapt. It would go to the same lever it has always gone to for food, and it would get shocked instead. Then, using its primitive reasoning, it would think that both levers are now designed to shock it. The mouse would probably stay away from both levers, trying to avoid a shock, and starve to death without ever thinking that the functions of the levers may have been switched. A person, on the other hand, would use his advanced intelligence and reasoning to adapt and figure the situation out. The ability to both reason and then adapt is what separates the human from the animal. For that matter, it also sets the human apart

from the machine. The world was astonished when IBM's "Deep Blue" supercomputer defeated the world chess champion. However, this machine, which was apparently "thinking," was actually doing no more than computing combinations at incredible speeds. The first of these chess playing supercomputers was defeated using a strange strategy. The computer was only programmed to compute combinations of moves that were likely to be made by an experienced chess player. However, its opponent chose *not* to make logical decisions on purpose. The computer was unable to adapt to this abnormal style of play and made mistakes because it didn't know what to do. The human chess player won the match because he was able to adapt.

4   Although computers lack many human characteristics of intelligence, they *do* possess one important one: the ability to perform tasks at accelerated rates. The human mind performs thousands of tiny tasks every second. Although this fact may sound improbable, it's true. The brain controls everything that happens in your body—the beating of your heart, the pumping of your lungs, and the twitching of your muscles. The slightest move of a finger involves thinking about the movement and sending a signal to the finger. Of course, when you move your finger, you don't think, "Ok, I'm going to move my finger now." Instead, it just seems to "happen." The autonomic system of the human body includes just about every task the mind performs that doesn't require conscious thought. It's what joins the mind with the body. So does the ability of a person to perform physical tasks reflect his intelligence? If so, then this would mean that the average klutz would be considered unintelligent because he can't perform certain brain-to-muscle operations fast enough. To a small extent, this theory is correct. For example, Michael Jordan is the greatest basketball player of all time. Did he get this way by training himself into being super-coordinated? No. He probably went to practice just like everyone else on the Bulls did. So what gave him his extraordinary edge over his opponents? It was his brain's ability to interact with his body at incredible speeds. Nobody on the court could match Jordan's moves nor, to a certain extent, his intelligence. While the typical "spaz" may be able to do a calculus problem faster than Michael Jordan, he wouldn't last three seconds on the court with him. This illustrates the contrast in meanings "intelligence" can have.

5   There are *many* levels of intelligence. In fact, there are *so* many levels that it is nearly impossible to define the term "intelligence." It can really only be broken down into a large cluster of categories and characteristics. Is Bob smarter than Phil? Such a question has no real answer. You could test both men, but intelligence tests only measure what is thought to be "intelligence." If ever there is found a true, accurate definition of the term "intelligence," it will surely involve these three fundamental abilities: the ability to reason, the ability to adapt, and the ability to perform tasks at accelerated rates.

Collaborative Activity

In small groups (three to five people), discuss each of the following questions.

1. Why does McPherson break intelligence into three classifications in his introduction? What are these classifications? How do they help him organize his essay?

2. Would McPherson consider a computer, such as IBM's "Deep Blue," intelligent? Why or why not?

3. Given his acknowledgement that "it is nearly impossible to define the term 'intelligence,'" what does McPherson hope to accomplish in his essay?

4. Do you find McPherson's decision to return to his classifications in the very last sentence redundant or conclusive? Explain.

Happiness

By Lauren Gibson

1   The dictionary defines happiness as the condition of being happy, or feeling as a person does when he or she is well or having a good time. In turn, the dictionary outlines popularity as the fact or condition of being liked by most of the people. Clearly, people can certainly be popular without being happy, and unquestionably vice versa, but are they? Today's society has adopted an attitude of "just do what feels good," or "live for yourself." Unfortunately, the narrow, shallow minds of high school students have yet to open up to this simple maxim. Will they ever?

2   The dictionary gives us a mere inkling of the definitions of the two words that I discuss. The way I see it, popularity is never having to walk alone during a class change. Popularity is never wondering, "what am I going to do this weekend?" because you're always invited to the biggest and best parties, and if you are not, this is due to the fact that you have to play starting quarterback or cheer at the front of the squad in the "big game." Popularity is having the best and cutest boyfriend or girlfriend and having all of your teachers wrapped around your little finger. You may think that I am exaggerating, but I have lived high school. I have seen teachers issue detention and then detain the student after class to shred the formidable yellow slip of carbon copy paper. I have seen the most beautiful and best dressed of my institution parade the halls with an entourage of groupies trailing behind. I have watched all of these goings-on with mixed feelings.

3   Now, happiness to me is being with my friends; it is achieving something I have been working toward for a very long time. Happiness

is babies, puppies, falling in love, spending time with the people I love, lazy winter days, sunny days, and rainy days. Happiness is being able to be a friend to someone when he or she needs me, and having someone do the same for me. Could I have been more happy during high school if I had been more popular? Of course. Would I have been happier? Perhaps.

4   My point is this: at my high school, I was never given the chance. I have attended school with the same people since elementary school, middle school, or our freshman year of high school. That has its advantages as well as disadvantages. For example, I have been friends with the same group of people for as long as I can remember. They are my stronghold; I cannot imagine the past seven years of my life without them. But anything "dorky" I might have done in third grade, or seventh grade, has followed me even to my senior year. I sometimes feel as if the elite of my grade have kept a record of everything everyone has ever done, kind of like your permanent record for your social status. Then again, on the advantageous side, if I were popular, I probably would not be friends with or even know the wonderful group of people with whom I have well spent my spare time these past three years.

5   Some may dispute that the cliques formed in elementary and middle school dissolve by the end of your freshman or sophomore year, but I do not agree. I often ponder this: If I got my break into the modeling industry or were discovered as an actress and signed to star in the next big teenage flick, would it be enough to get me an invitation to sit at "their" lunch table? Probably not. Would I even want to sit with the kind of people who exclude others anyway? I don't really know.

6   On the contrary, is everyone who is popular happy? I wouldn't know. Maybe the most sought after are not happy with the people who are their friends, but they continue to befriend those types of people to maintain their image as the most popular, or they just do not know how to befriend others. Maybe they do not enjoy being the representatives of our high school time and again, but they do not want anyone to take that "rite" away from them. Perhaps they do not relish upholding and maintaining an image—an image of perfection. For example, if I wake up one morning and do not feel like putting my contacts in or putting on makeup, then so what? The "elite" do not have that luxury. Ironic, is it not?

7   So would I have been more happy if I had been popular? Who is to say? I would not have the same friends, but then again I wouldn't have known any different. I wouldn't have dated the same people, thought about the events in my life the same way, or been treated the same way by others. In short, I would be a completely different person if I had held a different social status in middle and high school. And—while I may not love everything about myself or my life—in general, I think I'm pretty okay as far as people go. Yeah, I guess I like myself about as much as the next person, and when it comes to friends,

I couldn't have asked for any better than the ones I have. While it's impossible to say for sure whether or not I would have been happier if my life had been different, I think it's pretty safe to affirm no!

Collaborative Activity

In small groups (three to five people), discuss the following questions.

1. Why do you think Gibson links her discussion of "happiness" with a discussion of the word "popular"? Do her examples make this link seem wise? Why or why not?

2. Look at the connotative list of items that Gibson associates with happiness in the third paragraph. Why do you find the list effective or ineffective?

3. Does it bother you that Gibson acknowledges her knowledge of happiness is incomplete? Why or why not?

4. Comment on the degree to which Gibson uses first person in her essay.

Definition: Suggested Essay Topics

1. Define an emotion like envy, sorrow, compassion, courage, or love.

2. Define the concept of justice.

3. Define the concept of maturity.

4. An Essay That Compares and/or Contrasts

Picture this. You have just entered a grocery store, selected a shopping cart, and hurriedly begun picking up a few groceries. Since you are expecting your favorite cousin to visit tomorrow and you know she just loves fresh fruit, you slow down as you round the first corner in the store, which is filled with fresh fruits and vegetables. You don't usually buy grapefruits, but figuring your cousin probably would love one with her breakfast, you head to the grapefruit display. A woman with just a few pieces of fruit in her cart is there ahead of you, standing right in front of the display. She has one grapefruit in her left hand and is just now picking up another in her right hand. She slightly squeezes one, then the other. Then she sniffs first one and then the other. Next, she puts down the fruit in her right hand

and picks up a different one. She then repeats the process of squeezing and sniffing. Every now and then she drops a grapefruit from one hand or the other into her plastic bag. The entire process takes several minutes.

The picky shopper is an example of how we use comparison/contrast skills in everyday life. Notice that comparing or contrasting always involves our analysis of the qualities of two items. It may be two fruits we are comparing, two views of child rearing, the effects of a new drug on two different groups of people, or the marine life in a harbor before and after an oil spill. In other words, we must make comparisons all the time to function well as individuals and as a society. This is a given. Therefore, it is very important that we be able to organize our thoughts in terms of comparing and/or contrasting. When you emphasize the similarities between items, you are **comparing;** similarly, when you emphasize the differences, you are **contrasting.** Sometimes nearly an entire piece of writing is organized by this pattern of development.

The following assignment gives you practice writing a comparison/ contrast essay. Realize, however, that at times writers use the comparison/ contrast pattern in only a portion of an essay that is primarily organized a different way. For example, an essay discussing the effects of joining a sorority in college may include a brief comparison of living in a dorm and living in a sorority house. Likewise, an essay praising baseball as America's "national pastime" may briefly compare baseball's popularity in America to soccer's popularity in Chile. In either case, comparison/ contrast would be the secondary mode of discussion, but it could be the primary mode for other essays on these or a great variety of other topics.

The Comparison/Contrast Essay and the Communication Triangle

Comparison/contrast is a developmental pattern that you can employ successfully with various purposes and with many different audiences. Thus, you may find comparison/contrast useful, depending on the situation, when writing expressively, informatively, or persuasively, and also when writing about literature or other types of texts.

Organizing the Comparison/Contrast Essay

There are two ways to organize this type of essay. The first method is the **subject-by-subject** method. The second is the **point-by-point** method. If you choose to organize your essay subject by subject, you will say all you have to say about one item you are comparing or contrasting before moving on to say all you have to say about the next. If you choose point by point, then you will shift back and forth from one item to the other. In either case, you will first have to choose your **bases of comparison.** What does this mean? Well, have you ever heard anyone say that you must compare "apples to apples and oranges to oranges"? What this statement means is you must compare them using the same terms. This concept, though hard to explain, is relatively easy to grasp with a specific example.

Pretend that you are the doctor doing a study of a new medicine on two different groups of people. One group is taking only the new drug while the second group is taking an older drug and the new drug. If you measure changes in sleeping patterns, stomach upset, and blood pressure in one group, then you must measure these same items in the second group. You would not, for example, measure only percent of change of body fat and red blood cell counts in the second group. You have to use the same bases of comparison. Here is another example. If you were comparing your car and your friend's truck, you could discuss gas mileage, accessories, and legroom in both. You would not, however, discuss gas mileage, accessories, and legroom in one and price, maintenance, and safety in the other. To make a logical argument, you must use the same bases of comparison for each item.

A. The Subject-by-Subject Method. Here is an outline for an essay using the subject-by-subject method.

    I. Introduction
   II. My Porsche
        A. Physical appearance and accessories
        B. Gas mileage
        C. Cost of the vehicle and cost of maintenance
  III. My neighbor's pickup truck
        A. Physical appearance and accessories
        B. Gas mileage
        C. Cost of the vehicle and cost of maintenance
  IV. Conclusion

B. The Point-by-Point Method. Here is an outline of the same essay using the point-by-point method.

    I. Introduction
   II. Physical appearance and accessories
        A. My Porsche
        B. My neighbor's pickup truck
  III. Gas mileage
        A. My Porsche
        B. My neighbor's pickup truck
  IV. Cost of the vehicle and cost of maintenance
        A. My Porsche
        B. My neighbor's pick-up truck
  V. Conclusion

Two Student Models

The following are examples of comparison/contrast essays written by college freshmen. The first author, Gary Kimery, used the subject-by-subject method. The second author, Lynn Howard, used the point-by-point method. Regardless of the organization, though, notice how lively both essays read. Both use very specific details, action verbs, and careful word choice, all of which always make for good writing! Read each essay, and then in small groups answer the questions that follow.

A Time Honored Comedy Concept

By Gary Kimery

1   Unkempt Grog shuffles and aimlessly scratches at his Wooly Mammoth skin tunic. A statue-like Throk displeasingly looks at him and disgustedly states, "I told you to wear the Antelope." Laughter erupts from a crowd of Neanderthals. This prehistoric example may well be the beginning of a formula for comedy that is in use still today. Comedy teams are comparable to Sweet-tart candy. Initially sour and then sugary, the candy has contrasting taste characteristics. Similarly, duos use opposing personalities to create popular and enduring comedic routines.

2   The first ingredient of a comedy duo is the "straight" or "set-up" person. This individual can be frighteningly dull and impeccable in dress. The model of this character is Bud Abbott. In another version, the "straight" person is a good-looking heartthrob who woos the audience with dashing flare. Dean Martin typifies this incarnation. Oliver Hardy is a "set-up" person whose air of propriety is assaulted with mishaps until it pops like the buttons on his shirt. An essential element in the humor of a comedic partnership is the expectation of silly rebuttals, zany antics, and unintended disasters created by the "straight" or "set-up" person.

3   The polar opposition to the "set-up" person is the "funny one." While a very composed Bud Abbott explains the names of the players on his baseball team, his counterpart, Lou Costello, slowly becomes unraveled in both attitude and clothing. As the elastic faced and rubber limbed Jerry Lewis collapses in a contorted heap, the ever-dapper Dean Martin rarely has a single hair out of place. The tender hearted, well meaning Stan Laurel inadvertently triggers a chain-reaction of paint spills, falling ladders, and hammer smashed thumbs until Oliver Hardy explodes with rage. The "funny one" always has the perfect reaction, the right expression, or an unexpected comment causing the most laughter. The "funny one" springs the carefully placed comedic trap on the audience.

4   The formula for the comedic duo follows these principles. The "straight" or "set-up" person comes in all shapes, sizes, and personal-

ities. In the singular parallel between the two players, the "funny one" also comes in all shapes, sizes, and personalities. However, a conceptual requirement is that one is "sweet" and the other is "tart." In comedy partnerships, it is understood that the wider the contrast, the higher the potential for comedy greatness.

Collaborative Activity

In small groups (three to five people), discuss each of the following questions.

1. Explain why you agree or disagree with Kimery's decision to use the subject-by-subject method.

2. If you are unfamiliar with Laurel and Hardy, Abbot and Costello, or Martin and Lewis, think of one or two more recent comic duos. How do they fit or fail to fit into Kimery's comparison/contrast?

3. Notice the way the "sweet" and "tart" analogy appears in both the introduction and the conclusion. What does it contribute to your understanding of the subject?

4. Name a modern comic duo that you think will endure. What will make these two figures endure?

Miss Thrifty Meets Mister Own-It-All

By Lynn Howard

1   There are many things a couple must investigate prior to walking down the aisle and vowing to spend eternity together in marriage. We ask our future spouse important questions such as "How many children do we want?" "Where will we live?" "What church do we attend?" and "Can I have the right side of the bed?" However, sometimes we fail to inquire about the person's habits when spending and saving money.

2   My husband, Mark, and I have very different attitudes toward money. The pockets of Mark's pants are seared with black spots and holes where the money has burned straight through. My attitude is the exact opposite. I pinch pennies so tightly that Lincoln screams.

3   Mark believes that money is made to spend. He especially enjoys purchasing the latest in electronic technology. Our living room is a virtual movie theater. When he wants to view a movie, he turns on the thirty-five inch television screen, places a movie disc in the DVD system, and activates the surround sound system. With a recliner and a bowl of popcorn, he is in his definition of Heaven on Earth. The funny

thing about his purchases is that he is never awake to enjoy them. It amazes me how much money he spends on the latest gadgets just so he can snore through *Independence Day* as it plays loudly enough to rattle the windowpanes.

4   My spending habits are quite different. I am a bargain shopper from the start. I never pay full price. I will drive across town to save a nickel. I will wait for ages until a full priced item goes on sale before buying it. Saving money is much like a hunt to me. I am the proud lioness returning home, tired and bloody, from a day fighting for the last prized towel marked half off at Sears.

5   Since Mark's motto is "spend it before it gains interest," saving money is not an option for him. I can see it now; our two children will eagerly await the reading of Mark's will in order to find out what treasures he has bequeathed. They will be disappointed to discover that Mark has only equally divided the electronic devices between them. Of course, he will include an apology, "Sorry there is no money left, but what a great selection of DVDs."

6   I believe that we work in order to enjoy retirement. I understand the importance of saving money. Tax deferred contributions and company matching, stock options and mutual funds are part of the language I speak. I enjoy reading books such as *The Wealthy Barber* in order to improve my understanding of retirement savings. I have goals of a comfortable lifestyle in my golden years.

7   Although we have vastly different philosophies, Mark and I do recognize the extremes in our beliefs and take action to find a happy medium. Compromise is important in all aspects of a marriage, especially when dealing with financial obligations. Mark will continue to spend his allowance on gadgets, and I will continue to hold gadget yard sales to recover some of the expense. C'est la vie.

Collaborative Activity

In small groups (three to five people), discuss each of the following questions.

1. Do you agree or disagree with Howard's decision to use the point-by-point method?

2. Discuss the appropriateness or inappropriateness of Howard's use of humor to make her points.

3. Would you describe Lynn Howard's attitude toward her and her husband's attitudes about money as tolerant or intolerant? Explain.

4. Suggest a possible example of a compromise the Howards may have reached for their marriage to thrive.

Comparison/Contrast: Suggested Essay Topics

1. Write about a person or a place that has changed over time. Compare the way the person or place used to be with the way the person or place is now.

2. Write an essay comparing/contrasting two different teachers you have known.

3. Write an essay in which you compare the benefits of two different ways to study for an exam or two different processes for writing a paper.

C r e d i t s

Text

Maya Angelou. From *I Know Why the Caged Bird Sings* by Maya Angelou. Copyright © 1969 and renewed 1997 by Maya Angelou. Reprinted by permission of Random House, Inc.

Sandra Cisneros. From *The House on Mango Street* by Sandra Cisneros. Copyright © 1984 by Sandra Cisneros. Published by Vintage Books, a division of Random House, Inc. and in hardcover by Alfred A. Knopf in 1994. Reprinted by permission of Susan Bergholz Literary Services, New York. All rights reserved.

Peter Elbow. From *Writing With Power: The Techniques for Mastering the Writing Process* by Peter Elbow. Copyright © 1981 by Oxford University Press. Used by permission of Oxford University Press, Inc.

Bonnie Friedman. "The Paraffin Density of Wax Wings: Writing School" from WRITING PAST DARK by Bonnie Friedman. Copyright © 1993 by Bonnie Friedman. Reprinted by permission of HarperCollins Publishers, Inc.

John Garraty. From *A Short History of the American Nation,* Seventh Edition. Reprinted by permission of Addison Wesley Educational Publishers, Inc.

Marcy Gordon. "In Plain English: Feds Must Prune Prose" by Marcy Gordon. Reprinted by permission of the Associated Press.

Banesh Hoffman. "Unforgettable Albert Einstein" by Banesh Hoffman. Reprinted with permission from the January 1968 Reader's Digest. Copyright © 1968 by The Reader's Digest Assn., Inc.

Rachel Jones. "What's Wrong With Black English?" Reprinted by permission of the author. Rachel Jones is a freelance writer and editor in Washington, D.C.

Steven D. Kaye. "Save Now, Live Later" by Steven D. Kaye, et al. Copyright © 1996 by U.S. News and World Report. Visit us at our web site at *www.usnews.com* for additional information.

John Kessler. "Ah, Asian! Crossroads Flavors Are a Wonder." Reprinted with permission from The Atlanta Journal and The Atlanta Constitution.

David Leavitt. "The Hate Episode" by David Leavitt. Copyright © 1998

Photos

Index